Why is music composed by women so marginal to the standard "classical" repertoire? In attempting to answer this funda-mental question, this book examines the practices and attitudes that have led to the exclusion of women composers from the received "canon" of performed musical works.

Focusing on the tradition since 1800, Marcia J. Citron makes substantial use of feminist and interdisciplinary theory. After introducing the notion of canon and its role in cultural discourse, she explores important elements of canon formation: creativity, professionalism, music as gendered discourse, and reception. A final chapter provides a critique of many of these ideas with respect to the canon of the university music-history curriculum. Professor Citron shows how an understanding of canon forma-tion illuminates some of the basic issues that affect the discipline of musicology as a whole.

GENDER AND THE MUSICAL CANON

GENDER AND THE MUSICAL CANON

MARCIA J. CITRON

Rice University, Houston

Published by the Press Syndicate of the University of Cambridge
The Pitt Building, Trumpington Street, Cambridge CB2 1RP
40 West 20th Street, New York, NY 10011-4211, USA
10 Stamford Road, Oakleigh, Melbourne 3166, Australia

First published 1993

Printed in Great Britain at the University Press, Cambridge

A catalogue record for this book is available from the British Library

Library of Congress cataloguing in publication data

Citron, Marcia J.
Gender and the musical canon / Marcia J. Citron.
p.   cm.
Includes bibliographical references and index.
ISBN 0 521 39292 6 (hardback)
1. Canon (Music)   2. Women composers' music–history and criticism   I. Title.
ML3890.C58   1993
780′.82–dc20 92–2468 CIP   MN

ISBN 0 521 39292 6 hardback
ISBN 0 521 44974 X paperback

In loving memory of my parents, Leah & Aaron Citron,
who instilled a love of learning and a love of music

Contents

Preface

In the genesis of the project there were many who offered insights and support, and I would like to thank them here. First and foremost, my sincere gratitude to Suzanne Cusick for her detailed reading and perceptive comments on individual points and general matters of organization and tone. She has provided a kind of knowledgeable support that every author would like to have. To others who have commented on the whole, especially Eva Rieger, Jeffrey Kallberg, and Susan Borwick, I also express my appreciation. I received helpful advice during the early stages from Susan Cook, Philip Gossett, and Susan McClary. The many oral presentations of various aspects of the book, especially those drawn from Chapter 4, elicited thoughtful comments and suggestions, many of which led to significant changes. Although there are too many to list, I might mention in particular Jane Bowers, James Briscoe, Joke Dame, J. Michèle Edwards, Robert Fink, Sophie Fuller, Jan Hamer, Lydia Hamessley, Romy Kozak, Mitchell Morris, Leonard Ratner, Ruth Solie, Richard Taruskin, Judy Tsou, and Elizabeth Wood. For suggestions on the whole I am also grateful to the anonymous reader selected by the Press (you know who you are).

I would also like to express my appreciation to those institutions and groups that supported the project in other ways. Thus my thanks to the University of California campuses at Berkeley and Davis, Stanford University, and Texas A & M University for invitations to speak on the project. The three conferences on gender/feminism and music in the summer of 1991 (Utrecht, Minneapolis, and London) provided a special opportunity for sharing the project. The interest, enthusiasm, and support received at these meetings will be long remembered. Closer to home, I am indebted to the interdisciplinary Faculty Feminist Reading Group at Rice University for providing the entrée into feminist theory, without which I could not have even considered a project like this. My thanks also to Susan Clermont, Music Specialist at the Library of Congress, for assistance in locating documents related to gendered themes of sonata form.

I would like to express my appreciation to Bea Friedland and Da Capo Press for their permission to use excerpts of Cécile Chaminade's *Sonata*, Op. 21, from their reprint edition (1979). Mr. Michael Seeger kindly granted permission for a substantial quotation from Ruth Crawford Seeger's letter to Edgar Varèse of 29 May 1948. I make considerable use of a valuable survey published in numbers 1 and 2 of volume 20 of *Perspectives of New Music* (1981–2), pages 288 to 329, and I would like to thank the editor of the journal as well as composers Anne LeBaron, Annea Lockwood, Priscilla McLean, and Diane Thome for permission to quote from their responses.

To Penny Souster, music editor at Cambridge University Press, I owe a special word of thanks. And finally, to my husband Mark Kulstad, loving gratitude for the many forms of support during the ups and downs of the coming to fruition of this book. Your keen philosophical insights were especially helpful in the restructuring of the Chaminade analysis and the section on valuation.

Houston
August 1992

Introduction

While canonicity has long been an important concept in literature, it is a relative newcomer to musicology. Joseph Kerman's essay of 1983, "A few canonic variations," was one of the first significant explorations of musical canonicity.[1] Some four years later at the annual meeting of the American Musicological Society, a session devoted to the issue brought it to the forefront of the discipline. Diverse perspectives were offered: from Gregorian chant to contemporary music, from jazz and popular music to ethnomusicology.[2] My presentation the following year, "Gender, professionalism, and the musical canon," extended the conversation to women. Considered together, these explorations suggest that canonicity has become a central disciplinary concern. It offers a framework for posing questions about fundamental assumptions, values, and paradigms in music. It opens up possibilities for change. A study of canonicity has the potential to demystify the concept and clear a space for alternative historiographic models.

Canons in general have become a lightning rod for fierce cultural debate. No mere list of books, the literary canon has signified a field of struggle over vital social issues.[3] The canon is seen as a replication of social relations[4] and a potent symbol on their behalf. It provides a means of instilling a sense of identity in a culture: who the constituents are, where they come from, and where they are going. It can imply ideals of unity, consensus, and order. To adherents such ideals serve moral ends as they forge a common vision for the future. To opponents, however, they paper over the realities of social diversity and political dissent. Both sides would agree, however, that the canon creates a narrative of the past and a template for the future.

Given the high stakes it is no wonder that the rhetoric is partisan and passionate. Many believe that the controversy boils down to a struggle over power: who will decide what is studied, which in turn becomes emblematic of society itself. The literary professoriate, expectedly, plays a major role. But this is no monolithic bloc. It is a heterogeneous group with a wide range of opinions, and this has led to major curricular battles within departments. Across the larger academy the "Great Books" issue has become extremely controversial. Many colleges and universities are revising curricula as they re-examine their commitment to the classic tracts of Western society and its relationship, if any, to social considerations. A famous case in point are the curricular reforms at Stanford University. But the debate has extended well beyond academe. Influential voices of the government, especially William Bennett (former Secretary of Education) and Lynne Cheney (director of the National Endowment for the Humanities), have entered the fray. Such figures see themselves as needed correctives to the harmful excesses emanating from the academy, and their pronouncements betoken a shift in the power relationship between the government and higher education. Ironically this produces an inversion of traditional liberal–conservative positions regarding government interference.[5]

For all players ideology is critical. To conservatives ideology represents the partisanship and self-interest behind the assault upon the canon. In a clever rhetorical move some conservatives equate ideology with Marxist ideology in order to imply a dangerous leftist agenda. To liberals, however, ideology represents something positive – positive in the sense of inhering in everything. There is no such thing as value-free statements or behavior; whether implicit or explicit, a system of values is always present. Liberals believe that operative ideologies in an assumption, system, or institution should be acknowledged and analyzed. They accuse the conservatives of masking their own ideology in their claims of not having an ideology. While my characterizations may be extreme, they reinforce the notion that a major contest is under way for cultural authority.

Much of the debate concerns origins, particularly the cultural roots of the groups who constitute society. Demographics would suggest that the canon be representative. It should be democratic; it should respect and reflect differences. This multi-cultural approach, espoused by liberals, draws criticism from the other side. They say it contributes to social fragmentation. It undermines the preservation of Western civilization and promotes evaluative anarchy in its suggestion that European culture is not necessarily better than any other culture. Hence the charge of relativism. But this invites the response that quality is neither immanent nor universal, and therefore one has to inquire into the ideologies behind a given pronouncement of quality. It has been argued that those who make sweeping claims in the name of quality are elitist. Many see Allan Bloom, author of the influential *The Closing of the American Mind* (New York, 1987), in this light.[6] His curricular desires amount to a nostalgia for the past: a time when the white male ruled the roost, when uppity women and minorities steered clear of the pure pursuit of knowledge. The yearning suggests a search for a kind of idealized origins, perhaps akin to a fantasy, that some hope to recapture in their canonic quests. In this pursuit they are staking certain claims on the past. Proprietary propensities, however, are also to be found in those who favor a multicultural canon. One could argue that those who feel politically oppressed might fight hardest for canonic ground: they have farther to go and less to lose.[7]

Some charge that the calls for canonic change come from an urge to be intellectually "with it," to go along with the latest fad, whether it be multiculturalism, feminism, or deconstructionism. With its implication of opportunism the charge questions the intellectual honesty of the reformer. One might respond that those who favor the status quo are blind to the socially contingent nature of canons. Canons themselves do not remain the same over time, and theorizing about canons will respond to changing conditions. Even when a given work remains canonic, the reasons why it is canonic will change according to current value systems – what others might dub intellectual fashion. Thus faddism should be looked at very closely; it is more than meets the eye.

At first glance the stakes in musical canonicity might seem less compelling. Music, after all, appears to be removed from debates about social relations and cultural identity; it deals with abstract sounds, not concrete issues. But music is indeed socially contingent and participates in the dynamics of culture. Which music is deemed canonic says a great deal about the image a society has of itself. In the West the privileged position of art music of the European tradition is telling. It suggests a desire to hold fast to a venerated past. For the United States, especially, the association furnishes a means of affirming self-worth. We like to think of ourselves as a nation descended from Europe – this despite or even because of shifting demographics in favor of other areas, notably Asia and Latin America. Art music, like other European products, provides a useful way of expressing that identity. Its elitist cachet helps to demarcate social strata in a country relatively free of ingrained class divisions, ideologically if not in actual practice. This canon, however, is partial in more than its cultural exclusivity. It is partial in its gender composition: it consists almost entirely of works by men. While research of the last fifteen years has begun to make a difference in what is studied and performed, women's compositions still occupy a marginal position in relation to the canon.

The present study is a response to that asymmetry. It explores musical canonicity in terms of gender. More specifically, *Gender and the Musical Canon* is a feminist analysis of those concepts and assumptions in the canon formation of Western art music that have had a direct bearing on women's position with respect to the canon. While the project reflects growing musicological interest in canonicity, its roots lie at that intersection between feminism and the solid base of research into women composers that has established itself in the field. Feminism, a relative newcomer, has inflected discursive practices such that work on historical women, including newly discovered figures, need not focus solely on documentary recuperation but can utilize more critical approaches as well. I have a similar relationship to the project. After documentary investigation of individual figures, especially Fanny Hensel and Cécile Chaminade, I arrived at a point where certain questions began to call for frameworks beyond the scope of positivist musicology. This coincided with participation in an interdisciplinary feminist reading group at my institution, Rice University. The discussions not only revealed the richness of feminist theory, but provided a foundation for the launching of this project. Around the same time, feminism exploded on the musicological scene. The 1988 annual meeting of the American Musicological Society, with its many feminist papers and panels, marked a turning point,[8] and interest has only intensified since. Witness, for example, three major conferences devoted to feminism or gender in the summer of 1991.[9] My experiences in teaching both mainstream and gender-specific courses have also played a role in the genesis of the project. At some point I began to wonder about historiographic assumptions in teaching materials and the ways of presenting history with respect to those assumptions. Once I became aware of canonicity, I realized that many of these assumptions express aspects of canon formation and its problematic relationship with historical women. Thus I decided to do a study on canon formation as a way of pulling together many of the larger issues that concern historical women, in particular their absence from the canon. This resulted in the paper for the 1988 conference, which became an article.[10] The book represents a vast expansion over these forerunners: in length, breadth, complexity of argument, and incorporation of feminist theory. Happily, the gestation period for the larger study provided time for further reflection on the criterion of excellence.

The title includes terms that warrant explanation. Gender, a concept that has generated spirited debate, is used in its standard way: the social constructedness of what maleness and femaleness mean in a given culture. Thus gender is contingent on socio-historical context and is capable of affecting other conventions and codes. These attributes suggest that the meanings of what constitutes gender and how it interacts with society will fluctuate. They also raise the question whether the specific combination of characteristics that represent gender at a given time can be identified in a precise enough manner to justify its use. Despite this difficulty, gender has become a fundamental category in social analyses of women. As a marginalized group, women have been submerged in mainstream discourse because the undifferentiated subject has represented male experience. The category of gender acknowledges social difference between men and women and allows for analysis of women (and men) and their experiences in their own terms. For some, gender represents a continuum of possibilities between the end points socially male and socially female. For others, gender more closely resembles a male–female duality. While the two models might appear contradictory, I view them as complementary means of providing emphasis. Each is used in the study, depending on context.

The term "sex" refers to biological characteristics of male and female and implies bodily innateness independent of the cultural variability of gender.[11] In practice, however, distinctions between the two can be ambiguous. For example, biological sexuality can be framed in terms of cultural understanding and thus pertain to gender more than sex. This often occurs when sexuality is viewed from a wider perspective than the dominant mode of heterosexuality.

"Canon" also invites clarification. There are many canons in music and they interact in varied and often complex ways (see Chapters 1 and 6). I focus mainly on the repertorial canon of university music-history teaching, which in many respects coincides with the so-called standard repertoire. The core of the study, however, concerns canon formation of the central Western tradition more than any one kind of canon. In the final chapter the components of canon formation are funneled into the specific context of the teaching canon, and this serves as the focal point for alternative canonic modelings.

Women and their music occupy a central position in the narrative: from the vantage point of the composer (Chapters 2 and 3), the music (Chapter 4), and the listener (Chapter 5). Many discussions emphasize the experiences of women and allude to specific figures. While prose arguments make up the bulk of the study, one section is devoted to a lengthy analysis of a composition. I made a deliberate choice to use a work by a woman, for I believe it is imperative to put women's music into analytical discourse and take up the challenge of devising appropriate feminist frameworks. I also made a conscious decision to tackle an instrumental work. Most feminist analysis, understandably, has centered on compositions for which a text furnishes a concrete framework. Without that crutch one is forced to be original (to paraphrase Haydn) but one is left with a feeling of dancing through a minefield (to paraphrase Annette Kolodny). Nonetheless we cannot stop at the borders of texted music, and should try to break new ground for instrumental works. It is in this spirit of experimentation that I offer the analysis of the Chaminade *Piano Sonata* (Chapter 4). Although it has engendered a fair amount of controversy, it suggests that there are many ways of expanding analytic systems to accommodate different questions.

The temporal scope is approximately 1800 to the present. I concentrate on this period because it coincides with the rise and establishment of those institutions that fostered the formation of cohering repertories and eventually canons in the next century. Many discussions focus specifically on the nineteenth century because this is the time when many of our ideas towards canon formation originated. Occasionally I touch on earlier issues, for example Descartes's ideas on the mind–body relationship (Chapter 2) or Locke's on the relationship between kinship and the public–private spheres (Chapter 3).

These forays into philosophy exemplify the interdisciplinary reach of the book. This has two interesting ramifications. First, new historiographic insights can be acquired through approaches from individual fields. These can restructure relationships in music, which in turn affect how we think about history. Some examples are my borrowings from the field of literature, including the notion of the anxiety of influence (Chapter 2) and theories of response (Chapter 5). The second implication is that because feminism draws on many sources and takes what it needs from different kinds of theory,[12] it also utilizes supradisciplinary theory. This means important critical theory such as Lacanian psychoanalysis, Jaussian reception aesthetics, or Barthesian post-structuralism. In this study the marriage of critical theory and feminism has resulted in some useful analytical constructions. Since I summarize them retrospectively in chapter 6 I will mention only a few here, such as the postmodernist notions of multiple standpoints, contradiction, and non-unified subjectivity. These situate women socially and historically. Specificity of class and other social variables also provides an important anchor. It helps to counter the universalist tendencies of mainstream history, where male-centered narratives are assumed representative of everyone.

A related problem, common to feminist approaches to history, involves the tension between woman as a socially specific individual and women as a general group. History cannot embrace an endless string of anecdotes about specific individuals, and therefore generalizations about larger patterns of behavior have to be made. But there lurks the danger of essentializing women: of ascribing to women innate characteristics and thereby diminishing the importance of social context and individual difference. Like most feminists, I cannot claim to have found a totally satisfying solution to this daunting problem. Rather I see myself walking a tightrope as I work the narrative gingerly between individual and group according to context. The woman/women pair raises other potential difficulties. One involves a usage that distinguishes between woman as a transcendent signifier and women as real historical people. While the latter is self-evident and useful the implications of the former can be tricky. Singular woman here suggests an ideal or a stereotype, and this has the effect of eliminating differences among women or hindering their full(er) participation in society. How ironic that this use of the singular can essentialize much like the plural women described above.

As if these subtleties were not enough, there is another problematic dimension to the woman/women issue. It concerns the very existence of "woman" as a generic category – one that has little to do with singular–plural distinctions. Many feminist critics believe that it is very difficult to identify those social characteristics that define a woman (or women) as opposed to a man because women have been nurtured in a male-dominant society. They have internalized and appropriated many of the assumptions and conventions that could be dubbed male. Thus the category of woman is tainted, not pure, and theoretically impossible. Yet this deconstruction flies in the face of logic and experience. While I can appreciate the paradox, I believe that in the end the generic category "woman" has to be used to distinguish a female from a male. Perhaps the important thing to note is that the range of culturally constructed characteristics is wide and their combination complex and variable in relation to real women and real men. For this study, the more daunting issue is the negotiation of the contradictions inherent in the woman/women duo. I trust that my intent will be clear at each usage and the treatment consistent throughout the book.[13]

Gender and the Musical Canon focuses on the canon of Western art music. This implies a European tradition, and one representative mostly of white middle- to upper-class experience. The exploration of other musics and cultures is very important in connection with canonicity, but it will have to await other studies.

The outer chapters are devoted to aspects of canonicity, while Chapters 2 through 5 focus on canon formation and its relationship with gender. With the principal arguments in Chapters 2 through 6, Chapter 1 serves as backdrop to the forthcoming narrative as it relates what canons are, what they can do, and how they originated. Here I present a fairly straightforward view of canonicity, mainly for informational purposes, without a critique or proposal for change. The ordering of Chapters 2 through 5 is predicated on the seeming linearity in canon formation from the positing of creativity (Chapter 2) through the reception of the work (Chapter 5), with intervening stages of professionalism (Chapter 3) and the work itself (Chapter 4). Yet as the narrative suggests, such linearity probably represents an overgeneralization or even a distortion of the complexities within each stage. For example, reception and response not only follow but also act prior to creativity as they help construct the aesthetic conditions that shape the way a composer is trained and hence writes. In spite of the complexities, however, I decided to use this traditional sequence. For one, it creates an obvious organizational logic for the reader. But even more to the point, it provides a framework that can expose contradiction and demonstrate the need for paradigm modification based on the experiences of women.

Chapter 1, "Canonic issues," serves as an introduction to properties of canons. Canonicity exerts tremendous cultural power as it encodes and perpetuates ideologies of some dominant group or groups. These exemplary values establish norms for the future. Works that do not measure up are excluded or omitted and as a result potentially ignored. Canons are not intellectually pure but represent a variety of interests, not the least of which are commercial (e.g. publishers). Secular canons fall into two main types, disciplinary and repertorial, that interact in important ways, but this study focuses on the repertorial type. In fact, canons are *ad hoc* conceptualizations of paradigmatic repertories. In music such repertories were prompted by certain conditions of the early nineteenth century, particularly the rise of public music and a respect for the past. Cohering repertories helped foster the notion of the masterpiece, which has been further reified by notated anthologies. Scores and other physical embodiments of music, including recordings, point up the materiality of Western canons and suggest canonic dependence on writing and the visual for preservation. Women have had scant presence in the musical canon. Although recent pedagogical materials raise hopes for greater inclusion, we have to be wary of mere addition. This view will underlie one of the main arguments of Chapter 6.

Chapter 2, "Creativity," begins a group of four chapters that leave canonicity *per se* and devote themselves to a critique of those concepts, processes, and assumptions especially meaningful for women in canon formation. Creativity is a basic stage on a path to canonicity. In the nineteenth century it assumed transcendent status, and to a great extent it is still viewed that way. The chapter explores major themes of the restrictive traditions concerning women's ability to create, especially appropriation, and attempts to reframe them in feminist terms. For those who have composed the negativity has had psychological consequences. In many cases it has led to ambivalence and doubt – or what has been termed an anxiety of authorship.[14] Much of this anxiety is associated with a societal link between female creativity and the female body. Strategies for self-affirmation include a sense of a female creative tradition in the past, present, and future. The female composer may also have to commit a metaphorical murder of her depiction as a woman in previous works by men. This suggests texted works; in instrumental music more subtle codes may be operative.

Professionalism, the focus of chapter 3, has become a sign of seriousness and commitment. Worthy composers are assumed to be professional composers (and the converse). Thus professionalism has a lot to do with the chances for inclusion in the canon. It is a particularly compelling issue *vis à vis* women composers, many of whom have been devalued because they were not considered professionals. Yet criteria for professionalism are contradictory. The situation is further complicated for women because they have to negotiate their identity in the face of competing ideologies of woman and professionalism. Societal ranking of site, specifically within the dualism public–private, has played a role in women's visibility in professionalism. Yet like the difficulties in the notion of professionalism, public–private goes well beyond binary opposition and represents a mass of contradictions that need to be viewed within specific contexts. The gendered ranking constructed in the pair also implies an epistemological hierarchy that renders women that much less worthy to be vested with authorial authority. Publication is framed in terms of permanence, and I argue that this might cause ambivalence in many women. It marks a kind of public exposure that can problematize a woman's sense of who she is supposed to be. The next section discusses the author-function. The transcendent persona handed down from the nineteenth century has tremendous cultural power, and it has elevated the figure of the composer well-nigh to the top of the hierarchy in the semiology of music. I suggest that a partial de-centering of the author, while not totally unproblematic for women, may provide a way for female subjectivity to emerge even more strongly in professionalism. Thus professionalism can mean something different from its ideological definition. It has the potential to accommodate more successfully the experiences of women.

Chapter 4, "Music as gendered discourse," focuses on the work itself. The title suggests that music embodies gendered codes that participate in the narrative and communicative properties of music. It also implies music as a site for gendered discourse *about* music. "Discourse" connotes the ability of music to function as a means of cultural conversation and hence construct as well as reflect societal values. The first section concentrates on genre. Like canonicity, genre is a powerful category of categories that shapes values through pre-evaluation and exclusion, and tends to perpetuate itself. Hierarchies of genre carry gendered associations, and site and function form two of the major criteria in the determination of relative worth. The core of the chapter treats the sonata aesthetic and the related concept of absolute music. The interrelationship among ideology, representation, and practice is a major theme in these discussions. It becomes central to an exploration of gendered readings of sonata form in the nineteenth century and their implications for actual music. The first movement of Cécile Chaminade's *Sonata* for piano (pub. 1895) is analyzed in a framework of possibility with regard to these codes. While representation and gender of maker are clearly distinct entities, we discuss whether there are circumstances in which the gender of the composer could make a difference. Of course, essentialism lurks as a potential danger in such connections. It is also implicated in the burning issue of whether there is a specifically female style in music – a question that students and non-specialists pose with great frequency. In the final section, akin to a coda, I conclude that there are no stylistic traits essential to all women nor exclusive to women. But certain tendencies, perhaps related to subject positioning or socialization, seem to manifest themselves in many works by women. Such tendencies are also available to men. The absence of any specifically female style is another indication not only of the difficulty of applying absolute meanings to music, but of the fact that women have been socialized largely in male norms. Thus the possibility of definitive stylistic commonality among women becomes that much more remote. In general, the chapter suggests that an understanding of canonicity requires a recognition that gender is inscribed in music. To deny this is to misread music as human expression.

Chapter 5, "Reception," discusses the social and historic implications of the processes entailed in how music is received. A broad category, reception actually includes many issues discussed previously that serve as a theoretical foundation for the assessment of music – issues such as public and private, mind and body, and large and small. Canon formation itself can be viewed as a kind of super-reception. The term "reception" includes two distinct concepts: response, generally centered in an ahistorical individual, and reception, generally focused on the group in a historical context. Canon formation is more directly concerned with reception, while response can provide a framework for better understanding the behavior of individuals within the group. In the first section, on response, we discuss aspects of response theory that are particularly attractive for music. But response theory generally does not locate the respondent in a specific social context, and this is something that is needed in music as well as in literature. Although gender should be taken into account, it is important that the response of a female listener not be essentialized as behavior representative of all women. In the main section, on reception in its more limited meaning, we explore the notion of interpretive community as it pertains to the professional critic and to women. There may be a special subject–object relationship between the male critic and the female composer and her music. Several themes in formal reception have served to undermine the legitimacy of the female composer. While many have been aired in earlier chapters, we explore three here: the concept of genius, the paradigm of originality, and the strategy of sexual aesthetics. We consider the cultural significance of the fact that the music of women has been under-reviewed, and explore the implications for women of the centrality of written reception in canon formation. Written forms of reception provide only a partial view of musical activity of the past, and the challenge is how to find ways of accessing other formats and other kinds of written material to expand the historical vista.

Chapter 6, "The canon in practice," concerns the present and the university music-history teaching canon. After a brief section on institutions of power in canonicity I turn to the major topic of the chapter, and arguably the culmination of the book: a critique of many of the historiographic paradigms upon which the canon is based. Suggestions are offered for new canonic modelings that negotiate more successfully the positions, experiences, and contributions of women in history. Many discussions reinterpret toward practical ends many previous theoretical strands, for example a de-centering of the author and subject position. I discuss the problematic nature of periodization and of the "great composers," "great pieces" paradigms. After exploring how these relate to gender I suggest ways in which historical organization in music might be modified to reflect more effectively the experiences and contributions of women. The vertical approach in the Bonnie Anderson–Judith Zinsser survey *A History of Their Own* (New York, 1988) provides a good model and could be incorporated into a historical framework for women in music. It emphasizes function and place, and suggests the advantages to be gained from attention to social history. I also discuss valuation, an important aspect of canonicity, and argue that notions such as the criterion of excellence and the test of time are socially contingent. Yet contingency has to be considered in relation to aesthetic criteria and other variables of valuation, including the tension between autonomy and consensus. While there are not definitive solutions to this daunting issue, Gerald Graff's suggestion to adopt a standpoint of contradiction – to "teach the conflict" – provides a practical means of grappling with the difficulties. This idea is also applied to other issues of the chapter.

These critiques prepare the way for recommendations regarding the teaching canon. Women's music is often positioned as an either/or in terms of mainstreaming or separatism. While each has its advantages and disadvantages, I show how a perspective embracing both provides the best solution. This glorying in duality, affording a mobile subject position for both observer and historical subject, creates a kind of "double vision," as women's works are considered in relation to their own tradition and the mainstream. The inclusion of works by women and the new kinds of historiographic and evaluative questions they imply not only pertain to women, but permeate the canon as a whole and thus affect mainstream traditions. At the same time, canonic works by men need to be subjected to cultural analysis. This will illuminate the social values they represent and highlight their contingency. It is important that women are visible as teachers and scholars in order to confirm the presence of historical women. It is also essential that canonicity as a socially constructed concept be taught. I conclude that since we probably cannot eliminate canons or the preference-making behind them, the answer lies in modifying our desires as to what we want them to represent.

As the above suggests, the book covers a wide range of issues. This breadth is inherent in canonicity and especially in canon formation. But the breadth also reflects my interest in anchoring this study of canon formation in feminist theory, which offers a rich diversity of perspectives. I consider the multiplicity important. As of this writing, feminist musicology is still in a formative stage, trying to establish its strategies and its possibilities. Broad studies can serve as methodological models. On a general level they offer examples of how feminist theory in its various guises can be applied to music. More specifically they suggest how a given feminist theory might address a particular problem. Although more a result than a planned strategy, the study seems to serve this function, and I am pleased that many who have become acquainted with the project have commented favorably on this role. In keeping with this function I often provide explications of various feminist theories, which ensure the reader's understanding. If such theories lay in one's principal field, prior acquaintance could be assumed and clarification might not be needed. But given the complexity, diversity, and sheer magnitude of feminist theory – a formidable challenge even for those with longstanding acquaintance – I consider it critical to ground discussions in firm soil.

Despite or perhaps because of the comprehensive implications of canonicity, *Gender and the Musical Canon* is selective in its emphases. It does not pretend to offer an overarching theory of women and their relationship to canon formation, nor does it offer firm conclusions for many of the issues it introduces. In fact, the study probably raises as many questions as it answers. I do not consider this a drawback, however: it invites a more active involvement on the part of the reader. My hope is that the open-endedness of many of the discussions will spark further conversation on these important issues – issues that affect the very future of musicology as it enters the next century.

CHAPTER I

Canonic issues

According to *Webster's Ninth New Collegiate Dictionary*, "canon" traces back through Middle and Old English to Latin, and to Greek "kanon," to denote "ruler, rule, model, standard." Modern meanings basically expand on these definitions. A few entail church practice, including the concepts of "dogma" and a particular type of clergyman. The meanings most pertinent here are "an authoritative list of books accepted as Holy Scripture," and, even more germane, "the authentic works of a writer; *also*: a usually specified group or a body of related works." Another definition entails "a criterion or standard of judgment." From these one can infer that canons are exemplary, act as models, instruct, represent high quality, endure, and embody at least some degree of moral and ethical force.[1]

Secular canons have similar implications. In the sense of a specified body of works in a given field, canons exert tremendous power. By setting standards they represent what is considered worthy of inclusion. Works that do not measure up are excluded, either in the sense of deliberately omitted or ignored and hence forgotten. Canons are therefore exclusive. They represent certain sets of values or ideologies, which in turn represent certain segments of society. Canons self-perpetuate. As models to be emulated, they replicate their encoded values in subsequent exemplars. As canonic values become entrenched over time, the prescriptive and normative powers of canons become even greater. Their tenacity and authority create the ideology that they are timeless. As such it is assumed that they do not change. Yet the main aspect of canons that tends to remain constant is the ideology itself of immutability. In practice, however, the social values encoded in a given canon may change – not daily or monthly but over some larger period of time, perhaps every ten or fifteen years. This would entail overlapping modifications, not some concerted sea change. Individual works might change more frequently, especially with like-minded substitutions. All in all the dynamics of change in canons underscore their social constructedness and their powers of reconstruction. Thus it is vital to explore their workings as contingent entities, and especially with respect to women and their music.

In the present chapter we begin at the beginning, so to speak: an introduction to some basic properties of canons and canon formation. While music of course occupies the center of our discussions, literature functions as an important anchor. Thus many of the properties of canons are framed in terms of literature. This has the advantage of not only informing the reader about a correlate field, but even more importantly placing the behavior of musical canons in sharper relief. In "Properties of canons" I discuss the ontological implications of canons. The distinctions between disciplinary and repertorial types follow, after which I delve into the various kinds of interests that canons represent. The second section, "Canons in music," builds on previous issues. I discuss several types of repertorial canons and link the teaching canon with score anthologies. I explore the role of the public in canon formation, the historical context that led to the emergence of canons, and the impact of format and transmission on Western canonicity. The final section centers on women's relationship with the canon(s) of Western art music. This serves as culmination of the preceding discussions and pivot to the following chapters.

As a whole the chapter is intended as a curtain-raiser: a kind of overture to the book proper, where the main arguments reside. It provides an introduction to what canons are, where they come from, and what they can do. But a rehearsal of these properties in terms of practical application is reserved for the last chapter. In this sense the present chapter serves two roles: it complements the last chapter and provides a backdrop to the intervening discussions on canon formation.

PROPERTIES OF CANONS

In conceptualizing canon in the sense of a "specified group or a body of related works" we face the issue of whether it is a pre-existent notion into which one inserts works, or whether canon becomes meaningful only through *ad hoc* application to a coherent and identifiable repertoire. This is both a historical and philosophical question. In daily usage canon has come to mean a pre-existent entity. Historically, however, the concept of a canon followed the emergence of a repertoire of repeating "classics," which occurred in the nineteenth century. But the question also hinges on the legitimacy of the term iself. Should it be reserved only for *ad hoc* situations? Can we apply it to a repertoire prior to the introduction of the term in music, which occurred only in the last twenty years or so? Joseph Kerman, for instance, believes that "a canon is an idea; a repertory is a program or action." One is clearly *ad hoc*, the other is temporally ongoing. Furthermore, "repertories are determined by performers, canons by critics ... ."[2]

In order to avoid a lengthy discussion of these complicated issues I am going to assume the ontology of the category of canon for the purposes of this book – that canon exists as a distinct concept that we can use. In saying this I recognize the problem of taking a modern concept and applying it to processes that antedate its existence. In this case, however, I believe that the advantages to be gained through canon as a powerful analytic tool far outweigh the historiographic difficulty, although it is important to keep the problem in mind. While I appreciate Kerman's distinctions between canon and repertoire and even agree with them to some extent, I do not necessarily retain his usage throughout the book. First, there are many situations in which the differences are ambiguous and the line between repertoire and canon becomes meaningless. Second, the term "canon" is used rather freely in cultural discourse to mean a repertoire, what Kerman calls a canon, or a paradigm or ideal. This semiotic play can be advantageous in many situations, and thus I do not want to restrict its usage here. In addition I find Kerman's characterization of agency simplistic; the dynamics of cultural formation are much too fluid and complex for such a polar categorization.[3] It should also be noted that my acceptance of the ontology of canon in no way means that canon is no longer subject to critique, or that its utility is necessarily being endorsed.[4] What it does mean is that we can move ahead and subject canons, canonicity, and canon formation to analysis.

Like other powerful phenomena, canons have generated internal categories that articulate their behavior. As Barbara Herrnstein Smith notes, the kinds of categories that exist within a convention tell us a great deal about biases. In fact they act as a kind of pre-evaluation process that tends to be overlooked as such because of the seeming neutrality of the categorical array. Categorization groups like phenomena into the respective categories, but it also excludes those that do not fit. In canonicity the constituent categories are implicitly passing judgment on what sorts of things are culturally acceptable and therefore capable of being pre-canonic, and what sorts of things do not have a chance. Systems of categorization also shape what sorts of activities will be carried out in the future; as Smith points out, category names "foreground certain of their possible functions [and] also operate as signs – in effect, as culturally certified endorsements – of their more or less effective performance of those functions."[5]

As one might expect categories become entrenched, especially within a discipline. Sometimes they create problems. In an analysis of literary periodization, for example, Paul Lauter recalls that period names did not follow any one system of classification but bore either traditional titles or descriptive phrases with a point of view, for example "The frontier spirit." While this seemed inclusive, in practice works that did not fit were ignored. This revealed a major problem in American literature as a whole, but also suggests the problematic nature of periodization in general. In Lauter's view "such divisions are often used less to understand the dynamics of history than as convenient pigeonholes in which to place works in syllabi or anthologies." Being pragmatic he does not advocate the elimination of historical categories, but instead proposes inclusive categories that reflect cultural plurality. He hypothesizes that periodicity may be especially problematic for women because it emphasizes differences rather than continuities among periods. Female activity may depend more on regularity and continuity than does male experience.[6]

Whether or not we agree with Lauter's somewhat essentialist view of women's behavior, his case study suggests the kinds of problems that can arise with categories. A given array of categories tends to be accepted and therefore naturalized, and as such the individual categories assumed to be the only options. They become a basic part of the epistemological framework for dealing with important issues such as valuation. Hence it is easy to see why feminists in particular have been busy investigating the social and theoretical bases behind categories.[7] Similarly, much of this study is concerned with categorical configurations in canonicity: obvious ones like genre and periodization, but also more elusive classifications like creativity and professionalism. These have played major roles in the ongoing formation of the canons of Western art music.

Before proceeding we should note the existence of the second type of canon, namely the disciplinary canon. This refers to goals, methodologies, research conventions, institutions, social structures, belief systems, underlying theories, audience, language, subjects for study, and various other parameters that shape and define a discipline's self-view of what is standard, acceptable, and even desirable. These characteristics describe normative, prescriptive, idealizing, and excluding functions of canons, and they pertain to both types.

But who decides what is acceptable and what is unacceptable in canons – or more colloquially, what is in and what is out? This suggests the pivotal issue of the participation of interests in canonicity. Canon formation is not controlled by any one individual or organization, nor does it take place at any one historical moment. Rather, the process of the formation of a canon, whether a repertoire or a disciplinary paradigm, involves a lengthy historical process that engages many cultural variables. As a test case, if one took a canonic entity and wished to discover how it became canonic, one would first examine the paradigms constitutive of and reflected by that canon. One would explore various stages of the past to discover its relationship with the underlying paradigms. It would be necessary to go back to the time when the paradigm originated, if that is discernible, or even before, and investigate the conditions that gave rise to its birth. The Gadamer–Jauss ideas on the hermeneutic circle might be helpful in avoiding historiographic dogmatism.[8] But even without this mediation, my explanation may sound circular and is to some extent. For canons simultaneously reflect, instigate, and perpetuate value systems. They encode ideologies that are further legitimated through being canonized.[9] Through that legitimation canons achieve the seemingly wizard-like feat of self-perpetuation. As they bestow longevity upon themselves they tend to replicate themselves, for they now function as the yardstick against which precanonic works are judged. This process of serialized privilege suggests that canons tend to resist change; privileged interests will wish to remain privileged. Fundamental change may occur over an extended period of time, such as some multi-year period, reflecting an ideological shift. In the repertorial model individual members may be replaced more quickly, usually with similar works. Those with substantive difference might possess marginal status for a while or be accepted only tentatively. Nonetheless, as I suggest in Chapter 6, new works encoding other values have the potential for modifying the terms of discourse of the existent canon.

Agency in canon formation, however, involves real people more than the above might suggest. Canons embody the value systems of a dominant cultural group that is creating or perpetuating the repertoire, although it may be encoding values from some larger, more powerful group. Thus canons arise in a multi-cultural society of disparate power structures, where canons themselves provide "a means by which culture validates social power."[10] These empowered groups can be defined by several parameters, such as class, race, gender, sexuality, age, occupation, nationality, and political orientation. In literature in the twentieth century, for example, the professoriate – mostly white, male, and middle class – has served as the main canon-making group. But the base reaches beyond the ivory tower to incorporate functionaries of the marketplace. Publishers of classroom anthologies wield considerable power. They are not necessarily the principal arbiters of what goes into an anthology, however, unless they are skeptical of the marketability of the selections. As corporate entities publishers are driven by competition and will tend to eschew collections that deviate from their perception of what is canonic in academic literary circles. In other words, publishers assist in the perpetuation of the academy's notion of canonicity, which in turn reflects the professoriate's value systems, which in turn reflect their own training and the myriad social components that make up their world view, and so on.[11] We might more precisely characterize the principal canon-making group in literature as a professional–commercial coalition. But this is still a relatively small group to exercise such power, a concentration not atypical in canon formation.[12] It manages to retain power despite a limited base mainly because of the ideology of what a canon means and the prestige of the academy. Furthermore, as this example demonstrates, the empowered group need not be the principal ruling class; generally not, for instance, the moneyed upper class or the lawmakers, although their values may be mirrored at least in part.[13]

The public has an ambiguous role in the literary canon, and it seems to be more limited than in music. As described thus far, the literary canon pertains to the lists of "classics" utilized in the academy. These are made up mostly of works of the past. The public, however, tends to concentrate on current literature, especially those books that it helps to make "best sellers." Eventually some may become canonic and be immortalized in educational circles. But in general it is the institutional population and the relatively few independent "highbrows" that support literary classics. The public's fascination with the new, and with what becomes popular, resembles the situation in popular music. In both, currency and what is "hot" count for a lot. These will change relatively quickly – certainly much more quickly than the membership of traditional canons. Through the pocketbook the public influences the kinds of books that get published; public taste is simultaneously shaped by the kinds of books placed on the market. The participation of the public in musical canons will be discussed in some detail in the next section, but suffice it to say here that the public at large, through the standard repertoire, has a fair amount to say about what might become and remain canonic.

In general, the values encoded in a canon affirm a particular cultural group or groups and are not necessarily meaningful for other groups. Thus by virtue of its particularity a canon is not universal. Nor is it neutral. In its representativeness it is partial, and partiality precludes neutrality. In other words, its selectivity translates as a particular point of view. Furthermore, a canon is not invariable. Even though ideological values represented by a canon can be fairly static, individual members can change often. Yet if a work is canonic over a long period of time its supporting values tend to change, resulting in differing works in terms of their meaning. In other words, the work of art as an ontological entity changes as its supporting values change, so that over time it is actually a succession of works rather than one immutable embodiment of value. This is Jane Tompkins's explanation for the phrase "test of time": a work of multiple ontologies based on fluctuating interpretations that reflect (and construct) value systems of various eras.[14] This contrasts with the general understanding of the term: a work that has remained popular over a long stretch of time and thus proven its ability to withstand the vagaries of fashion. It presupposes that a work could be fashionable for awhile but fade when tastes changed. This would occur because its quality was not sufficiently high. Quality, it seems, is at the heart of the matter. It apparently has to be put to a test, and longevity indicates worth. Another tacit assumption is universality: that the best works are those that can speak to people in various historical contexts, and that traits that can bind people to each other are to be valued. It can imply that people of different eras are responding favorably to the same characteristics, and that there are immutable traits in the work. Perhaps all this stems from liberal ideologies of the eighteenth and early nineteenth centuries of democracy and brotherhood. Translated to later eras it suggests a demographics of unity. While this might seem laudable, it could be construed as an obliteration of cultural difference.

Universality, neutrality, and immutability: difficult myths to counter or even recognize as such, especially since the interests represented in a canon are generally content to let those myths stand. Other cultural groups tend to internalize the immanence of universality to such a degree that they may offer little resistance to the canon and in fact assist in its longevity. In the past twenty years, however, with attention to ethnicity and the inception of a postmodernist climate, several groups have noted their exclusion from particular canons. This results from a growing awareness of the cultural constructedness of canons, and thus it is natural that disenfranchised groups, motivated by self-interest but also concern for a more balanced view of human culture, function as agents of canonic deconstruction.[15] Such muted groups will tend to see canon formation for what it is: a political process with high stakes for shaping discourse and values. Women, blacks, and native Americans have been among the most vocal in this regard.[16] Similarly, my perception as a woman of women's marginalization in musical canonicity is partly responsible for the present study.

CANONS IN MUSIC

As in literature, the many canons in music fall into two main categories: disciplinary and repertorial. In musicology, for instance, we can identify such disciplinary paradigms as Western art music, Schenker analysis, sketch studies, archival work, documentation, objectified language, era periodization, historical emphasis, and scholarly journals. With additional thought we would realize that other concepts would probably not fit our list, at least easily, such as slang language, rap music, or MTV.[17] Many of these, however, are being challenged as musicology approaches a new century.[18] Because of the multiplicity of musical disciplines, such as the recording industry, the music-publishing industry, the music-book publishing industry, and performing-groups organizations, disciplinary canons in music as a whole are difficult to identify. If one were to compare in a systematic way the nature of disciplinary paradigms from one area to another the results would yield some fascinating insights into the sociology of music. What mainly concerns us here, however, is the discipline of musicology, although other musical areas affect the discourse of the canon formation of art music.

Repertorial and disciplinary canons might be easy to define as separate entities, but in practice they interact in flexible and fluid ways. To illustrate: without the accepted disciplinary convention of preparing musical editions, many pieces of early music, for example masses of Dufay, would not be canonic. Similarly, disciplinary paradigms are both shaped and supported by canonic repertories. For example, sketch studies might not be considered paradigmatic if Beethoven's music were not already deemed canonic.

Repertorial canons exist in many forms. There are canons of works performed by professional groups and individuals, and each performing area has its own canon. Furthermore, there are canons for groups that inhabit a particular historical niche. Early music groups form an important type. Because of their dependence on scholarship for the production of musical scores, early music performers tend to have close ties with the musicological community and its disciplinary paradigms. The other principal type is new-music groups. In the United States these usually flourish in the university, around active composers, or in a few instances as independent groups in large cities. If the group really presents *new* music then one cannot speak of a canon, i.e. a repeating repertoire, for new, previously unperformed music is being emphasized. New compositions, however, can qualify as pre-canonic: they could become canonic at some later stage. In the sense of a disciplinary paradigm, what is "canonic" in this context is that new compositions are receiving a first hearing. If, however, the group takes a chronologically broader view of contemporary music, as a repertoire that is not confined to world premières and can include "classics" such as Boulez and Babbitt, then a repertorial canon, in various stages of formation, is in evidence.

A paradox emerges from the relationship between new music and canons. I suspect that at least some contemporary composers do not believe in the efficacy of repertorial canons. In perpetuating music of the past canons have made conditions that much more difficult for the creation and acceptance of new music. Yet composers want their music to be performed, and not just at a première. But once repeatability becomes a norm the spectre of canonicity looms as a possibility (although statistically not a very likely one) and historicism takes hold, thus reinforcing the bias against new works. Perhaps composers would wish to have their works performed many times, and perhaps they might say that the war-horses could yield to a model of diversity. That might involve significant changes in patronage, financing, function, and the general position of the composer in society. "Canonic" would not mean what it does now, and perhaps a new vocabulary would have to emerge to reflect the modified structures.[19]

Recordings represent another type of canonic repertoire. They are an important medium for the dissemination of music to the wider public and thus possess potent cultural force. The powerful recording industry controls the production and distribution of who, what, and by whom is recorded. For art music, only one component in the industry, recordings act as a cultural barometer and negotiator. This shows up in which compositions are issued and re-issued, how many different versions exist, and the nature of the promotion. Of course recordings reflect the membership of other repertorial canons. They particularly play off mainstream performing institutions such as symphony and opera, but can reinforce or even instigate membership in other repertorial canons, particularly those of "marginal" areas like early music and new music. Kerman has perceptively noted how the recording has replaced the live performance as the principal performing medium for many pieces of new music.[20] As in the case of scores, this exemplifies the substitution of a tangible, physical object – the physicality of the recording itself – for the more ephemeral phenomenological realization. Another property of recordings is their ability to convert phenomenological experience into a text subject to aural analysis, upon repeated "readings" (i.e. hearings).[21] They can also construct the paradigmatic aural version of a given work.

Another type of repertorial canon occurs in the academic teaching of music, in the classroom. Here I am referring mainly to music history pedagogy.[22] This canon is largely material. Aural renditions occur in the form of recordings and occasional live performances, although recordings can become material upon repeated hearings. Textbooks and anthologies, as the repository of the canon, wield enormous power as determinants of canonic status. Although theoretically free to use any materials, most instructors rely heavily on published materials for repertorial examples. Textbooks, like anthologies, emphasize specific works and composers, but most provide some latitude by mentioning additional figures. The limitations posed by anthologies, however, can be formidable. Imagine: if one is teaching a survey course and finds none of the anthologies suitable, one is left to cull from hither and yon. This is not only time-consuming but raises the likelihood of copyright infringement, thus creating a legal problem. A more feasible outcome is dependence on an anthology for most of the examples and then either supplementing (somehow negotiating the copyright problems of duplication) or dispensing with scores for a few works. Whatever the compromise, it is not difficult to see how the decisions of a relatively small group of individuals – anthologizers, textbook authors, and the publishers with whom they work – can shape the behavior and tastes of a large population of listeners, performers, composers, and scholars. But we may be too quick in assigning such power to authors and publishers. Their aim, after all, is to sell copies, and that is dependent on giving the target consumers, i.e. the academic community, what they want. So the system operates in both directions. On the one hand, musicologists' tastes and musicological culture at large affect what is offered in pedagogical materials. On the other hand, musicologists' desires as individuals were molded at least in part by textbooks (and also anthologies, for the younger generations), and their current pedagogical practices are shaped by the realities of what is available. But in the past few years, publishers have been responding to fresh breezes of change in musicology, and this has resulted in the inclusion of a few female figures (more in this chapter and Chapter 6). Thus forces of the marketplace and the academy interact in the complexities of negotiating value systems for the present and the future.[23]

Music anthologies intended primarily for the pedagogy of music history and theory began to flourish in the twentieth century. Arnold Schering's *Geschichte der Musik in Beispielen* (Leipzig, 1931) was one of the first, and its title indicates the growing interest in the study of music through actual pieces.[24] Other important collections were the two-volume *Historical Anthology of Music*, edited by Willi Apel and Archibald Davison (Cambridge, Mass., 1946); and *Masterpieces of Music Before* 1750 (New York, 1951) and *A Treasury of Early Music* (New York, 1958), both compiled by Carl Parrish (the former with

J. F. Ohl). These collections, once considered historically comprehensive, are devoted solely to music composed before 1800.

Coverage of later music in anthologies did not become routine
until the 1960s, and several reasons account for the change. One is the
appearance of Donald Grout's landmark study, *A History of Western
Music* (New York, 1960). This was perhaps the first major English-
language survey to define music history in terms of style. Issued
without scores, Grout's text created a need that publishers began to
fill. The second reason also concerns the market. Beginning in the late
1960s college populations, at least in the United States, grew
dramatically and so did the numbers of students in music courses.
Publishers seemed to recognize the power of later music to attract
students to the courses and materials. The third reason mirrors
general musicological culture: music after 1800 began to be
acceptable for serious historical study. The rationale for the delay is
that sufficient time had to pass to ensure historical objectivity. But
this represents a partial explanation. Perhaps a more telling factor
was the modernist embarrassment over the emotional and rhetorical
excesses of Romanticism. These may have been linked with the
feminine, and through the connection provided yet another motive
for extended suppression of the repertoire. Such an attitude reveals a
great deal about the power of modernism, of course, but it also
suggests a close connection between historiography and gendered
discourse in music.

Anthologies have stressed Western art music and generally ignored
other idioms, such as folk music, popular music, and world music.
Music by women and other "minorities" in Western culture has also
been overlooked, and this shows the biases in gender, class, and race
that are inherent in the seemingly comprehensive label "Western art
music." Like other dominant structures, the *de facto* emphasis on that
repertoire has not necessitated that it be culturally specific. In other
words, as the assumed repertoire Western art music does not have to
identify itself as such. While this may seem convenient, the
assumption of the dominant mode implies a false universality. This
results in the marginalization of other musics and masks the
particular social parameters of the Western tradition. But as we move
beyond this dominant-muted issue, the question remains whether
Western art music should so consistently occupy exclusive place in
broad-based music instruction.[25] This is a major topic of discussion in
forums such as the College Music Society. Recent job lists suggest

that universities are eagerly hiring non-Western specialists and responding to cultural diversity on a global level. This is all to the good.

What relationship does the teaching canon have with the so-called "standard repertoire"? This is a complex issue. One challenge involves the definition of standard repertoire. Perhaps a working definition would be that it refers to the repertoire of major performing groups and performing areas, notably the symphony orchestra, opera, standard chamber ensembles, voice, and piano. In practice it pertains mainly to music of the common-practice period and those pieces performed most often. The teaching canon encompasses many if not the majority of its works. One area of difference, for example, might be virtuosic concerti by someone like Wieniawski; these would be in the standard repertoire but not the teaching canon. The teaching canon, however, has greater historical range and stylistic variety. Extending at least as far back as the Middle Ages, it comes fairly close to the present and embraces a wider range of genres. I suspect that the two interact in a variety of ways. For example, they both grow out of a common performance history, which in turn is based on shared ideologies and value systems. The teaching canon, however, has been fashioned most directly by musicologists (analysis anthologies by theorists and composers), and this raises the question of the extent of musicology's relationship with performance structures geared toward the general public. Certainly there is interaction and certainly there is awareness in the discipline of what is being performed. Some research has been catalyst to revisionist performances, such as Philip Gossett's editions of Rossini's operas. Many scholars write program notes and other essays, present lectures or give interviews for the media.[26] But anthologizers often take independent stances from the standard repertoire. Leon Plantinga, for instance, includes scenes from an opera by Meyerbeer, an opera transcription for piano by Liszt, and a scene from Berlioz's *Damnation of Faust* in the anthology that accompanies the textbook *Romantic Music: A History of Musical Style in Nineteenth-Century Europe* (New York, 1984). Plantinga apparently considers these works important, at least for illustrative purposes, even though they might not be viewed as prominent members of the standard repertoire. As for the influence of the teaching canon on the standard repertoire, the most obvious consideration involves the role of university education in shaping the aesthetic values of future professionals as well as audience members and consumers of music. After all, the values students internalize will underlie their professional choice of repertoire, whether as soloist, ensemble player, conductor, or possibly concert manager or music journalist. As audience members they can contribute to the shaping of the standard repertoire through the power of the purse. Thus the teaching canon, as a major influence on future musical culture, is extremely important. It is this canon, with its increasingly fluid relationship with the standard repertoire, that serves as the main but not exclusive canonic focal point of the book.

The public can play a significant role in canon formation. It provides forms of support and resistance, often with profound consequences.[27] As Henry Pleasants notes in a scathing critique of contemporary music (1955), "Audience taste still determines the selection of the standard repertoire; for it is the standard repertoire that sustains the expensive institutions identified with serious music. Here the public cannot be ignored" (p. 9). Pleasants and several composers sounded the alarm around mid-century because of their belief that the public had become disenfranchised from newly composed music. From our vantage point some forty years later we can see the issue in broader perspective. The public has had its say in what it wants to hear and has often prevailed. This has had an impact on the repertoire and also resonated on living composers and their very reasons for composing. For some it has meant sobering reappraisals of what it means to compose. Furthermore the public has probably had a hand in the movement from modernism to postmodernism – a shift that can be seen as a recognition that music is first and foremost communication between composer and audience. To be precise we should point out that in relation to new music the public does not pass judgment directly on the canon, for that is more of an *ad hoc* concept, but raises its voice about which repertoire is acceptable and hence could become canonic in the future.

Several twentieth-century composers have been forced to recognize the power of the public. Arnold Schoenberg, for example, seems to have had a love–hate relationship with the public. Some of his writings indicate a yearning for public acceptance; many reveal a desire to be part of a venerable historical lineage. While an essay like "Brahms the progressive" is a defensive strategy against charges of radicalism, it is also Schoenberg's way of forging a personal link to the pantheon of acknowledged greats. George Rochberg has speculated that this historical self-consciousness had a destructive effect on

Schoenberg's career: he felt overwhelmed by the burden of posterity.[28] It could also be dubbed the tyranny of the canon.[29] Many
aspects of Schoenberg's career, however, show a retreat from the
public. As he acknowledged in 1930, "Called upon to say something
about my public, I have to confess: I do not believe I have one."[30]
The process of mutual alienation began earlier. His humiliation at
performances such as the London première of the *Five Pieces for
Orchestra*, in 1912, led to a defensive posture. Thus the founding of a
private society (1919) for like-minded visionaries.[31] Ironically, this
rejection of the public in favor of a circle of connoisseurs in some ways
marked a return to one of the major social contexts for music before
1750. Yet given the modern time frame the private gathering had a
very different meaning. Schoenberg's retreat resulted from the
public's perception that his music was too intellectual and abstract,
and hence incomprehensible. Even now the public at large considers
it difficult. Although many professional musicians deem Schoenberg
the most influential composer of the century, it might be fair to say
that he has not won a place in the standard repertoire.

Other major figures have also engendered resistance. Like Schoenberg, Elliott Carter sought acceptance in his early years and did not
get it. The public's rejection of his First String Quartet (1950), an
extremely difficult work, was decisive. As the composer recalls,

From that point on I decided that I would write whatever interested me,
whatever expressed the conceptions and feelings that I had, without concern
for an existing public. Now I'm aware that these attitudes can lead to
"disastrous" results, that you can have terribly angry people and terribly
angry performers on your hands – and I have. I'm aware of this when I
write my pieces; but I've decided that the fun of composing ... is to write
pieces that interest me very much. I don't expect them to be very successful
when they're played ... .[32]

While elitist tendencies can be read between the lines in Carter's
writings, they are mild in comparison with the strong views of Milton
Babbitt. A mathematician as well as a composer at Princeton,
Babbitt was firmly convinced of the desirability of the withdrawal of
the composer from society at large. The university provided the ideal
refuge – a paradigmatic affirmation of the "ivory tower." Babbitt
saw the composer as a specialist and compared him to the scientist
engaged in advanced activities well beyond the ken of the layperson.
He advocated "total, resolute, and voluntary withdrawal from this
public world" to a private realm "with its very real possibility of

complete elimination of the public and social aspects of musical composition."[33] Babbitt seems to have been granted his wish. His is a name known mainly to specialists, and his importance seems to lie largely in his esoteric writings.

While Babbitt's position was extreme, it nonetheless expresses the climate of alienation around mid-century. Pragmatists like Aaron Copland and Roger Sessions recognized the crisis and wrote about it in several essays addressed to the general public. In 1970 George Rochberg specifically rejected Babbitt's scientific analogy and reaffirmed the centrality of the human element in composition, including the composer himself.[34] The idea that the humanity of the maker is vital to the understanding of the work hearkens back to Romantic historiography, of course, but also presages one of the central tenets of the postmodernist aesthetic.

A particular tension characterizes the modernist struggle between composer and public. Rooted largely in expectations, the rhetoric often focuses on the responsibility of each party towards the other. Blame is assigned both ways. Carter and Sessions, and by implication Babbitt, have criticized the public for not being educated enough to understand their music. The onus is on the public to bridge whatever gaps are made evident by the composition. Sessions softens his position by calling for a "willing ear" to understand modern music, and believes that the composer's honest intentions, and not neccssarily success in communication, are what makes a work of art meaningful. On the other side, Hindemith and Rochberg have castigated some composers for being too intellectual and composing for themselves while ignoring the public and its needs. It is the composer who must ensure effective communication, not the listener.

Of course the performer plays a major role in the communication with the public. Let us recall Carter's passing remark about resistance to contemporary idioms from performers. Even Carter, whose scores are renowned for their performing difficulties, recognizes that the realities of financing and learning new music render such resistance understandable. In this regard the university is much more congenial for contemporary music than the concert hall. Students (and generally faculty as well) do not have to be paid for rehearsal time and tend to learn new works in a spirit of discovery and cooperation. There are other reasons why the concert hall may not be the most feasible location, for example a problematic fit between style and the size of performing forces. It should be noted, however, that Carter has attributed much of the public's difficulty with new orchestral music to bad performances caused by insufficient rehearsal time. Performers then become frustrated over performance quality. That can lead to a chronic case of negativity and eventually structural resistance that can hinder performances of new works.[35]

The public invests a great deal in its aesthetic decisions and the question could be posed why it does so. In other words, what does the public "get" out of the canon? Many of the general stakes in canonicity were laid out in the "Introduction," but here we might discuss them more specifically in terms of music. Perhaps most importantly, the public seems to look to canons for setting standards of taste. If the work is in the canon, assumes a layperson, it must be good and something I should be familiar with. Furthermore, I should "appreciate," if not necessarily like, it and similar works. This can be illustrated by two examples. One is the case of the classical music "expert" on public radio, who over the course of several months presents his list of the basic record library that a music lover should own. The listener tends to take that advice as canonic: the expert surely knows what is good and what is not. The list will guide purchases and how one reacts at concerts. A second example is the situation when one turns on the radio in the middle of a work, does not know its title, and suspends judgment on whether one likes it until the name of the composer is given. This can also happen in a museum when glancing at a painting without knowing the name of the artist. In all these instances, "canonically correct" knowledge confers a kind of moral imprimatur on its possessor. Somehow one is a better person with that erudition. One not only feels ennobled but also identifies with a particular segment of the culture. In the case of Western art music the link is with a European heritage and its elitist cachet. The canon, and especially the standard repertoire, serves as a means of preserving that connection.[36]

As noted, "canon" has only recently been applied to music. But the processes of forming paradigmatic repertories, which precede more formalized canons, existed some time before. Musical historicism functioned as one of the prime ingredients in creating paradigmatic repertories. And once repertories were fashioned, the idea of potential retention of old works and potential incorporation of new works came into existence. Nonetheless, in the early stages, shortly after 1800, composers were still more concerned with a direct than an enduring success for their compositions. Some still considered themselves craftsmen, although the changed nature of patronage made it less clear why and for whom they were composing. But most probably thought little about some paradigmatic repertoire that would confer exemplary status on their work and ensure its repetition some unimaginable number of times. Perhaps Wagner provided the turning point at mid-century with his artwork of the future: a philosophical ideal implying repetition, longevity, and idealism.

Still, the concept of canonicity lay in the future. If we were to mark its inception we could say it started with the Bach edition in the last half of the century and the other sets of complete works and monuments that followed. Or we could go back to the growing nineteenth-century predilection for repeating works of past composers, especially Mozart and Haydn and then Beethoven, a practice reinforced by their adulation as subjects of numerous essays.[37] Or we could attribute its beginnings to the issuing of musical anthologies, in the second or third decades of the twentieth century. Or we could take heed of which composers and compositions were emphasized when style became the basis of history, especially in Riemann's contributions *c.* 1900. If we had a broader definition of canonicity we might agree with the ideas of William Weber. He argues that it began in the later eighteenth century, especially in England, after many older works had become part of a repertoire of repeating classics.[38] These are all candidates. A "right" answer might depend on one's precise definition of canon. But I suspect that each represents an important moment in musical canonicity; perhaps one should not worry excessively about exclusive origins. Nonetheless, I see anthologies as markers of one important stage in *ad hoc* canonicity. Anthologies have traditionally devoted themselves to presenting works that the compiler considers worthy of being included, whatever the specific purpose of the anthology and whether or not quality is a stated criterion.[39] This indicates a self-conscious sense of active selection from some larger pool of works the compiler believes exemplary toward the achievement of his or her ends.

Anthologies tend to confer the status of masterpiece on their constituent members. Conversely, once a work is deemed a masterpiece it raises the status of the collection in which it appears. Together they constitute a circularity akin to canonicity itself. Historicism and a growing respect for the past implicitly created the notion of masterpiece: a work worthy of being repeatedly performed, published, and written about, eventually acquiring a permanency comparable to a painting in a museum.[40] Many in the twentieth century have lamented the situation. Aaron Copland, for example, complained that "it leaves a minimum of wall space for the showing of the works of new composers, without which the supply of future writers of masterworks is certain to dry up."[41] In the nineteenth century, repeated works were only individually called masterpieces and even more rarely considered paradigmatic within some defined repertoire of masterpieces. What I am suggesting is that a sense of canon was not possible until individual masterpieces were joined with others in a discrete repertoire and viewed as a group that embodied whatever paradigmatic traits one thought were exemplified by that repertoire. This does not mean that individual works before 1900 were exempt from adulation as masterpieces or great works. We know of many pieces that were considered exemplary or great. But these were mostly individual cases, not part of some larger paradigmatic repertory or canon.

The formation of repertories grew out of a confluence of favorable conditions at the end of the eighteenth century. Social power moved from court and Church to the public arena, and traditional patronage and the functional reasons for writing music began to wane. The careers of Haydn and Mozart typify the vagaries of this gradual changeover. Arguably the most significant shift occurred with the commercialization of music, which was rooted in capitalist ideals of free enterprise and the market-driven economy. Many segments of musical life were shaped by the new mercantile emphasis: music publishing, music magazines, concert series, instrument makers, critics, entrepreneurial composers, and independent performers and performing groups. Behind it lay the Enlightenment notion of the autonomous individual with unlimited potential if unfettered by socio-political restraints. But in practice this universalist ideology pertained mostly to the experiences of the dominant cultural group, namely the white middle- and upper-class male. As we shall see later, women's experiences and talents often flourished in their own kinds of social structures, with their own paradigms.

The music business fed off a growing moneyed class with time and means for the consumption of music. The extent of the commercialism varied. With a strong mercantile tradition, London probably fostered these institutions the most; with a conservative and repressive climate, Vienna tended to absorb the new institutions more slowly.[42] Taking their cue from the influential *Allgemeine musikalische Zeitung*

(1798–), music magazines were important in promoting music to a growing public: reporting on concerts, reviewing and publishing new music, and presenting articles on miscellaneous topics of interest. Features on earlier composers, theorists, and musical practices were especially significant in creating a respect for the past. This historicizing slant acted as a means of instilling "correct" aesthetic values in the readership – values that could influence taste in the consumption of music. It can be argued, in fact, that historicism in general was motivated by a "concern for the taste of the present."[43]

Contents of reviews were instrumental in shaping taste, of course. But the very fact of which pieces were selected for evaluation itself advanced a point of view. This was not always an aesthetic matter. Many leading magazines, for example *Allgemeine musikalische Zeitung* and *Revue et gazette musicale de Paris*, were owned by publishers of music (Breitkopf & Härtel and Schlesinger, respectively). These provided an obvious vehicle for promoting financial interests in the works chosen for review. Indeed, perhaps it is not unreasonable to suggest that historicism arose partly in response to the needs of entrepreneurs to create viable markets in music – ones that would appeal to the growing middle class. For written media in particular new music may not have sufficed, and thus the past became the repository of additional works and figures to fill up the pages.[44] We should also note that the concert review in the daily newspaper was another means of shaping taste.

As Kerman has suggested, music critics in the early nineteenth century grew out of a literary tradition. Many influential writers, such as E. T. A. Hoffmann, extended their aesthetic outlook to encompass music. This took the form of reviews, but the work was represented by a score rather than a live performance.[45] Perhaps this had something to do with the fact that music was now considered one of the fine arts,[46] and as such might take on some of the tangibility of other art forms. This type of judgment not only constructed an ontology of the score but also reinforced the power of material media to define music. As written documents they acquired enormous weight in their capacity not only to be read and re-read, but preserved for some future readership. Accordingly, composers had to pay more attention to being judged. In earlier days a performance would take place, a patron would assess a work verbally, and the judgment would evaporate and elude permanency. With written criticism, however, the nature of creative accountability changed.

Instead of a direct kind of responsibility, composers were now answerable to an impersonal group known collectively as the public. Were they supposed to please the public, edify the public; was there a moral imperative?[47] Who was the public: was it that large amorphous body or was it really the individuals who dispensed written judgment to and on behalf of the public? It was critics, after all, who were making the kinds of pronouncements that strongly influenced public opinion.[48] Critics were also shaping public taste in their essays on other musical topics. It is interesting that some composers functioned as critics and thus propagandists of their own aesthetic. Perhaps this served as a way of neutralizing the creative anxiety many must have felt *vis-à-vis* the changed dynamic involving the evaluation of their music. On a societal level the ideology of transcendent genius may have functioned as another means of alleviating anxiety. As for female composers, they probably did not experience this kind of creative anxiety to the same degree because many worked in the private sphere, beyond the purview of the critic.[49] In any case, a collective literature began to accumulate. This created its own literary history, and with this the door opened wider to the notion of historicism.

An important factor in the rise of public music was the increased non-functionality of the musical work. In the old system a piece was created for a specific occasion with a specific set of listeners. The composer knew with reasonable certitude the values and ideologies of the listeners, and these generally coincided with the function of the work. But with the gradual dissolution of the traditional reasons for writing music, composers must have begun to feel unsettled about which styles might work. As noted, their livelihood now depended upon acceptance by a public–commercial machinery. I believe that as the century progressed, the various agents in the music business, including the entrepreneurial composer, began looking to previously acceptable stylistic conventions as one means of achieving security. This may explain, for example, the continued vitality of the sonata aesthetic.[50] Perhaps some considered the public fickle and unpredictable, and the idea of repeating a "sure thing" would seem attractive. The social composition of the public, mostly middle class, probably contributed to the standardization of aesthetic values at some median level – this despite a competing ideology of novelty. The standardization could foster audience expectations for stylistic familiarity – not necessarily uniformity – which in turn would prompt repetition of musical works in performance. Perhaps this desire mirrors larger concerns of the later nineteenth century. It might express a societal yearning for security in the face of the challenges of secular political power, a new reality for much of Europe. Or perhaps it represents a means of social consolidation at a time when colonialism underscored the existence of foreign cultures and hence potential encroachment of a cultural Other. At any rate, historicism served as a strong impetus for repertorialization, and this formed the basis for the notion of canonicity at a later stage.[51]

There is more to be said about repeating classics. Weber believes that they arose as a means of fighting the crassness that accompanied the commercialization of music.[52] It is an interesting theory that ties in nicely with the efforts of Schumann and others to combat philistinism and uphold the good and true in music. But commercialism was more than an impetus for a defensive posture. Indeed, commercial interests seem to have supported the notion of repeating classics: by publishing older music, promoting their performance, and writing about them. While further research would have to be conducted on the details, commercial interests apparently found older music profitable. It was a way to make money. Although seemingly contradictory, the two theories highlight two facets of the musical markets in the nineteenth century. Many kinds of music were available for public consumption, a fact too easily forgotten when we focus on the canon of works handed down to us. I suspect that both processes were underway simultaneously, and this shows the complexities of the interrelationship between aesthetics and economics. The composer, meanwhile, was looking for a means of legitimation in the loosened social structures in which he found himself. The notion of past "masters" provided a sense of identity, and it placed him in a line of descent that could affirm the evolutionary ideas circulating at the time. The public was also involved. Edward Dent has suggested that the public very much wanted to be a collective patron. But it was not able to do so, for two reasons: first, it did not have the financial resources to support new music; and second, the public did not understand what patronage meant. It could support older works, a less expensive proposition, and this was one of the main reasons for its affinity for repeating classics.[53]

Another factor in the movement toward canonicity is the nationalistic tendencies of the late eighteenth and nineteenth centuries. As a given culture sought to engender a sense of unity and common purpose, it looked to the past for symbols of its heritage. Music could serve that purpose. I am not implying that this was one of the major reasons for repeating classics. But I do think that it probably figured in the social dynamics that affirmed the past. For example, even as early as the founding of the Paris Conservatoire in 1795, one goal was an aesthetics that replicated the politics of democracy touted in society at large.[54] Across the Channel the Handel Commemoration of 1784 was an important event in the celebration of a specifically English (*sic*) music.[55] Or moving to the late nineteenth and early twentieth centuries, we see the beginnings of national collections such as *Denkmäler der deutschen Tonkunst* and *Denkmäler der Tonkunst in Oesterreich*. It is also important to remember that musicology itself is implicated in the process. As we know, it arose as a result of the historicist movement of the nineteenth century. But once established, its own growth helped sustain the trend toward canonicity into the next century. It is hard to imagine the entrenchment of the canon without the historicist work of musicologists. Musicology supplied "scientific" legitimation.

The understanding and meanings of canonicity are bound up with format and transmission. In Western art music textuality has virtually become inherent in compositions.[56] Instead of functioning as visual representations of an aural experience in time, maps to the realization of the piece, or symbols of its essence, scores are often considered first and foremost the pieces themselves.[57] This creates at least two ontologies for any composition: the texted version and the aural realization in performance. The latter, of course, subdivides into a separate ontology for each performance. Musicology has focused mostly on the texted version, using it as the basis of historico-stylistic analysis. Indeed, musicologists and music theorists resemble literary critics in this regard. Literary critics, however, tend to subject the texts to cultural analysis as a matter of course, which is partly explainable by the more obviously narrative content of literature. In any case, traditional musical analysis has remained mostly within formalist discourse. In the academy, where musical analysis occupies such a central pedagogical role, score anthologies resemble literary anthologies. Although there are some significant differences, a score can be read through like a piece of literature. We even talk about notated versions in terms of grammar, vocabulary, and themes. Although we want our students to realize that such technical analysis relates in important ways to actual performance, usually their principal musical activity, still we might have to admit that the formalist emphasis can create a greater intersubjective space between performer and performed than desirable. It also suggests that the piece exists mainly for its own sake and has little to do with larger social implications. All in all, the emphasis on music-as-physical-object that arose in the early nineteenth century was instrumental in paving the way for the notion of canon.

Canons have a great affinity for a written tradition: they thrive on such visceral data. But writing is not the only means of preservation. In dance, for example, transmission still occurs principally from choreographer to dancer who in turn becomes choreographer. This human sequence bears some resemblance to the human chain of an oral tradition, discussed below. Nonetheless, traditional methods in dance have been buttressed by a written idiom in the form of notations that map out the steps. More recently, dance preservation has also begun to depend on filmed or videotaped realizations. Although not literally "written," these visual representations are material, and like material forms of music can be read, held in one's hand, and physically accessed. This visual text performing itself, or being interpreted as performing,[58] has its counterpart in videos of musical works. These kinds of recordings convey the oral–aural dimension, the principal sensory element in music, but reify the visual to a prominent position akin to the dance video. Of course, for certain kinds of musical works on videocassette, such as opera, one could argue that the visual rightfully occupies a prime position and thus its form as a visual text is entirely appropriate. Like its incarnation as aural text in traditional recordings, the musical work as visual text implies permanence because of tangibility and repeatability. These characteristics can define the paradigmatic interpretation that will be emulated by others. This tends to challenge the ontological multiplicity of performances. Whatever the ontological implications, however, the video revolution helps to reinforce the traditional privileging of the visual over the aural in Western culture. Some have argued that this reliance on the visual represents a male epistemological mode, and by implication perhaps a suppression of female experience.[59]

Given that the Western musical canon relies so heavily on written transmission, one might wonder whether canons can emerge in oral traditions. Folk traditions, for example, are mostly oral. Expectedly, the temporal and geographical range of transmission will vary from work to work. One might be tempted to consider those with greater saturation part of a repertorial canon. Such works, however, might be better categorized as merely popular, important, or highly representative of their cultures. If we had a sense of a coherent and delimited group of pieces we might label them a folk repertoire. In the absence of some tangible record, such as a notated version or even a recording, it would be difficult to consider them part of a canon.[60] Even if there were a notated version, the meaning of the notation in that context would be critical. If, for instance, it were an exemplar of one of many possible versions of a folk song, it would serve mainly a utilitarian or referential function. This would not be *the* definitive version – there would not be one. Instead it would be one of many possibilities and take on a multiplicity that strips away the veneer of moral authority vested in the ontology of the definitive version.[61] The casual status would indicate that oral traditions stress process over material object – written versions are the exception. Similar kinds of problems would arise with recordings. While we cannot take the time to go into these complex issues, we can re-emphasize the material basis of canons and point out that they are most pertinent to cultures or sub-cultures in which writing and literacy are fundamental: in creating, transmitting, reproducing, and allowing reference to a work. This suggests an obvious class bias in favor of the educated, at least in the Western sense.[62]

Another aspect of an oral tradition deserves attention. An oral tradition propagates works that lack a strongly defined sense of an individual creator. The absence of notated versions removes one of the most obvious ways that an author becomes identified: the name on the score. Oral transmission in some cultures seems to promote changes to the work as it gets passed on, and this complicates the question as to what *exactly* constitutes the piece. In effect there are numerous creators: each person in the process who makes changes. The situation bears some similarity to improvised traditions in Western music. Not coincidentally these declined in the nineteenth century as historicism and individualism gained a foothold. The concept of multiple creators, whether specific individuals or community effort, contrasts with the ideology of the individuated composer so valued in the West, at least after 1750.[63] It has become canonic in musicology[64] and in general strengthened the ontology of music as material object: music in the one version created by the composer and then visually reproduced.[65] This ideal, however, is tempered by the fact that notation can never be absolutely specific, and thus there is always the question of multiple versions. I am talking mainly about an ideology – that somehow a visual representation is definite and precise, and more preservable and reproducible than other media. Such a tangible lineage makes the canonic process more feasible.

It should be noted, however, that there are various theories of oral transmission, as a result of several factors. First, there are many cultures in many eras, and one's hypotheses about trends may apply only to a relatively limited repertoire. Second, there are usually few documents to work with in oral transmission, and this makes the task of conducting historical research more difficult. Third, there is the anthropological challenge of applying a Western mindset to the study of another culture. Another complicating factor can emerge if the culture is in transition and oral and written transmission co-exist. All of these suggest the difficulty in making definitive statements about the relative behaviors of the two modes of transmission.

The relationship between written and oral transmission has been re-theorized in recent years. It has been suggested that the two modes are so intertwined in certain repertoires that it is a distortion to speak of them as distinct processes.[66] Another revisionist theory concerns oral and written modes in Western art music. Specifically, before the advent of written notation in plainchant, oral transmission necessitated the retention of the music in memory. This meant that change was relatively slow. Written transmission, in contrast, has allowed for relatively rapid change because the permanence of the notation eliminates the need for human retention.[67] "Change" here denotes broad stylistic changes over a culture rather than changes to a particular work over time. Indeed, in a very general comparison between the two types of transmission, one could infer that oral transmission tends to promote changes within a given work as it gets passed on; written transmission would keep a given work constant yet encourage a multiplicity of styles within the culture. Written transmission means there are numerous works preserved, each in the definitive version, in potentially numerous styles.

But what lies behind the strong desire in the West for preservation? Why has it become such an ideal, indeed an emblem of high culture? Perhaps it stems from a male wish for self-reproduction, as Suzanne Cusick has suggested.[68] Perhaps it involves the related notion of a narcissistic urge of the male to see himself reflected indefinitely in institutions and objects. Both provide a comforting sense of immortality. Another factor could be the fear of encroachment by competing groups and ideologies. A means of maintaining control over disenfranchised groups would be exclusion through the reification of writing as the privileged medium for cultural communication. Similarly, the reification of certain values and conventions may have functioned as an effective means of suppressing a female presence in music.

WOMEN AND THE CANON

Perhaps the reader misses a female presence in the largely gender-neutral perspective of the previous discussions. Because the semiotics of canonicity and the formation of canons from cohering repertories have taken place mostly within dominant ideologies, I have had little need thus far to make distinctions in terms of gender. The more obvious reason is that women have exercised minimal power in the formation and semiology of the canons of Western art music. If they had a greater voice in canonicity, then gender would have figured prominently in the narrative. This of course does not mean that women have been silent as composers, performers, and participants in other facets of music. It does suggest that what we might call mainstream canonicity has derived mostly from male structures and conventions, and canons have provided a powerful tool for their self-perpetuation. For a complex set of reasons women have generally been omitted or excluded; thus the canon is still overwhelmingly male in its membership. This is true whether we are referring to the teaching canon, the standard repertoire, or other major canons of Western art music, even though music by women is beginning to affect the values behind current canons and position itself for eventual incorporation into canons with a more pluralistic set of values. This will take time. Meanwhile, the increased presence of women in musicology and the substantial number of studies devoted to women and feminist issues are diverting disciplinary canons away from exclusive focus on male subjects and a positivist approach to history. In particular, the subtle link between musical women in the present and the past should not be underestimated for its potential in effecting change.[69]

As noted, anthologies play an important role in the teaching of music history and can serve as a barometer of canonic culture.

Unfortunately an overview of some standard anthologies yields disappointing results for women composers and their music.[70] Probably the most influential collection, the *Norton Anthology of Western Music* (New York, 1988), which accompanies the fourth edition of the Grout–Palisca *A History of Western Music*, contains only one piece out of 163 by a woman, a *canso* by the medieval composer the Countess of Dia. In addition to the extremely low percentage I am struck by the fact that women are missing from later periods of music, eras in which more composers have been identified and for whom there now exists a relatively rich pool of music. Plantinga's anthology *Romantic Music* is similarly disappointing in this regard, including no works by women, although the accompanying textbook provides brief discussions of two composers, Fanny Hensel and Clara Schumann, and a reference to another, Corona Schröter. The third and fourth editions of *The Norton Scores* (1977, 1984), a series widely used in music surveys for majors and non-majors, include a work by a woman, a movement from Ruth Crawford Seeger's *String Quartet* of 1931 (a different movement in each edition). Although I have not conducted a comprehensive survey, I suspect that the representation cited here is characteristic.

But related materials of more recent vintage offer encouraging signs that the influence of women's increased visibility, historically and professionally, is beginning to pay dividends. Thus the recordings that accompany the sixth edition of *The Enjoyment of Music* (New York, 1991), ed. Joseph Machlis and Kristine Forney, contain a work by Clara Schumann. In addition, two survey textbooks offer greater coverage of women. K. Marie Stolba's *The Development of Western Music: A History* (Dubuque, Iowa, 1990), intended for music majors, discusses women relatively often in comparison to older surveys. These include well-known figures like Hildegard, Schumann, and Seeger; and the "less familiar," such as Barbara Strozzi and Alma Mahler. Intended for the more general student, R. Larry Todd's *The Musical Art: An Introduction to Western Music* (Belmont, Calif., 1991) similarly mentions many women, and accords Schumann and Ellen Taafe Zwilich fairly extended analytic treatment. Robert Winter's *Music for Our Time* (Belmont, Calif., 1991) also makes a solid effort to incorporate women. I suspect that future texts and anthologies will continue in this direction.

Yet as I applaud the trend – it is crucial to expose students to women and their music – I have some concerns over the basic approach to women in these materials. It resembles what Karin Pendle has termed "add and stir":[71] the addition of a few new women to the old historiographic recipes, a technique that does not significantly change the batter or the finished product. While Pendle mainly applies the phrase to the need for separate histories of women's experiences, I find it an apt metaphor for the dangers of merely inserting women and their music into existing structures without at least questioning them in terms of gender. While some existent paradigms may be applicable to gender others will probably not, and may in fact reinforce women's position as Other to the mainstream canons of Western art music. Chapter 6 discusses these issues at great length so I will not explore them further at this point. But suffice it to say that it is critical that women's activities be understood in their own terms, and not only with respect to existing categories, conventions, and figures – classifications that play a critical role in canonicity in general. Yet a crucial first step involves identification and analysis of the complexities of these elements in terms of gender.

As we have seen, canonicity is a powerful concept that implicates a multitude of factors rooted in culture and history. How Western society has viewed creativity, that most basic property behind the birth of a composition, provides a good starting point for our study.

CHAPTER 2

Creativity

Virginia Woolf tells the story of Judith Shakespeare, an imaginary sister of the famous playwright.[1] Extremely talented, adventurous, yet denied education, forbidden to pay attention to books, and forced to marry a local tradesman, Judith rebels and runs away to the big city, to London. Here she lives her fantasy by hanging around at stage doors and hoping to become a part of the life of the theater, like her brother William. She meets a man of the theater, who befriends her, and soon she is pregnant. Now in a state of shame and isolation she has nowhere to turn, especially back to her home, and she commits suicide. Thus the fate of sixteenth-century women who dared challenge patriarchal codes. This story, however, is not too different from later images of women. Particularly in the Romantic period, female characters who dared flout convention and transgress male limits of their sphere of creativity often ended up mad, confined, or dead.[2]

Daring to write, daring to compose: at the least a challenge facing talented women, at the most an act of rebellion. A positive response has the potential for meaningful personal expression and hence enormous satisfaction. But should the decision be made not to create, in spite of talent, then works do not emanate. That woman is lost to posterity, to that accumulating history from which repertories and later canons are made.[3] Of course it is impossible for us to know how many Judith Shakespeares of composition we have lost – women who wanted to write music but were discouraged, forbidden, or subtly channeled into other, more "womanly" paths of life. We shall also never know how many others were detoured even before they arrived at the point of knowing they wanted to compose.

In the Western art tradition women have fashioned varied connections to the creative act. There are many important questions to be asked. What are the foundations and manifestations of those

44

connections? From what kinds of positions have women had to negotiate the legitimacy of their creativity? How have they dealt with symbolic and rhetorical strictures aimed at creative suppression? What kinds of tangible constraints have they faced? How have psychological factors affected self-confidence and what has that meant for the larger historical picture? And what are the personal and historiographic implications of the notion of a female tradition? These will form the basis of discussion in this chapter.

Creativity has assumed several meanings. Most fundamental is the sense of making or fashioning. This often implies making something where little or nothing existed before. Thus the created product and the maker gain status on account of the distance traversed from the starting point to the completion of the task. A second sense involves the characteristic of talent, as in "one is creative." For example, a person has a good sense for selecting matching fabrics and wallpaper, or for devising some unusual solution for a challenging repair. A third meaning applies to acts considered special or highly meaningful by society, as in the creation of a painting or composition. A quality of transcendence often adheres to this type and it is part of the legacy of the nineteenth-century view of the artist.[4] It still holds powerful sway in helping to maintain structures of art in Western society – classical music, museum art, ballet – which became repertorialized in the late nineteenth century and canonized in the twentieth. A fourth sense of creativity connotes authorship: being an author and what it means to be an author – for the individual, the created entity, and society at large. In the course of the chapter I will be discussing aspects of creativity that rest on one or more of these meanings and I hope my intent will be clear in the given context.

GENDERED THEORIES OF CREATIVITY

Patriarchal society has captured the concept of creativity and deployed it as a powerful means of silencing women. Literary critic Susan Stanford Friedman has summarized the gendered wordplay associated with creativity.[5] Creation, which involves the mind, is reserved for male activity; procreation, which involves giving birth, is applied to women. Labor refers to men's production, to women's reproduction. Conceiving for males is mental and takes place in the head; conceiving for females is physical and occurs in the womb.[6]

The pairs share a gendered split between activity of the mind and of the body, and clearly privilege the former. The imagery for male activity is celebratory, for female activity negative. In this modeling entities once-removed are favored over the *ur* material, namely life itself. Culture is privileged over nature. The distinctions imply exclusivity: not only that men cannot (and should not) partake of women's bodily kind of creativity, but that women are unable to partake of men's intellectual kind of creativity.

As these pairs suggest, artistic creativity has been linked with the creation of life. It could be argued that attitudes towards the relationship between gender and artistic creativity are derived largely from beliefs surrounding the creation of life. Both are characterized by male appropriation. This reflects a variety of concerns, rational and irrational, among them a desire for social power, a fear of female hegemony, and a fear of women's body and its mysterious powers.[7] An important part of this appropriation is discreditation of the meaning of women as givers of life and creators of art. This leads to suppression of the feminine. Fortunately it has not meant that women have dared not compose. Many have, and often with great success. But it has often been difficult for women to move beyond the negative metaphors, and there have been considerable psychological costs.

Ideas on the creation of life begin with God. In the Bible God is the first creator of life – the prime progenitor. God is actualized as male and referred to as He, Lord, and King. This forms the basis of the connections between creator and male, divinity and creativity, and divinity and male. Created in God's image, man assumes the potential if not the actuality of these characteristics. Consider, for example, the observations of Anaïs Nin on the impact of the lineage. She notes that some male friends speak of "the necessity of 'I am God' in order to create," but believes it really means "I am God, I am not a woman." She continues, "This 'I am God,' which makes creation an act of solitude and pride, this image of God alone making sky, earth, sea, it is this image which has confused women."[8] Besides addressing creative legitimation, Nin raises the issue of identification. She hints at aspects of socialization and subjective positioning that make it difficult for women to imagine themselves in the role of creator; these will be discussed later. Of course, the genderless or gender-inclusive God that has been introduced in liberal denominations can mean new implications for the line of descent. But this is relatively recent and still considered radical. While it may carry weight in some quarters, societally it cannot compete with the mainstream view of a few thousand years, which says that God is male. Perhaps it might make a difference in the future.

The male progenitor of the Judeo–Christian tradition is often a female in other traditions. In ancient Greece, for example, the ultimate authority for fertility and generation of life resides in female goddesses. Often identified with the earth, some goddesses bear the iconographic attributes of roundness, pliancy, darkness, and comfort. One sees figures like this in Mayan art, African art, and other older civilizations. In musical terms I am reminded of Jacques Chailley's cosmology of female signs in *The Magic Flute* or of the very character of the goddess Erda in *The Ring*.[9] The basis for the connection between deity of creativity and women is obvious: women physically give birth. Then why a male God in the Judeo–Christian tradition? No doubt this is a controversial issue among biblical scholars and feminists, and no simplistic answer will do. The issue is further complicated by the fact that many believe that scriptural authority is absolute and therefore beyond cultural analysis. We do not have the time to go into any detailed discussions on the matter. Perhaps one factor is that historical conditions were such at those times when the Bible was formulated and translated that the institution of a male God was believed critical to maintain the social order. This is a kind of male appropriation.

God's association with the creation of life is not total, however. Certainly it is metaphysical, prestigious, and symbolic; it is bound up with the notion of life as a miracle sanctioned by the divinity. But it is semiotically removed from the mundane realities of life-giving, namely biology and sex, and has even less connection with the gestation period and the pain of giving birth. These areas are linked with women, and more specifically with women's body (intercourse also with the male body). The physical workings of women's body – giving birth, menstruating, nursing, and so on – have evoked feelings ranging from awe to jealousy to terror. These stem largely from a fear of the unknown. Women's bodies are different and mysterious, possibly threatening, and hence must be contained. The denigration of women – symbolically, rhetorically, and materially – is a powerful part of that control. So also are the limitations imposed by the state on women's reproductive freedom.

The ideology of the untamed female body – a "natural" body, beyond the civilizing effects of culture – has led to measures intended to curb her role as life-giver. As the first woman and mother, Eve has made a useful symbol. Her moral weakness in allowing herself to be tempted caused the downfall of humankind. While this could have been interpreted as human error it has been ascribed to her femaleness. Many, including John Milton in *Paradise Lost*, indict Eve's sexuality and her ability to create life. In the Renaissance some women rewrote the Eve story to allow themselves morality and creativity.[10] At least one recent interpretation has recast the issue as Adam's "womb envy."[11] Performance artist Laurie Anderson retells the story from a woman's point of view in "Langue d'amour."[12] But mainstream rhetoric has deployed the story to help sustain a discreditation of women's bodies and their importance to the birth process. In the seventeenth century, for example, the mechanist theory of reproduction was revived. It effectively obliterated women's participation in the creation of life by holding that women were merely transitory vessels until the delivery; God and man were the true agents of procreation. It was also around this time that the medical establishment began to appropriate the job of birth attendant, a task previously in the hands of midwives. This represented more than just a contest between lay women and professional men for control of the birth process. It meant pathologization: a further objectification and dis-embodiment of the female body. It probably confirmed society's fears about the evils of women's body. In Western countries today, a woman typically has her baby in a hospital – a place meant for sick people. What is fundamentally a natural process has been brought into the arena of culture under the watchful eye of the male medical establishment.[13]

Despite the appropriation, the fact remains that life issues directly from women's bodies. Men cannot change that[14] but they have found other ways to control creativity: as creators of art works. In a sense these function as substitutes for the real thing; art works are entities once-removed. This moves the arena of creativity to the level of culture: culture as the power structures run by men. Culture, indeed, has been positioned in Western discourse opposite nature. Culture is privileged and associated with men, while nature is inferior and linked with women. Culture encompasses knowledge and human-made social structures. Nature implies a pure state unmediated by intellect. While Rousseau and others have praised nature for its moral innocence, nature has often been construed as a negative sign. Sometimes the feminine has been used to affirm its weaknesses.

Francis Bacon, in the early seventeenth century, believed that nature had to be tamed by science, and he often used gendered metaphors to describe that process. Bacon "united matter and form – Nature as female and Nature as knowable. Knowable Nature is presented as female, and the task of science is the exercise of the right kind of male domination over her."[15] Science in this construct represents an emblem of culture. Others have used the nature metaphor to characterize essentialist weaknesses in women. Nietzsche, for instance, remarked that "Woman is more closely related to Nature than men and in all her essentials she remains ever herself. Culture is with her always something external, a something which does not touch the kernel that is eternally faithful to Nature."[16] Such rhetoric acts as a self-fulfilling prophecy as it keeps women outside structures of acculturation and preserves male power. Nietzsche went on to stress the need for men to express their creativity "artificially, through the medium of technology and symbols. In so doing, he creates relatively lasting, eternal, transcendent objects, while the woman creates only perishables – human beings."[17] While an affirmation of my argument regarding men's relationship to creativity, Nietzsche's statement adds the element of permanence: longevity, even if artificially constituted, is preferable to life itself. This says a great deal about the value systems of Nietzsche's time and his place in them. Perhaps the Wagnerian rhetoric of the artwork of the future still resonated for Nietzsche when he made the statement. Perhaps not coincidentally, this was also the time when cohering repertories were becoming more prevalent and responding to a cultural desire for permanence.

As noted, culture and nature have been constructed in Western thought as a hierarchic relationship.[18] Because of the negative consequences for women this might suggest that it would be best to dispose of the paired concept. But I think this is a good case where revelation of biases and suggestion for reconceptualization are more feasible than elimination. The culture–nature hierarchy is a deeply entrenched ideology and would not disappear just because it is thought to be prejudicial. We might heed the advice of anthropologist Sherry Ortner, who did pioneering work on exposing the cultural implications of the pair. She suggests the model of a continuum, which plots gradualism rather than either/or opposition. On this view women (and men) stand at various positions in the middle. We could structure the continuum as a circle and thus provide unity and continuity. The terms could be plotted in innumerable ways with respect to the intervening degrees. In addition, the two distances might have different meanings, e.g. varied rates of movement. Ortner conjectures that women might function as mediators along the continuum. This idea is attractive because of its holistic implications and its sensitivity to the needs of particular situations. It also suggests an interactive rather than static model.

As itself a product of culture, the culture–nature hierarchy has functioned as a rhetorical means of excluding women from the creation of art. The relegation of women to the lower natural sphere reserves the higher level of culture for men. Creativity is wrested from the natural and housed in the more prestigious cultural. Thus artistic creativity forms a "natural" association with men. Again we might ask, why? What are the personal and societal needs for the exclusion of women from artistic creativity?

One obvious reason is political: the fear that women could become successful as creators and crowd out men. As Christine Battersby observes, "Men would not have insisted that creativity is a male prerogative unless women created – and unless men were afraid that women's creations would be taken seriously."[19] This should be seen within the context of the societal perception that art itself is linked with the feminine (and also the effeminate). Masculinizing the arts, which includes the obvious strategy of keeping women out, can lessen the threat of that association.[20] It has been suggested, for example, that modernism arose as a means of countering the feminization of literature and music. This placed men in the uneasy position of having to react to foremothers, thus presenting a fundamental problem for Oedipal resolution. One outcome of this male dilemma was the formation of an aesthetic intended to exclude women, namely modernism.[21]

Appropriation also provides a means for the suppression of the female body. This is obviously a more intangible reason, but arguably the need lies at the heart of the psychological anxieties towards women. We have observed that the reproductive powers of women have evoked strong feelings. The womb has been feared for its mystery, unpredictability, and potentially magical powers: something beyond rational social control. If kept out of the realm of artistic creativity it is that much less of a threat. The awe/terror also derives from the fact that it is this very body that men themselves come from. Thus there is no clear "natural" separation between men and women, and the suppression of that female physical source becomes all the more urgent. Yet as there is a fear of sameness – that men could be considered women[22] – there is also the recognition of the sexual powers of the female body *vis-à-vis* men. Here there is difference. This difference has often been represented as the power of women's sexuality to "swallow up" male sexuality. This could be especially harmful given the metaphorical connection between male virility and creativity. In the Renaissance, for instance, male sexual potency was considered the basis for creativity, which could be depleted if expended in sexual acts. Even as late as 1888, Van Gogh advised an artist friend not to "fuck too much"; this will make the paintings "all the more spermatic."[23] There are two interesting implications for women. One is that they cannot be creators because they lack a male's sexual equipment. The other, more indirect, is that as the recipients of sperm in the sexual act women are somehow robbing a man of his creative powers. This is reminiscent of the old belief that in the act of receiving semen women were weakening a man – enervating him, stealing away the life force. How fascinating that the moment of climax, popularly understood as a conquest, could be construed as a metaphor of sexual victimization.

In the process of deconstructing the sexual connections to creativity feminists have devised some apt metaphors. Thus the pen in literature and the paintbrush in art have been termed a metaphorical penis.[24] In music the pen used to notate music is comparable. Probably more vivid are the phallic performative symbols of the conductor's baton and certain instruments, notably the woodwinds. Predictably, women were prohibited from playing instruments held directly in the mouth. The phallic symbolism of the baton captures the realities of historical male presence at the head of orchestras. All of these symbols may be another indication of male appropriation. Largely through the sign of their bodies women have been displaced from artistic creativity.

Given the masculinization of art it is interesting to consider what happens when a woman decides to become a creator. Susan Gubar believes that the de-feminization may lead female creators to perceive the creative act as a male violation of their bodies. "If artistic creativity is likened to biological creativity, the terror for inspiration for women is experienced quite literally as the terror of being entered, deflowered, possessed, taken, had, broken, ravished – all words which illustrate the pain of the passive self whose boundaries are being violated."[25] Some of this terror and pain is expressed in ambivalence, to be discussed later. While Gubar's position may appear extreme, it points up the power of acculturation for women in male society. The internalization of the link between creativity and male cultural power may be so strong for women that engaging in creativity means being taken over by the sexual potency of men. This might feel like sexual violation. But while I see the value in this interpretation I have two reservations. One is the graphic nature of the metaphor, whose language implies rape. I find that inappropriate here and in a broader sense worry that excessive use of such language can dilute the horror of what rape is when it actually occurs. Second, Gubar's metaphor may imply an undue victimization of women that hinders their chances for creativity. But, to repeat, on the positive side it underscores the complex psychological ramifications of the privileged link between artistic creativity and male sexuality.

Male appropriation of creativity has depended on another ideology for its success: the link between creativity and the mental. This has been an important element in naturalizing that appropriation. The mental, or the mind, has been considered fundamental to creativity. While this might seem odd given a general understanding that art deals in emotions, an oppositional concept to mind, the emphasis has provided a means of excluding women. The mind–body duality has been of longstanding interest to philosophers and exerted considerable cultural force.[26] In general, "rational knowledge has been constructed as a transcending, transformation or control of natural forces; and the feminine has been associated with what rational knowledge transcends, dominates, or simply leaves behind."[27] Reason has often served to express and privilege maleness.

Plato was one of the first to propose the separateness of the mind and body. For him the body was a disruptive entity to be conquered, as a master would conquer a slave. It contained the soul, struggling to escape. Transcendence beyond the body was possible only when the soul departed at death. Nonetheless, the body did possess the potential to inspire efforts toward the attainment of knowledge, in the realm of the mind. In the seventeenth century, which saw the scientific appropriation of the female body, the theories of René Descartes signaled a radical reformulation of the mind–body relationship. He theorized mind and body as two distinct substances, oppositional and incapable of merging. According to philosopher Susan Bordo, "The mutual exclusion of *res extensa* and *res cogitans*

made possible the conceptualization of complete intellectual transcendence of the body, organ of the deceptive senses and distracting
'commotion' in the heart, blood, and animal spirits."[28] The rarefied
realm of the mind was totally isolated from daily concerns, which
were linked with the body. This was not only a reinforcement of *de
facto* gendered roles but a means of "opening the way to the idea of
distinctive male and female consciousness."[29]

The deceptive body came to be seen also as the source of emotions
and emotional instability, which were linked with the feminine. For
centuries women have been considered too "emotional" to create –
an ironic observation given that emotion is arguably a major
component of art.[30] Emotional meant irrational, and the dualism
rational–irrational emerged alongside mind–body. The rational
described the activities of the mind, associated with men, and the
irrational the body or the emotions, linked with women. Many
philosophers would deploy the hierarchical analogy to limit the
participation of women in creative life, e.g. Rousseau and Kant in the
eighteenth century and Hegel and Schopenhauer in the nineteenth.[31]

The mental–rational has had a powerful means of expressing itself:
in Logos, or the power of the word. This "became the paradigm of
male creativity, indeed the foundation of Western patriarchal
ideology."[32] It has sustained those structures that shape and govern
Western society, and it is arguably the main vehicle for exercising
cultural power. While Logos has assumed both written and oral
forms, it is the written that has been more important in the
negotiation of societal attitudes and paradigms. Its ability to create
permanent documents has made it privileged, and, as discussed in
Chapter 1, that can be critical in the formation of canons. Because of
many factors, to be discussed throughout the book, women have been
denied full access to Logos, or more broadly the power of expression.
This takes in artistic creativity but could also include the various
modalities of expression that are to be found in music, for example
performing, speaking about one's own music, or writing about other
music.

As a means of finding an equally powerful communicative vehicle
situated specifically in women, some French feminists have theorized
a fascinating metaphor for negotiating the space between a woman's
body and her creative powers. *Ecriture féminine*, or "writing the
body,"[33] centers on woman and proceeds from something intrinsic to
her – the fact of her body, which is uniquely "woman" and thus her

own. It celebrates the body as the source of her spirit, creativity, and strength. Some American feminists, however, have questioned its vagueness, its impracticality: how does one *literally* "write the body"? Is this a process of transforming the personal and social meanings of one's (female) body into a written text? How does one convert physical sensations into writing? How does female sexuality figure in the process? Proponents might respond that in order to find a means of female expression we have to move beyond the rational of patriarchy and create a discourse that luxuriates in that which makes women women. While this strategy veers into potentially dangerous essentialist waters, it helps to rescue the female body from its position as "Other" in mainstream culture.

For American feminism, with its pragmatic bent, "writing the body" may be most useful for its suggestiveness; it can help reconceptualize harmful ideologies.[34] Indeed, the negative imaging of the female body has taken its toll on creativity. An anxiety of body has fed an anxiety of authorship.

ANXIETY OF AUTHORSHIP

Many female composers of art music have expressed an anxiety of authorship,[35] with authorship defined here as the state of writing or having written a piece of music (we will explore another sense in Chapter 3). The anxiety often translates into ambivalence: contradictory statements or actions about one's relationship to the creative process. The ambivalence usually indicates a lack of confidence. Emma Lou Diemer (*b.* 1927), for example, notes that "it has been necessary sometimes to work on my confidence as a composer." And an anonymous respondent to a questionnaire sent to women composers in the early 1980s writes about the "Biggest problem for women composers: not enough emphasis in woman's upbringing on ego, courage, and independence. Affects self-image as composers. This is a bigger problem than outside prejudice and/or male chauvinism."[36]

While recent composers may be more self-conscious about the nature and causes of creative ambivalence, earlier figures also expressed self-doubt. Fanny Hensel (1805–47), for example, wrote to her brother Felix Mendelssohn in July 1829 about an eight-voice piece she had just written for her fiancé, the painter Wilhelm Hensel:

It won't be much but it will be something … . You know how concerned I always am that my imagination will run away from me, so therefore I'm happy if I succeed in writing down some notes, without having much of an idea at the start as to how it will turn out afterwards. Later, of course, I fret if it's bad.[37]

A year later, after the lengthy "confinement" that culminated in the birth of her son Sebastian, Hensel lamented that "I haven't composed anything yet; I had plenty of ideas when I wasn't permitted to compose, but now I'll probably undergo the familiar dearth of inspiration, which I pick up from the weather" (*Letters*, p. 106). And some ten years later, on a trip to Rome, she noted that "no ideas strike me any more – nothing good and nothing bad. *Dio mio!* Abraham is getting old" (*Letters*, p. 288).

Hensel's lack of confidence resulted from many factors. Limited space prevents a full airing of the issues and I refer the reader elsewhere.[38] But especially in letters to her more well-known brother, which constitute the bulk of her available prose, it is clear that Fanny often viewed herself as Other to the gaze of the self embodied in Felix. She saw that gaze as controlling and determining her creative worth. In mid-career, for instance, she wrote to him,

I don't know exactly what Goethe means by the demonic influence, … but this much is clear: if it does exist, you exert it over me. I believe that if you seriously suggested that I become a good mathematician, I wouldn't have any particular difficulty in doing so, and I could just as easily cease being a musician tomorrow if you thought I wasn't good at that any longer. Therefore treat me with great care (*Letters*, 30 July 1836, p. 209).

When Hensel was contemplating the major step of publishing under her own name, she asked not only for his opinion but his approval:

With regard to my publishing I stand like the donkey between two bales of hay. I have to admit honestly that I'm rather neutral about it, and Hensel, on the one hand, is for it, and you, on the other, are against it. I would of course comply totally with the wishes of my husband in any other matter, yet on this issue alone it's crucial to have your consent, for without it I might not undertake anything of the kind (*Letters*, 22 November 1836, p. 222).

Here the subjective gazes of two important men in her life – brother and husband (her father had died the year before) – were vying to supplant Hensel's own subjective gaze: a process in which her view of her creative panorama was intercut with a notion of self emanating from another individual, placing her subjectivity in the objectified position of Other. It is no wonder that such internal struggle between inherent self and cultural other expressed itself in ambivalence. Yet Hensel resisted the objectified other status by reinstating her own self: she did go ahead and publish and would do it again nine years later.[39]

In a few instances Hensel transferred her own gaze to that of Mendelssohn. She told him to report every detail to her, for he was her eyes, during his *Bildungsreisen* to Weimar in 1821 to see Goethe, and to Paris in 1825 to see the capital of musical life. Nonetheless, Hensel assumed a strong self in certain circumstances, as when Mendelssohn sent his pieces to her for criticism. Athough he would tease Hensel for being a harsh critic, Mendelssohn did not express anxiety about his creative abilities after harsh judgments. He does not appear to have taken on objective status; perhaps he transferred that status to the piece under question and thus removed himself from the self-object dyad. But, unlike Fanny, Felix did not have to fight internalized prescriptions about what the "Other" gender should be doing. Hensel also assumed a strong self as leader of bi-weekly musicales, which showcased her abilities as performer, conductor, and composer. As a structure built on interconnectedness and community, the *salon* functioned as a brilliant socio-intellectual locus for gifted women. Occasionally she felt ambivalent about her pianistic abilities. Yet such expressions were usually associated with performance in the public arena (this began in 1838 and was rare) or a situation that would subject her to direct comparison with Felix. In short, it appears that Hensel's subjective self felt most threatened when creativity was at issue.

Clara Schumann (1819–96) also displayed a split sense of selfhood: a strong subjected self when it came to performing, a self tending toward objectified Other when it came to composing. Like Hensel, Schumann felt like Other to close male figures: first her father, the domineering pedagogue Friedrich Wieck (1785–1873), and then her husband Robert (married 1840). For example, regarding her splendid g-minor Trio, Op. 17 (1846), Schumann recognized some good passages but went on to say that "naturally it is still women's work, which always lacks force and occasionally invention"; a year later she compared it negatively to Robert's Trio, claiming that hers "sounded quite effeminate and sentimental."[40] Schumann's negative feelings had been echoed even before she felt the weight of a male-composer-as-spouse. In 1839 she wrote in her diary,

I once believed that I had creative talent, but I have given up this idea; a woman must not wish to compose – there never was one able to do it. Am I intended to be the one? It would be arrogant to believe that. That was something with which only my father tempted me in former days. But I soon gave up believing this.[41]

This intriguing statement raises questions. What factors caused Schumann to lose her confidence? Did being a grown woman instead of a girl signal the closing off of possibility? This could force her to acknowledge prejudicial ideologies that were easier to ignore as a child. How decisive was the recognition that she apparently knew of no successful women composers (successful, of course, could mean many things)? Did Robert's ambitions to make it as a composer in the late 1830s play a role? This could have intensified her understanding of societal notions of proper roles: men create, women re-create. And finally, did great success as a performer somehow make creative success that much more remote? Perhaps society could sanction or tolerate a successful woman in one area but not in two. Exceeding that boundary could have moral repercussions.

Schumann's statements imply a moral awareness: a woman's understanding of the impropriety of taking up the pen, almost in the sense of transgression. Two late eighteenth-century composers, Corona Schröter (1751–1802) and Maria Theresia von Paradis (1759–1824), had made similar remarks.[42] Schumann uses the word "arrogant," which implies unseemly pride and self-assertion. She speaks of "women's work" and as such identifies woman as Other in relation to the masculine creative act. Schumann, to a lesser extent Hensel, and many other women creators thus internalized the philosophical tradition of creativity situated in the rationalized subjectivity of man. The physicality of woman as the true creator of life is suppressed as Other. By extension the female persona is denied legitimacy as a source of creativity.

An interesting question is why Western women have taken up and continued to take up the pen to compose given their ambivalence.[43] In the nineteenth century this means mainly white women of the middle to upper classes, but a much wider range develops later. Some recent composers, for example, come from a lower middle-class or blue-collar background. In addition, many more women of color have become art composers, for example Florence Price (1888–1953). Particularly in light of this growing diversity, it would be foolish to attempt any one answer to our question, as individuals do things for a variety of reasons. Nonetheless we might be able to posit some hypotheses. For one, composing may function for many female composers as a prime means of self-expression: not just *a* means of expression but as the main way to channel their inner selves into some tangible form. This might be different from the situation for males who compose. As the privileged gender in Western culture, men possess many more outlets for self-expression in addition to that of the art work. For women, perhaps, composing *per se* has existed as more of a necessary activity; arguably this is the case for the imaginary writer Judith Shakespeare. In addition, for women the creation of a work may bring body and mind together and thereby resist the negative implications of the mind–body split.

Given the potential for expressive satisfaction in composing, it might be useful to reconsider statements of creative ambivalence. Perhaps such expressions convey an impression of creative disability – that ambivalence has paralyzed compositional activity. But I do not mean to imply disability, at least for those whom I have quoted, who have achieved some degree of success. Perhaps the ambivalence is best understood within a particular context. I am thinking specifically of the situation where a woman and her music are being judged. This involves such structures as publications, commissions, competitions, performances, and reviews – in short, the public arena. These trappings of professionalism might evoke negative self-analysis. In other words, the fact or prospect of being judged in public – of being tested according to some standard of quality – often causes ambivalence. Of course, doubts about compositional talent can strike either gender. But women assume artistic creativity from a potentially different set of subjective positions to men, at least in terms of societal rhetoric about proper roles. They undergo a double test, as it were: as ideological outsiders and as composers of music. The very fact of challenging the stereotype of the male composer has its psychological costs. In addition, the moral stigma still resonates, even if it is hushed. Most women today, however, would probably not feel as though they were committing a sin or transgressing by being composers. Minority women attempting to create in the Western art tradition, still a white bastion, would feel the conflict more strongly. In general, we might conclude that the main reason a woman composes is the same reason a man chooses to compose: women have something to express, and expressing it in musical terms is important. But *how* a woman expresses herself can be linked with aspects of her gender and their intersection with cultural and aesthetic conventions (more on this in Chapter 4).

How a musician becomes a composer involves a music education: the fact of that education, the nature of that education, and the meaning of that education. Most musicians would agree that a music education functions as a necessary ingredient in composing, at least in the Western art tradition. Traditions that are more oral and improvisatory, such as folk music or jazz, depend less on formal education and may in fact be able to dispense with it entirely. Other structures, such as apprenticeship, play a greater role. In the West two constraints are noteworthy. First, some aspiring composers have faced parental opposition, usually paternal, to serious music study. Ethel Smyth (1858–1944), for example, locked herself in her room for days in order to convince her father of her determination to study at the Leipzig Conservatory. Hippolyte Chaminade would not permit his daughter Cécile (1857–1944) to attend the Paris Conservatoire, although he allowed her to study privately with some of its faculty. Rebecka Clarke (1886–1979) had an ongoing battle with her strict father to become a musician. With her mother's support, Germaine Tailleferre (1892–1983) attended the Conservatoire over the objections of her father. In the case of Augusta Holmès (1847–1903) it was the mother who objected to music study. After she died Monsieur Holmès secured instruction for his daughter.

Second, some women were barred from classes or programs open to men only. American composer Mabel Daniels (1878–1971) tells the amusing story of the astonished reactions of the male students to her entrance into a classroom one day: she was the first woman admitted to a score-reading class at the Munich Conservatory. She also notes that "until five years ago [1897] women were not allowed to study counterpoint at the conservatory. In fact, anything more advanced than elementary harmony was debarred."[44] At the Paris Conservatoire women were apparently excluded from advanced theory and composition classes until well into the century, and only in the final decades admitted into programs in these areas.[45]

But even with *de jure* equality, *de facto* acceptance into needed educational structures has taken a long time. Rejected as a composition student at the Oberlin Conservatory in 1944, Edith Borroff (*b.* 1925) recalls that it was very difficult for a female to find a teacher who would agree to take her on in composition.[46] Ethel Smyth observed some ten years earlier that "There is not at this present moment one single middle-aged woman alive who has had the musical education that has fallen to men as a matter of course, without any effort on their part, ever since music was!"[47] Just as when talent goes unrecognized, it is impossible to estimate how many women never managed to become composers because they received little or no training.

In general, the kinds of instruction one is expected to acquire function as canonic constructs. They reflect ideologies of what is considered good and what kinds of training will produce that result, and simultaneously perpetuate those same ideological values because the desired kinds of music embodying those values continue to be composed and praised. Structures of education, especially their categories and emphases, both shape and predict outcome. They are specific to social factors such as class, race, and gender.[48] Western music over the past few hundred years, for example, has stressed complexity in texture, timbre, and harmony. This has tended to privilege largeness: more notes, more sound sources, more performers, more volume. Arguably these pertain to general cultural paradigms, especially the political expansionism of the nineteenth and early twentieth centuries. As these paradigms become reprivileged through music education and the next generation of pieces, they become reified on the social level as well. Thus continues a multi-directional process that involves music and society.

It is useful to compare music with other creative fields. Western art music since *c.* 1750 has required skills that one can acquire only through some kind of formal training, whether in a school or privately. Literature also requires literacy and a familiarity with other works. But it does not necessitate a comparable array of specialized skills. It is, Ethel Smyth notes, a "relatively simple matter ... to become a writer. You can teach yourself to write by reading, by watching life, by taking flights on your own and inflicting the result on such of your friends as have patience and discrimination." The novel has proven especially felicitous as a vehicle for female self-expression.[49] Art, however, is more analogous to music in the need for training. Although women were barred from important educational institutions at various points since the Renaissance, the most critical exclusion was their prohibition from life anatomy class. This involved sketching the male nude from a live model. The exclusion was particularly problematic in the nineteenth century because the skillful rendering of the human body still formed the basis of the history painting, and the history painting still occupied top position in the hierarchy of painterly genres.[50] This situation resembled women's exclusion from advanced theory and orchestration classes – this at a time when music was valued for its complexity and size.[51] In the next century subtle discrimination replaced statutory restriction. Katherine Hoover (*b.* 1937), for example, was steered away from composition in college because of her gender.[52]

Encouragement is crucial, particularly in the family. As noted elsewhere, women composers, at least those who actually became composers and whom we know about, usually came from musical or artistic homes.[53] Several have written about the importance of encouragement for the creative act and for continuing to create, particularly since women have had to depend upon assumptions other than that of their own tradition to understand the place and function of their contribution. What may rank as the most egregious piece of discouragement comes from none other than Gustav Mahler. With a fragile ego and a heightened sensitivity to potential competition, Mahler forbade his fiancé Alma Schindler (1879–1964) to compose. He must have realized she was a creative force to be reckoned with. "He considered the marriage of Robert and Clara Schumann 'ridiculous,' for instance. He sent me a long letter with the demand that I instantly give up my music and live for his alone."[54] Mahler's change of heart several years later apparently stemmed from fear that his wife was about to leave him. Although we cannot be sure, it seems as if the independent-minded Alma Mahler continued to compose during the forbidden years. Gustav's death in 1911 freed her from an oppressive father figure. Although she apparently did not go on to compose a great deal of music, her proto-modernist songs might be said to express an *Angst* that derives partly from a suppressed creativity.[55] Near-contemporary Lili Boulanger (1893–1918), in contrast, enjoyed enormous support and encour-agement for the development of her creative imagination. She was surrounded by a family of musicians that included women who had been professionals (mother, grandmother) or were now aspiring to professionalism (her sister Nadia). In this favorable environment, in spite of enervating illness, Boulanger captured the Prix de Rome, in 1913. She was the first woman composer to win the competition.[56]

Boulanger's case of strong and assumed female creativity hints at the importance of the female bond in establishing an enabling sense of self. Feminists have spoken particularly of the mother–daughter bond. This was distorted in Freudian and other classic psychoanalytic accounts because it was viewed as an offshoot from the central theoretical concern – the relationship between the son and each of his parents. Studies of early child development have also tended to focus on male behavior, although they often fail to acknowledge the gendered limitations of their results. Nancy Chodorow in particular has done groundbreaking work in rebutting male-focused Freudian theory and, even more important, positing models that specifically center the subjective status of female development. Rejecting Freud's attribution of male and female developmental differences solely to their sexual makeup, Chodorow locates gender difference in the mother–child relationship. As those generally responsible for the care of young children, mothers are socially geared toward the care and welfare of other people – toward connectedness with others. As they interact with their female children they feel a special sense of interconnectedness because of gender identity. Young girls feel likewise towards their mothers. This leads to flexible ego boundaries that enable connection with the outer world. There is a lessened sense of differentiation from others. Boys, however, "come to define themselves as more separate and distinct, with a greater sense of rigid ego boundaries and differentiation ... . The basic masculine sense of self is separate."[57]

An influential study that has cast a wide shadow, Chodorow's *The Reproduction of Mothering* (Berkeley, 1978) has been criticized for its universalizing tendencies. But psychological studies are often transhistorical and culturally ambiguous, and in certain contexts could imply universalism. This contrasts with recent feminist preference for social specificity.[58] As for the present context, I am aware of the dangers of utilizing psychological theory but see important mitigating factors. First, my study is focused on a specific social group: white, Western, middle- to upper-class women over the past two hundred years. Arguably they share many of Chodorow's developmental features. Second, although I can appreciate the view that this is a diverse group socially and temporally and that it could be misleading to apply developmental theories without further qualification, I am afraid that such restrictiveness would preclude psychological theory except in the most limited of cases. Yet it can be instrumental in illuminating important aspects of gender, especially in broad historiographic discussions. Third, Chodorow's work is based on patterns of socialization and not on inherent traits. It can be socially grounded within a given context and thus minimize generalizing tendencies. Indeed, I try as much as possible to do so. Thus in spite of potential difficulties I have decided to weave Chodorow's ideas into the argument. But they are only one strand in the conceptual fabric.

With a few notable exceptions, most investigations of female composers, mirroring scholarship and culture at large, have ignored formative female figures: mothers in particular but also other female relatives and friends. This reflects the conditioning of most scholars, of both genders. The internalized message is that history-worthy influences consist mainly of known figures, virtually all of them male. They are likely to be defined by male culture with certain kinds of historical criteria. But as feminists have asserted, when questions are posed that lead to new criteria for what is important and therefore history worthy, new figures and kinds of information emerge as important parts of her-story.[59] One such previously hidden figure is the mother. Unfortunately it is still difficult to tell many maternal stories for female composers because there is very little information available. But for a few composers we have at least a fairly good sense of the importance of the maternal link in fostering the creative impulse.

Although seemingly molded solely by her father Friedrich Wieck, Clara Schumann became who she was in no small measure by virtue of her mother, Marianne Tromlitz Wieck Bargiel (1797–1872).[60] Bargiel, who married Wieck in 1816, was a professional singer who performed regularly in Gewandhaus concerts; she was also a fine pianist, better than Wieck, who was known mainly as a pedagogue. Unable to withstand Wieck's tyrannical nature, Bargiel left home in May 1824 and within eight months obtained a divorce. In that period the five-year-old Clara was wrenched from her mother and taken to live permanently with her father, in line with the law. Although Clara only saw her mother from time to time and occasionally wrote her during her formative years, the bond between them was important. Nancy Reich surmises that Clara's strength and determination, not to mention her considerable musical gifts, came from her mother.[61] Clara had in front of her a glowing model of a professional woman who was extremely active in many areas of musical life. While growing up Clara probably carried a vivid belief in her own powers as a female musician largely because of an identification with her mother. As far as I know, however, Bargiel was not a composer. Perhaps it was the inability to identify with her mother as a musical creator that formed the basis of Clara Schumann's ambivalence towards writing music.

Fanny Hensel, in contrast, had the good fortune to be the product of an extremely stable family.[62] Born into the rich matrix of post-Enlightenment Jewish culture, Hensel had a mother who provided musical, intellectual, and spiritual nourishment. Lea Salomon Mendelssohn (1778–1842) was herself a musician, having studied with the Prussian composer–theorist Johann Philipp Kirnberger.[63] Said to have declared at Fanny's birth that her daughter had "Bach-fugue fingers," Lea Mendelssohn served as Fanny's first music teacher, in piano. She made sure that her daughter had the finest musical education. This included piano lessons with Ludwig Berger, and with Marie Bigot when the family visited Paris (1816); and theory instruction with the renowned pedagogue Carl Friedrich Zelter, at least partly at his Singakademie. In short, it was apparently Lea Mendelssohn who made sure that Fanny received the kind of training that a talented boy would receive. This is borne out by the similarity of Felix's education. Her support went beyond education, however. It was Lea who wrote to Felix on Fanny's behalf in mid-1837 to ask him to assist Fanny in the publication of her music; he declined to do so. Lea Mendelssohn not only believed strongly in the creative talents of her daughter but, unlike her son, apparently saw no real or imaginary barriers towards a full flowering of Fanny's compositional aspirations.[64]

Hensel also had several other strong female role models in the family, on both sides. Among these were her mother's aunts. Sara Levy (1761–1854) was a pupil of Wilhelm Friedemann Bach, a fine harpsichordist, a famous *saloniste*, and a patron of W. F. and C. P. E. Bach. Fanny Arnstein (1758–1818) was a leading Viennese *saloniste* and philanthropist, and a founder of the Gesellschaft für Musik-freunde (Fanny was named after her and her sister, Caecilia Eskeles). Whether directly or indirectly, these sophisticated women, which also included Lea's mother Babette Salomon (1749–1825), had a hand in shaping Fanny's activities. Their pluck and independence were matched by two sisters of Fanny's father. There was Dorothea Veit (1764–1839), who left her husband and ran off with Friedrich Schlegel, and thence became one of the real-life "heroines" of early German Romanticism.[65] And there was Henriette Mendelssohn (1768–1831), brilliant *saloniste* and headmistress of an exclusive finishing school for girls in Paris. Ten-year-old Fanny must have spent a great deal of time with her during a lengthy stay in the French capital. We should also not underestimate the importance of her close relationship with her only sister, Rebecka Dirichlet (1811–1858). A talented soprano, highly educated, and especially good at languages, Rebecka may have provided a steady on-site support that was indispensable to Hensel's commitment to composition. In fact, some future study of the interrelationships among the four siblings (the youngest, Paul, was a gifted cellist) would be quite useful.

We might wonder why Hensel experienced creative ambivalence given such a strong female heritage. But there was still the dominating presence of her father; he had made it clear early on that Fanny's role was to be housewife and adornment, not professional musician. And there was Felix, who perpetuated patriarchal authority after Abraham Mendelssohn's death in 1835,[66] not to mention societal ideals about woman's proper activities. Despite female strength and power in abundance, familial authority for artistic creativity resided in men. Nonetheless, as we have seen, Hensel resisted and eventually reappropriated creative authority by publishing *en masse*.

Closer to the present, Edith Borroff has spoken fondly of her mother, composer–pianist Marie Bergersen (1894–1989), and of her central position in the regular musicales that took place in their home.[67] Around the age of three Bergersen herself was already participating in the family's musical gatherings, which her mother had begun. Borroff tells of the participation of the entire family, each person contributing his or her particular skills to the musical fun, and of her own entrée in the 1920s. Benefiting from a strong female tradition in her family, Borroff seems to have acquired her basic aesthetic views in this environment: the potential for quality in all kinds of music; the non-dominance of Western art music; and a decided preference for the performance experience itself over the texted representation of a score.[68] This holistic view of music may characterize a female aesthetic perspective and parallels the developmental profile sketched above, with its emphases on connectedness and flexible boundaries.

These women, as well as others too numerous to detail here, reaped enormous benefit from maternal figures who understood what they were about and themselves formed a crucial part of a female tradition with which women musicians could identify.[69] Of course, a maternal figure need not necessarily be a blood relation; Ethel

Smyth, for example, was a maternal presence for the younger Virginia Woolf.[70] As Gilbert and Gubar have noted, an important strategy for a woman coping with the anxiety of authorship is finding a tradition in which she has a place.[71] A familial tradition, as important as it may be, functions as only one component in a composer's sense of situatedness and identity. Female colleagues, precursors, and successors, or at least the understanding that there will be successors, together make up a present, a past, and a future that are a crucial enabling of the creative act for a woman.[72] For example, New-Zealand born Annea Lockwood (*b.* 1939), in the United States since adulthood, has written of the importance of mentors and community. Recalling the "electricity" of meeting Elisabeth Lutyens (1906–83), the first female composer with whom she came in contact, Lockwood remarks that "I think it would have been very good for me to have had more contact with older women composers, particularly." Furthermore, "had I had close contact with a woman composer during those years, I would have become aware of the cultural imbalance much sooner and it might have enabled [me] to see what I thought were personal problems in a truer and broader context." By the late sixties and the onset of the feminist movement, "I badly felt the need of other women artists around me. A friendship with Pauline Oliveros ... made such a deep difference to my life, as a later friendship with the composer Ruth Anderson is doing now." But Lockwood is optimistic and points to the "delights of the developing community of women composers which now exists [*c.* 1981] – communities really, but many are interconnected."[73] Composer Anna Rubin (*b.* 1946) also affirms the importance of collegial community. Organizations for female composers, such as the International League of Women Composers (founded 1975, and merged with the International Congress on Women in Music in 1991), provide support and perhaps serve "to validate and make easier the transition to professional status for younger composers." I find the validation function compelling. If the female composer feels that she exists as a *unicum* there always lurks the spectre of illegitimacy: of lacking social or even moral justification for being a composer. The situation reminds me of Lockwood's statement above about being able to place problems into truer perspective once she mingled with other women composers. Rubin also singles out Oliveros as an important role model but notes that the "dearth of women in academia" makes her angry.[74] Not only does this absence confirm what students internalize from their music history and theory classes – that there were/are no women composers – but as statements by Lockwood and Rubin imply, it fosters an undue sense of isolation, alienation, and creative anxiety in female composition students that could be alleviated by female mentors.

The situation for black women composers of art music assumes two aspects of identification with a past. Margaret Bonds (1913–72), for example, could forge dual connections in her composition studies with Florence B. Price. Although Bonds studied with Price at a relatively early age and with others as she progressed in her musical education, the presence of a mentor in two areas of "Otherness" probably played a major role in her desire to become a professional composer.[75] A fuller discussion of this notion of doubled Other – or possibly tripled Other, if one considers American music a muted tradition – to the mainly male, white canon of Western art music will have to await another study. It will also be important to explore the dynamics of black women in relation to white women composers. What is the impact of class as well as racial difference? How did segregation affect music education? What forms of support and resistance do black women art composers receive from the black community? In short, how does the fact of racial Otherness complicate the already complicated picture of canon formation in the Western art tradition?

The presence of a past can go a long way toward assuaging creative anxiety. But which past does the female creator relate to: some neutral or universal past, a male past, or a female past? Perhaps she might want to relate to more than one tradition. But if one of them is a female tradition the problem is that there is still no fully formed female tradition to relate to. Music by women is performed occasionally but still has not acquired the status of a meaningful tradition. As statements by many women suggest and as I have been arguing in this book, relating to a neutral past can mean marginalization and subordination to the ideologies of dominant culture, which is male culture. This may be especially true given that women are socialized in dominant culture. In fact, there is no such thing as a neutral, universal past; every past represents a later reconstruction that selects what it wishes to emphasize.[76] Can a female find a place in a male tradition, i.e. can she relate to male figures, male stylistic paradigms? Can she locate her identity in a tradition that has been male? Obviously, in the sense that for women before *c.* 1950 a male past was "the only game in town," a woman had to relate to that tradition. With rare exceptions she learned music only by men and studied only with men (at least theory and composition); history books spoke almost exclusively of men. Yet how could a woman composer feel validated psychologically if she had no history, no precursors? Virginia Woolf put the situation well, in 1929, when she noted that for the female creator who had no female past, the choice was either to demur to men, claiming she was "only a woman," or protest that she was "as good as a man."[77] By asserting the latter she might be consciously rejecting her femaleness. Only by marking herself as different from what patriarchy considered inferior or by being perceived that way could she hope to gain acceptance. Symbolically this might resemble an inverted Oedipal killing: woman killing the female culture she came from.

This might have been especially understandable around 1900. Aesthetic conditions were such that women might be praised for sounding like men and criticized for sounding like women. There seemed to be an understood typology of gendered musical traits. Knowing this, a female composer might want to mark herself off from other female composers and women in general. But being forced into this situation places her in a terrible psychological bind. It has the practical effect of draining her creative energies; it forces her to spend time concentrating on something extraneous to the work itself. Psychologically it splits her subjectivity into an internal struggle for selfhood, a battle unknown to males.[78] Perhaps this occurred with the following kind of review, written in 1903 after a performance of Ethel Smyth's opera *Der Wald* at the Metropolitan Opera in New York (the first opera by a woman performed there). The writer observed that with respect to strong climaxes and full brass writing "the gifted Englishwoman has successfully emancipated herself from her sex."[79] We tend to think of Smyth as a tough-minded individual, with a fluid sense of gender identification. Yet despite her pragmatism I suspect that such rhetoric could cause Smyth at least some measure of internal conflict.

It might be useful to make a few comments on the meanings of a female tradition. What is under discussion here is literally the presence of female composers, and the cumulative effect of their presence in constituting a tradition that is distinct from a tradition made up of men. In another usage, however, a female tradition could be problematic. It could have essentialist connotations if understood as a tradition that is pure in terms of style. That suggests that women's music is different from men's, and that it will possess womanly traits from one female composer to the next. One difficulty is that music as sound material seems to defy gender typing in any totalizing way. As to compositional strategies that might refer to gender, these might involve representation and deconstruction. But none would be essential to only female or only male composers. Part of this has to do with the fact that there has been a common stylistic language in music, available to all. Women, like men, are socialized into this language. A composer might devise a strategy in a particular piece to reveal some aspect of gender. But it would be an individual choice and make few if any claims on how other composers of the same gender fashion their musical language. Nonetheless, as a result of societal and technological changes and growing numbers of female composers, perhaps sometime in the future it might be possible to speak of a female tradition in terms of style or aesthetic.[80]

While many women experience internal conflict in negotiating the mainstream tradition, which is male, many men find themselves in a struggle that is more likely to befall them than women. It is what literary critic Harold Bloom has dubbed the "anxiety of influence": the creative anxiety one feels when confronting one's precursors. It proceeds much like an Oedipal killing.[81] The male needs to remove the onus of the (male) precursor's style and presence, and the only way to do so is to destroy, to kill that ontological weight. The theory seems predicated on the desirability and necessity of a strong sense of an individuated creator, who must establish his authority through separateness, difference, and by extension originality.[82] It appears to grow out of a profile of male psychological development. In its unconnectedness to others and an environment, and its concern with style, it seems to smack of modernism. Furthermore, its emphasis on an individuated creator who has to be original derives from nineteenth-century Romantic paradigms. The female creator, in contrast, has little place in an Oedipal relationship. Not only do the gender terms not apply, but Western women's socialization toward connectedness probably precludes or at least lessens the kind of competitive urge that would necessitate the metaphorical destruction of a precursor. Furthermore, women can look forward to becoming foremothers of their own traditions. As Gilbert and Gubar so aptly put it, "The son of many fathers, today's male writer feels hopelessly belated; the daughter of too few mothers, today's female writer feels that she is helping to create a viable tradition which is at least definitively emerging."[83] In music the analogous situation would involve the male composer, who at least since the early nineteenth century has been exhorted to be original, to mark himself off as a creative individual. While women composers might have been judged in those terms, and often found wanting, the fact of so few known female composers would be comparable to that of women authors. Thus Oedipal anxiety would not create pressure on women for stylistic differentiation. On the other hand, as Libby Larsen (*b*. 1950) points out, a woman composer may end up writing works that differ from currently favored styles. As compared to the male composer, "you don't expect to be heard, you don't have to fit into a tradition .... That frees you a bit."[84] This sense of being apart from the mainstream reminds me of Haydn's famous dictum on how he was forced to be original because he was isolated. In fact, this was as much historical as geographic. For Haydn the focus was on the present and getting the job done. Except possibly for his last years, past and future counted little in his conception of his place in music. He did not have to confront the past. Like women composers in general, male composers prior to the rise of self-conscious historicism were probably implicated minimally in this Oedipal "anxiety of influence."[85]

But even though women creators need not destroy precursors, they might need to destroy their own portrayal in works by men. In art, for example, the female nude and its objectification of women is a tradition that the female artist probably has to overcome in order to create. Rozsika Parker and Griselda Pollock show how some artists, especially Paula Modersohn-Becker (1876–1907) and Suzanne Valadon (1865–1938), redefine the meanings of female nudity and thereby reconstruct the tradition in which they are working.[86] On a societal level, the secret group Gorilla Girls exists for the express purpose of deconstructing and subverting discriminatory practices in the content and structures of art. In literature, male depictions of women also assume powerful symbolic force and become normative and prescriptive in defining women. The point is that a female creator herself is defined in terms of those male characterizations of women, with potentially devastating psychological results. Two literary images have been identified as particularly harmful: the "bogey" of John Milton's *Paradise Lost* and the virtuous "angel in the house" of much Romantic fiction. It is these, according to Myra Jehlen, that the female writer must destroy. She must commit this double murder, and, in general, "all women must destroy in order to create."[87] An ironic variation on this theme is Otto Rank's comment to Anaïs Nin that "to create it is necessary to destroy. Woman cannot destroy... that may be why she has rarely been a great artist."[88] Rank's target of destruction has little to do with women's negative depictions, however. He is probably referring to the paradigm of originality and how greatness means the metaphoric destruction of previous style through creative innovation. He seems to be describing an Oedipal struggle, pertinent to male development, and affirming Harold Bloom's ideas on the anxiety of influence, discussed above.

In music women who are composers (or theorists or musicologists or critics, etc.) might have to destroy their definition in compositions by men. They also need to murder their image as muse to male composers, a significant ideology of the late nineteenth century. The idealization of musical women as inspiration for male creativity and as re-producers of their music provided a means of displacing the threat of female creativity.[89]

Deconstructing these portrayals is a first step, and feminist scholars are beginning to tackle this enormous task.[90] The following discussions give some idea of how men have written women in representational music. I have chosen Mozart operas because I have discussed them at length in graduate seminars and find them rich. Above all I love them, and it is probably this more than anything that leads me to critique them. Overall I do not find Mozart particularly negative toward women, especially compared to other composers. Nonetheless, there are some problems, and as major works in the canon they need to be discussed.

We have already noted the misogynistic treatment of the maternal Queen of the Night in *The Magic Flute* (see note 9, above). Other Mozart operas contain negative portrayals of women, even though the composer is often sympathetic to his female characters (Susanna in *The Marriage of Figaro* is a good example). Arguably the most problematic of the Da Ponte operas, *Così fan tutte* has drawn heavy criticism since its première in 1790.[91] It should really be titled *Così fan tutti*: thus does everybody, males and females alike.[92] The seemingly small orthographic change is telling. *Così* is not really about female fickleness and deceit, nor women's weakness in allowing themselves to be persuaded to replace their lovers. It is, rather, largely about male duplicity. It is about Don Alfonso the manipulator, the cutout about whom we know virtually nothing as a person – a character whose questionable moral sense finds it amusing to play a cruel joke on the women and also, as it turns out, on the men. It is about Ferrando and Guglielmo, whose fragile male egos transcend a concern for their loved ones and who allow themselves to become pawns in Don Alfonso's malicious game.[93] Furthermore, the supposed duplicity of the women is paralleled in the actions of the men. In particular, the great duet "Fra gli amplessi" (No. 29), between Ferrando and Fiordiligi, tells us that in spite of themselves at least one of the men has become as deeply attached to his new lover as the women. In addition, the opera leaves us uncertain as to the pairing at the end. Perhaps the libretto's subtitle, *la scuola degli amanti* ("The school for lovers"), should represent the work: it implicates all four lovers, of both genders. Perhaps we should point the finger at Da Ponte rather than Mozart. But the composer has assisted in assigning moral blame to the women. This occurs mostly near the beginning of Act I, in the first appearance of the two sisters (No. 4). Musical lines of parallel thirds or sixths in the second half of the duet convey a sense of shallowness and hence lesser moral fiber. By the middle of Act II Fiordiligi and Dorabella will emerge as distinct personalities. But it is as if their "normal" state, which returns near the end of the opera, is one of mutual dependence.

Such traits have laid the groundwork for audience acceptance of the opera's title – this even though all the characters betray human frailty by the middle of Act II, and the ultimate moral salvo should be fired at Don Alfonso. Unfortunately most directors have internalized the message of the main title. Hence they have emphasized Don Alfonso's cynical view of women without pointing up its hypocrisy and the shared moral weakness of the six principals. Some recent productions, however, have spread the blame more equitably. These include Peter Sellars's version presented on American public television in early 1991, and the Goeran Jarvefelt and Harry Silverstein staging presented in Houston in April of the same year. While the former is an updated setting in a Westchester diner, with questionable success, and the latter a period piece, both give a sense of a morally reflective Don Alfonso. If such productions are indicative of current thinking about the work, we can look forward to more humane interpretations. They also suggest that women might have to consider additional structures as repositories for negative portrayals: performance history and critical reception. Indeed, it is often difficult to discern the line between the work itself and the work as embodied in a given production. Opera is especially susceptible to this ambiguity. Although there are limits, a director–producer can do a great deal in constructing the meanings and impact of a work. Thus the trappings of performance and reception need to be considered in a more expanded notion of the structures that convey negative images of women.

Don Giovanni (1787) also provides food for thought. Of paramount significance is the validation and near exaltation of rape: Giovanni's violent attacks on Donna Anna and Zerlina and his pre-opera violation of Donna Elvira. Giovanni is presumably punished for his sins at the end of the opera. Yet during the course of the work the seductions elicit laughter and admiration. We are goaded to view Giovanni as heroic and courageous (even though he is always unsuccessful, thus metaphorically impotent). A misogynistic feature are the exaggerated lines of Donna Elvira, as in her first aria (No. 8) – or rather, it is more correct to say that these lines have been interpreted in a misogynistic manner. Wide leaps and jagged rhythms have often signified heroism and courage in Western music. Yet for Elvira they are also seen as a lack of moderation and judgment. In general her music includes a fair amount of coloratura and some repetition; perhaps she is beyond rational control, taken over by bodily passions. These characteristics suggest female hysteria – a powerful sign of female madness that stems from medieval notions of the degenerate womb ("hysteria" back to Greek "hystera," meaning womb).[94] It is one of the most effective ways of discrediting a woman. Yet Elvira may be the most rounded and humane figure in the opera. It is she, after all, who engages Giovanni as a moral equal. Many directors, such as Von Karajan in the Salzburg production broadcast in 1989, dilute her credibility through physical movements that make her seem silly. A notable exception is the Donna Elvira conceived by Peter Sellars in the production aired on American television in January 1991. In this updated treatment grounded in urban violence and drugs – what Sellars dubs "a night in Hell" – Donna Elvira is a sympathetic and courageous character who faces down the knife-wielding Giovanni. Like the production in general she does not get laughs. This is a life-and-death contest for survival, and Elvira figures as one of the key players.

Idealistic pronouncements by influential Romantics helped construct the misogynistic interpretive tradition of *Don Giovanni*. These include E. T. A. Hoffmann's conception of Donna Anna as purity incarnate and Kierkegaard's view of the Don as embodiment of the realization of desire and hence of the life force itself. Hoffmann projects onto Donna Anna a male fantasy of desire: what a man in the early nineteenth century desired a woman to represent. Perhaps this was a secular replacement for the Holy Virgin in a self-consciously secular age – a version of the "eternal feminine." In general the nineteenth century paid much more attention to Anna than Elvira: the former could be idealized and controlled while the latter threatened ideologies of social relationship. Kierkegaard constructs yet another male fantasy: the man whom all women so desire that he is the *sine qua non* of life itself.[95] Frequently performed and arguably the opera revered most by musicians, *Don Giovanni* encodes the elevation of male violence and the objectification of woman as Other to the empowered male. The "beauty" of the Sellars production is that it foregrounds the inherent violence and subversiveness of the work.[96]

How do women respond to such denigrations of themselves? Many feminists have raised that very question and suggested that reactions are diverse: confusion, shame, denial, inferiorization, ambivalence, and, more recently, anger.[97] For such stories, telling of male experience from a male point of view, imply a male receptor. A female receptor, however, often ends up being forced to adopt a male point of view and thereby take a stand against herself and effectively participate in the conspiracy. She identifies against herself as she is swept up and sutured into male narratives and patterns of desire.[98] As Lawrence Lipking notes, illumination of such bias means that many works Western culture has valued are now uncomfortable or embarrassing.[99] As a woman I can affirm that kind of reaction for several works whose messages I first internalized along with those of patriarchal society, but which I now consider demeaning or harmful to myself and other women.

One such work is "Batti, batti," one of two arias for Zerlina in *Don Giovanni*. As Zerlina entreats Masetto, usually coyly, to beat her I wince and fidget. The aria conveys some harmful images: woman as a little girl to a patriarchal boyfriend who can punish her through violence; and woman's victimization in sexually masochistic acts, internalized to the point of willing submission. I have discussed this with many audience members, both male and female. Although both genders feel embarrassed and even puzzled (younger listeners), women tend to experience such feelings more keenly and painfully.

One successful but disturbing resolution occurs in Sellars's production set in the drug culture of the south Bronx (see also discussion above). In the preceding recitative Zerlina is beaten, offstage, by her jealous fiancé. This is deadly serious. When the aria proper occurs, therefore, Zerlina's words assume a meaning that is as far removed from coyness as one could imagine: she sarcastically asks to be abused some more. The victimization is much more direct than in traditional productions. Rather than embarrassment or discomfort, a female viewer (and a man) tends to experience feelings of fear and empathy. They hit close to home and are born of the contemporary realities of physical abuse of women and rampant violent crime, at least in American cities. Cute has been replaced by scary, but with a scary that is morally honest rather than demeaning.

After these critiques I think it is only fair to contextualize my remarks. I realize that I am imposing some modern standards of drama on the two operas, particularly realism. *Così*, especially, may have been intended largely as parody, and its artifices of plot and music (e.g. No. 4) could be considered appropriate to this dramatic framework. The didactic implications of the subtitle ("la scuola degli amanti") further suggest another plane of reality. Sellars's productions (also for *Figaro*) and much of my positioning to these works are rooted in expectations of realism. While *Don Giovanni* has been famous for its naturalism and thus ripe for such treatment, with *Così* a desire for realism could be a wish for something that the work cannot deliver. This aesthetic discussion could go on at length but that is not possible here. In any event, every era reinterprets works for itself, and in Mozart operas the richness of musical characterization makes possible connections to the present-day world. Perhaps that makes us expect more; we might *demand* contemporary relevance. Women might not accept as easily the misogynistic conventions that "passed" in earlier eras. As a means of mediation, perhaps what is important is that we try to understand the bases for our tastes and biases and still keep in mind the historical context of the work, to the extent that we can ever do that without intrusions from the present.

For women creators a potential means of expurgating the negative myths of women in works by men is the construction of a female aesthetic: women composers creating their own definition of self. But this may be highly problematic (see discussion above and at length in Chapter 4). The expurgation also takes place cumulatively through the institution of a female tradition. We have seen how many contemporary women composers are rejoicing in the community of a tradition in the present. Two questions arise: what was the relationship in the past, e.g. in the nineteenth century, between women composers and a female tradition? And what are some of the historiographic ramifications for women's music of the existence of a female tradition? As to the first question, in doing research on nineteenth-century women composers I have not seen an awareness of a female tradition. For composers of the early part of that century, of course, the absence of such knowledge is not surprising; European composers in general were only beginning to uncover past repertories. But I have not sensed a feeling of community with female-composer contemporaries, at least from the written records I know. Nonetheless we do have isolated statements, such as Clara Schumann's quoted above, that show an awareness that women have at least attempted to be composers. Recognition of the possibility of a past female tradition may have become important around the end of the nineteenth century. Smyth was certainly aware of its implications.[100] Female composers probably found community and support in female friends, some of whom may have been composers, and in social structures other than those patriarchal history has emphasized.[101] We do not know much about such sub-cultures for several reasons: the women composers we know of did not find such things important enough to write about, the documents in which they recorded such things are lost or destroyed, or such evidence has yet to be looked at or deemed significant.

Several composers have explained why a female tradition is crucial. American Amy Fay (1844–1928) noted in 1900 how male composers formed a tradition based on imitation. She believed that women should have the same opportunity: "If it has required 50,000 years to produce a male Beethoven, surely one little century ought to be vouchsafed to create a female one."[102] Some thirty years later Smyth raised the issue of critical mass: "You cannot get giants like Mt. Blanc and Mt. Everest without the mass of moderate-sized mountains on whose shoulders they stand. It is the upbuilding of this platform that is impossible so long as full musical life is denied to women."[103] In 1981 Priscilla McLean also utilized the building metaphor, noting that "the adage of a 'pyramid' effect building excellent composers is true. There must be a large base of women composers to assure the development of good works. This base has been developing for the last twenty years, and now is beginning to show some fruits."[104]

Women have developed other strategies for asserting their creative voice in patriarchy. One strategy involves resistance: resistance to stylistic norms, social institutions, behavioral and creative prescriptions, and to the internalization of the gendered codes embodied in Western art works.[105] Another strategy entails secretiveness: keeping one's creative fruits unseen by others, perhaps akin to a diary or some other form of personal expression.[106] Although the work might lose its meaning as inter-subjective communication, it could gain enormously as affirmation of self as the work became an extension of self or a communication between one's self and an alter ego. On a societal scale such self-ownership could be subversive. If pervasive, the Western ideology of a body of works to be shared and enjoyed by some larger constituency would be subverted. It would mean fundamental reconceptualization of the meanings of art in society. Given Western structures as they actually exist in the production and re-production of art, such self-appropriation would result in non-publication, non-performance, and hence probable preclusion from pre-canonic status. Thus the historiographic dangers. On a personal level, secretiveness could deny the composer the real joy of communication with an audience; for some this might be one of the main motivations for composing. Practically, of course, it suppresses what few structures exist for financial remuneration and makes composition a hobby. Thus while it may reflect what many female composers were forced to do as a result of discriminatory practice, the idea might be more of a fanciful abstraction than a strategy for creative satisfaction. Perhaps its applicability depends on one's conception of the necessity of communication in artistic experience.

Finally, an important strategy involves women creators establishing and working in their own sub-cultures: their own kinds of outlets for dissemination, their own audiences, their own structures for support and encouragement. This centers power in women and re-appropriates artistic creativity. It implicitly deconstructs many of the harmful dualisms discussed earlier, especially culture–nature and mind–body. "Composing the body," as it were, might be an apt metaphor. Yet as contemporary composers enjoy such structures, many worry about consequent marginalization and trivialization.[107] Some resist the term "woman" composer: any qualifier can imply specialness and therefore lesser competence. But many consider gender-specific structures necessary for strategic and psychological reasons at least until such time that "composer" is gender-blind and works by women receive as much attention as those by men. That might be the best of all possible worlds. Radical feminists, however, might view things differently: they might fear a solution that neutralizes the tensions of gendered difference. For in such a scenario the less powerful could be subsumed again under the more powerful, but with the critical difference that the less powerful would not think that a power differential exists any longer. As for myself, I am not in either camp but positioned somewhere in between. Practically I lean to the former, however. Improvement within the world as it is seems the more feasible strategy.

CONCLUSION: POSITIVE IMAGES FOR FEMALE CREATIVITY

Certain themes have threaded their way through the chapter, and they serve as the underpinnings of a positive view of female creativity. Denigrated in the mind–body split and other Western dualisms, the female body functions as a source of creative strength in its potential for childbearing and other creative acts, including giving birth to works of art. It has provided a societal pretext for male appropriation of creativity. White Western women of the middle and upper classes have generally been socialized to view their bodies and themselves within structures of connectedness: connectedness with their minds, their emotions, their activities, and with others in the external world. This connectedness corresponds to their psychological development; it enfolds continuities and inclusiveness largely because of women's positive gender identification with a nurturing mother. The psychological connectedness fosters the reaching out to others, especially females, without the barriers of hard-and-fast categories: personal rather than positional identification. For this reason and others, female creativity has a great need for communal support. This comes from family but is crucial in the form of external social structures, notably friends and colleagues. A sense of relating or belonging to a palpable tradition is crucial: a tradition of the past, on which one can build and to which one can look for models and validation; a tradition of the present, especially support groups promoting women composers and their music; and a sense of a future tradition, for which one can function as a precursor to subsequent women composers, many of whom the female composer hopes to train and mentor today. This chronological swing from past through present to future nurtures a sense of psychic and social locatedness and creates space for the unencumbered subjective gaze across the historical horizon. It also challenges the mainstreaming model of canonicity and opens up possibilities for models based on multiplicity. A bigger question arises: to what extent the concept of canon as presently defined can accommodate such flexibility. This awaits the final chapter, "The canon in practice."

CHAPTER 3

Professionalism

Professionalism has generally been considered a goal of a nurtured and practicing creativity in music. It has functioned as a powerful sign of success. Indeed, being a composer in the West may be equivalent to being a professional composer. That is, from a practical and ideological standpoint, composition as an activity carries little cultural weight beyond the frame of professionalism. To be a professional composer is to be taken seriously in one's own time and possibly in the future. It involves reputation, authority, and the circulation of a name within culture. How and why it circulates have a lot to do with preservation and the formation of canons. Thus professionalism forms a natural part of our study.

Yet what I have just described is merely the tip of the iceberg – the result of many practical and sociological factors that go into the making of a career. Critical reception is one, and that is reserved for a later chapter. Talent is of course another, and assumed as a given here. Professionalism also involves having one's music published, performed, and written about. These are obvious ways to bring compositions to the attention of the public. Such practicalities might suggest that professionalism is at odds with the ideology of canonicity. For canonicity implies high-minded characteristics like transcendence, disinteredness, and aesthetic distance. But these describe an ideology and not the realities of canonicity; this distinction, in fact, is one of the basic arguments of the book. Furthermore, it is these very practicalities that make up an important part of canon formation itself. There is also a natural link between canonicity and professionalism as emblems of prestige. Although different in kind and degree, both exude a moral authority that commands deep respect.

Behind the practicalities of professionalism lies a number of assumptions about the identity of the composer and his [*sic*] relationship with culture at large. The most obvious is that the professional composer is male. Another assumption, or perhaps better understood as a symbol, is that of the composer as social outsider. A legacy of nineteenth-century ideology that saw the composer as genius, it is a status that many composers still live with. Today it might be experienced more as alienation or isolation. In any event its Otherness seems to contradict the prestige inherent in professionalism. Yet these are not necessarily contradictory. It could be argued, in fact, that outsider status can actually contribute to the prestige of professionalism. For in some ways professionalism operates "outside" mass culture, passing fads, and bourgeois conventions; it prides itself on difference and moral superiority. Yet while outsider status has often worked well with(in) the paradigm of the male composer, the female composer has not generally enjoyed the benefits of professional Otherness. She actually stands as a doubled outsider to society. As one who does not fit the assumption of the male professional she bears an added layer of Otherness. While this can be advantageous in terms of subjective mobility (more in later chapters), it can cause serious problems of self-image and identity.

The notion of professional composer is not static but varies in structure and meaning. It participates in the dynamics of culture and will negotiate ideals of gender, class, ethnicity, and so forth. In the approximately two hundred years under discussion here professionalism has undergone several changes. At the end of the eighteenth century the European composer began to move away from the patronage system. He (mostly) helped sustain an entrepreneurial system centered in publishing and other commercial structures, including performance and journalism. In the twentieth century the state occasionally functioned as a kind of super-patron, as in Soviet Russia. In contexts with meager state support, such as the United States, the university has become the major support system for composers of art music. It provides basic subsistence, which can be augmented by grants, commissions, recordings, and private teaching. This history, however, is reflective mostly of male experience. With a few notable exceptions, most before the rise of public music,[1] women have faced formidable obstacles to professionalism. These stem from prejudicial attitudes and resultant practices that have excluded women from professional positions and the various processes that funnel into them: what Ethel Smyth has dubbed the "musical machinery."[2] In the nineteenth century, particularly, women did not fare well. This would seem paradoxical given increased educational opportunity for women. Yet the growing gendered split between public and private brought on by industrialization often caused women to fall further behind, especially middle- and upper-class women.

The powerful musical structures, such as orchestras and music publishers, were public and market-based. As such they were generally off-limits to women who attempted to function in them as individual agents. At the least, codes of decorum controlled women's movement; perhaps this arose from a fear of women's power should they utilize their education and political freedom toward professional ends. A sizeable proportion of male composers latched onto the public institutions and this facilitated their entrée into professional life. Felix Mendelssohn, for example, conducted several orchestras, including the Leipzig Gewandhaus, and could present his works and keep his name before the public in newspapers and magazines. For Schumann and others the power of the pen provided an effective means of enhancing authorial subjectivity. I do not know of major female conductors or journalists in the nineteenth century.[3] As for the present, today's university composer is typically male. Although women composers inhabit many music departments, they are still under-represented in academia in general.[4]

Professionalism has thus eluded many a female composer. This is one of the main reasons why so few are known. Yet lest professionalism be viewed as a tidy concept with clear-cut characteristics, it is important to point out inconsistencies. These suggest that its position as a major criterion for canonicity should be reconsidered and the concept conceived more broadly to embrace the experiences of women. In a commonly held view, professionalism implies commitment to a profession or an occupation that is one's primary or exclusive occupation – in this case the composing of music. This is problematic, however. In point of fact, the Western composer has usually been involved in other musical activities as well, be they teaching, conducting, performing, or writing. One could argue that these often constitute the principal professional pursuit, at least in terms of time. Bach and Haydn, for example, may have devoted more hours to other musical activities that were required under their respective contracts. Many university professors spend more time discharging academic duties than composing. Thus the myth of a full-time commitment crumbles. Another typical criterion is remuneration and the degree to which one relies on composition for subsistence: the lesser the reliance then presumably the lesser the degree of professionalism. Yet this does not obtain for academia or for figures like Berlioz and Ives. Perhaps intentions are critical: whether one intends to be "serious" about composition. This is an elusive quality that might depend on regularity and longevity of activity. But how regular does regularity have to be? How long does longevity have to last? Furthermore, can one be considered professional without signs of success, namely performances, commissions, and publications? Could professional status be accorded a "closet" composer with an independent income who composes steadily over many years, and is therefore "serious," yet who chooses or is forced to keep pieces private, unperformed, unpublished? While these conditions might seem hypothetical, they suggest that certain signs of success in the commercial world weigh heavily in the determination of professionalism. They also imply that cultural meanings beyond semantic labeling are inscribed in the notion of professionalism, in what Michel Foucault has termed the "author-function" in Western society. As the preceding demonstrates, professionalism in the West is complex and often contradictory. It should make us wary of entrenched dualisms like professional/amateur that privilege one member over the other.[5] In spite of contradiction and exclusiveness, however, professionalism has generally been assumed desirable.

For any meaningful reconceptualization of professionalism there has to be a recognition of the subtleties of women's relationship to professionalism. Many involve identity, and this will form a major focus of our discussions. The complex relationship is always challenging, often problematic, and occasionally satisfying. It can be understood within a model of exclusion that nonetheless shows some signs of inclusiveness, especially recently. We will discuss how the relationship affects canon formation. This is influenced by women's expectations toward professionalism and themselves, and societal expectations toward professionalism and women. The negotiation of the spaces among these sets is the process that women as individuals have to go through to find their own place in professionalism. But it is fraught with psychological risk. Being a professional composer and a woman may mean an uneasy location in contradiction.

The first section discusses ideologies of woman and professionalism, and possible meanings of their coming together under the notion of professional female composer. It considers practical factors that relate specifically to women and their identity: their roles within the family, the timing of their careers, and the names they go by. In many cases these add up to an empowered self that finds a satisfying relationship to professionalism. In others, however, empowerment is partial and identity as a professional uncertain. "Public and private" explores practical and metaphorical aspects of the division between the public and private spheres. Special attention is paid to the *salon*. In the next section we discuss the meanings of exposure to the public in the form of publication. Finally, "The author-function" takes up the ideological implications of authorship in Western culture and wonders about their usefulness in promoting female professionalism. Whether or not one favors centered authorship, it is imperative to understand its power and its relationship with the processes involved in the circulation of a name within culture. This can tell us a great deal about how canons are formed.

EXPECTATIONS AND PRACTICALITIES

I cannot help feeling a keen schism at times between the composer, who is a more generalized and abstract part of my self, and the woman, who is daily aware of, and made aware of, what it means to be a composer *and* a woman. I do believe that, for all the ambiguity and complexity which impact this double identity, it is possible and necessary to separate the two.[6]

Composer Diane Thome (b. 1942) has obviously internalized two distinct ideological messages: one for professional composer and one for woman. We have mentioned some of the basic features of professionalism but there is a lot more to be said. "Professional" of professional composer implies an expectation of success. An ambiguous term, success can be seen as some combination of career advancement, critical acclaim, public acknowledgment, commercial reward, and personal satisfaction. There is no uniform formula; some elements may be missing or barely evident in a "successful" composer. Yet there are further ambiguities. Who ascertains success and when it applies? Is a composer successful if ignored in his/her lifetime yet famous sometime later? Whatever the answer, success since the middle of the nineteenth century has meant a reputation in the public at large. This can entail intense scrutiny and subjective exposure. It suggests vulnerability. Yet in return for potential psychic intrusion the composer is invested with authorial authority. He is presumed a repository of knowledge and skill – someone with epistemological expertise. By the mere fact of being a professional the composer commands respect. While we should note, parenthetically, that some view professionals in general as hacks, as mechanical doers as opposed to intellectual thinkers, my remarks are made within the context of ideologies of professional in the arts.

A significant feature of the ideology of professionalism is that professionalism marks an advanced stage in acculturation. Claude Lévi-Strauss's metaphor of raw–cooked is useful here. Nature, the "raw" state, needs to be improved, and it is civilization that turns it into a palatable or "cooked" form. In this case it is like taking creativity, itself appropriated into culture, and embedding it even further in culture. Many steps beyond raw and even processed creativity, professionalism means that many layers of culture have been applied to effect a polished, or cooked, product. And as noted in Chapter 2, culture is associated with male power.

On a more practical level, the ideology of professionalism fosters the notion that professional status has been arrived at through a deliberate decision. It is well beyond casual experience and chance. It represents the culmination of a lengthy process that requires planning and awareness. Perhaps this helps prevent a dilution of standards: where would professionalism be without a presumption of quality? In a further interpretation, perhaps the ideology of deliberateness also means an awareness of the cultural ramifications of deliberateness. This makes professionalism even more of a calculated decision.

Ideologies of women inflect their social construction, and many are discussed elsewhere in the study. Perhaps most pertinent here is that a woman's identity is defined primarily in terms of context, in a particular structure of relationship. She is rarely seen as autonomous. Ideologically she is identified with family. This implies nurturing, reproduction, and nature. Since the family is centered in the home, woman is linked with the private. Her familial power has limits, however. She may have power over her children but she is not the head of the family. She is subservient (to a man). This implies a reactive rather than pro-active relationship to the world, especially since it is the husband who is vested with authority conferred by his dealings with the outside world. In her nurturing role woman is expected to be honest, ethical, and virtuous – important traits to pass along to the young. More generally, the ideology of woman stresses purity. This makes her sexuality a problem. As a result she has often been constructed within a framework of extremes: either the purity of the Madonna or the promiscuity of a whore. This duality has been extremely damaging to women; it has impugned their moral legitimacy and thus had a negative impact on their participation in culture.

With such defining ideologies stored in memory, what attitudes and assumptions might women composers bring to professionalism? As Thome's statement implies, for some women professionalism problematizes their womanhood. It can threaten their image of themselves as women. It might imply such a strong commitment to composition that familial nurturing, of whatever form, is ignored. It could suggest an emphasis on success and reputation such that one identifies with men more than women. Perhaps because of the potential for feeling that one is becoming a socialized man and crossing the boundary of who one is supposed to be, many women fear success. It may be a tangible sign of crossover. Fear of success is not only a matter of feeling uncomfortable with notoriety in the public sphere – of exposing female subjectivity when women are supposed to remain in the background. Fear of success includes a real fear of failure. Those fears become more intense once one has placed oneself in a structure that has been traditionally male. Before that little is risked. Or perhaps the fear of success/failure is as real as it is because failure means much more than "ordinary" failure: it may signal the futility of having even thought one could succeed in a masculine profession. As mentioned elsewhere in the study, this problematized position makes for contradiction. It is important, however, that a fear of problematizing one's womanhood not be taken necessarily as a sign of confusion regarding female gender. It can be a positive statement on those traits that a particular woman associates with women, which may or may not coincide with attributes passed on in societal ideologies. She may want to make it clear to herself and others that she values these traits, and that becoming professional does not mean their abandonment. But she would still have to come to terms with the messages of ideology on who she is supposed to be.

In a more general sense, the coming together of these ideologies in the concept of the woman composer has some interesting connotations. Because the ideologies sketched above, in somewhat extreme form, seem oppositional, an inference could be drawn that woman and composer do not or cannot belong together. This is probably a basis of Thome's belief that it is "necessary to separate the two."

Oddly enough, her strategy can act as an affirmation of harmful dualisms like culture–nature or mind–body. A historiographic consequence of the inference is that those women who do become professionals in composition are the exceptions. They are exceptions to typical women and to typical composers. They defy the incompatibility of the ideologies as they attempt to live the professional life. But being an exception has psychological costs: a woman might have to reject women in general and positive aspects of the ideology. Another outcome of the exception thesis is that the normative power of the ideologies is strengthened, as are presumably the messages contained in them. It is likely that future women will continue to be positioned in outsider status. Exception status also denigrates activities of women in which women are the norm. Of course, there is also the alternative of questioning the model of ideological incompatibility, and in a sense much of this chapter is concerned with the deconstruction of that ideology. In any case, the apparent non-congruence promulgated by the model can itself be an ideology that has been useful for society to perpetuate. Women as professional composers may be considered subversive – a threat to the cultural order. Behaviors beyond prescribed boundaries may appear as excess or display, and suggest a womanhood beyond social containment. An ideology of incompatibility can stave off the threat. It can help to ensure the longevity of the ideologies of woman.

Before we leave this issue we might note a potential consequence: the strategy of the masquerade. A woman may feel compelled to assume another set of characteristics to play a role that does not come naturally. I am not talking about essential traits but about socialized behavior patterns that might be naturalized by ideologies. For a female composer this kind of mediation may mean donning subjective attributes foreign to her socialization, especially those likely to contribute to authorial authority. This could be an empowering move, but like other accommodations of identity it might engender psychological conflict.

An obvious aspect of the joining of woman and composer is the meaning that the word "woman" inflects on the term "composer." Miriam Gideon (*b.* 1906), for example, believes that the use of a qualifier such as "female" in front of composer "implies in my mind, at least, some limitation." It places you in a smaller group, which presumably would be unnecessary were you good enough to be a top player in the more competitive "major leagues."[7] Perhaps some fear that the qualifier also means an implicit acceptance of traits or behaviors characteristic of that group – in other words an essentializing straitjacket. It is easy to understand resistance in such circumstances. We also have to understand why older women in particular would shy away from the term. They aspired to professionalism at a time when they were truly exceptions. Only a handful of women were successful and there were few if any female support systems in music. Hardly any female figures of the past were known to them – certainly much less so than today. Ideologies of womanhood such as those sketched above were much more entrenched. As a result an aspiring female composer had little to identify with in musical creativity that was female. She was practically forced to identify with male-defined structures and practices, and of course with males themselves. It was necessary to prove that she could do as well as men; she would not want to have a designation that would mark her off from them. The label "woman composer" would be a decided liability. Psychologically it would mean "immasculation" – the process of counter-identification theorized by Judith Fetterley in which a woman is forced to identify against herself.[8]

While some worry about the term "woman composer," many resist the implications for professional women of a larger, related concept: gender itself. Barbara Kolb (*b.* 1939) and Laurie Spiegel (*b.* 1945), for example, do not believe in its applicability to their professional self-definition. Here again, personal experience may be significant. Shulamit Ran (*b.* 1949) and Gideon both question its validity as a category. Ran, in particular, wonders why gender is singled out as especially significant when classifications such as ethnicity, nationality, and age are as critical to the molding of the individual.[9] Feminists would probably agree with the last part but add that this is not a reason to ignore gender; they should all be taken into consideration in the formation of identity.

Composer Nicola LeFanu's observations may offer a practicable solution to the thorny issue of the term "woman composer."[10] We might call this a strategy of accommodation: accommodation to the realities of socialization and discrimination. LeFanu discusses her initial resistance to labels and structures that mark her off from composers in general. But with the realization that being a woman *is* a fundamental (not essentialist) aspect of her identity, she recognizes that somehow that fact is expressed in her music. It is not women's music, it is music composed by an individual who happens to be a woman (and British, and a daughter of a mother who is a composer, etc.). It is true that some descriptors would not be affixed to "composer." But the numbers and the common problems covered by "woman" make this a reasonable term. For LeFanu, the adjective "woman" makes sense until such time that diversity is fully celebrated in composition. Meanwhile, the label helps draw attention to women's contributions and solidify the bonds among women who are writing music. Among other composers who recognize the importance of gendered support are Nancy Van de Vate (*b.* 1930) and Annea Lockwood (*b.* 1942).

While such support systems are enormously helpful to women composers, they do not obviate the need for other responses. Women composers have to negotiate individual solutions to identity in the spaces between woman and professional as represented in ideology. A fundamental area of negotiation involves the family. For some women, the ideological expectations of wife and mother – of primary caregiver – are felt very strongly. Anne Le Baron (*b.* 1953), for example, writes that she had to "whittle away" at that "wife/mother conditioning that bred resentment since childhood."[11] While Le Baron rebelled against the ideology from an early age, many others seemed to internalize the expectations without conflict, at least while they were young. Later on things could become more complicated. As Priscilla McLean recalls,

I was brought up to believe that all composers were men, and that women, to work at all, should take a temporary "service" position, such as nursing or teaching, until they inevitably got married and had children. Then they were to quit and take care of the home. Even hiring a babysitter ... while the mother composed was considered "unnatural" and perhaps immoral!

She attempted to follow this path, with disastrous personal results, and eventually gathered up courage and embarked on the road to becoming a composer.[12]

We do not have much autobiographical insight on how nineteenth-century women felt about such conflicts. But in a few cases we can draw reasonable inferences. Clara Schumann apparently resisted societal pressures of motherhood because of strong emotional needs for continuing her concert career.[13] Yet this seems to conflict with the fact that she continued to have children – eight in all. What was the reason? While we may not know with certainty – many personal issues were not written about then – we could venture some hypotheses. One could be the power of the ideology of the virtuous and dutiful wife. Even though Schumann was an independent woman, conventions of class might have instilled strong notions of the meanings of married woman. She obviously forged her own path with regard to work. But the duty of having children may have struck a particularly resonant chord. There is also the possibility that birth control devices and information were unavailable, or if available were not utilized because of moral proscriptions against interfering with reproduction. Although Fanny Hensel seemed to enjoy motherhood immensely we do not have a clear picture of any conflicts she might have experienced.[14] For a while, at least, she seems to have found a satisfying psychic space for the personal and professional aspects of her life. Until the late 1830s, when her son was older and she felt an urge toward the public arena, Hensel created her own version of professionalism. Although extremely prolific, her works were mostly for private consumption and thus confound the paradigm of success as measured by public acclaim. For Hensel in this period, satisfaction as a composer meant a redefinition of professionalism.

Nearer the present, Marga Richter (*b.* 1926) expresses gratitude that "I didn't have commissions coming in and deadlines to meet while the kids were growing up. To tell them to go away, I'm busy – I don't think I could have done this."[15] Many composers mention the heavy time commitment of raising children and its impact on sustained work. This can come at a particularly crucial time in women's careers. Yet an anonymous respondent to the 1981 survey finds childcare a stimulus to creativity:

Effects of motherhood … on composing: necessity for constant outward extension seems antithetical to isolation of daily composing; however, close touch with life outside very energizing: strengthens desire to communicate; increases need for clearing away the trappings and being direct. Less time to work means clearer faster decisions, greater intensity and commitment, elimination of other unnecessary activities. Connection with child's future respect. Mothering analogous to compositional energy; struggling, waiting, watching, reacting, looking for clues, followed by many glorious moments to make it all worthwhile.

The shared, negotiated space of childcare and composition described here resolves the ideological dissonance between woman–mother and composer. This woman has found a kind of harmony that many composers, men and women, might envy. Such a solution also dismantles harmful dualisms such as culture–nature and mind–body (see also Chapter 2). But lest we look upon this as an ideal solution, we should bear in mind that the statement provides only a partial view of professional life. We do not know, for instance, about the circumstances surrounding publication, remuneration, and expectations for success.

Women have reacted in various ways to the impact of actual or contemplated marriage on their professional lives. Given a more diverse array of work models it seems less of an issue now than in the past, say before 1960. As previously noted, marriage carries a lot of ideological baggage for women. Deciding to get married might fulfill one expectation for women, but it would bring them into direct confrontation with the ideology of motherhood. Being a married woman without children can make you a lesser woman. Yet having children and being a professional presents a formidable challenge. There is also a potential practical complication brought on by marriage. In past eras, especially, a husband might not allow his wife to be a professional (see Chapter 2 on Alma and Gustav Mahler). A working wife could be seen as an insult to the image of the husband as provider, not to mention a potential source of competition.

Because ideological expectations for men have emphasized success and power, professional men have generally experienced considerably less conflict at the prospect of marriage. A home life forms less of their ideological identity and therefore marriage can be accommodated more easily with their professionalism. Perhaps Brahms counts as a famous exception. I suspect, however, that the romanticized accounts of his longings for marital stability and his inability to reconcile those desires with his professional life mask other factors yet to be discussed by musicologists. Was the ambivalence a sign of homosexuality, for example? While I cannot answer this question (in any case it is more of an aside), it is fair to say that women have expended a great deal of psychic energy on the decision to marry. Cécile Chaminade, for example, firmly believed that only a certain kind of man in a certain kind of marriage was suitable for a woman of talent. She needed the freedom to pursue her profession unencumbered. Her platonic marriage in 1901 to Louis Carbonel, some twenty years her senior, probably provided the desired environment. Chaminade had already established herself professionally when she married at age 54. Her family later believed, however, that the years she tended her ailing husband – a time of great aesthetic change in music – cost her reputation dearly.[16] The British composer–violist Rebecca Clarke (1886–1979) also married late, at age 58, to pianist James Friskin (1886–1967), but Clarke virtually stopped composing after her marriage. The reason is unclear: whether the marriage itself, the performing tours with her husband, or some other factor accounted for the change.[17] In some cases marriage had a decidedly negative impact on professionalism. It was detrimental to the career of Germaine Tailleferre (1892–1983); her first husband thwarted her opportunity to collaborate with Charlie Chaplin on films in Hollywood.[18] The first marriage of Texas-born Radie Britain (*b.* 1899), who was advised not to marry if she wanted to be a "serious composer," also collided with her career. She felt that her husband did not understand what it meant to be a composer.[19]

The professional path of Ruth Crawford (1901–53) took an interesting turn after she married her teacher, Charles Seeger, in 1932. Well on her way to becoming a "star" of the emerging modernist movement, especially after a productive Guggenheim year in Paris, Crawford gave up the composition of art music and turned to American folk idioms. She joined her husband in research at the Library of Congress and also made arrangements of this music. On the surface it seems that marriage put an end to her career.

A few points should be considered, however. First, Ruth and Charles were swept up by the populism of the 1930s in the aftermath of the Depression. Second, they became parents, to four children (Charles also had three sons from a previous marriage). As a mother, Crawford probably had little if any time for sustained concentration on composition. In addition she may have wanted to relate her musical activities to the lives of her children (the folk arrangements were used for pedagogy). Third, it is possible that Seeger may have encouraged the change. He did admit in a later interview that in those years he had believed "that it was a bit absurd to expect women to fit themselves into a groove [the tradition of Western music] which was so definitely flavored with machismo ... ."[20] Fourth, Crawford herself was aware of the difficulties that marriage could pose to the career of a composer who was a woman. As of 1927, before she met Seeger, she had apparently decided not to marry.[21] Judith Tick offers the metaphor of the "straddler," a phrase used reflexively by the composer, to describe Crawford's often contradictory relationship to her desires for career and family.[22] "Straddler" conjures up a subject position of potential: of the not totally flexible position from which one can move in either direction. Perhaps the complexities of Crawford might suggest a subject positioning of possibilities in more than two directions. And finally, as suggested by J. Michèle Edwards, the decisive turn away from professionalism may have resulted not from marriage but from an earlier event: failure to complete a large-scale orchestral work during the Guggenheim year. The grant was not renewed, and Crawford returned home and married Seeger. Edwards thus shifts the usual focus of attention from the marriage–career dyad to the vagaries of professional advancement, in this case institutional insistence on the significance of the large forms. Crawford wrote several works during the grant year but not the desired "masterpiece."[23]

From the vantage point of 1948 Crawford herself reflected on the stylistic changes, in a letter to Edgar Varèse:

... I am still not sure whether the road I have been following the last dozen years is a main road or a detour. I have begun to feel, the past year or two, that it is the latter – a detour, but a very important one to me, during which I have descended from stratosphere onto a solid well-traveled highway. ... Until a year or so ago I had felt so at home among this (to me) new found music that I thought maybe this was what I wanted most. I listened to nothing else, and felt somewhat like a ghost when my compositions were spoken of. I answered no letters pertaining to them; requests for scores and biographical data were stuck in drawers.... Whether I ever unfold the wings and make a start toward the stratosphere and how much of the dust of the road will still cling to me, is an interesting question, at least to me. If I do, I will probably pull the road up with me.[24]

Even earlier, in 1941, Crawford had considered resuming her career. Daughter Peggy observes that Ruth may have had to complete the mothering phase before she could return to professional composition.[25] Crawford unfortunately died before she had the chance to test her potential new direction. The issue may suggest some interesting questions about gender and its relationship with modernism, accessibility, and exclusionism. But this letter suggests that for several years Crawford seems to have divorced herself psychologically from her earlier self. Perhaps this was her way of dealing with the contradictory ideologies of professional composer and woman. She had found happiness in a family life that matched societal paradigms of womanhood. Perhaps the internalization of those messages necessitated that she stay away from structures that imply a lesser woman. While it may be fruitless to speculate, one can only wonder how Crawford might have resolved competing expectations had she lived in a later period.

But to return to the main issue, we should hasten to add that some women have found considerable support and encouragement from their partner for their professional lives, for example Agathe Backer-Grøndahl (1847–1907).[26] Priscilla McLean hails the advantages of a dual-composer marriage, a phenomenon that may become increasingly common. For McLean, who decided to forgo children because of financial considerations and the necessary commitment of time, the giving up "a normal life with social activities and children of one's own: this is the choice given to a woman. Is it, however, the choice a man has to make?"[27]

As we have seen, considerations of marriage and family have led to varied solutions that often resist conformity to prevailing male patterns. Another area of negotiation involves the timing of the career path. Carolyn Heilbrun has observed that many literary women blossom into professionalism when they are older: "Men tend to move on a fairly predictable path to achievement; women transform themselves only after an awakening. And that awakening is identifiable only in hindsight."[28] Such an awakening might come with life experiences that bolster confidence. It could signal active engagement with limiting ideologies – what Heilbrun calls "confronting society."

In composition this process could involve the paradigm of the carefully thought-out career plan. As a profession in the arts composition implies talent, devotion, and high-minded seriousness. These in turn imply a concentrated focus that is recognized in college or perhaps earlier and intensively cultivated, without major interruption. In this model someone would not chance upon composition as a career at some later stage in life. It would require advance planning, with the goal clearly in sight. While there have been many exceptions to these paradigms, they are nonetheless part of the ideology of the professional composer. But the ideology is based on male patterns. Societal expectations for women follow different patterns and many do not fit the professional paradigms. Until recently, women were typically not socialized to focus on a plan for their career. The idea of upward mobility toward specific career goals was mostly foreign to them. Some might think about a given occupation they wanted to pursue, and many more would think about their education. But the goals might stop there. If asked a common question put to men as to where they see themselves in ten or fifteen years, many women would say they do not know – they have not given the matter much thought. Some might say they suppose they will be married. Some might embark on a career and drift upward to higher levels, through hard work, but it might be more of an *ad hoc* occurrence than a calculated plan conceived in advance. Perhaps this is part of a resistance to challenge societal notions of womanhood – one feels comfortable going only so far.

The ideology of the typical career path implies continuity; there are no major time-out periods. For women, of course, this can create problems, particularly for those who wish to have children. Even under the best of circumstances childbearing and childraising occupy a fair amount of time; under typical circumstances they may make a full-time commitment to the profession impossible. But a further complication is the timing: women have children in their early adult lives. And this is the crucial period when a career is established. As LeFanu points out, many structures that can make or break a career are specifically for composers in their twenties or thirties, such as competitions, prizes, and commissions. But if a woman is busy with young children she may not have the time or powers of concentration to devote to full-time composition.[29] This could mean professional oblivion. After all, conventional wisdom has it that if one has not been recognized then one's work is of lesser quality than someone who has been recognized. This can have serious consequences for the woman who becomes a professional after raising a family. As Van de Vate observes, such a woman

is frequently pushed back into the category of amateur. This wouldn't happen to a man because no such category exists. He can't be pushed back into the circuit of women's clubs. He's either a student, a developing composer, or a professional. And if he's a student, university faculties are interested in him rather than in the older woman, who is sometimes regarded as a bit of a nuisance.[30]

She may be viewed as a dabbler because she interrupted her career for non-work-related activity or did not have the necessary burning commitment when young to stay with it. This view is predicated on a desirable split between art and life, between culture and nature. While professional women today are attempting to bridge that gulf, with individual solutions, they still have to work against a powerful ideology of the totalizing commitment. Older women entering composition may also have to fight societal images of themselves. In a culture obsessed with youth and beauty the aging woman is often ignored and trivialized. The white-haired man becomes wise and distinguished, the white-haired woman haggard and expendable. Perhaps with changing demographics and power structures the older woman will come to be seen as a source of authority.

In the changing climate, meanwhile, some structures are becoming more inclusive of diverse career patterns. In musicology, for instance, the Committee on the Status of Women in the early 1980s effected a change in the criteria for the Einstein Award given by the American Musicological Society. With the grantors' intention that the prize go to a junior scholar, the original criteria stipulated an age limit. This reflected the typical male path of continuous education through to a job. But after it was argued that the age limit excluded women who might raise children and then complete their Ph.D. and get a job, the rules were re-written with junior status now defined as a certain number of years after the degree. Incidentally, some groups of men were also excluded under the old regulations, including those drafted into the military in the midst of graduate school. Perhaps similar changes could be made to definitions of "young composer" in competitive structures in composition. Subtleties of attitudinal discrimination, however, are much harder to fix.

As identity is negotiated in terms of contradictory ideologies, the professional female composer contends with the issue of what to call herself. With what name will she be known to the public? This becomes important because her subjectivity is exposed and she can be in an extremely vulnerable position. For a woman, the circulation of her name within culture can mean an admission and affirmation of difference from woman as constructed in ideology. The "unusual" activity is no longer concealed but open for everyone to see; there are witnesses, so to speak, to excessive behavior. This behavior can lead to censure, and it can also result in public success – a condition often feared, as we have noted. Given the high stakes, it is no wonder that women who become professional have conceived various strategies to negotiate the exposure of that conflicted subjectivity. One strategy has involved concealment of gender through the use of some alternative identity. It has usually assumed the form of male gender or androgynous gender assumed to be male, although anonymous, ambiguous, and absent identities have also been adopted. Heilbrun notes shrewdly that "women have long been nameless. They have not been persons. Handed by a father to another man, the husband, they have been objects of circulation, exchanging one name for another."[31] This helps ensure patriarchal succession.[32]

The Western tradition of nominative fluidity for women has had a major impact on societal perceptions of the transitoriness of female identity. It has apparently played freely into the consciousness of many women as well. If her name is exchangeable perhaps she herself can appropriate the power of naming and proceed to name herself. In this way she can have more control over her location in the spaces between professionalism and woman. She can adopt a pseudonym, keep her present name, or if married return to her maiden name. She might even decide on a strategy of multiplicity, like Joyce Carol Oates–Rosamond Smith. We should remember, however, that "one's own name" in northern Western culture means a patrilineal, not matrilineal, surname.[33]

Literature contains numerous examples of male pseudonyms. The practice began to flourish in the nineteenth century: women were daring to take up the pen but the feminine ideal precluded strong subjectivity and public attention. Elaine Showalter underscores the impact of Georges Sand on women's adoption of literary pseudonyms.[34] Sand had begun the crossover through crossdressing, with a practical aim: to allow for the kind of physical mobility that was restricted by standard female attire. According to Gilbert and Gubar, this soon became a kind of male impersonation and apparently facilitated acceptance by male writers. George Eliot and the three Brontë sisters, among others, also adopted male pseudonyms. "Disguised as a man ... a woman writer could move vigorously away from the 'lesser subjects' and 'lesser lives' which had constrained her foremothers."[35] Victorian ideals of femininity prescribed what the nineteenth-century female author could write about in order to remain within bounds of female decorum. A pseudonym thus opened up vast literary and psychic possibilities. Not only could she now treat otherwise taboo characters and themes, but she could feel empowered through a sense of freedom upon throwing off the shackles of Victorian propriety. She could assume that her work and authorial authority would be taken seriously, without the interference of gender as a factor, whether expressed as criticism or flattery.[36] It may have acted as an equalizer of class: the upper-class woman writer (which most of them were) entering the world of commerce much like her lower-class sister in the factory.

In music we know of several women who assumed alternative identities. Irish–French composer Augusta Holmès (1847–1903) is said to have used the name Hermann Zenta for her early published works.[37] Rebecca Clarke took the pseudonym Anthony Trent after she composed the viola sonata (*c.* 1919), and the concealment apparently brought her works greater attention. In another twist on identity, Clarke relates later how some questioned the existence of a Rebecca Clarke given the quality of the works. The situation became more entangled when they were thought to be under a female pseudonym for Ernest Bloch.[38] Several years later Edith Borroff had the following discouraging experiences:

After earning the degrees in composition I found that performance and publication of my music were inseparably linked with my sex: all works that I submitted with my right name were rejected (all but one unopened – and that with a letter saying that my work was "deserving of performance" and yet not offering to perform it); conversely, the two that I submitted with male pseudonym were accepted. When I gave up the subterfuge on principle, I virtually relinquished any chance for significant activity as a composer until the late 1960s, when attitudes began to change.[39]

Van de Vate's experience with concealed identity is similar, although Van de Vate retained her surname and an initial in place of her first name.

I remember the very first [composition sent off under this name] was an orchestral work that a major symposium accepted, and were they amazed when I showed up for the performance! I followed the same procedure several times, always with an orchestral work, but Van de Vate is a distinctive name, and after I became known a little I couldn't do this any more.[40]

Other forms of alternative identity have been used by women. In earlier eras, prior to the emphasis on individualism, anonymous authorship occurred with some frequency. Perhaps at least one of the famous "Anonymous" authors of medieval music treatises was a woman. I have no particular evidence for this, but just as Hildegard of Bingen (1098–1179) was hidden for many years so too there could be another nun who functioned as a learned man and wrote treatises. The anonymous response to the Barkin questionnaire of 1981, however, indicates that some women (and possibly some men as well) still wish to mask their true identity. There have also been instances of ambiguous authorship. A famous example is the joint Lieder collection of Robert and Clara Schumann, Op. 37/12 (his Op. 37, her Op. 12), where no specific attribution is given for any of the pieces. Then there is absent authorship, exemplified by Fanny Hensel's contribution of three Lieder respectively to her brother's Opp. 8 and 9 collections. Only Mendelssohn's name appears as author. This curious situation has given rise to various theories. The only pertinent information I have found is Hensel's ambiguous statement regarding Op. 9 in her letter to Mendelssohn of *c.* 22 May 1830 that "I shoved them down Schlesinger's throat" (Schlesinger was the publisher). Thus it seems that Hensel took part in the ruse. I suspect, however, that the situation is probably more complicated. Perhaps further information might turn up sometime in one of Hensel's diaries.[41]

Another interesting kind of authorial absence has emerged in the past few years. In many cases the "woman behind the man" turns out to be the actual author. For example, Princess Wittgenstein may have penned several writings formerly attributed to Liszt. And more recently, in spring 1990, there emerged a revisionist view of Albert Einstein and his wife: she may have played a major role in the formulation of the theory of relativity. These examples suggest questionable appropriation of women's professional identities. Once done, the ideologies meant to suppress women are perpetuated.

Carolyn Heilbrun's use of pseudonym represents perhaps the most positive kind of alternative identity for a woman: re-birth as another woman. This wonderful metaphor symbolizes female solidarity and union as identities are exchanged from woman to woman. It also means that gender identity is strengthened, not suppressed. For Heilbrun, who replaced her academic literary-theorist identity with that of mystery writer Amanda Cross, there was now an expansion of her subjective gaze. The gaze also embraced her lead character, academic sleuth Kate Fansler. Heilbrun could invest both of these new personas with aspects of herself that were hidden or submerged. With a wonderful sense of exhilaration, Heilbrun has realized the importance of her detective: "creating Kate Fansler and her quests, I was recreating myself. Women come to writing, I believe, simultaneously with self-creation." In Kate, Heilbrun "sought another identity, another role. I sought to create an individual whose destiny offered more possibility than I could comfortably imagine for myself." In short, Heilbrun "created a fantasy."[42] She explains candidly how she needed such an alter ego at that time of her life, even though she seemed comfortably settled professionally and personally. The enhanced "psychic space" afforded through the assumption of another identity provided great power, and she relished the exercise of that power. I almost laughed aloud as she told how she would write letters as both Heilbrun and Cross to the same person. Thus secrecy and its heightened sense of resilience served as a base of power, not a reactive locus of confinement. That secrecy can be desirable provides an intriguing alternative to the professional paradigm of exposure and renown. It also raises questions about the public–private relationship and about the ownership of an art work.

PUBLIC AND PRIVATE

Since the middle of the nineteenth century the public domain has generally been viewed as the terrain of the professional, the private of the non-professional. Immediately we encounter difficulties with this simplistic distinction. As noted earlier, clear-cut definitions do not adequately express the notion of professionalism, and by extension it is problematic to assume categories of non-professional to describe what those would entail. Furthermore, the public–private dualism raises several thorny issues. What do we mean by public and private? Are they distinguished by agency? Do they imply economic or political sites? Do they involve governance? What types of social configurations make up the two domains? And are they really domains or a symbolic representation of something else? Such questions bear directly on women and their music. Certain assumptions about the relative worth of public and private have become a fundamental part of musical valuation and thus figure in canon formation.

Feminist philosopher and social historian Linda Nicholson has written about important philosophical foundations of the public–private division in the West.[43] Her argument begins with the Lockean split of the old kinship system into the two spheres of family and state, in the late seventeenth century. Previously, Western society had been organized according to a system of kinship – that is, according to blood relationship. Many societal functions, such as economic production, health care, regulation of crime, and sexuality, were centered around and governed by relational ties. It is important to distinguish this system from the concept of the family. According to

Nicholson the critical factors are relationship and living proximity: the family refers to a group of individuals living together and forming a unit, who incidentally could be related by blood; kinship need not entail proximity. In any case, in a response to one Robert Filmer, John Locke wrote of the need for a separation into two distinct spheres, each with its own functions. In part he based his theory on the claim that women required protection by males that would be best served by the institution of the family. Nicholson points out that Locke's influential ideas implied universal and transhistorical validity, and that constitutes a serious flaw.[44] She argues that the relationship between public and private is a changing dynamic, subject to socio-historic context. Because of an absence of historical grounding in Locke's formulations, the roots of family and state in kinship have been buried. The perception of their separation as universal has only intensified ever since.

As liberalism gained currency in the next two centuries, the individual became the center of a new kind of economic organization: private enterprise. It was "private" in that the commercial activity was not owned by the state. But it took place in a public, not a "private" (domestic) setting and thus clouds any simple definition of what "private" means.[45] With the displacement of the family as the fundamental socio-political structure, the individual has functioned as a private unit, such that "the private has increasingly come to be defined as that which concerns the individual alone."[46] Thus agency and site are two significant variables in private and public. Private has referred to the ontology and agency of the individual person and also described the home; public has pertained to the communal body politic known as the state but also connoted economic activity that shuns state participation and places a premium on individual initiative.

Western art music since the early nineteenth century has reified the public marketplace as the favored locus of activity. Yet we see it is the individual, as a "private" socio-economic entity, who rose to prominence in this period: the solo performer, the free-lance composer, the orchestra conductor, the impresario, the music critic. Of course, as Janet Wolff points out, these seemingly autonomous individuals interact in larger interlocking processes that contribute to the production of an artwork.[47] Nonetheless, the model of the autonomous (private) individual marketing his talents in the market-based (private) economy increasingly became the standard for determining professional status. Even though the private individual operated in a private economy, this favored model was dubbed the public sphere and privileged over the non-public, or domestic sphere. The hierarchy, in theory, corresponded to the dominance of the masculine over the feminine; the home – the moral haven from the turmoils of the male (public) world – was linked with the feminine.[48] While especially transparent around 1900, the gendered division has typically been denied or ignored in later periods. In any case, many women were involved in economic activity in the home, thus bringing "public" work to the private realm. Many, particularly those of the middle to upper classes, actually traveled and thereby challenge the myth of womanly confinement to the home. In addition, a significant number of lower-class women were beginning to take employment in the factories – thus partaking of the "public" world of "private" enterprise.

From these discussions we are left with a sense of the subtleties and contradictions of public and private. As Nicholson and Michelle Rosaldo urge, we must be careful to examine the concepts contextually and be ready to posit precise links if appropriate, or possibly abandon the terms altogether and devise other relational models that better reflect the dynamics of the particular situation.[49]

Musicological culture of the last fifty years has tacitly reinforced the hierarchical dualism, at least for music after 1800. This has come mainly in the disciplinary emphasis on public structures and the de-emphasis, and in many cases wholesale dismissal, of private structures. To put it another way, musicology has paid attention to canonic works and paradigms, and in turn affirmed their value. As said many times, the public arena has been privileged, and its activities have been chronicled, preserved, and praised. Often removed from written scrutiny, the private has been given much less attention. Perhaps this results from the fact that the dynamics of the private call for different questions to be asked, and until fairly recently they were not posed. In any event, there are ways of escaping the tyranny of the dualism. One involves the elimination of public and private as realms of normative or prescribed societal activity. We have already seen how the terms in practice describe contradictory characteristics, yet how they are deployed frequently, without qualification. Particularly injurious is the retention of the feminine with the "lower" private and the masculine with the "higher" public. Even today the Western paradigm of professionalism means public activity, and we have seen how it has been difficult for many female composers to fit the demands of their familial lives into the prevailing public models of the professional composer. Alienation would be less of a problem if public and private figured less prominently in notions of professionalism. The negotiation of contradictory ideologies might be less difficult.

Another way of dealing with public and private is to alter the implied relationality of the pair, so that private means something different from merely a poorer relation to public. In this line of argument, private stands for a rich realm of activities that yield insight into much previously untapped socio-historic activity. Like our proposals for gender and for culture–nature, a possible model could feature a continuum between the two concepts, with a smooth and imperceptible transition from one to the other. But this would still assign the concepts some distance from each other, and without qualification suggest opposition between end points. Perhaps a circle would provide a better model, much like that described in Chapter 2 *vis-à-vis* nature and culture. Among its advantages is the ability to return to the other concept via a different arc. That arc could pass through multiple points and entail different rates of movement. One could also imagine some kind of three-dimensional modeling that accounts for the multiple variables implicated in the pair, including individual, communal, state, corporate, and domestic. Such a complex model demonstrates that no simple description suffices.[50]

The career of Chaminade after approximately 1888 illustrates the contradictions in the pair and the need for more complex modeling. She performed in both public and private venues. Her pieces were written mostly for private settings, the non-professional, and women. She was a public figure in that the overwhelming majority of her pieces were published, for a large clientele, and she was reviewed (occasionally). For her only appearance in the United States, between October and December of 1908, Chaminade performed in public, in major cities, to large audiences. These audiences were made up mostly of admiring women, who would perform or teach her works in private settings. Virtually every concert was reviewed at length in major newspapers. A commercial firm handled the tour, and there was publicity prior to each event. Thus public and private intermingled in ways that defy an oppositional model. I would suspect that Chaminade herself made few distinctions between the two, if she even would have conceived of her activities in those terms.

But to return to ideological considerations, it is important to note that the gendered associations of public and private mean more than site, agency, and societal status. They have important metaphoric and epistemological implications as well. They symbolize psychic space: women and private as reined in and bounded, men and public as free and open. Men have fewer restrictions on their behavior. Public represents an epistemological space without limits, and therefore privileged. Private suggests boundaries of knowledge and access to knowledge; it implies a lesser justification for knowledge and authority.[51] Musical activity rooted in the private, therefore, has less cultural justification and presumably less value than the workings and agents of the public sphere. Similarly, practitioners of the private are lesser. Of course, it is instructive to consider the model of private before the middle of the nineteenth century. Private meant select, elite, aristocratic. But it did not have public as an oppositional term. Public did not function as a serious competing ideology, at least with regard to art music, and so "private" did not have the implications it has today. In other words, what we call "private" was the typical venue for secular music-making and was not viewed as "Other." The historical comparison demonstrates, once again, that notions of private and public require contextualization, and that the hierarchies they imply need careful investigation. The dualism is not universal, nor are its meanings.

The salon

The *salon* has functioned as one of the important institutions of private music-making for women. It became prominent in the nineteenth century, a time when various institutions supplanted court and church as sites of musical activity. We have already noted the dramatic rise of public music around 1800. The business of music, centered increasingly around entrepreneurial activity, now catered to a broader clientele. Nonetheless the aristocracy, ever more independent from the court, held on to its class privileges by continuing the practice of smaller, restricted musical gatherings, now known loosely as *salons*. The term itself came from seventeenth-century France, when large rooms in palatial settings began to be called *salons*. At the end of the century, particularly at Versailles, the term also connoted musical performances in such rooms. But *salons* apparently originated with women, who hosted literary gatherings. The earliest, at the Hôtel de Rambouillet, lasted from 1608 to 1659.

Politics and music also occupied a niche. In the eighteenth century philosophy found its way into the gatherings, and it was in that century that the word *salon* entered the German language.[52]

Like much of the upper class, the aristocracy of the early nineteenth century wanted to cling to French culture and its elitist cachet.[53] Many of Beethoven's chamber-music works and piano sonatas, for example, were introduced in private gatherings hosted by aristocrats. In the 1830s and 1840s Chopin thrived amid the rarefied atmosphere of the Parisian *salon*. Many *salons* exuded a feminine tone, arguably a general characteristic of French aristocratic culture. The ambiance probably resulted from other factors as well, including the large number of female participants, the opulence of the surroundings, and the kind of music performed, which was often lyrical and expressive.[54] Furthermore, even though financed by male aristocrats, the *salon* located itself in a residence. And the home, even if palatial, tended to be a female domain. Thus despite its role as replacement for the masculine preserve of the court, the *salon* represented an important site of feminine culture.

But *salon* pertained to a variety of cultural settings. In Germany, for example, some interesting developments were taking place. In the waning years of the eighteenth century, several Jewish women of newly emancipated families carved out a cultural niche for themselves as hosts of private gatherings that included leading artists. These *salons* were not successors to the court, however; the roots were in upper middle-class commercialism rather than the aristocracy. Furthermore, women led these *salons* and continued a tradition of almost two hundred years of female cultural leadership as *salonières*. This offered gifted Jewish women arguably their prime outlet for intellectual and artistic expression. As post-Enlightenment Jews recently emancipated from the ghettos, they continued to face discrimination from German culture at large. Even Jews who converted to Christianity, like the Mendelssohns, were still viewed as Jews, and they tended to retain values from their Jewish heritage and socialize with other Jewish or newly converted families.[55] For Jewish women in particular, many of whom received an education comparable to men but who were constrained from engaging in commercial pursuits, the *salon* afforded a unique vehicle for the expression of their minds and hearts. Women such as Fanny Arnstein in Vienna, and Henriette Herz (1764–1847), Rahel Levin (later Varnhagen von Ense; 1771–1833), and Fanny Hensel in Berlin, shone in their *salons*. What could have been merely a reaction to restrictiveness became instead a sparkling showcase for the considerable talents of some brilliant women.[56]

The class implications are quite interesting. On the one hand, these women came from families with substantial wealth and learning: the elite of the emancipated Jewish community. On the other, familial roots in commercialism, especially banking, placed them within a bourgeois framework. This linked them more closely with the emerging middle class than with the "old money" of aristocracy. Yet as outsiders they found a comfortable fit with neither the gentile middle class nor the nobility.

Hensel's activities in the *salon* provide an interesting look at this thriving musical culture. Having grown up in a home that hosted leading artistic figures on a regular basis, Hensel took charge of the bi-weekly *Sonntagsmusiken* at the family's splendid residence in the early 1830s. She acted in various capacities: organizer, composer, performer (solo and chamber), contractor, conductor, and chronicler. This holistic immersion in the creative–performing process apparently proved very satisfying to Hensel, who chronicled many of her experiences in diaries and letters to her brother.[57] The *salon* helped maintain a life-long interest in composition, an activity that produced over four hundred pieces even though publication and public performance were barred through paternal proscription. Although it is impossible to state with complete accuracy, a substantial number of Hensel's compositions were performed at her musicales. Apparently she also circulated works to a wide circle of friends, who were noted performers in Berlin. In the early 1830s Hensel wrote orchestral works for the gatherings, for which she hired the musicians, and on at least one occasion conducted her own composition.[58] Thus in a private, self-directed, non-commercial musical enterprise, Hensel may have experienced as wide a variety of musical activities as the professional in the public arena. But since the public arena formed the basis of written reviews and repertorialization, activity in the *salon* has sifted through the filters of history and been devalued. For fine musicians like Hensel, however, the *salon* functioned as a meaningful sign of creative authority.

Another type of non-aristocratic salon revolved around the bourgeoisie, typified by Schubert's circles in Vienna in the 1810s and 1820s. Compared with the Jewish *salons*, these gatherings involved people with modest socio-economic status, with a provincial background. The term *salon* does not apply here. They apparently consisted mainly of men and provided a social framework for the homosexual culture of Schubert and his friends.[59] While the dearth of female participation might be expected given the gay environment, it also conveys a sense of educational realities of the time. Privileged women were the typical recipients of a good education. Bourgeois women would be occupied with domestic concerns and have little preparation or time for intellectual activities. As the century progressed, however, women benefited from increased educational access. This helped effect a growing middle class, with ever increasing social clout. The social democratization was paralleled in the democratization of the *salon* as the middle class assumed control. In Britain and America the site was often called drawing room or parlor. This change marked a demystification of French culture and a turn away from the elitist associations of the *salon*. The democratization also meant a broader participation of women.[60]

By 1900, particularly in the United States, the parlor also functioned as a great musical equalizer. Women and men of various ages and talents might perform for each other. Edith Borroff fondly describes such a gathering, a family event, in which all kinds of music were heard – from "classical" to popular to improvisation.[61] Music functioned as entertainment in this eclectic environment and shed elitist pretensions. In some ways it recalled practice of the late eighteenth century, for both made fewer distinctions between serious and popular. Of course, some styles in the nineteenth century, such as Italian opera, capitalized on popular elements. But I am focusing mainly on the hegemonic Germanic tradition, which gained the upper hand in music historiography and established a hierarchy of high art music and low popular music.[62] This ever-widening division also developed by way of modernism. In its formative stages around 1900, modernism favored the abstract, the impersonal, and the separation of art and life. Popular music, by definition, would reflect the values of a broad segment of the population. In doing so it would engage the listener much more directly and tend to blur divisions between art and life: a challenge to precepts of modernism. Yet modernism was instrumental in shaping twentieth-century historiography, and this power partly explains the century's denigration of popular idioms as not being serious. Perhaps this is a tautology, or seems like a tautology because of internalized understandings of the terms. But one could argue that seriousness should be eliminated as a criterion because it is inappropriate, or if it must be retained it should be re-defined in ways that avoid elitism.[63]

Many women active as composers or performers around 1900 have been linked negatively to the *salon* (or drawing room or parlor).[64] Chaminade provides a case in point. Extremely popular through 1910, Chaminade's reputation was soon tarnished through mere association with the *salon*. *The New Grove Dictionary*, for example, basically repeated the pejorative assessment of the second edition that her music is intended for the drawing room.[65] Nicholas Slonimsky, for example, has also deployed the *salon* as a sign of trivial music.[66] These accounts typify the pervasive twentieth-century association of women with the *salon*, and the *salon* with marginal artistic activity. The social and stylistic democratization in the *salon* has reinforced negative gender associations. It is possible that around 1900 male society began to fear the *salon* as a site of female power. One effective means of suppression is discreditation: denigration of the mixing of the personal and the artistic within the home. Such a mixture flies in the face of modernism's separation of life and art. Furthermore, the perceived threat may have hinged also on the age-old fear of woman's body: woman inhabiting the *salon* is tantamount to control of artistic activity by her body. As Leslie Dunn shows for the Renaissance, male fear of the female singing voice arousing male desire may have something to do with the relegation of women to separate spaces where they perform for each other.[67] Symbolically, therefore, the *salon* can represent and be represented by body: both are hidden, to be kept out of public view. But for women active in the *salon*, the site afforded rich opportunity for creative artistry and a place where professional identity could be expressed according to different standards.[68]

PUBLICATION

Just as it is generally assumed that professionalism represents a status and identity to be aspired to, especially by the middle class, so most practitioners of Western music history assume that composers view publication as a universally desirable goal. But given the fact that women historically have had fewer pieces published than men, we might start to wonder about the assumptions behind that statement. Why has it been assumed desirable to publish? Why does a composer publish music? Might there be reasons why a composer might not wish to publish? What are the larger implications of such a choice? Are women problematized through ideological conflicts arising from publication?

Since *c.* 1750, publication has been the principal means of circulation of Western art music. It has brought pieces of music to a greater number of people than was possible through manuscript distribution. But publication has assumed a life of its own as a commodity of the marketplace; it is no accident that music publishers began to proliferate in the industrial revolution. Furthermore, publication has been closely tied to other elements of the canonic process, including public performance, reviews, and historical retention. A published piece of music is a document, a physical object. It can be held, referred to, analyzed, and reproduced visually in an exact form (see also Chapter 1). Moreover, publication offers the work to the public in a way quite different from manuscript circulation or non-circulation: the potential for permanence and for broad recognition. What this means is that unpublished works of women (and men) elude the historical filters that depend on physicality for their source material. Without this the potential for canonicity drops markedly. Sometimes, however, extraordinary measures can rescue an unpublished work from historical oblivion, such as Robert Schumann's discovery and promotion of Schubert's C-major Symphony. But such exceptions, if anything, only reaffirm the canonic power of publication. Publication also raises interesting questions about the composer's proprietary relationship to the work once it is published.

Composers have wanted to have their pieces published because publication works hand in hand with other musical structures and increases the potential for canonicity. Publications earn money. Today they can also generate income indirectly through broadcasts or recordings. Yet there may be psychological consequences of circulating one's work to the public. For a woman, in particular, publication may expose her in ways that problematize her self-identity. Because publication itself is considered a distinguishing characteristic of professionalism, many of the problematic aspects of professionalism are similarly problematic with publishing. Women might be forced to counter or at the least stretch societal ideals of themselves. By placing a woman and her subjectivity in the open, publishing highlights the contradictions between ideology and her professionalism. As mentioned earlier, her identity as a woman may be problematized; she may be seen as a lesser woman, a fraudulent woman, or even a lesser man. Because this can affect her sense of herself, her confidence as a composer can be undermined. She might fear the exposure that published authorship brings.

Ironically, Felix Mendelssohn's restrictive views on published authorship are instructive. It is summer 1837 and Mendelssohn is responding to his mother's request that he encourage his sister, Fanny Hensel, to publish her music:

I hope I don't need to say that if she decides to publish anything, I will help her all I can and alleviate any difficulties arising from it. But I cannot persuade her to publish anything, because it is against my views and convictions. We have previously spoken a great deal about it, and I still hold the same opinion. I consider publishing something serious (it should at least be that) and believe that one should do it only if one wants to appear as an author one's entire life and stick to it. But that necessitates a series of works, one after the other.... Fanny, as I know her, possesses neither the inclination nor calling for authorship. She is too much a woman for that, as is proper, and looks after her house and thinks neither about the public nor the musical world, unless that primary occupation is accomplished. Publishing would only disturb her in these duties, and I cannot reconcile myself to it. If she decides on her own to publish, or to please Hensel [Fanny's husband], I am, as I said, ready to be helpful as much as possible, but to encourage her towards something I don't consider right is what I cannot do.[69]

Even though Mendelssohn's remarks propose limits on the musical activities of his sister, he is nonetheless correctly assessing the ideology of what a published composer means and what a real woman means, at least in his time. He affirms the separation between the public world of the professional and the domestic world of women. For Mendelssohn, the difference between creating works and being a professional seems to lie in publishing, in that subjective exposure to the public. Publication implies regular and continuous activity, characteristics mentioned earlier in regard to professionalism.[70] Incidentally, one modern interpretation of Felix's views is that he was trying to protect Fanny from the unpleasantness of public criticism.[71] If so he was conforming to societal ideals of manhood and womanhood: women are to be protected, men are to protect women, and it is up to men to decide when to invoke the protection. As in this case, such intervention would be needed when women's actions suggested they were trespassing in the public arena and leaving the domestic world where they are ideologically situated.

Women may also have a fear of the implications of permanence that inhere in publication. Creating a work is one thing, but having it in a form that suggests permanence is quite another. Permanence implies a centered position in culture – as if the permanent entity is somehow representative of and constitutive of that society. While women are raised within mainstream society, they are socialized at least in part as cultural Others. Their subjective positions can range from inside to outside and they often feel contradiction or am-bivalence from conflicting ideals. As a result, women may not be comfortable assuming the center through a permanent version of a work; they might fear the contradictory spaces they might need to inhabit. Part of this may have to do with women's sense of their subjective positioning in history: they are outsiders. As compared to men, therefore, women composers might be more likely to shy away from thinking of their works in terms of future history. And future history depends in large measure on the longevity of physical documents. The published composition is just such a document. It is also a requirement for professional success, at least as the system is presently structured. Yet if many women harbor a fear of success because of potential ideological conflicts and a fear of living up to that success, then publications can be a cause for ambivalence and confusion. We must remember, however, that discriminatory prac-tices often made that stage of decision-making moot. Women were not expected to publish and their works were excluded from many of the structures that lead to publication.

A related issue is why works should be perpetuated beyond their original milieu. Perhaps they should not; perhaps that is a cultural distortion of the work. Since the nineteenth century, however, there has been an expectation of permanence. In terms of ideology, therefore, cultural displacement does not spell cultural distortion. But perhaps that ideology disregards the desires of women. Ideologies of domesticity may promote the expectation of adaptation to local circumstances. As a result women may feel more comfortable conceiving a work for a knowable context. Potential use in an ambiguous future could arouse insecurity and doubt. In short, the permanence of the published composition may be a mixed blessing.

Publication may signal yet another kind of anxiety: an anxiety of separation. If women are idealized as nurturers and caregivers in the family, they might experience a special sense of loss when the created object goes out into the world as a published work. While it may be extreme to say that it resembles a grieving process, it might not be far-fetched to compare it to the anxiety that accompanies weaning a baby or having a grown child move out of the home: the musical child, as it were, is leaving the nest.[72] The special bond between creator and created is now appropriated, in a way, by an amorphous public or posterity. For who "owns" the work once it leaves the purview of the composer herself? While publisher and/or composer retains legal ownership, in a certain sense the piece now belongs to every potential member of the public who hears it, performs it, and studies it. The composer is still inherent but cedes some control to others. And it may be this loss of control that engenders anxiety. This can happen to any composer, female or male. But I would suspect that social conditioning may make it easier for a man to let his piece go. Indeed, he may be eager to have the work enter the public's consciousness. This can increase the chances for canonicity and a secure place in history. Men, after all, generally feel more centered in history than women and see themselves as a natural part of historical succession. They will be more comfortable seeing their creative progeny go into the world as a published work. As Suzanne Cusick suggests, these "sons" will be sent out into the world and launched in a profession with paternal encouragement and blessing.[73]

Having aired the possible anxieties that women composers may experience toward publication, we should recognize the other side of the ambivalence. Publication can mean a kind of professional affirmation that is extremely satisfying to a composer. It opens up greater possibilities for expression and communication. In practical terms publication can mean a greater likelihood of sustaining a career in composition. Given that publication is *de facto* such an important sign of professionalism, the putting into public circulation of women and their works can be critical towards modifying societal ideologies of women and of professionalism. Yet as the preceding discussions suggest, publication as a universally desirable goal can be problematic, at least for women. For those women whose output was only thinly published, particularly in the nineteenth century, at some level the act of not publishing could have operated as preference and not merely reaction to patriarchal oppression. If we view publication as a structure with certain ambiguities and biases we will be better able to construct models of canon formation that put publication into a truer perspective. We cannot assume, for instance, that if a work has not been published it is of inferior quality. There are too many contingent factors that go into the publishing of a work. Publication does not rest unambiguously on absolute standards of quality.

THE AUTHOR-FUNCTION

As the composer's name circulates in society and becomes known it signifies much more than itself. This "author-function," as Michel Foucault calls it,[74] has assumed great import in Western culture since the rise of liberalism in the eighteenth century. As both signifier and sign it has conferred status not only on itself but on numerous structures of culture. It has come to represent a subjectivity that transcends boundaries. The timeless persona of the author (here including composer) achieves a mythic status that is difficult to concretize. Yet its semiotic power plays a major role in canonicity and needs to be understood. In particular it is important to ascertain its relationship to women composers *vis-à-vis* canon formation. How does the author-function color perceptions of historic worth? Are there ways in which women have been disadvantaged through the cultural implications of the concept? And if so, might there be ways to reconfigure the notion to improve the situation?

In Western music the figure of the composer has been privileged above most other structures. This larger-than-life entity stems from Romantic notions of the composer as genius.[75] Creativity is likened to divine miracle and removed to a metaphysical plane beyond rational empiricism. The composer, as divine agent, becomes an object of awe. Ideologically he inhabits the sublime and as such is distanced from the trivialities of daily existence. This contributes to an aura of timelessness. Semiotically this transcendent author infuses numerous modes of discourse with meaning. The aggregate of meanings is much greater than the sum of an individual's life and works, and seems to transcend individual ideologies. The author takes on a kind of disembodied form beyond social specificity. In short, the transcendent author of the author-function is quite powerful.

The hegemony of the composer has its roots in societal emphases on the individual, a process we have noted on several occasions. In addition to the many new roles based in the individual, a powerful critical establishment advanced the cause of individualism through frequent writings on composers. Composers would be mentioned in reviews, of course, but there were also biographical essays and monographs. Even the earliest issues of two important magazines, the *Allgemeine musikalische Zeitung* (1798) and *Dwight's Journal of Music* (1852), included lengthy studies of individual composers, Mozart and Chopin respectively. Monographs such as Forkel's study of J. S. Bach (1802) and Nissen's biography of Mozart (1828) helped generate the great interest in composers' lives. By the late twentieth century, indeed, composer biography is considered a standard genre to the extent that one *expects* to find at least one study of a given figure.

In toto, such writings have helped create an ontology of author. But it has been argued that the authorial emphasis has gone too far. Louis Althusser, for example, believes that the author notion in the West means an existential author: one whose subjectivity strives toward ultimate personal freedom, without thoughts of community or societal responsibility.[76] This suggests a selfishness and self-absorption that could be harmful to the larger social fabric: social good sacrificed to personal gratification. There are also criticisms specific to music. In the late twentieth century, for example, Elliott Carter complains how it is "the public image of the composer [that is] the real item of consumption.... [The public] must think – and perhaps rightly – that the musical work is intended to help his public image through reviews and reports in widely circulated periodicals, and thus lead the composer to more important positions in domains peripheral to composition, but more remunerative."[77] Carter is clearly chagrined over the inversion. He has become a media personality – an important element in the recent workings of the author-function. Yet exploited commercial object is probably not what he had in mind when he became a professional. Roger Sessions says it well when he expresses concern over "what has seemed to me an overemphasis on the composer – both individually and collectively – and his problems, even, one might say, at the expense of attention to his music itself."[78] Yet these famous (dare I say "popular"?) composers are part of a relatively small group of celebrity composers. Perhaps many another composer would envy their fame and be happy to find themselves in such a position.

While Carter and Sessions focus reflexively on the present, Edward Dent has made some insightful observations that link past and present.[79] The composer of the past is invested with an inflated persona that is appropriated by present-day conductors and solo performers. This takes place through the performance of canonical works. It is an "iniquity of the virtuoso conductor, or of any virtuoso interpreter; he trades upon our childlike reverence for the classics in order to get some of that reverence transferred to his own person." And this, Dent asserts, has a preventative effect on conductors' willingness to take up new works. If they did, they would give up that reflected glory. In a new work attention is focused mainly on the work itself; the composer is inherent but has not yet accrued the awe that comes with historical longevity. In fact, the composer may well be present literally at a performance of a new work, and she or he will absorb much of the acclaim that would ordinarily go to the conductor or performer. For Dent, in 1937, the contemporary composer is subordinated to the egotistic persona of the conductor and solo performer. For Carter and Sessions approximately thirty years later, the contemporary composer can become a captive of the media, while the music is ignored. In both, the cultural power of the transcendent subject to shape patterns of identity is evident.

Thus the author-function has come to represent meanings well beyond the sum of the author's works. Like categories in general the author-function is descriptive, classificational, and pre-evaluative.[80] Descriptive suggests all the attributes, opinions, and relationships that fall under the name of an author. When the name is used these will enter the semiotic field of possibility. If we take the name of Beethoven, for example, attributes such as great, genius, and powerful might come to mind. The author-function is organizational in that it groups similar and diverse elements, and eliminates irrelevant factors. Beethoven is associated, for example, with the symphony, German music, and Romanticism; serialism or concerto grosso would be excluded by his name. The author-function also acts as a means of pre-evaluation: it establishes expectations for judgment based on prior knowledge of the figure. Beethoven's name would imply a giant in Western art music and therefore someone whose music is first rate. This level of aesthetic authority would confer great moral force on an author. But even lesser authors of the past who have remained canonic are vested with a moral veneer that places them above the category of mere historical person. It might be this quality that lies at the heart of Dent's theory about modern appropriation of the reverence accorded canonic composers.

In musicology the author-function exists as a category of research and a category under which one can find information, even on non-biographical matters (such as style and aesthetics). It has been instrumental in defining historical organization; witness titles such as *The Age of Beethoven* (1982) in the *New Oxford History of Music* series or *The Sonata Since Beethoven* (1969) in William S. Newman's series on the history of the sonata idea.[81] The composer's name can be socially prestigious and commercially valuable. Today, for example, symphony concerts and individual recitals are usually advertised according to the names of the composers (or conductors or solo performers) even more than the titles of pieces. Similarly, recordings are classified according to the author's or performer's name. These figures are the stars of the "classical" world in much the same way that Madonna or Sting functions in the pop world. Should we need further evidence of the power of the author-function we might imagine the fate of a work that lacks an authorial signature. We might not know how to handle it for it lacks many of the signs that we depend on for contextualization; it almost seems illegitimate. A probable result is canonic exclusion.

The author-function has been internalized to such an extent in the West that it might be difficult to envision other systems for organizing the signifiers presently under the author's name. But there are other possibilities. Foucault mentions emphases on the idea of the work and on *écriture* – writing. The former is certainly paradigmatic in musicology. We need only think of research on individual compositions, for example Beethoven's *Eroica* Symphony or Stravinsky's *Rite of Spring*. Of course, my inclusion of the composer's name as a possessive reveals my own internalization of the author-function. Indeed, a work virtually belongs to the notion of its author. This is yet another kind of ownership from the types discussed previously and it suggests a reason why some composers might be reluctant to part with their works. For many women, in particular, literal possession of the work may be the only kind of proprietary relationship they have with it. The ownership inherent in the author-function may not pertain to them because their names have not been circulated on the societal level to any significant degree, at least until recently.

As to *écriture* the analogy with musicology is more ambiguous. If *écriture* implies the style of the written work then it clearly does serve as a major focus in the field. The musical work is taken as a visual object and subjected to much the same grammatical and syntactical manipulations as a semantic text. If, however, *écriture* entails process, in particular the process of writing, then the links with musicology are not as strong. To be sure some analytic approaches emphasize process, but most focus on the finished product. *Ecriture* may also suggest social processes that "write" or inscribe the work in culture. Canon formation itself might qualify under such a definition. If so, then musicology has recently expanded its models to emphasize process as well as static structures. But the older paradigms still have a firm grip on the discipline.

Another strategy to replace the author-function calls for the elimination of the author altogether. This is favored by Roland Barthes, among others.[82] One of the reasons given is the fallacy of the Western notion that the author *precedes* the work; he believes the author originates simultaneously with the work. What he seems to be saying is that the cultural meanings of the author are not, or perhaps should not be, a pre-existent category but come into being when the work comes into being. For Barthes, at least as of 1968, it is the reader, not the author, who creates literary meaning and thus the reader is the more important element.[83] Another possible replacement for the author-function would be a structure grounded in community. The individual, with a transcendent subjectivity, would no longer serve as the basis of meaning. Meaning would now derive from shared structures, made up of more than one person. Lawrence Lipking dubs this a structure of "affiliation" and believes it would be particularly suitable for women.[84] As discussed in Chapter 1, many oral traditions exhibit this characteristic. Another illustration of Lipking's multiplicity can be seen in some curricular designs.[85] Here material is organized according to larger categories instead of individual names. In one kind of arrangement, several names are placed in each category and it is up to the instructor to select which one she or he would like to use in a given year. This subverts the transcendent quality of the author-function; the interchangeability of authorial identities suggests an equivalence that tames the exaggerated persona of any one of them. Nonetheless, even in this model the author-function is present. It is just that it has been checked within boundaries that make room for other ways of approaching the material under study.

Lipking's idea also suggests the broader question of the meaning of the author-function for women authors.[86] One observation we can make is that women composers, for various reasons, have barely reached the nominative classificational function. There are very few women composers, for example, in *The New Grove Dictionary* and hardly any in the Grout–Palisca *A History of Western Music.*

Furthermore, the descriptive and pre-evaluative aspects of the author-function are less relevant to women composers; they have not yet received the accumulated critical exposure that gives their names the semiotic power to describe or to participate in evaluation.

So in light of these difficulties, is the author-function as presently understood – what we could call the "centered author" – a useful construct for women? I think the answer is mixed. It is easy to attribute women's canonic exclusion partly to musicology's emphasis on the category of the individual creator – on the author-function. For it is men who have been canonized through the various processes involved in canon formation, and it is men's names that presently signify quality and universality. Those whose names are not known, including many who are women, are then considered wanting in those desired qualities. Thus it seems that we would wish the elimination of the author-function, possibly in favor of some other kind(s) of emphases, for instance on the work or on the text. But as mentioned earlier, we already place significant emphasis on these areas as well. Furthermore, the elimination of the author introduces some major problems. First of all, the destruction of the category "author" would leave a huge hole difficult to fill. What would account for agency, for example? What would account for the ideological importance of the author in current historiographic practice? In addition, from a practical standpoint it is not easy to disrupt entrenched belief systems without gradual modification. For women in particular there are other reasons to resist the elimination of the author. It could close off an important source of cultural authority, and just at the time when women are beginning to make inroads into historical prominence. As Nancy Miller and others have noted,[87] men have long enjoyed authorial prestige and thus it might be easy for Barthes and other men to call for the elimination of the author. Perhaps the timing is no coincidence; perhaps it is motivated at least partly by the fear of female encroachment when a real threat is sensed. This would make it both a pre-emptive and reactive move. The elimination of the author would prematurely preclude recognition of female achievement, and the net result could be further suppression of women's artistic contributions.

Yet the female authorial voice has not fared well under present ideologies. It can be argued that the hegemony of the author-function has crowded out other ways of dealing with artistic activity. The author-function is a kind of take-over plant, like kudzu, that spreads rapidly into other forms and then emerges on the surface as the only viable structure. Yet other forms, with differing textures and emphases, are eager to re-emerge were it not for the aggressiveness of the invader. The main difference with the plant analogy is that the author-function seems to have been a "natural" part of the cultural landscape since *c.* 1800. Even if not a foreign invader, however, it has still suppressed other conventions that can influence our ideas on valuation and history. For example, the elevation of the reputation of reviewed composers has implicitly devalued the contributions of composers and performers (and patrons and audience members) who worked in non-public venues and therefore were not reviewed. It has suppressed aspects of social specificity like gender and class and implied a unitary model of artistic activity. The centered author of the author-function has crowded out alternatives and potential competitors to its exalted position.

But if the author-function is problematic and so is its elimination, is there any viable solution for women? One answer lies in a de-centering of the author.[88] This means displacing the semiotic weight of the author-function by a lessened emphasis on the transcendent subjectivity of the author. This can happen through greater attention to social context, including factors of gender and class, and to process. The author would be situated in a specific time and place, and subjectivity would share space with process and context. Such a de-centering could benefit musical women. First, it would help demystify the universalism of present structures. Second, it would provide more flexible models in which to situate women and their work. A de-centering in the way described here could actually enhance female subjectivity by enabling the opening of windows to its exposure. It could foster closer identity with models of professionalism because the models themselves would be inflected with a more contextualized view of the composer.

The kind of de-centering called for here will not strip away individual subjectivity but move it toward equilibrium with other factors that figure into historiography. There will be greater flexibility in approaching the past, dealing with the present, and preparing for the future. Professionalism will be capable of multiple models. As a result of this diversity women composers may well find themselves swimming in new mainstreams that re-define what being a serious composer in Western art music is all about.

CHAPTER 4

Music as gendered discourse

The previous chapters focused on the figure of the composer in those first stages needed to bring a name into the arena of culture. In the present chapter we add the critical element of the work itself, arguably the principal content of a canon. While we might be tempted to make a clear distinction between composer and work, it is important to understand the work as a comprehensive notion that includes the idea of the author as well. Although this may not have been the case when canons, or rather repertories, were first starting to cohere, it seems to be the situation at present. What this means in terms of the organization of this study is that while we are dealing with an entity that makes sense within a linear progression from creativity through criticism – a seemingly reasonable path of canon formation – it also suggests an elasticity that upsets the neatness of the model. We might recall, for example, Roland Barthes's observation that the author does not precede the work but is born with it.[1]

Several assumptions underlie the chapter. One is the idea that music, like its sister art forms, grows out of a specific social context. It expresses in various ways fundamental assumptions about the culture in which it originates. Aesthetically music entails communication, and this can take place at many levels and in varied combinations of work, composer, performer, and receptor. As to the composer, she or he is embedded in particular cultural circumstances and assumptions, and these affect the way a piece is written. The receptor is similarly grounded. This indicates that meaning(s) imputed to a piece of music vary not only from one historical period to the next but within a given period, based on crucial factors such as gender, class, race, ethnicity, sexuality, and nationality. In addition, a receptor might or might not read in the same meanings or signs that a composer intended, consciously or not, in a composition. In fact, she or he probably will not, at least in their entirety, for one's understanding of a piece depends on one's present semiotic context and how it interprets the signs of the past. Nonetheless, it is generally useful to attempt to discover as much as possible about the aesthetic and social context surrounding the composition of the work and to mediate that with present culture. The strength of the present may be such, however, that one cannot really know the past; it is always inflected with the present and further tainted by the very process of examining it. If we are to study history, these are inescapable problems we have to live with. Recognizing them and accounting for them, however, go a long way towards lessening the difficulties. In any event, these assumptions on cultural embeddedness act to repudiate the notion of aesthetic autonomy in a piece of music. As we shall see later, even aesthetic paradigms that posit autonomy, such as "absolute music" of German Romanticism, are still, in that very positing, expressing something fundamental about contemporary social processes and the way men view themselves within emerging bourgeois culture.

As these assumptions suggest, the musical composition does important cultural work. Through the author-function it circulates the reputation of the composer. But more importantly for society as a whole it can function as a discourse that reproduces societal values and ideologies. Through that process it also constructs values and ideologies, and it becomes difficult and perhaps fruitless to attempt to discern which is which. These operations mean that a work and the musical conventions that govern a work are socially biased in certain ways, even though it can be extremely difficult to figure out how, especially in instrumental music. Important social variables such as power, class, and gender can be inscribed in a work. A likely possibility is that they will be mapped to function as a means of representation: to represent societal ideologies of desirable status and behavior. Inscriptions of gender typically function as strategies of representation and often aim to expose in some way the ideological paradigms concerning socialized women and men. It is important for us to distinguish societal ideals from the experiences of real women and recognize that strategies of gendered representation typically treat ideals rather than lived experience. An incidental advantage of this framework is that it avoids the danger of essentialism that can arise when a gendered code is thought representative of actual people. This would suggest that all real people behave this way or believe in the validity of the code for all members of their gender. In the ideology model, however, there is the space between ideals and reality, and in that space can be negotiated numerous theories that accommodate individuals and their particular circumstances. But even more than that, it makes practical sense that a gendered strategy would direct its attention to the level of societal paradigm. If change or at least eventual change is the implicit goal, this is where it probably can do the most good. Of course, I have just described a strategy of exposure that is implicitly an act of criticism. There are also inscriptions of gender, especially in larger musical conventions, that are meant to reinforce ideologies, not question them. These could be more difficult to identify because of the absence of disruption.

This chapter explores some of the ways in which gender is expressed in music and its codes, and how that relates to societal ideologies of gender and its effect on the experiences of real women, especially women who write music. These issues are significant for canon formation. They shape attitudes towards, and understandings of, influential conventions in music, many of which form the underpinning of theories that determine what becomes canonic. In other words we are talking about valuation: about the relative rankings among conventions and how some will be perpetuated and others ignored. They reinforce the notion that the variables that make up canon formation are neither absolute nor insular but shaped by ideologies that grow out of society at large. This underscores the contingency of canon formation itself. While these properties might seem obvious, especially by this point in the study, we should recall that the ability of music to embody meanings in reference to society is an idea that has been implicitly denied in the twentieth century, at least until recently. It is a way of keeping music pure, in the realm of the mind, and thus ideologically (and as a consequence practically) away from women. The exaltation of the composer (and conductor and solo performer) into a transcendent persona has also assisted in the repression of social referentiality in music.

The first section focuses on the category of musical categories, i.e. genre. This is an example of a convention whose internal divisions are based on criteria that reflect social values, such as a preference for largeness and for non-functionality that implies transcendence. The criteria establish hierarchies that are linked with gender: maleness with the large, the non-functional, and the intellectual, which are valued; femaleness with the small and the functional (and the private), which are devalued. In analogies with art history, we see how ideologies of gender in genre affect how women practice in these fields and how that affects their location in canonicity.

The bulk of the chapter treats gender in aesthetic conventions. Most of the space is devoted to aspects of the sonata aesthetic, one of the major organizational systems of the past 250 years. It includes the notion of absolute music and also sonata form. We see how absolute music serves to affirm ideologies of gender within culture. This is further reinforced in an unusually overt expression of gender relations in ideology: the gendered codes of sonata form. Here the ideological subordination of woman is reflected in a musical template, which in itself represents a kind of ideological or idealistic projection of musical materials. Subsequently we take a sonata movement, by Cécile Chaminade, and analyze potential challenging strategies to the gendered representation inherent in the codes. While there is no essentialist connection between woman composer and compositional strategy, we still have to wonder whether Chaminade's subject position as a socialized woman, even with all the contradictions that implies, might have a bearing on her approach to the codes. We also have to consider the relationship between the ideological sub-ordination of women in the codes and the anxieties and oppression that actual female composers have had to deal with. While these codes were not "real" in terms of describing what actual women experienced, they were nonetheless a real part of the history of ideas and conveyed a powerful ideology for women. Thus it is reasonable to assume that these kinds of messages exacerbated the anxieties and other difficulties of women, as described in preceding chapters.

We also take up the possibility of a female aesthetic. Here we confront potential essentialism, and we have to consider carefully whether the gender of the maker can make a difference in how music is composed. We might even say that the category itself is questionable. But it is a burning issue and something that needs to be discussed.

It will become clear that the issues covered in the chapter extend into the area of reception. While I hint at it in the Chaminade analysis, it is left mostly to the next chapter, which is devoted solely to the issue. Thus to a great extent Chapter 5 complements the present chapter, and the reader should bear this in mind when proceeding through the arguments here.

THEORIES OF GENRE

We do not move about in a raw universe. Not only are the objects we encounter always to some extent pre-interpreted and preclassified for us by our particular cultures and languages, but also pre-evaluated, bearing the marks and signs of their prior valuings and evaluations by our fellow creatures. Indeed, preclassification is itself a form of pre-evaluation, for the labels or category names under which we encounter objects not only … foreground certain of their possible functions but also operate as signs – in effect, as culturally certified endorsements – of their more or less effective performance of those functions.[2]

Thus Barbara Herrnstein Smith identifies one of the most crucial functions of genre: pre-classification as pre-evaluation. Classification sets up certain expectations and assumptions based on culturally understood meanings of value of the particular category. For musical genre this entails parameters such as function, style, scoring, length, site of performance, intended audience, manner and nature of reception, decorum of the performative experience, and value. Classification validates and supports the right to existence of works within its boundaries. Works beyond tend to be excluded, ignored, and consequently devalued. The very choice of what categories exist predicts what will be produced and how thinking about them will proceed – creative, critical, historiographic. The classificational array will imply the questions to be asked and how they are framed, and set the agenda for the aesthetic and intellectual issues that become central. It will structure the stylistic and evaluative expectations listeners bring to the works of a given genre.[3] Contemporary understanding of a genre will become predictive of subsequent exemplars in that same genre. This perpetuation of paradigms resembles the perpetuating function of canons, and this is not surprising given that generic classification occupies a major position within canon formation. The predictive function of genres and canons is bound up with the normative function. The traits considered basic to the genre – those that define the particular genre and distinguish it from others, and those that populate many examples of the category – will become norms, whether stylistic, performative, or social, that provide the guiding framework for future forays into the category. Genres, of course, are subject to change. While they conceivably might disappear, they are more likely to undergo modification that alters their style, their function, their mode of transmission, their audience, or other parameters, including their very name.[4]

The exclusionist property of genre is critical toward understanding its cultural power. If, for example, we take the genre of the symphony, with its traditional definition as an orchestral piece in several movements, then where do we place a piece such as Berlioz's *Damnation of Faust* – a work with strong narrative content, a cast of characters, a wealth of pictorial scenes, and an unusual structure? What happens to pieces like this that challenge generic norms? One practical consequence is that they may not be performed very much; our performing structures have reflected and helped construct our categories of genre. Furthermore, this piece would have a greater likelihood of being omitted from studies or classes focusing on the symphony than, say, a Brahms symphony, and might well be excluded also from forums on the cantata, oratorio, or opera. This illustrates a major weakness of generic classification: exclusion and implied devaluation of works that do not fit the categories within the system. Generic classification can thus turn its Janus-like face to reveal an unredeeming rigidity that can prove fatal to musical works.

Carl Dahlhaus, who has written extensively on genre,[5] observes that not every piece fits into a recognized genre and implies that it need not do so. While I certainly agree with the first statement and wholeheartedly concur with the second in principle, in practice many works that do not fit accepted generic categories have suffered oblivion, neglect, or devaluation because of their differences from the established categories. In a related issue, Dahlhaus notes that generic diversity of scoring in a publication of music or a concert program gave the impression of a lack of seriousness for the endeavor. I would conjecture that the reasons for the criticism could entail a perception of certain aesthetic transgressions: in aesthetic decorum, organicism, autonomy, and non-functionalism. The very fact of having to pay attention to purely performative matters could encroach upon pure aesthetic contemplation. Perhaps a solution is to go beyond genre categories and resist the impulse to classify. Another strategy is to restructure the criteria behind the categories, which we will do shortly. "Mixing" of genres can also take place within a given piece. As Jeffrey Kallberg observes, composers often mixed genres within a composition for some deliberate reason. Just as deliberately they might obfuscate or counter some basic attribute of a genre. This might play a role in the Chaminade analysis later in the chapter.[6]

As Dahlhaus notes, before 1800 the notion of genre figured prominently in the fundamental conception of a piece of music. Genre was defined largely according to the particular function underlying a composition, such as liturgy or dance. Although generic differentiation was still important in the nineteenth century, lack of functionality and a new emphasis on the autonomy of the individual work meant that genre was proportionally less important. While there was clearly tension between the individual work and the inclusive category, Dahlhaus believes that the weight shifted increasingly toward the concept of the individual work, a trend that recalls the growing semiotic importance of the author-figure. The tendency toward uniqueness and aesthetic autonomy intensified to the point that genre holds little meaning for music written after 1900.[7]

Two aspects of Dahlhaus's ideas warrant comment, however. First, he assumes a narrow view of functionality, one in which utility has to be obvious and direct. But functionality also expresses less tangible purposes. Autonomous music, for example, exhibits this kind of functionality. In the nineteenth century, autonomous music provided a social outlet for the increasingly moneyed middle and upper classes. It also validated bourgeois power that now lacked monarchy and church for legitimation, and served as a vehicle for moral edification in a secular age. Second, Dahlhaus's statement about the relative unimportance of genre for music composed after 1900 presupposes a fairly inflexible notion of genre. It is as if the proliferation in compositional types and the apparent decline in functionality meant that the generic categories of the past were no longer valid. Thus genre as a system was no longer applicable. But as Dahlhaus himself observes, genres in general respond to cultural fluctuations and mediate among a variety of determining factors: composer intentionality, stylistic paradigms, performance circumstances, and class. In this broadened framework, genres can regroup in a variety of ways. Perhaps the proliferation in scoring types after 1900 was indeed problematic within conventional notions of genre – scoring, after all, was traditionally one of the main defining criteria of genre. Perhaps a more meaningful basis of classification would entail social factors, such as intended audience, performance site, or mode of transmission (e.g. electronic, audiovisual, conventional). In any case, the situation exemplifies the need for flexibility in assigning relative weight to the critical criteria. Social factors must be considered in any meaningful approach, of whatever period. This can help structure the presence of gender in canon formation.

Another aspect of genre that often goes unrecognized is the relative valuing of genres, or the hierarchy of genre. Perhaps hierarchies have arisen as an inevitable consequence of Western categorization, which has emphasized differences more than similarities.[8] Yet lest this sound totally rigid, the criteria for relative valuation have undergone changes in response to social context. The étude, for example, rose in status during the first half of the nineteenth century from a technical exercise to a concert piece.[9] In literature the biography occupied a high position in the eighteenth century, whereas the novel – a new genre, catering primarily to women – stood decidedly lower on the scale. In the nineteenth century, poetry ascended to generic heights, probably because of the considerable emphasis on personal expression and spiritual transcendence. The novel, now more firmly in the domain of women, lost ground.[10]

Art has also witnessed hierarchical fluctuation, especially in connection with gender, and its experience can be instructive for music. The principal hierarchy in art has been a division into fine arts (high) and decorative or applied arts, or crafts (low).[11] Although the split began in the Renaissance, it may not have been felt in some quarters until considerably later. In the nineteenth century, for example, Englishman William Morris worried about negative consequences of such a hierarchy:

It is only in latter times and under the most intricate conditions of life, that [the great arts and the so-called Decorative Arts] have fallen apart from one another; and I hold that, when they are so parted, it is ill for the Arts altogether: the lesser ones become trivial, mechanical, unintelligent... ; while the greater, however they may be practised for a while by men of great minds and wonder-working hands ... are sure to lose their dignity of popular arts, and become nothing but dull adjuncts to unmeaning pomp, or ingenious toys for a few rich or idle men.[12]

The "great arts" to which Morris alludes were architecture, sculpture, and painting, each subdivided into genres. In the last category, the history painting ranked supreme. It stressed a monumental, sculptural depiction of human anatomy in mythological or Classical setting. Higher genres idealized mankind: a humanity beyond vagaries of daily existence, beyond divisions of class. The identification of the individual with heroes and gods divorced from temporal specificity promoted a sense of moral superiority. Lesser genres, in contrast, were rooted in class divisions of contemporary society and often portrayed life of the middle class, with flaws in evidence. So-called "genre" painting depicted scenes of daily life, for example gatherings in the home (Vermeer, Chardin, Hogarth) or still life. The term itself is curious. Perhaps it signifies a theoretical link between an overt admission of the existence of categories or genres, and a particular category that was ranked relatively low. In other words, art that was highly valued may have been considered beyond the bounds of category, while art of lesser value could be categorized: thus the term "genre painting."[13] In any case, lower art has tended to stress practicality, the present, and plurality of class. The higher arts have prided themselves on timelessness and non-functionality, although their efforts at going beyond contemporary referentiality have themselves constituted a particular function. Functionality is probably inescapable.

Supported by the emphasis on the human figure in the art academy, the history painting maintained its high status well into the nineteenth century. Sketching from the nude formed the principal means of acquiring mastery. As noted earlier, women were excluded from such classes and thus *de facto* relegated to the periphery of the fine arts.[14] An interesting story in this regard concerns the French painter Rosa Bonheur (1822–99). Deprived of acquiring the skills for the history painting, Bonheur became interested in rendering animals in a monumental manner. She wished to depict horses in bold action: in a sense a replacement of animal monumentality for human monumentality, or one kind of "masculine" aesthetic for another. This would challenge the ideology of gendered subject matter and its appropriate maker. But Bonheur still needed direct visual study. Since the sites of horse trading were off-limits to women, Bonheur had to apply for permission to visit the establishments, and for personal safety donned male clothing to conceal her sexual identity.[15] These efforts resulted in the magnificent canvas "The horse fair" (1853), which hangs in the Metropolitan Museum in New York. It was the largest painting of animals to date. Bonheur's "masculine" rendition of masculine subject matter paved the way for similar works by women, such as Lady Elizabeth Butler's "Scotland for ever!" (1881).[16]

Although Bonheur and other women gradually gained fame with masculine themes, many women constructed links with the ideological feminine.[17] Flower painting flourished in the sixteenth and seventeenth centuries and counted as an art form rich in metaphor and symbolism, like much pre-modern art. Women as well as men participated as makers. In later eras critics and scholars identified nature as the basis of a commonality between women and flower painting and in the process denied flower painting a rich intellectual heritage: nature represented an inferior state to culture. Consequently, the genre and women's contributions to the genre were devalued. According to Parker and Pollock, modern critics apply to flower painting "exactly the same terms that are used to justify the secondary status accorded to crafts, which are similarly described as manually dexterous, decorative, and intellectually undemanding."[18] In contrast, the prestigious history painting was seen as a representation of culture. Its portrayal of human figures in idealized guise captured the nobility of the civilizing effects of Western society.

Embroidery (or needlework) is another example of a feminized art form. In the Middle Ages men and women of the privileged classes – royalty and aristocrats, monks and nuns – practiced needlework, which functioned as a means of glorifying power. In the late Middle Ages male guilds took over a considerable share of the activity. Around 1700, economic configurations of family and kinship changed, and as a result women were associated with needlework as domestic activity. In the eighteenth century the work became a defining symbol of the home and the gentility of the emerging bourgeoisie. Needlework "began to embody and maintain a feminine stereotype."[19] As such it became the butt of male satire, and women themselves grew ambivalent because of its restrictive connotations.

Needlework has been categorized as craft: it was strongly functional, and produced and consumed in the home. The fine arts, in contrast, have purported to be functionless, originated in more formal circumstances, resided in the public sphere for their consumption, and existed largely for aesthetic purposes.[20] Parker and Pollock assert that the label "craft" has had little to do with the product *per se* or its quality. Furthermore, they believe that gender has played only a symptomatic role in the art/craft division. I would suggest, however, that it has often acted as a causative factor. This idea is strengthened by their own thesis that many areas of art previously practiced by men or both sexes lost stature after women became the chief practitioners – as in the cases of flower painting and needlework.[21] But regardless of whether gender figures as cause or as effect, hierarchical notions of art forms have had a close relationship with societal constructions of gender: gender has informed societal notions about higher and lesser art, and conversely hierarchic notions have served as a barometer of women's participation in various levels of the artistic pecking order.[22] Generic stature can also suggest epistemological legitimacy.

The art–craft division corresponds in music to a division between Western art music and other types such as popular music, folk music, jazz, and world music. I realize that this ranking is culturally chauvinist, but I am constructing it from the point of view of a partisan of Western art culture.[23] Like its fine-arts counterpart, art music has had its own generic hierarchies. The criteria resemble those within fine arts, with the important distinction that music adds a component generally absent from art: the performer as necessary mediator between the maker and receptor. This is a significant consideration in the aesthetic valuation of music.

Since *c.* 1800 art music has generally placed greater value on the larger forms (genres). Symphony and opera have occupied the top rung of instrumental and vocal music, respectively.[24] This suggests that size in two senses – quantitative and temporal, or vertical and horizontal – has played a decisive role in the determination of value. The desire for large numerical size may be reducible to something as fundamental as the desire for greater volume: more performers, more sound. As Leonard Meyer has observed, size is "a sign of power."[25] Perhaps greater size compensated for the decrease in utilitarianism in nineteenth-century music. Nationalism and imperialism served as political pretexts for the deployment of large musical forces. French grand opera, for example, glorified France in the midst of political instability at home and territorial expansion abroad. Teutonic preoccupation with massive symphonies and music dramas reinforced strong urges toward nationhood, and arguably laid an aesthetic foundation for desires for world supremacy in the next century.[26] In their nineteenth-century incarnation, these genres represented masculinist more than feminine societal values: emphasis on political might and expansionism. Because of the power of the ideological associations, male composers have produced symphonies, operas, and other large-scale pieces in proportionally greater numbers than women, although there is certainly no essentialist reason why women cannot write in the large forms. Other factors, however, may underlie the quantitative difference. These include restricted access to music education and other components of the musical machinery, and negative stereotyping of women's creative abilities (see Chapter 2). Nonetheless, it is important not to underestimate the cultural referentiality of genre.

The so-called lesser genres have generally entailed fewer performers and considerably shorter duration. Song and solo piano fall naturally into this category, although internal distinctions have to be made. Song, for example, can range from folk-like simplicity to the complexity of Hugo Wolf's Lieder. The former, often excluded from the broad category of art music, would be considered a lower genre, while the latter would occupy a much higher position.[27] Place of performance would play a role in the ranking: Wolf's Lieder belonged in the concert hall, the temple of high art,[28] while folk-style resided in the home or some other informal setting. The domestic site would convey lower rank because of non-professional performers and listeners, a large population of women, a markedly less devotional tone during the musical experience, and the greater likelihood of utilitarianism as a reason for the activity. As in the case of the folk-like song, domestic or parlor music (or salon music, at least after mid-century) generally meant simpler musical style, especially in comparison to the complexities produced in the concert hall.

The distinction between complex and simple style has served as a fundamental criterion in the relative valuation of genres and sub-genres. The ranking rests on the assumption that complexity is desirable: it shows skill and competence, qualities deemed necessary for "good" composition. Yet why does complexity automatically spell quality? Why is the demonstration of skill a necessary component for a good composition? Skill is a relative term, and the demonstration of skill "to whose satisfaction" is an open question. Valued in Western society as a symbol of dedication, learning, and hard work, skill can assume many forms. One could, for instance, be extremely skilled at constructing an unaccompanied tune, like Hildegard of Bingen or other clerics of the Middle Ages. But pure tunesmiths have not been highly appreciated in Western art music of the past two hundred years. Furthermore, skill has carried the connotation of formal learning. Since *c.* 1700 this has taken the form of display of multi-part techniques such as counterpoint and orchestration, skills from which women were often educationally excluded. The cases of music and art both suggest that the greater value placed on complex art forms, which required formal education, may have been a way of keeping out women. The circular relationship between education and product illustrates Barbara Herrnstein Smith's thesis that structures of education, like canons, construct behavioral and evaluative paradigms that replicate themselves and thus reconfirm their own validity.[29]

The respect accorded stylistic complexity after 1800 may result from a socio-political fabric that was itself becoming increasingly complex.[30] In this post-aristocratic era there was greater personal opportunity, but the potential was much more relevant to men than women. This difference could partially explain the interest of nineteenth-century women in musical simplicity and their frequent avoidance of complex musical structures like symphony and opera. Many female composers and listeners seemed to prefer musical simplicity, at least as gauged by the many tuneful songs and piano works composed by women. Such works would be considered lower genres, particularly if performed in private settings. Of course, they might be performed there just because of the simpler style, as well as for reasons of custom and access. The works might be assigned dismissive judgments, for example that they do "not rise above charming salon music," which appears in the entry on Cécile Chaminade in *The New Grove*.[31] Furthermore, as noted in art, women's attraction to more "natural" genres – those stressing melody, for example – could be used to justify their exclusion from the higher realms of "culture." This was likely to result in the perpetuation of those ideologies that could produce creative and professional ambivalence in women.

SONATA FORM, ABSOLUTE MUSIC

Sonata form is one of the most important structural plans of the last 250 years. But it has often connoted more than an abstract organizational scheme. Some descriptions have included analogies with societal notions of masculine and feminine. These metaphors probably first appeared in A. B. Marx's *Die Lehre von der musikalischen Komposition* (1845). An influential how-to method, especially in its attention to sonata form, Marx's treatise went through many editions and apparently retained the gendered description, through the fifth edition of 1879. Hugo Riemann included the description in the question-and-answer *Katechismus der Musik* (*Allgemeine Musiklehre*), first issued in 1888. It appeared in subsequent editions, at least through the ninth of 1922. Meanwhile, in France, a voluminous manual on composition devoted considerable space to sonata form. Vincent D'Indy's *Cours de composition musicale* (1909) took the gendered metaphor quite seriously and used it as a basis of an extended discussion of sonata form. I would assume that the metaphor has appeared in many sources I have not consulted. But lest it be inferred that it faded away in the early twentieth century, we should note its inclusion in the venerable encyclopedia, *Die Musik in Geschichte und Gegenwart* (1955), where it is mentioned in connection with sonata form in the article on "Form."

These codes, or rather the ideology represented in the codes, have had considerable staying power. Basically the two themes of the exposition are set up as a hierarchy that exhibits stylistic traits considered characteristic of man and woman, respectively. These are constructed in various ways, as we shall see, but the basic model is one of ideological domination of man over woman. It seems to be an extension of general societal notions of ideal man and ideal woman and their proper relationship.[32] Given that these were pervasive ideals, it is not difficult to understand why aestheticians adopted them to make their points. Conversely, it is not difficult to understand why they might have couched the power relationships of the two themes in such a hierarchic manner: the themes themselves were apparently strongly imbued with a sense of oppositional dualism, as inculcated by contemporary notions of male and female and probably by other dualisms as well. Certainly it is possible to imagine sonata form described differently, for example in terms of the second theme growing out of the first, or in terms of tonality, which was done in early descriptions of the form. Today we tend to ignore gendered descriptions. Whether or not we believe in the ideology conveyed in the codes is beside the point. What is important is to understand their implications in the history of ideas and their potential impact on practice.

Derived from binary form, one of the chief structural plans of the Baroque, sonata form served as the organizing principle in the overwhelming majority of first movements of multi-movement instrumental works in the Classic and Romantic periods. In modified clothing it also underlay the first movement of the concerto. Sonata form came to be known loosely as "first-movement form" ("sonata allegro form") because of its prevalence in that position. It would also appear in the last movement, sometimes combined with the rondo principle, or in modified form in another movement. Over its extensive history the form underwent changes. In early descriptions tonality was the main criterion of structure, whereas by the mid-nineteenth century thematic treatment took on that role. Tonality was still important, of course, but it depended on its links with the themes.

We have noted how nineteenth-century society constructed stereotypes of femininity, and have hypothesized that such paradigms arose out of a need of the newly emergent bourgeois society to assert and maintain social control over women. Sonata form became a metaphor for the gendered struggle, and once entrenched probably acted to reinforce and re-construct that gendered ideology in Western society at large. We are mainly talking about the Austro-German musical tradition, where the sonata aesthetic was of great importance. In other countries sonata form played a lesser role. Yet there were pockets of interest elsewhere. For example, France at the end of the nineteenth century was influenced by Germanic ideals, and D'Indy's comprehensive treatise comes out of that climate.

While Marx's description of gendered themes appears to have been the first, an earlier compositional treatise hints at considerations of gender. Antonin Reicha's *Traité de haute composition musicale*, of 1826, uses the word "mère" for the themes: "Motif ou première idée mère," and "Seconde idée mère, dans la nouvelle tonique" (no comparable "père" is used). The term connotes significance and generativity: that these important musical ideas give rise to the content of the musical discourse occupying the movement.[33] While the adjectival "mère" could be ascribed merely to conventions of language, it is nonetheless highly suggestive. Maternal creativity assumes ontological significance in a revered aesthetic. Might this be a glaring exception to, or contradiction of, the prevailing stereotype of female creativity, one that debases the female–body association rooted in her childbearing capability in favor of exaltation of the male–mind linkage? For more on this see Chapter 2. But however we approach the question, we might keep in mind that the concept of mother (or motherhood) is not synonymous with the concept of female. It is merely one culturally constructed, potential attribute of femaleness. Perhaps Reicha's usage represents an idealization of the concept much like the Romantics' "eternal feminine," and in that sense functioned as a means of objectification.[34] This could result in greater distance between women and their creative involvement in sonata form. In any case, Reicha's explanation of sonata form did not include gendered distinctions between masculine and feminine themes; this is Marx's contribution some nineteen years later.

Marx's description of the themes in sonata form reads as follows:

In this pair of themes ... the main theme is the first one, therefore first and foremost the decisive one in freshness and energy, therefore the one constructed more energetically, more vigorously, more completely – the dominant one and the decisive one. The subsidiary theme ["Seitensatz"], on the other hand, ... serves as contrast, constructed and determined by the preceding, thus by nature necessarily the gentler, cultivated more flexibly than vigorously – the feminine, as it were, to that preceding masculine. In this sense each of the two themes is different and only with the other becomes something higher, more perfect.[35]

Marx's conclusion seems to suggest a model of organicism. Yet the higher unity embodied by the whole is made up of parts that are unequal. The first is dominant, decisive, and prominent through position. The second has lesser agency and is dependent on the first for its legitimacy. Yet Marx goes on to contradict the implications of this paragraph by stating that the themes are equal in importance and receive comparable musical development. Perhaps he did not interpret dependence as inferior status and thus saw little discrepancy between the two descriptions. It is also interesting to note that the gendered metaphor is set almost as an afterthought to the musical characteristics. But the gendered duality could have been fundamental in structuring the characteristics of the purely musical description.

Riemann's depiction is rather short: "As a rule sonata form is laid out with a strong, characteristic, first theme – the representative of the masculine principle, so to speak – and a contrasting, lyrical, gentle second theme, representing the feminine principle, usually in a different but related tonality...."[36] Riemann drops the organic ideal but still speaks in terms of opposition and dualism. For the recapitulation he discusses how "the second theme is softened in its opposition to the first [theme] by the assumption of the latter's tonality or the closest approximation to the same."[37] This is a taming of a disruptive Other. While it replicates ideologies of control, it also reflects and affirms societal practices that in fact controlled women: economically, politically, and sexually. Furthermore, Riemann's terms "masculine principle" and "feminine principle" suggest a heightened essentialism that was in fact in evidence at the time.

D'Indy also makes reductionist statements. His description intensi-
fies the earlier traces of essentialism through a kind of philosophical
justification: an appeal to natural law. Because it is such an
interesting statement I quote it in full:

To the extent that the two ideas exposed and developed in pieces in sonata
form perfect themselves, one notices indeed that they really behave like
living beings, submitted to the inevitable laws of humanity: liking or
antipathy, attraction or repulsion, love or hate. And, in this perpetual
conflict, which reflects those in life, each of the two ideas offers qualities
comparable to those which have always been attributable respectively to
man and woman.
    Force and energy, concision and clarity: such are almost variably the
essential *masculine* characteristics belonging to the *first idea*: it imposes itself in
brusque rhythms, affirming very nobly its tonal ownership, one and definitive.
    The *second idea*, in contrast, entirely gentle and of *melodic* grace, is affective
almost always by means of its verbosity and modulatory vagueness of the
eminently alluring *feminine*: supple and elegant, it spreads out progressively
the curve of its ornamented melody; circumscribed more or less clearly in a
neighboring tonality in the course of the exposition, it will always depart
from it in the recapitulation, in order to adopt the first tonality occupied
from the beginning by the dominant masculine element, alone. It is as if,
after the active battle of the development, the being ["l'être"] of gentleness
and weakness has to submit, whether by violence or by persuasion, to the
conquest of the being of force and power.
    Such seems to be at least, in sonatas as in life, the communal law, despite
several rare exceptions where the respective role of the two ideas seems less
settled, sometimes even inverted.[38]

His is a kind of organicism too: the themes take on human qualities
that follow the laws of behavior. Here we see contingency stripped
away: this is an ideology based on irrefutable authority. This
naturalizes difference, and it implies that inherent traits, especially
biology, define identity. Like his predecessors, D'Indy still makes use
of opposition as a fundamental relationship. I am especially intrigued
by his remarks concerning the recapitulation. Like Riemann he
discusses how the tonality of the second theme is resolved to the tonic.
But the images of submission, violence, and conquest hint at sexual
domination gone awry – possibly rape. While this reading is influenced by my own cultural context, with its greater awareness of
physical abuse, still the combination created by D'Indy is at the least
curious and more likely suggestive of male sexual conquest of women.
Violence is specifically mentioned. Overall, this treatment of
gendered themes is perhaps more dualistic and oppositional than in

previous theorists. This may reflect the fact that ideologies of woman as passive and dependent intensified as the century progressed. Nonetheless, the final disclaimer shows awareness of some practical difficulties. But no explanation is offered as to how this can mesh with the reified ideologies of absolute male and absolute female just discussed.

As we jump some fifty years into mid-century, we see the following description of gendered themes in *MGG*:

Two fundamental principles of humankind are given form in the two main themes: the active, extroverted, masculine first theme and the quiet, introverted, feminine second theme.... [The second theme]...is above all supposed to be a "subsidiary theme" ["Folgethema"], one of lesser independence, adapting to the first and yet a contrast in expression.[39]

While it drops the violence of the D'Indy, it still relies on natural law for authority, although to a lesser degree. This description is not intended as a historical statement of how sonata form was described in the nineteenth century. It is a straightforward account of how the workings of sonata form are to be understood. This is particularly striking, given that in the mid- to late twentieth century the ideology of gendered themes has generally been ignored, or refuted on the grounds that actual sonatas do not behave that way. Charles Rosen, for example, attempts to discredit gender in sonata form by asserting that many sonatas have lyrical themes before bold themes, and there are "hermaphrodite" themes. While a gallant effort, the strategy tends to affirm rather than refute the notion of gendered themes.[40] An effective critique from this point of view might assert that gender has no place at all in the disposition of themes. The tendency to ignore the codes may stem from a cynicism concerning the applicability of the metaphor, or embarrassment over the intrusion of gender in "pure" music. Whatever the reason, it is a mistake to ignore the codes; history and historiography speak loudly against their suppression. They did exist and they tell us a great deal about the representation of women and men in society, how ideologies affected how music itself was conceptualized and described, and how music had close ties with ideals and processes in society. We also have to consider what effect the perpetuation and circulation of these ideologies in music has had on actual female practitioners of music.

There are other aspects to consider in understanding the cultural meaning of these readings of sonata form. A kind of double legitimation may be taking place. The appeal to widely accepted gender ideologies legitimates how the analysis of sonata form is being framed. At the same time, however, the gendered ideology itself is further legitimated by association with a form-type of high status, and this is especially relevant in D'Indy and *MGG*. The notion of status suggests historicism. Marx, Riemann, and D'Indy were all codifiers of traditional practices and each seemed to take it upon himself to serve as advocate for the past: to propagate the high values of a musical tradition. This is not so much a comment on the gendered descriptions *per se* but an observation on the general context in which they are found. In Marx and Riemann, Beethoven is clearly the referential figure for sonata form, and examples from specific Beethoven sonatas are given. In D'Indy, there is a lengthy analysis of the "Hammerklavier" Sonata, and this includes indications of masculine and feminine themes. In this treatise one could argue that Beethoven, more than the sonata, is the real topic of interest. Marx and D'Indy may have felt a need to propagandize this hero from the past. In these theorists, at least, historicism may be a major impetus for codifications of sonata form.

Pedagogy is also a prime reason for such treatises. The D'Indy, for example, states that it is based on "notes taken in composition classes at the Schola Cantorum in 1899–1900."[41] This raises the question of the purpose of the descriptions of sonata form. Are they mainly idealized formulas for theory students and hence removed from what actual composers are doing? While the answer is uncertain, I think that the respective authors attempt to ground the theory in real music – witness the numerous Beethoven examples. But there is still a sense of abstraction from real practice, only intensified through the incorporation of an ideology of gender that is distinct from lived experience of actual people. Once again, I believe that one of the subtexts in these descriptions is historical. The depictions provide a means of upholding the good musical values of the past. While this strategy is probably a reaction to a perception of aesthetic decline, there may well be another reactive strategy at work in the gendered descriptions. It could be motivated by a fear of the feminization of music. Around the time of Marx and through the nineteenth century, lyricism and expressivity became prominent through the music of Chopin and others, particularly in the character piece. To some this might be perceived as a feminine assault on the masculinity in the music and persona of Beethoven and others, and by extension on the masculinity of the (mostly male) practitioners themselves. A link between a revered form-type, especially in terms of Beethoven, and an ideology of masculine domination could help preserve male control of music and what were thought of as masculine values in musical style. It could have the practical result of keeping women practitioners in subordinate roles and dependent on men.

As articulated in the nineteenth century, the two themes of sonata form with their respective gender associations still carried particular tonal functions. The tonal functions of tonic key and other key (or others) suggested a hierarchical relationship, even if the structural implications of that hierarchy were not as crucial to the basic aesthetic of the composition as they had been earlier. It is significant that the key of the masculine first theme, or principal theme, retains its tonal hegemony throughout the movement, whereas the tonally disruptive female theme, or subordinate theme, is chastened, so to speak, in the recapitulation as it finds its proper place within the tonal sphere of the masculine first theme. How ironic that the typical key of the first appearance of the feminine theme, at least in major-key movements, is called the dominant, for in the end the dominant is subordinate. As the Riemann and D'Indy readings suggest, what has happened is that the male tonal principle, situated in the home key, has asserted its dominance over the disruptive female element, located in a contrasting key: a triumph of masculinity. In terms of a Freudian metaphor, the "lack" embedded in the feminine theme in the exposition – its lack of the more "active" musical traits of the masculine theme and its lack of the overall identifying tonality – is now partially compensated for by its infusion with the tonality associated with the masculine first theme.[42]

To view the situation from another perspective, the narrative implications of gendered sonata form posit an Other who has to be reined in to dominant discourse so that the movement can regain stability and necessary closure. The tonic of the masculine must close the movement, otherwise deeply inculcated patterns of narrative desire will be frustrated. As Susan McClary has pointed out, such desires must not be denied, and thus the feminine has to be sacrificed, as it were.[43] She believes that Western art music seems to have a need for the construction of an Other within a work, whether it be associated with the feminine or some other object of ideological subordination. While I am not prepared to comment fully on the theory here, it is significant that in the case of sonata form what could be considered an element of musical Otherness is infused in many readings with the label feminine and all the semiotic baggage that that bears in society at large. Consistent with McClary's larger thesis, this Other must be squelched so that the inexorable dominance of the tonic emerges as victor. This is a given of Western music, at least before Mahler. Perhaps the territorial imperialism, as it were, of the masculine over the feminine replicates contemporary expansionist desires in the West. In addition, the inevitability of the drive to tonal closure as a result of a "perfecting" process, an expression used by D'Indy, may mirror contemporary ideals of progress and evolutionary development.

It is interesting that McClary adopts militaristic metaphors as a rhetorical device to describe what she considers to be a violent narrative process. We have seen how gendered readings of sonata form employ opposition as a basic conceptual strategy. This kind of language also appears in more recent references to sonata form. For example, German musicologist Ernst Meyer, in a Marxist critique, characterizes the replacement of two opposing themes for the more monothematic practices of the Baroque as a representation of an aggressive spirit in the rising middle class.[44] In 1980 Charles Rosen writes that the exposition "presents the thematic material and articulates the movement from tonic to dominant in various ways so that it takes on the character of a polarization or opposition. The essential character of this opposition may be defined as a large-scale dissonance."[45] At times a competitive tone colors the rhetoric. Donald Francis Tovey observes that transitions in J. C. Bach have been "wittily described as 'presenting arms' to the new key"; James Webster claims that one can often view the arrival of the recapitulation "as a triumph over difficulties."[46] By difficulties Webster is referring to the tonal and thematic conflicts waged in the development section, which can be considered an intensification of the tonal–thematic–sexual polarization of the exposition.

What happens to these accumulated conflicts in the recapitulation? Some writers view the recapitulation much like a Hegelian site of synthesis.[47] On this view, the contrasts introduced in the exposition between the two keys and between the masculine and feminine themes are successfully resolved, presumably mainly through the tonicization of the feminine theme. But one wonders whether that tonal process actually constitutes a Hegelian resolution, for Hegel proposed a synthesis that fashioned something new out of elements of the original two entities. In sonata form, however, the feminine theme in the recapitulation remains largely intact but now stands within the masculine tonality. A true synthesis into a new entity, such as a tonality mediating between the original tonic and dominant of the two themes, has not taken place. To view the situation another way, the feminine theme entered the movement in second position, in a second key. As implied in A. B. Marx, although stated quite differently, given semiotic and ontological meanings of openings the feminine theme may be doomed to compromised treatment.[48]

But beyond the ideological message of female subordination, the question has to be asked, again, as to what body or bodies of music is assumed in the codes. As mentioned, the target could be student replications of existing prototypes, especially piano sonatas by Beethoven. Because the codes apply to certain pieces only and not to many others, they do seem like an idealized abstraction. Their incorporation of ideological representation of man and woman further underscores the abstract level on which they operate. Thus, the extent to which they do or do not apply to any given sonata becomes somewhat moot. To frame the issue another way, we might say that the fact that there are so many sonatas that do not exhibit masculine and feminine themes according to the treatises does not at all undermine the "validity" of the gendered themes. If they were not designed in the first place to apply to most cases of real music, then not having them in a given piece does not undermine them. To repeat what was said earlier, these codes are "real" in that they existed as an embodiment of ideological representation of man and woman. We may not agree with the content of the ideology or its applicability to actual pieces, but they existed nonetheless as a real phenomenon in the history of ideas and are thus important. Furthermore, representational codes of masculine and feminine may also apply to other kinds of pieces but not formalized as such in writing.

Sonata form functions as a major component of a larger concept: the sonata aesthetic. By sonata aesthetic I mean a composite idea that encompasses sonata form, the sonata as a genre, and the myriad works that utilize sonata form in one or more movements. Such compositions, generally multi-movement, can belong to a host of genres, including symphony, concerto, and chamber music. Having helped displace the supremacy of vocal music, the sonata aesthetic has carried enormous semiotic meaning ever since. In the early part of the nineteenth century, particularly in Germany, writers and literati constructed the myth of autonomous music. Autonomous music could transcend the vagaries of daily existence better than any art-form and catapult creator and listener into some timeless, placeless realm of pure aesthetic contemplation. Without the interference of text and fixed meanings, such music amounted to an embodiment of the absolute – hence the term (although it was not called this until Wagner coined the term).[49] While Romantics denied the existence of content in the kinds of music they considered absolute, they simultaneously elevated the concept of "pure idea" and intellectuality ("Geistigkeit") that they considered the heart of such music. In the quest for transcendence, absolute music placed utmost faith in the higher faculties of the mind. In this regard it affirmed the ideology of the mind–body dualism and the resultant devaluation of the body.[50] Connotations of body tie in with the feminine and with the debasing and morally lesser associations of female sexuality. The notion of absolute music, therefore, has acted as an ingenious means of elevating the masculine notion of mind while at the same time suppressing the body, sexuality, and the feminine.[51] I call it ingenious because it has done so under the guise of professed autonomy from underlying social referentiality and thus made its agenda that much more subtle and difficult to identify.

Yet the metaphor of gendered themes as it pertains to an important aspect of absolute music indicates a breaking of the decorum of absoluteness. How interesting that theorists turned to societal ideology to express the musical relationships. Of course, at the same time that the merits of absoluteness were praised, composers tainted the ideal with a poetic idea and this resulted in programmatic music. Taken together these suggest contradictory desires as well as possible resistance to the notion of absolute music. As implied above, its importance may lie more as an aesthetic ideal than as a viable foundation for sustained composition.

Ironically, the ideal was also sullied by the exaggerated rhetoric used to describe it. Early Romantics such as E. T. A. Hoffmann and Ludwig Tieck, adopting the devotional hyperbole of Wackenroder's writings of 1797 and 1799,[52] seemed to contradict the desired goal of "Geistigkeit" through their gushing excesses in praise of the aesthetic. This was an obvious insertion of sensuous contemplation, of the body. Was it a dangerously close touching of the feminine? Was the threat sensed or recognized later in the century and as a result rejected as mere Romantic excess? Perhaps early German Romantics expressed more of a feminine component than they were aware of. And consequently, since the notion of absolute music resulted more from rhetoric than inherent qualities, a feminized rhetoric could undermine the inviolability of absolute music as well as its autonomy.[53]

The hyperbole bore a strong devotional tone, and music began to assume the seriousness of religious experience. Not only did the locale and circumstances of performed music undergo change, but composers were transformed from skilled craftspersons to divinely inspired creators removed from everyday society. As such they were replicating God the creator. These musical embodiments of secular religion that cropped up around 1800 functioned as a replacement for the declining power of official religion and also served as a kind of institutional anchor for the social validation of the rising middle class. These processes legitimated male interests. In the composer's new personal identification with God, the male composer was the assumed participant, for only a male could identify with a male God: he, not a she, was created in His image. Women composers would be metaphorically excluded from the cultish emphasis on art-as-religion in the first half of the nineteenth century.[54] This accorded with the very practical consideration of women's longstanding exclusion from creative and institutional power in the Church.

The transcendence vested in absolute music also connoted a metaphysical ability to transport one to the infinite beyond all barriers. Not only did that portend a link with the infinity of God, it also suggested a psychological profile open to reaching out beyond learned boundaries. Carol Gilligan hypothesizes that male psychological development in the West has typically followed a course in which the boy breaks away from the mother and the female world she represents. While one can question the applicability of transhistorical pronouncements to a particular cultural context, especially when remote, Gilligan's theories are nonetheless useful for laying out some general lines of development, even as we acknowledge that they are subject to historical fine-tuning.[55] Gilligan claims that the boy attempts to break the strong infantile link by finding his male identity beyond the female environment. In so doing he is reaching out into the beyond. Customs of socialization further encourage male exploration and quest through the validation of curiosity and individualism. In capitalistic societies like the United States, this has been reinforced through the ideal of unlimited opportunity for all. In practice, however, numerous structural constraints, including race, gender, and class, play a not inconsiderable role in restricting opportunity. But for the boy, transcendence and quest come to be natural and comfortable. The three great literary themes of Don Juan, Faust, and Don Quixote, for example, express these from various perspectives. In a similar way, the ethos of absolute music embodies the psychological path of quest and transcendence laid out for the male. The white, Western female, on the other hand, has tended to identify with her mother, her primary nurturer and also a female, and therefore feels less need to transcend the world represented by her mother or reach out into the infinite. Meaning and identity might be more readily found within the complex of signs associated with mother and other females.[56] Consequently, the ethos of absolute music might be more unfamiliar and alien, and possibly even repugnant.

Yet the training and musical socialization of actual women composers would probably instill a respect for absolute music. Many women have written pieces of absolute music, although not in great numbers. One of the more interesting works is the *Piano Sonata*, Op. 21, by Cécile Chaminade, published in 1895. In the following discussion we focus on the first movement. In this exploration of possibility I suggest that the work may reconceptualize the ideologies of masculine and feminine as encoded in gendered readings of sonata form. By choosing a work by a woman I am not implying that such challenges are available only to women. On the contrary: they are available to any composer, male or female. Nor am I suggesting that there is some essentialist relationship between a woman composer and woman-as-Other in the codes of sonata form. What I am suggesting is that this is a work that exhibits distinctive behavior in its treatment of themes, and this could signal a reconfiguration of the ideological relationship between masculine and feminine. No doubt there are many sonata movements in the nineteenth century, including many by men, that could be analyzed in this way. The fact that they have not been approached from this standpoint does not mean that they do not mount similar challenges. But given the makeup of the current canon, I believe it is especially vital to place women's works into analytic discourse. And Chaminade's work is one of the few sonatas by women composers that is readily available, in score as well as recording.[57] But beyond altruism, availability, and the fact that it is a fine work, another reason for focusing on a work by a woman is the possibility that the subject positions and socialization of women may inflect their challenges to codes of representation. This potential relationship is complex and not without methodological risk. Yet it raises important issues that might help us understand why some women composers seemed to shy away from absolute forms. This, in turn, has a bearing on canon formation. Restrictions in access and education are important considerations, of course, but this discussion may suggest more subtle factors as well.

CECILE CHAMINADE'S *SONATA*, OP. 21

This analysis is an exploration of possibility: the possibility that the first movement challenges the representational model of domination encoded in masculine and feminine in sonata form. It is not intended as an explanation that accounts for everything that goes on musically in the movement, nor even everything that might be considered the most significant aspects of the piece. To a great extent, of course, these are matters of judgment. But what I am trying to emphasize is that this reading is meant as an added layer of meaning to a work capable of many interpretations and analytical frameworks. It is possible, perhaps even likely, that it may partially contradict important ways of viewing the work. But I do not necessarily view this as a drawback. In fact, it can be an advantage, for it persuades one to view the work as a complex field of signifiers, of diverse kinds: historical, stylistic, aesthetic, and ideological. It also underscores the temporal multiplicity of interpretations – mine, made from the vantage point of the present, will be quite differently grounded from those ten, fifty, or one hundred years earlier. These may not agree in detail or in basic approach, yet each in a sense is "correct." The work is enriched, as it were, through the varied strands of meaning, and this can affect our views on how pieces become memorialized in canons.

There are difficulties in analyzing an instrumental work in terms of codes of representation. One involves a potential conflict between their analytical implications. Analysis of so-called "common practice" instrumental works has typically stressed the structure in purely musical terms; harmonies, tonalities, and similarities and differences among themes have formed the basis of the approach. Perhaps the insularity has resulted from the absence of semantic reference and from a modernist reaction to excessive programmatic interpretation in the nineteenth century. In any case, there is presently little in the way of models for an analysis of ideological constructions of gender in instrumental music; work by Susan McClary and Jeffrey Kallberg is notable in this regard.[58] One difficulty in the present case is that the nineteenth century did not codify affects formally as in the Baroque, although in some ways the readings of gendered themes in sonata form are fairly explicit. These codes are steeped within a structural context, and this suggests an analytic approach based on structure. The methodological implications of the two may imply contradiction: the one grounded in subjective inference, the other in objective data. I prefer, however, to view these as complementary tendencies that can enhance each other and provide insights that might not be evident were there a more unitary framework. This probably means certain moves of accommodation. There may be greater risk of ambiguity. But the sites of contradiction and ambiguity might themselves spark further discussion on representations of gender and suggest ways of dealing with works that negotiate such representation.

As discussed above, the behavior of the gendered themes in A. B. Marx and others represents an abstraction that is often removed from practice. What is "real," however, is that the gendered characteristics of masculine and feminine that they are purported to contain do pertain to palpable and powerful ideologies of masculine and feminine in society at large. These characteristics as they then define how a theme is constructed musically are significant, as is the resultant power relationship played out in the form. Another important consideration for our analysis is that even though the sonata aesthetic was mainly an expression of the Germanic tradition, D'Indy's treatise *c.* 1900 shows that it was important in France as well, at least in certain circles.

As to compositional practice, the last half of the century witnessed varied approaches to sonata form and the sonata as a genre. Harmonic practice was expanded and the architectonic function of tonality became less important to the definition of the form. Developmental procedures were often luxuriant and yielded to melodic and sonorous considerations. In general there was a great deal of experimentation, and arguably the sonata (and sonata form) became an anachronism in the late nineteenth century. But we could also say that both the genre and the form were experiencing changes that might be expected when a convention is long-lived. They do not necessarily signal decline or aberration, but may mean that a later exemplar may require a more flexible analytical approach than in the more typical form of earlier days.

Chaminade's *Sonata*, Op. 21, her only sonata for piano, was published in 1895 but may well have been composed in the 1880s. The last of the three movements is clearly earlier, having been published in 1886 under the title "Appassionato," as the fourth of the *Six Etudes de Concert*, Op. 35. The first movement dates from May 1893 at the latest, based on the fact that she performed it in London shortly thereafter,[59] and I suspect that it was actually composed well before that, perhaps as early as 1888 or 1889. I base my estimate on the fact that with the exception of the *Concertino* commissioned by the Conservatoire as a competition piece (1902), Chaminade's major pieces of absolute music – two piano trios and a *Concertstück* for piano and orchestra – all date from the 1880s (1880, 1886, and 1888, respectively). In her output overall, character pieces account for the overwhelming majority of the works for piano, which total approximately two hundred. Songs (*mélodies*) and to a lesser extent choral works and miscellaneous genres make up the two hundred or so other compositions. The *Sonata* is dedicated to Moritz Moszkowski, a supportive friend who was to become her brother-in-law.[60] It is possible that he was a decisive Germanic influence in the genesis of this singular work.

The first movement, the longest and most complex, features a flexible treatment of sonata form. Often ambiguous, the structure may result from a mixture of three conventions: sonata form, character piece, and prelude and fugue. Sonata form, of course, is still the expected form-type for a first movement, even at this late date. Prelude and fugue may stem from Chaminade's systematic counterpoint training and the practices of a revered compatriot, Camille Saint-Saëns. As to character piece, this is a genre with which Chaminade was very familiar through her prolific output for the piano; most works, in fact, fall into this category. While the mixture in sonata form might seem unusual, precedents do exist. For example, the famous last movement of the "Jupiter" Symphony incorporates a fugal exposition within the first group of the sonata exposition. Here the fugal texture is clearly subsumed within the sonata-form convention and does not pose the kind of structural disruption that it

Example 1 Chaminade, *Sonata*, First movement, measures 1–8

does in the Chaminade. We might recall the fugue in Liszt's innovative *Sonata* for piano (1853). We might also recall the varied deployment of fugue in late sonatas of Beethoven, for example in Opp. 106, 110, and 111. Models for prelude and fugue, however, are harder to find in earlier sonatas. As for the character piece, its influence can be felt in the many experimental sonatas of the second half of the nineteenth century. This includes such common traits as leisurely pacing, extended developmental techniques, and a casual treatment of functional tonality; structure might seem more resultant than planned. We should remember, however, that in general the relationship between norms and actual exemplars is not clear-cut. Even in the heyday of the sonata and sonata form, from approximately 1780 to 1825, departure from norms was a commonplace, and perhaps even expected. This suggests that there can be a broad range of practice within a norm.

Nonetheless, the first movement of the Chaminade displays strong connections with sonata form. It is, after all, the first movement of a typical three-movement cycle (fast–slow–fast) of a composition entitled "Sonata." Even given the date one would still expect firm links to the typical form-type for a first movement, although one would not be too surprised should it turn out to be something else. In addition to this semiotic connection there are telling signs of sonata form in the music itself. One is the opening theme (see Ex. 1).[61] Its tonal clarity and functionality, especially in establishing the tonic immediately, and its thematicism, periodicity, tempo, and rhythmic regularity connote a stability that could indicate the start of a movement in sonata form. As further confirmation this music comes

Example 2 Chaminade, *Sonata*, First movement, measures 36–48

back verbatim, late in the movement, after considerable harmonic and thematic development, as a clear recapitulation. It is a strong and dramatic return to the material and tonality of the opening. The main elements that depart from sonata form are the tonal organization, the proportions, and the disposition of themes.

Table I shows the basic organization of the movement. One can see the topheavy first part, roughly comparable to a sonata exposition, and the relatively brief second and third parts, roughly development and recapitulation. The ratio approximates 5:1:2. Among the striking aspects of the exposition in addition to its relative weight are a second theme begun in the tonic and introduced as a fughetta (see Ex. 2), and a closing tonality in the tonic. Thus the idea of tonal progress, a mainstay of sonata form, is subverted in favor of emphasis of home key: tonal stasis, if you will. Put another way, a major aspect of desire is being denied.[62] C minor does not govern the entire exposition, however. Other tonalities are implied, such as E flat major (relative major) briefly in an episodic passage of the fughetta, and especially A flat major, as a lengthily prepared goal never firmly reached. We begin to expect A flat as the modulatory goal of the subsidiary tonal area of the exposition. Instead it is denied, and Chaminade takes us back to where we started, to c minor.

Another means by which Chaminade marks the unusual nature of the second theme is that it is not led into smoothly and gradually with

Table 1. Chaminade, *Sonata*, first movement

SECTION I 133 measures			SECTION II 25 measures	SECTION III 52 measures		
First theme: (35 measures) Tonic	*Second theme:* fugue & immediate aftermath (43 measures)	*Themes in fragmentation* (46 measures) First theme (80–83)	*Tonally static* (25 measures) Second theme: in 3 stable statements	*First theme* (35 measures)	*Second theme re-call* (4 measures)	*Coda* (13 measures): Built on first theme
CLOSES IN TONIC	THEME IN TONIC Aftermath in E♭ and A♭ Ends A♭ 6–4	Second theme (83–97) First theme (97–126) [133] Closing flourish (126–33): similar to last 7 measures of piece ENDS IN TONIC	(134–45) Build-up to first theme (146–58)			

T ——→ T T ——————→ Ambiv.   Ambiv. ——————→ T

Tripartite subdivision

Example 3 Chaminade, *Sonata*, First movement, measures 30–35

music that implies continuation. Instead it is preceded by a grand flourish of runs and *fortissimo* cadential chords that spell closure: not just tonal closure but structural closure of a movement or composition (see Ex. 3). Thus when the fughetta begins we have a sense of a new piece beginning – as if the previous music has been a grand preparatory gesture for the main music at hand, perhaps similar to a prelude-like section that precedes a fugue. Yet this impression might not replace our initial one as we experienced the music in time, for on that hearing the material at the beginning was clearly thematic and structural, not merely introductory. In addition, Chaminade uses it later as the basis of substantial thematic development. In totality, the start of the fughetta marks the juncture of at least two conventions: sonata form, and prelude (introduction) and fugue. The intersection marks a departure from textbook ideals of sonata form.

Let us explore the second theme more closely. "Second theme" here signifies something different from its usual meaning of a musical idea that first appears in a contrasting key and has been reached by modulation. In this context second theme merely means the theme that occurs second in the movement; it has been stripped of other semiotic meanings. It is interesting to see whether the second theme conforms to nineteenth-century descriptions of the "feminine" theme, particularly since the first theme in this movement embodies the attributes of a masculine theme and thereby reinforces expectations for a contrasting, feminine second theme. What we get, however, is ambiguous: a theme with features of each gender. It seems to have feminine traits in the "tranquillo" indication, the

Example 4 Chaminade, *Sonata*, First movement, measures 195–8

lyricism, softer dynamic level (*mp*), and thinner texture (only one voice initially). The masculine, however, emerges in the retention of the home key, the strongly functional harmonies after the other voices enter, and arguably the fact of a fughetta.[63] This structural and gendered ambiguity challenges ideologies of sonata form as understood in the nineteenth century. The convention is further challenged in the recapitulation. Only a brief hint of the second theme appears, and it behaves in a tonally ambiguous way in its unison sonority and initial turn to E flat before a bridge takes us back to the tonic (see Ex. 4). A concluding section in the tonic, which includes the flourishes that closed the introductory section and the exposition, ends the movement.

In its brief appearance in the recapitulation, however, the second theme has appeared in a different guise from its fugal disposition when first introduced. Marked "Andante," it constitutes one of the many places in the movement where thematic transformation has altered the character and meaning of the second theme. The length and lyricism of this brief occurrence resemble other appearances of the second theme after the fughetta. The earlier statements, however, conveyed even more markedly the sense of a different mood – a more gentle, lyrical, "feminine" mood, if you will – from the fughetta theme. See, for instance, mm. 57–60, conceivably a relaxation after the fughetta; or especially mm. 134–44 in the development, marked Meno mosso, containing three statements with three respective harmonizations, implying A flat, f minor, and A flat (see Ex. 5). The latter section is also interesting for its staticness: a feeling of floating and of non-functionality, of emphasis on pure sound and color.[64] This sensuous luxuriating in pure sound acts as another means of arresting the progress of sonata form, especially since the passage occupies approximately half of the development in number of measures and possibly well over that in psychological time. And it occurs within feminized versions of the second theme. Thus the feminine acts to

Example 5 Chaminade, *Sonata*, First movement, measures 134–45

challenge an important driving force of sonata form. Its disposition is an important indication that many of the attributes of a character piece are in place.

It is useful to step back for a moment and discuss the theoretical link between the mixed genre we see here and the gendered readings of sonata form. The gendered codes in Marx and others represent musical appropriation of ideological notions of masculine and feminine (and vice versa). The readings exist largely on the level of abstraction, particularly as they might pertain to actual pieces or movements in sonata form. And even pieces considered to be squarely in sonata form typically depart from the idealized definitions that perhaps of necessity are reductionist. By extension, I am suggesting that the power of the societal ideologies of masculine and feminine and the flexibility of actual pieces in sonata form imply that one can still infer masculine and feminine themes in a mixed musical convention grounded in sonata form. Understandings of masculine as strong, bold, rhythmic, and assertive, and of feminine as lyrical, gentle, soft, and diffuse do not evaporate when a movement deploys themes in an individual way. Naturally there are limits as to how far one can stretch the boundaries, stylistically as well as historically. I would not, for example, take a piece like the Samuel Barber *Sonata* (1949) and speak of gendered themes, at least in reference to nineteenth-century treatises. The work is obviously too remote historically and aesthetically from those ideologies and codifications. But as for the Chaminade, I believe that the fundamental aesthetic and historical framework makes such a connection reasonable and appropriate.

Having laid this groundwork, I would like to proceed with further observations on the challenge to gendered codes of representation in the Chaminade. The movement seems to avoid the objectification of the feminine created through tonal Otherness. The feminine is supposed to appear in another key and drive the narrative toward final closure by allowing itself to be reined back to the tonic, the key of the masculine, in the recapitulation. But the movement does not really establish an Other key. It passes through and hints at contrasting keys, such as the relative major (E flat) and the submediant (A flat), but denies their full-bodied definition. The tonic, representing the masculine, re-appears at those places where we would expect strong cadences in another key. The masculine is clearly defined in this movement, the feminine is not. This is not to say that the feminine is not a major presence in the movement. Actually it appears much more often than the masculine, but it is configured as a diffuse gesture that will not let itself be a tonal Other. The masculine is unproblematic in its construction and behavior. Overall, what we may have in this movement is a resistance to the hierarchical relationship between masculine and feminine as articulated in the gendered codes of sonata form and even more importantly in the ideologies they represent. This is expressed through a reconceptualization of the feminine: not an obliteration of the feminine, and not an inversion of power relations, but in a sense a refusal to play by the rules laid out in ideology.

For the sake of interest, I would also like to offer a more speculative analysis of the gendered implications of the work. This is suggested by a more restrictive view of sonata form. In such a framework, the first movement of the Chaminade is not in sonata form. By extension, the applicability of the gendered readings of sonata form is highly questionable – perhaps to the extent that they no longer apply. Instead, the movement is thought to behave like a character piece, especially since the category is fairly broad and ambiguous. But despite the non-applicability of the gendered codes as specifically associated with sonata form, there is a recognition nonetheless that the ideology of masculine and feminine was generally very powerful in the nineteenth century, and that it may well be inscribed in other music even if not formalized as such in writing. Or to put it another way, what may have been understood as masculine and feminine traits in musical language over a very broad spectrum of art music happened to have been codified in writing for one particular form-type, primarily for pedagogical purposes. But the musical characteristics and their ideological associations were available and indeed found in many kinds of music in the nineteenth century. On this view, even if the first movement is considered a character piece, the musical signs of masculine and feminine are still in evidence. Of course, the details of the relationships between musical masculine and feminine might vary in different form-types, based on internal expectations. But one would still be able to construct patterns of behavior in terms of masculine and feminine gestures.

This proposal is not without risk, however. For one it could essentialize the understanding of music to an undesirable degree. For example, lyrical would equal feminine and rhythmic equal masculine regardless of context. Rather than an additional layer of meaning in an exploration of possibility, it could actually exclude potential readings by affixing absolute meaning to particular musical behavior. Of course, this could be minimized by a careful framing of the analysis in terms of possibility, and careful attention to other factors that could inflect the viewpoint away from absolutism. There is also the risk of further confirmation of gendered dualism and hierarchy. If they are confined to sonata forms, then the ideology can be contained and minimally reinforced. But while this containment solves some problems, I do not actually believe that the gendered understandings were (or are) confined to themes in sonata form. At this point, however, I cannot prove it or argue convincingly in its favor. Perhaps others will wish to take up the issue.

To return specifically to the first movement of the Chaminade, there is yet another issue to be discussed: whether the fact that Chaminade is a woman has any bearing on the analysis or the strategy of representation. As frequently noted, there is a clear distinction between gender of maker and strategy of representation. Any composer, male or female, can interpret gendered codes, and strategies such as reinforcement, resistance, disruption, challenge, and reconceptualization are available to each. There is no essentialist connection between gender of the maker and the representation of that gender within a given code. Therefore, with regard to the particular piece under discussion, there is no inherent reason why the reconceptualization of the feminine and the resistance to masculine domination could not have appeared in a work composed by a man.

Yet this model of equivalence may be naive. An ideology of masculine domination did exist in society and it was pervasive. It affected and mirrored many aspects of women's lives. Depending upon country and time period, women were restricted legally, economically, politically, and sexually. Women could not own property, sue for divorce, inherit, or vote. Legally they were property of husband or father and had few rights as individuals. Sexuality and reproductive freedoms were also controlled. It is important to place women composers in this general context. In previous chapters we have discussed attitudes and practices that have limited their participation and produced anxiety toward their own creativity and professionalism. Repressive societal ideologies and their codification in schemata such as the gendered themes of sonata form have probably contributed to the difficulty. In addition to the conflicts and contradictions that affect self-identity, the objectification can create a subject positioning that may be different from men. It will vary from woman to woman. But in comparison with men, it has a greater likelihood of location in cultural Otherness. This position might be more likely to elicit strategies of resistance than one that is centered. To put it another way, female composers may be more likely than men to mount strategies of resistance to gendered codes in music that suggest women's domination by men.

But the situation is more complicated. While there are many good reasons for a location in Otherness, there are also good reasons why at least part of women's position is centered. This has to do with socialization. For women who have trained to be composers, socialization has taken place largely in male conventions and norms. Women probably identify in many ways with male mentors and colleagues, and with customs and traditions that grow out of the expectations and experiences of men. The process can lead to what Judith Fetterley terms "immasculation": taking on the viewpoints of men and identifying against women.[65] It means that socialization is not pure. Subject positioning does not lie entirely in Otherness, therefore, but also inhabits some centered cultural structures. Debilitating feelings of contradiction and conflict can result. But they can also lead to an empowered subjectivity of multiplicity or mobility.[66] This signals positive appropriation and control. Nonetheless, it is important to keep in mind that socialization in male society does not mean that women come out socialized men. However much they wish to identify with male institutions, they still have to deal with societal messages constructed for biological women. Even if they reject the content, the very fact of having had to think about them means that they are involved in the dynamics of what woman and man mean in society. Thus, despite complexity and contradiction it seems reasonable to expect that women are more likely than men to challenge women's negative representation in gendered codes in music.

In the case of Chaminade, the potential resistance in the first movement to ideological masculine domination may be replicated on the level of the work. Curiously, this is her only sonata for piano within an output of approximately two hundred works for the instrument. It was her last multi-movement instrumental composition; after this she concentrated more exclusively on character pieces and *mélodies*. Even more striking is the fact that she seems to have avoided performing it in public. Chaminade would typically compose a piano piece with the express purpose of bringing it to the public's attention in her recitals. This would spark sales of the published version. With the *Sonata*, however, I have come across only one performance, and only of the first movement (London, 1 June 1893). Perhaps all these circumstances suggest that Chaminade did not feel comfortable with the work. Perhaps the genre did not suit the communicative needs of her audience, which consisted mainly of middle- to upper-class women. As a type of absolute music the sonata might seem alienating to women.[67] Ideological connotations of transcendence could remind them of their exclusion from intellectual endeavors and of denigration of the body. As a composer, Chaminade might feel uncomfortable inhabiting a genre with expectations of stylistic complexity, at least for the first movement. Her popularity rested on a tuneful, simple style that accorded well with the needs and desires of female practitioners in a domestic setting. Perhaps the *Sonata* was a compositional experiment for Chaminade, the final work in what we could view as a Germanic phase in her career. Like French music in general in the 1880s and early 1890s, Chaminade may have been strongly influenced by Germanic aesthetics, perhaps through Moszkowski. It was in 1888, for example, that she produced the highly successful *Concertstück* (note the Germanic title!), whose opening perhaps not coincidentally bears a striking resemblance to the opening of *The Flying Dutchman*. Of course, we should not discount the possibility that Chaminade did not perform the *Sonata* because she did not like the work or considered it an artistic failure. But even this could be linked with a feeling on her part that the sonata aesthetic did not fit the needs of her musical environment.

Perhaps Chaminade's view of her *Sonata* exemplifies a discomfort that several women composers may have felt towards the sonata and similar genres. Eva Rieger points to Clara Schumann, for example, who wrote only one piano sonata and apparently hid it away before it was finished.[68] She did not perform it, and probably was advised by Robert not to have it published.[69] In addition, Schumann avoids thematic contrast in the piece, as she does also in the Piano Concerto. As Rieger surmises, it is possible that nineteenth-century women composers found it difficult to assume the role of compositional subject given that the masculine occupies that semiotic role in the understanding of the form. She sees this as part of a general crisis in the piano sonata after Beethoven. But given that women were becoming more active as composers, although not necessarily as professionals, and that they had long-standing links with the keyboard, the crisis takes on a gendered component that is vital to any meaningful consideration of the genre.

In closing this section I would like to offer the following as a theoretical summary. There are many kinds of meaning in a piece of music, and each has the potential to contribute something important toward a fuller understanding of culture. Instrumental music poses formidable challenges to analysis that attempts to move beyond the insular framework of the work. The difficulties, contradictions, and ambiguities entailed in such an approach, particularly in terms of social referentiality, are not insurmountable. But they do suggest the need for new questions and new associations. Yet ultimately the methodological model might rest on contradiction or ambiguity. This is not necessarily a drawback, however. The complexity, indeed, might more closely resemble the workings of real life than does the abstraction of a unitary or unified point of view. As for gender specifically, no essentialist relationship exists between the gender of the maker and gendered codes of representation. But while they are distinct, subject positioning and socialization have the potential to affect the relationship such that the gender of the maker can make a difference as to how the codes are manipulated. Nonetheless, in doing such an analysis we have to be careful to avoid essentialism: that what we find in a given piece is automatically presumed characteristic of others in the same group. Effects of socialization and subjectivity in the meanings of the work are critical. To leave them out of considerations of how canons are formed is to marginalize those voices that lie outside the dominant group.

CODA: IS THERE A WOMEN'S STYLE?

A person brought up as a woman can never occupy the same social or artistic space as one reared as a man. However superficially similar, her words, works and perceptions will never be the same as those of a man, and are likely (whether she knows it or not) to have features in common with those of other women.[70]

Does this statement, by Christine Battersby, imply that there is a female style in music? That compositions written by women can be recognized as such and share qualities that are distinct from those in compositions by men? We have been warning against the dangers of essentialism and can make a similar plea here. There seems to be no essentialist female style in music, at least in the following ways. There is no style that issues from inherent traits in female biology. It cannot be claimed that every female composer writes in a style that all women composers utilize, that is unmistakeably their own, and that cannot be found in works by men. Without additional information or the presence of a text, it is extremely difficult to discern via style whether a work is by a woman or a man. Other clues, however, might guide us to the gender of the composer, e.g. genre or function. This suggests that socio-cultural factors might play a role in gender identification, especially aspects of socialization, subject position, and ideology. But these affect style indirectly. Perhaps this can be clarified by noting the difference between saying that there is no interval or chord used exclusively by male or female composers, and that women were likely to compose tuneful piano pieces for the *salon*. While certain codes of gendered representation might grow up around a particular chord in a particular context, composition itself is basically a technical discipline whose language is available to men and women alike; an interval or a chord is not inherently gendered.[71]

As to the *salon* example, we can see how a cultural factor, not inherent style, forms the basis of the association.

What might be feasible and meaningful, indeed, is a theory that considers gendered style mainly as an outgrowth of certain cultural factors. In this move style becomes much more than local events as it takes on larger implications of music such as process, function, and categorization. Aspects of socialization, subject position, ideology, and historical traditions play a major role in the connections between women and musical conventions. Rieger has made some perceptive observations about female compositional practices in this regard.[72] They are not proposed as essentialist traits but as tendencies that grow out of certain social conditions. One is that many women make the most out of a limited amount of material. While this could apply to minimalism in general, an aesthetic practiced by many male composers, it can also pertain to women's compositions for the *salon*. Although relatively short works, they fulfilled an important role functionally and expressively in that environment. Many women have also exhibited a tendency toward compositional flexibility. This may relate to their dual socialization in dominant and muted cultures, and to a subjective mobility that can negotiate the contradictions and ambiguities to best advantage. Women may also develop flexible ego boundaries, as Nancy Chodorow suggests.[73] Furthermore, ideologies of motherhood and other womanly roles emphasize nurturing, which in itself means a flexibility in response to the needs of others. Rieger observes that contemporary female composers may sense a flexibility in female compositional traditions of the past, and thus absorb the tendency themselves. One potential difficulty in this interesting idea, however, is that many women may not be aware of past female practices in music. Finally, another observation of Rieger is that women composers, in comparison to men, are not as concerned with newness in their music. "Originality is not fetishized, but rather subordinated to the total conception."[74] This may have to do with a lesser need to deal with an anxiety of influence. As discussed in Chapter 2, this has come to be a burden to the male composer. He feels an Oedipal need to "destroy" the historical weight of predecessors by establishing his own musical identity. A new style can effect that break.

While ideology lies behind many tendencies that relate to women, it could also be considered a basis for codifying historical periods according to gender. It is not that a given period is somehow displaying essentialist characteristics of real women or real men in its music. It is rather that ideologies about feminine and masculine and about their representation in music characterize the creative productions of a given period. The question of whether these labels are objectively true is not the point. What is important is that they have actually been applied to certain eras and key figures, and that they are based on ideologies that lay behind musical conventions. The early nineteenth century, for example, might be considered a period of varying musical gender: the masculine vigor of Beethoven's music and the feminine, or perhaps effeminate, grace of Chopin's compositions. We could consider the Italian lyricism of Mozart in the late eighteenth century a feminine trait, to be quashed by the masculine energy in Beethoven. In the 1830s and 1840s the feminine elegance of French culture takes hold in much of the music of Chopin and Mendelssohn. The 1850s witness an upsurge of masculine imagery in the Teutonic power of the Wagnerian music-drama, and this continues through post-Romantics like Mahler, Strauss, and Bruckner. Debussy and company reassert the feminine around 1900. Soon modernism brings masculine qualities to the fore and casts a wide shadow over twentieth-century aesthetics. It is possible that some of the swings, particularly to the masculine, were instigated in response to a perceived feminization of culture.

While musicologists may theorize about the possibilities of a women's style, it is important to hear the views of composers. We have little input from the past. There is a statement by Fanny Hensel in which she complains about her "tender style": a possible reference to the ideological feminine.[75] Modern composers have been more voluble. In general there is a diversity of opinion that ranges from outright rejection of the idea that compositions by women share any specific qualities to a sense that there may indeed be characteristics that are particular to women. No one, however, can identify precisely what those are; they remain in the realm of tendency. The responses come from the 1981 survey published in *Perspectives of New Music*.[76] On the positive side, Miriam Gideon and Marga Richter believe a woman has something special to say, something quite different from what a man would express. As Richter puts it, "After all, I am a woman, and I express what I am." Gideon ventures the idea "that women are freer and more generous about expressing emotion than men (wow!) and this often seems to carry over into their music. They seem (again, often) unwilling to settle for systems or schemes unless guided by a strong emotional impulse. (Maybe I'm just thinking about myself.)'" This ties in with the idea that women composers seem to eschew stylistic newness. Sandra Cotton, perhaps as surprised as Gideon at her own response, wonders whether her articulation of female musical qualities merely reflects predilections in her own music. Very tentatively, as she puts it, she identifies certain traits that might characterize a female style: "Pacing seems to be more organically a function of evolving material, breathing seems longer, and the architecture seems more fluid in contour." These might relate to flexibility, discussed above. Annea Lockwood and Ruth Anderson single out as specifically female a propensity for a holistic approach to composition. But most of these women sense the uncertainty, unprovability, and non-universality of their ideas, and seem to offer them as a way of characterizing their own compositions as well as many works by other women. In this regard, Cotton and Richter perceptively observe that a sense of what constitutes a female style will probably become much clearer "when we have a female tradition" (Richter). Perhaps we still have too small a sample from which to draw meaningful generalizations.[77] In any case, some composers evince womanly pride in being linked with female traits. As Lockwood states, "'Sounding like a woman' is taking on other connotations now ... at least amongst women. To quite a few of the people I talk with it implies that vague term, a sense of wholeness in the work, and strongly centered work. A positive term."

Other tendencies have been proposed for a female aesthetic. One is a "fascination with process": an intuitive, whimsical approach that might stress fantasy and experimentation outside accepted structures and techniques.[78] Perhaps this relates to Gideon's statement that women composers tend to avoid esoteric compositional systems. Lyricism might qualify as another female trait. This is a case where societal ideologies of the feminine underlie musical associations with women. The connection is further affirmed in the styles practiced in such female spheres as the *salon*. Other associations can be made. Lyricism generally embodies long lines and horizontal connectedness. The latter might be related to women's psychological development in the West, but this component may need greater contextualization. The former might pertain to female sexual rhythm, but the specific connection between the two is difficult to concretize. Furthermore, the sexual premise has so many potential exceptions as to be highly questionable. But lyricism may not always imply a positive relationship with women. Metaphorically its position in homophonic texture is problematic. Homophony constructs a hierarchical relationship between its two members: a dominant melody over a subordinate accompaniment. This arrangement might represent the power structure of the late eighteenth and nineteenth centuries. Men, here in lyrical guise, are dominant over less privileged groups, including women and the working classes. But in the search for a texture that is affirming for women, Renée Cox proposes heterophony. It allows for multiplicity of voice without the kind of slavish imitation found in counterpoint and avoids hierarchic vertical relationships. Heterophony is also a highly process-oriented texture, one that can accommodate improvisation and considerable experimentation. Yet even though her study takes a world view, Cox realizes that heterophony might not easily find a place in Western musical traditions.[79] Nonetheless, the idea of heterophony is suggestive. Given their subordination in male culture, many women might be attracted to the political implications of an aesthetic of equality.

Yet like many other potential structures, equality may represent an abstract ideal that bears little relationship to the realities of women's socialization. Acculturation according to dominant norms and conventions is a major part of their socialization and thus it becomes difficult to speak of a female mode, whether it be epistemology or aesthetics. In response, anthropologist Edwin Ardener offers the concept of the "wild zone" to account for that portion of women's socialization that lies beyond the boundaries of dominant culture.[80] While an attractive idea, it may be impractical because the two areas may be impossible to disentangle from one another. Another theoretical solution may lie in the realm of the pre-symbolic. This represents the early stage of child development that precedes the acquisition of language and the onset of acculturation. As Susan McClary observes, the uncontrolled, untamed pre-symbolic resembles the uncontrolled, untamed nature of aesthetic experience. It shares with music in particular an irrationality beyond the control of semantic reference and mind.[81] Perhaps it is in study of this stage that we can find out more about aesthetic experience. One difficulty is that the pre-symbolic might not prove useful for a gendered aesthetic, particularly a female aesthetic; the Lacanian version posits gender differentiation *after*, not during, this amorphous stage. For Julia Kristeva, however, the timing of the pre-symbolic as prior to patriarchal rule, and with a close mother–child bond, may suggest a possibility of femaleness imprinted before the entrance into culture. And this imprint may remain in the unconscious until adulthood and then reappear.[82] From the standpoint of music, research into this area would be challenging, to say the least.

In conclusion, the notion of a women's style is difficult and elusive but fundamental to questions about how music becomes a part of the canon. While it may be too early to tell if there is a specifically female aesthetic, at present most hypotheses put forward are grounded in elements of culture. The complexities of subject positioning and socialization are powerful. They must be considered in any attempt to find connections among the creative accomplishments of women.

CHAPTER 5

Reception

Reception seems the last element in a succession from creation through evaluation within canon formation: a work is composed and later received. Thus it forms a chapter at this point in the study. Yet reception in the broad sense infuses every stage of canon formation and is itself constituted by many of the assumptions that go into the making of a canon. We have been talking about aspects of reception since Chapter 1. For example, notions of public and private, mind and body, and large and small genres shape patterns of reception and are themselves shaped by previous patterns of reception. Indeed, many of the choices a composer makes as to style, genre, purpose, and audience are based on assumptions as to how the work will be received. A positive reception can mean affirmation of the original choices in other works by the individual and in compositions by other composers. Like several issues in the study, therefore, reception exhibits a circularity akin to canonicity. The absence of a written form of reception can mean exclusion from the canons of Western art music.

Reception has received a great deal of attention from literary theorists and linguists. It embraces a variety of approaches and is often expressed by the term "response." Before we proceed it is necessary to define the two more precisely, although distinctions between them are not entirely clear. Literary theorist Robert Holub describes the difference more in terms of schools than content: reception theorists are centered in Constance, Germany, while response theorists are elsewhere, particularly in France and the United States.[1] But there seem to be substantive distinctions as well. Reception theory usually deals more specifically with aesthetics. It pays greater attention to history and to collectivity in the sense of a public or an audience. Response theory, in contrast, appears to be more ahistorical and focused on the individual. Nonetheless, these are broad generalizations, and I often found the distinctions reversed in the sources consulted for the chapter.[2] I will try, however, to keep the meanings distinct. Reception will refer to the issue in general, as in the title of the chapter, and to the more collective and historical aspects of how works were (and are) perceived and evaluated. Response will pertain mostly to the level of the individual and to a context in which history plays a minimal role.

But good intentions notwithstanding, inconsistencies may arise. For example, if one is discussing the theories of Hans-Georg Gadamer and Hans-Robert Jauss, the two major exponents of *Rezeptionsästhetik* in Constance, one runs into problems of terminology. The theories emphasize a dialectical manipulation of historical perspective and thus fall under reception. Yet agency is located in an individual who could belong to any historical period. This idealized individual lacks social specificity and has no obvious connection with a group or an audience. Officially the ideas of Gadamer and Jauss are categorized as reception, yet some elements could be considered response. In the present study, even if the usage is not entirely consistent, I hope that the reader will be able to understand what I am trying to emphasize in a given context.

Because of its historical and collective implications, reception is the main focus of the chapter. But response is also relevant. Canon formation can be thought of as a subtle interplay between the individual and the group. The individual is located within the societal framework and partakes of societal assumptions and ideologies. But the individual is also a source for those assumptions and ideologies. The shifting relationships among those postures make for a complexity that cannot be easily separated into either individual or group. Similarly, response of the individual and reception of the group are not easily distinguished. The critic, who plays an important role in formal reception, is after all an individual. While he or she represents the group and is steeped in cultural understandings of music, the critic responds on many levels as an individual. Is this a man or a woman? What is the critic's previous acquaintance with the composition? Is knowledge of the work from a performance or a score (or recording)? What are the age and class of the critic? And so forth. Furthermore, this architect of formal reception replicates or substitutes for the individual responses of numerous audience members. It is a collectivity born of individuality. Speaking for many individuals, the critic also speaks to many individuals and helps shape their individual responses.

Of course, the critic is not the only agent in reception. As we saw in Chapter 1, the audience can have a great deal to say about how a work, composer, or aesthetic is received. While we can think of the audience as a conceptual bloc, it is composed of individuals. Their individual reactions and how they process musical experience form the basis of those collective reactions and judgments that may have an effect on history. Defining the makeup and behavior of the individuals in the group can therefore make a difference in formal reception. This can illuminate other basic questions about the compositional process: who is the composer writing for? How does it affect the style of the work? What is the temporal relationship with the intended audience? Furthermore, if the composer is responding to the reactions of critics and of audiences as groups and individuals, then we have another case of individual response. Like other elements in the complex process, the composer is part of groups yet also operates as an individual. The responses that prompt compositional choices are partly individual and partly collective and are extremely difficult to separate. In a sense it is pointless to try to do so. But some understanding of what goes into individual response can help us comprehend how reception works and ultimately how it influences the formation of canons.

While it can be difficult to distinguish between response and reception, it is also difficult to define reception itself. It can mean formal criticism of music, especially in the form of reviews: Eduard Hanslick's excoriations of Wagnerian music drama or Franz Liszt's adorations of the same. It can include interpretive essays in diverse media: Susan McClary's essay on Janika Vandervelde's *Genesis II*, originally written for a composers' newsletter, or Andrew Porter's critiques of eighteenth-century opera, written for *The New Yorker*. It can include criticism in musicological journals, for example Richard Taruskin's "Resisting the ninth" or Carolyn Abbate's "What the sorcerer said."[3] In a sense, of course, all musicological writing, even the more objective, is a form of reception. Obviously there is a difference in the historiographic implications of a review written at the time of a première and an essay written about a work of the distant past. But each type tells us how a work is being "received" or viewed in a given period. This means much more than an evaluation of perceived strengths and weaknesses. It means an expression of some of the fundamental metaphors of the culture. The very fact of written evaluation in a public forum is itself evidence of the cultural preference for written media. Conversely, the written format itself valorizes the content and accords music a kind of permanence that it has been seeking ever since the early nineteenth century (see Chapter 1). Reception not only gives expression to cultural metaphors but also provides for their control. The power of the pen can shape mightily how these metaphors are disseminated, understood, reinforced, or modified. A good example is the emphasis on largeness that colored reception of nineteenth-century music, which in turn reinforced expansionist ideals in society at large. I am not saying that music reviews directly influenced decisions on whether to colonize other areas of the world. What I am suggesting is that the reviews contributed to a mind-set favorably disposed to bigness and transcendence, and this probably reaffirmed tendencies already in existence in society.

Reception reflects and establishes the criteria by which music is judged, and as such plays an obvious role in valuation. It represents a structure with considerable power in the forming of canons. It serves as the framework in which pieces are reviewed and marked off for attention. This attention implies that the work must be worthy of attention and therefore important. Even if the assessment is negative, an implied significance is present that is missing when a work is not reviewed. Attention in print can lead to further performances and potential canonicity. A review can also shape categorization. First, a review implies that the work belongs to an important category, for it is worthy of being discussed in print. Second, a review might impose categories on the work or the composer, be they in terms of genre, function, or style. A review summarizes the expectations of the audience and shapes them at the same time. It affirms cultural associations between the respondents and the performance, including site, class, and gender. A review also sets a moral tone that confers status on the musical experience under consideration and the individual readers of the review.

Yet reception may be much more than written evaluation. It may also include those informal, unwritten responses to music that elude permanence yet affect practice. Many involve a path that departs from the mainstream. As we have seen, the pipeline from creation through professionalism through public performance and public review leaves out a great deal. For example, how were Chaminade's works received in music clubs? How did their reception in those circles affect subsequent compositions? What about unpublished works that were performed in private? How were Hensel's compositions received in the private musicales in Berlin? Did the fact that they were intended for a limited audience influence their style? The "receivers" in such settings were not professional writers and the sites were not public. Thus the mechanisms of music reviewing did not apply. One reason for the canonic exclusion of such works is that the performances were not reviewed.

Actual reception of music may also involve factors beyond the realm of critical evaluation – factors that may be difficult to locate or identify. I am thinking of the subtle reactions that individuals, including individuals as part of groups, may experience in music. What about physical, sexual, or affective reactions to music? What about pleasure?[4] While I realize that these may imply individual response rather than reception, we are also talking about group reception, in a historical context. For example, a work like *The Rite of Spring* contains stark physical and sexual imagery. It infuses the story and the dance, and arguably is suggested by the musical gestures themselves. Yet should we stop at the borders of the work to find meaning? Might there be corresponding physical or sexual components in the audience's reaction? These could reflect tendencies in society at that time and resemble responses evoked by contemporary art works. Similarly, the affective reactions of audiences to much film music forms an interesting area of reception. Opera produced on film might also be explored in this manner. What I am trying to emphasize is that reception is expressed in many forms and we have to be careful lest we assume that written evaluation constitutes the only kind of reception. The non-written and the non-intellectual have an important part to play in the understanding of the past. One difficulty is that they can be ephemeral and are not easily accessed. Furthermore, they may implicate the body and its ideological association with the feminine more than society wishes to acknowledge. But this does not negate their existence and their importance.

As the above suggests, reception has a lot to do with many of the central issues of this book. In a sense, canon formation is a kind of super-reception itself that selects, processes, and advances those values it wishes to perpetuate. Thus many issues discussed previously represent assumptions, metaphors, or ideologies that have shaped how music has been received: for example, the large over the small, the public over the private, the mind over the body, the masculine over the feminine. Reception has formed a subtext in other chapters. Accordingly, the present chapter does not explore in depth many of the details involved in reception, especially those discussed previously, and as a result is shorter than the other chapters.

The organization is simple. The first section focuses on response and summarizes many of the significant aspects to be considered in an understanding of who that individual is that potentially makes up the collective group that receives a work. The second and principal section explores various aspects of reception. In general, the chapter demonstrates that reception is temporally diverse and forms a foundation for the writing of music. There is a fascinating tension between the individual and the group, and the two standpoints have to be considered in any meaningful approach to reception. As noted, reception involves much more than formal criticism. With regard to women, it is very difficult to show that there is a female "voice" (ear?) in reception or in responding to music in general. Music is a technical discipline that may lie beyond gendered differentiation in style. Additionally, women have been socialized in male culture and may have little basis for a response that is specifically female. Of course, as discussed earlier (see Chapter 2), the narratives of texted works may draw different reactions from women. But in instrumental music it may be difficult to discern essential differences. Finally, we should recall that reception is a crucial element in the dynamics of culture and forms a fundamental part of any understanding of music as social practice.

RESPONSE

Theories of individual response come mainly from literature and linguistics and have occupied literary practitioners for many years. In music, studies on the listening process began in the middle of the century and most stress the phenomenal side of music. They tend to focus on the individual, on psycho-physiological response, and on stylistic properties of the music. *The Rhythmic Structure of Music* (Chicago, 1960), by Grosvenor Cooper and Leonard Meyer, typifies this approach. Its exploration of the complexities of expectation as a listener moves through a piece of music paved the way for other studies. But as sophisticated as many have been, including Walter

Frisch's more recent *Brahms and the Principle of Developing Variation* (Berkeley, 1984), most have continued to operate under an assumption of insularity from social meaning. The analytic frame has usually stopped at the edges of the composition. This forecloses links with socio-historical context that might play a significant role in the understanding of music. The listener has been proffered as some generalized persona without social location. Is this, for example, a present-day listener? A listener in the composer's day or twenty years later? A "knowledgeable" listener? A listener at a live concert? A first-time listener to the composition? A listener who has read a review of the work or the performance? A performer listening to his or her playing? A male listener? A non-Western listener? As this list suggests, the notion of a non-specific, non-situated listener presents many problems to a meaningful theory of response. Each type of listener might relate in a particular way to a given piece of music. Yet recent work is beginning to pay attention to social coding in music, and the 1987 collection *Music and Society: The Politics of Composition, Performance and Reception*, ed. Richard Leppert and Susan McClary, is a landmark in this regard.

But if the field of music has been slow to break out of its insularity and bridge the gap between sonar abstraction and social referentiality, it can look to the field of literature for guidance. The lively debates among theorists of varied persuasions have produced a wide range of ideas. They include the theories of E. D. Hirsch, a fierce backer of authorial intention *vis-à-vis* reader subjectivity; of Wolfgang Iser, an exponent of phenomenological priority in the communication of meaning; of Jauss, an advocate of historical specificity in an aesthetic of reception; and of Roland Barthes, an iconoclast who nearly destroys author and text in the priority accorded the reader's construction of meaning. These names can only hint at the richness and complexity surrounding response.

The many theories that have attempted to define the reader generally make no distinction as to gender and *de facto* assume a male reader. But gender is an important component in that definition and forms a basic category in the work of several feminist scholars. The main impetus has come from literary criticism and includes Elaine Showalter, Jane Tompkins, Judith Fetterley, Peggy Kamuf, Lillian Robinson, and Patrocinio Schweickart. Their insights have sparked feminists in other fields, and they include Jill Dolan in theater, Rozsika Parker–Griselda Pollock in art, and Teresa de Lauretis and

Tania Modleski in film.[5] But because music (particularly Western art music) has been considered abstract, elitist, and insular, musicologists are only beginning to theorize connections between gender and response/reception.

It is not the purpose of this chapter to discuss in detail the many theories of literary response. But we can produce a kind of "wish list" of characteristics that provide a useful framework for further analysis of musical response. Such a structure can form the basis of a collectivity that characterizes reception. As a performative medium, music can benefit from phenomenological theories of response (Wolfgang Iser, Stanley Fish). The emphasis on the reading process as the site of the production of meaning has much in common with the listening process in music. Temporality is a key factor, as the responding process unfolds over time. Its adoption for literary response not only provides a new mode of conceptualization for literature, but affords musicians a broader meaning of aesthetic temporality and assists us in finding commonalities with supposedly non-temporal media like literature.[6] Fish in particular considers the very act of reading the prime element in the construction of meaning of a work; it ranks above the independent work and also above the agency of the author. Although I value response and agree that it precedes as well as follows creation,[7] I do not go as far as Fish and others in assigning response such an exclusive role in the production of meaning. The composer still counts as an important figure, although we need to balance the notion of the author with greater attention to social context (see Chapter 3); response forms a major component in that social context. The work is already receiving a great deal of attention in musicology, although our emphases on formalism are too restrictive. On a practical level, Iser's notion of gaps in the work that are filled in by the respondent during the reading process is attractive for music. Relying upon memory of past events in the piece and expectations of future events, the listener continually constructs and re-constructs relationships and meanings where they are not explicitly stated. How these gaps are filled also depends on the musical experience and cultural makeup of the individual.

The phenomenological emphasis suggests the notion of response as creation. Listening not only engages the listener actively in a fluctuating dynamic with the composition, but it also creates the piece.[8] This creating by the listener does not usually negate or supplant the creativity of the composer who wrote the piece.[9] Instead it creates another ontology of the work – a realized version, replete with meaning for that listener, as distinct from the notated version that the composer created. Dual ontology also suggests the figure of the performer, a crucial presence between maker and listener. No mere static relay point, the performer serves as (re)creator and respondent all in one.[10] As a respondent, the performer responds to the visual and cultural implications of the notated version of the piece to create meaning and then transmits that re-created version via the performed interpretation to a listener. Of course, in an ensemble piece, the performer might bring response and creativity into closer temporal alignment as he or she reacts to the response/creativity of the other performers. The performer also responds/creates on the basis of previous interpretations by others. Thus Joan's rendition of a Chopin nocturne is influenced by Sue's recording, as well as by many other factors. Although it is a performer rather than the composer, this is another facet of how response precedes creativity. In these situations the performer is playing for other listeners. But one often performs for oneself, without any other ears. Then the creation/ response function appears closer to the literary model; just substitute reader for performer.

When the performer is playing for others, each listener will be creating once again another ontology of the work. This newly constructed version of the piece probably does not coincide in all respects with the performer's understood version or with the composer's. This non-congruence resembles Barthes's concept of ruptures, or breaks within the system involving maker and re-spondent. There is nothing to guarantee that constructed notions of meaning in a given ontology of a work will communicate themselves obviously or totally to others. But perhaps we could fall back on the idea of an interpretive community – a collectivity based on shared cultural values – as a way of minimizing such ruptures. Yet since interpretive community has only been loosely conceived, the concept may be too vague to help us pin down cultural commonality. Furthermore, incongruity, breakage, and similar traits that resist conformity may serve beneficial ends: they inject interest and texture into processes of response and reception. Another factor that undermines a theory of consistent response is that response varies within an individual from hearing to hearing of a given piece. This could even happen when the stimulus is relatively constant, as in a recording. Multiple response may be related to multiple subjectivity. This Barthesian notion seems to arise from an awareness that the individual is situated in history, and this location can have its own ruptures that affect subjectivity. Contradiction may result, but this is not necessarily a problem. Rather, the important thing is that contradiction and multiplicity are recognized. These can enrich an individual's response.

But precisely who is the music respondent? Who is the individual referred to in the above-mentioned dynamic processes? In actuality there is no unitary model of listener but rather a multiplicity of listeners, differentiated by factors such as historical era, gender, class, race, nationality, age, and prior experience with music. These do not connote hierarchy in the sense of a particular affiliation yielding a "better" kind of response. Rather they suggest difference shaped by social and experiential factors that an individual brings to the meaning-producing processes of response. The work created through the process of response circles back to influence and modify the very construction of those social categories. Music resembles literature in that the intended respondent(s) is already contained, or inscribed, within the work. Such a figure is no socially neuter presence but rather an individual defined by social location, especially gender, class, nationality, sexuality, and race. This does not mean that the piece holds less meaning for some other kind of respondent, but rather *different* meaning.

The notion of inscribed respondent also does not mean that the work will not "hold up" in a later context – a consideration that slides into matters of reception. What it does mean is that the relationship between the work and the new listeners will change, and that the values delineated by original respondents will be modified or replaced by others more pertinent to the newer situation. It also seems to imply that the original and newer values may not coincide and may actually contradict one another. But this dissonance can enrich the work. Succeeding generations will have the benefit of cumulative traditions for their current interpretations. Whether consciously or not, they are interacting with previous theories and thus invoking Gadamer's concept of a fusion of horizons. Current notions of valuation and history are tempered by notions of the past and thereby avoid the kinds of errors that can result from exclusive reliance on current historiography. As to the relativism that could result from the plethora of interpretations, we can recoup Gadamer's idea of the "hermeneutic circle": checking and comparing our own interpretations with those of others. It is not the purpose of the process to persuade an individual to change his or her ideas. It can place one's interpretation in greater relief and sharpen the reasons for certain evaluative decisions. Nonetheless, the validity of the individual's interpretation can stand at face-value. At the very least, it represents an assertion of personal subjectivity: a statement of individual agency and social constitution. Patrocinio Schweickart describes it well when she observes that "we can think of validity [of interpretation] not as a property inherent in an interpretation, but rather as a *claim* implicit in the *act* of propounding an interpretation."[11]

Yet there is always a danger of anecdotal excess if attention is given solely to the experiences of countless individuals. A surfeit of individual cases provides a mass of details that may not produce meaningful patterns of behavior. But without the attention to numerous individuals as individuals there is the danger of overgeneralization, universalism, and even essentialism. In music, much more so than literature, response/reception operates around the two poles of individual and group. This is beneficial, and we should try to keep the two in balance when considering how music has been received.

If we consider gender and its relationship to response, we might wonder about the issue of individual response as a woman. Can gender make a difference in individual response? Is there such a thing as a woman's way of listening? And if so, what is the epistemological basis of such a mode and how is it configured? These are difficult questions and there are no simple answers. Jonathan Culler provides a means of negotiating the issue in his essay "Reading as a woman." One of the chapters in his monograph on deconstruction,[12] the essay offers a structure that we can apply to music as well. The line of inquiry I am pursuing here implies that a better understanding of how response works for the individual *vis-à-vis* gender can have a bearing on our approach to reception. It could, for instance, suggest ways of dealing with modes of reception that lie outside the mainstream.

In "Reading as a woman" Culler claims that female experience cannot serve as the basis of a theory of female reading. This is because there is no such thing as female experience. Like Fetterley, Culler believes that women are socialized into male culture and hence a pure female mode does not exist. Socialized women are divided and show the traces of the dividedness. Consequently, should a woman want to function deliberately as a woman then she is playing a role that is modeled on what a woman's point of view is supposed to be. The process is like a data loop, akin to Derrida's chain of deferred meaning. As Culler states, "For a woman to read as a woman is not to repeat an identity or an experience that is given but to play a role she constructs with reference to her identity as a woman, which is also a construct, so that the series can continue: a woman reading as a woman reading as a woman."[13] Grounded in a *hypothesis* of a woman rather than a real woman, Culler's theory simultaneously recognizes the potency of ideologies of woman and realities of socialization. But in spite of its attractiveness it still has a serious drawback: it denies the existence of real women and the validity of their experiences. It undermines their agency and questions the basis upon which women are to live their lives.[14]

Culler might respond that this is not what he is doing. In the attempt to find a basis for an aesthetic standpoint he faces built-in traps: the essentialist trap that says there is a female experience which all women share, and the purity trap that claims it is confined to women only. It is a major challenge to devise a theory of response which can apply to such a large yet limited group. Despite the fact that Culler is sympathetic in the essay to the validity of female experience, the fact that he feels compelled to reject it in the end could demonstrate the difficulties inherent in the project. For what is there ultimately in his theory upon which to base a practice of female response? Not much, I am afraid. Signification is deferred indefinitely, and there is a gaping hole left vacant by the presence of real women.[15]

Another aspect of Culler's theory deserves comment. The word "as" implies equivalence between the substantives "reading" and "woman," and also action "in the role or guise of" a woman. Unlike the term "like," "as" does not immediately suggest imitation or role-playing, or if it does the implication is muted. But "as" can suggest representation: that a woman is reading as a representative of the larger class "women." For me this has advantages and disadvantages. I am attracted to the idea of responsibility to the larger group and to the possibility of commonalities between an individual and the group. Yet this very commonality could mean essentialism among all members of the group. The relationship can also imply that the single representative is some idealized being which has little to do with actual women. I suppose this is indeed what Culler is claiming when he refutes the validity of experience as a basis for aesthetic response, although he comes to that conclusion through a different line of reasoning. The tensions between individual and group, and between ideology and reality, underscore fundamental difficulties in working through feminist issues.

The problems engendered by Culler's theory are not alleviated in music. If anything, indeed, they become more complicated because of an absence of semantic meaning in the materials of the art form. Can we even consider experience as a basis of a theory of musical response, much less female experience? What has experience to do with a sound medium? One answer may lie in representation: a woman listener responding to her representation as a woman in music. Like literature, this can take the form of reaction to her portrayal in texted works, where there is a clear narrative. This obviously resembles what Culler and others are talking about in literature. But as we saw in Chapter 4 for the gendered themes of sonata form, certain musical conventions encode societal ideologies of a woman. These can prompt a response from any listener, man or woman. But a woman's particular range of subject positions, which are potentially different from those of men, might predispose her to react to those codes in a way that comes from the fact that she is indeed a woman, even one socialized in contradiction. Perhaps Culler would interject here that since there is no such thing as a pure woman it is pointless to even refer to her in such terms. "Woman" does not carry subjective integrity in patriarchal culture and is not capable of acting as an agent in its own terms. I have two comments. First, as suggested in the "Introduction," this is a theoretical location that flies in the face of common sense. There are indeed living, breathing women in the world, and everyday experience tells us that the concept "woman" is valid because women exist all around us. And second, to answer the objection in theoretical terms, I am not suggesting that a female experience is pure. I am accepting contradiction. This becomes a part of, and even strongly defines, a likely female subject positioning. It is this that can serve as the basis of a woman's response to music.

A woman might respond to more than her own representation, however. She might respond, in subtle ways, to the very fact that she has been constructed as Other to the canon. Few works by women populate the canon, and this could lead to problems of identity. After all, how is a woman listener supposed to respond to a tradition in which she has had little visibility? In which she has been outsider? The following are possibilities for her response to this difficult question. First, women, like men, have been socialized to think of music as an art-form beyond gender, and that includes its composers and its history. Until recently, music history was conceived as a history of composers, not a history of *male* composers. So a woman might not recognize that there is a problem. Second, men and women have become accustomed to the idea that men populate music and its history. A woman might not have missed the presence of women because men were the "natural" practitioners. In this option there is also little awareness of a problem. As a third possibility, a woman might experience the psychological effects of historical invisibility but not be aware of them. And last, a woman might be consciously aware of her position outside mainstream history and experience problems of identity as a result. I am not suggesting that these potential reactions are necessarily exclusive. It is entirely possible that a woman might react differently at different times. What is clear, however, is that there is no essentialist female way of processing music. Yet in many cases a woman has become part of an interpretive community of women that has participated in musical reception.

RECEPTION

Reception operates more directly in canon formation than does individual response. Generally articulated in written form, reception focuses on collective response and its relationship with history. A class of professionals – the critic – has occupied the center of reception, and this forms an interesting contrast with the social plurality of the individual respondent. Reception can affect whether a work becomes canonic. Similarly, the values inscribed in reception have the affirming and perpetuating properties of a canon. Reception, in short, is a means of controlling many of the central metaphors of a culture. Those works or structures left out of formal reception are headed down a different path from the mainstream. But as discussed earlier, some musical contexts have other modes of reception. Although difficult to access, they form an important part of actual musical practice.

Formal reception creates meaning in each review or essay that is written and published. But it also forms a body of interpretation with signifiers and signs that spill over the boundary of a given essay into another, and even beyond. The intertextuality means that reviews make semiotic even if not literal reference to each other and to other pieces and composers. These unarticulated referents may be inscribed within the essay and function as assumptions upon which the given work is based. Of course, the temporal relationship with the composition/composer and the previous tradition of writing on that work or figure can make a difference in the semiotic framework. For example, a review of one of Brahms's earliest compositions, when he was an unknown, will embody a very different set of referents than one written after, say, the one-hundredth performance of the work. Thus the terms within the intertextual system will change. But in general the persona of the composer forms a major element in the system. As mentioned in Chapter 3, this is so powerful that the reverence accorded a given work of a composer spills over to others by the same person, even if they are not very good.[16] The cultural meanings implied by the signifier Beethoven, for example, connote high quality, genius, and respect. The use of his name in criticism suggests a level to be aspired to and a realm of Serious Art and Deep Meaning. Intertextuality also operates on other aspects of musical practice. For example, in the area of ideology, the use of the word "feminine" around 1900 signified a separate and lesser kind of music. The term "feminine" within sonata form also connoted lesser status. While the semiotic implications of formal criticism are too vast to be explored here, the important point is that written reception should be seen as a signifying network of great import. A particular review does not merely create meaning in and of itself. It passes and receives meaning from a long tradition of reception and from contemporary forms of meaning within and beyond the field of music.

Since *c.* 1800, when public music became important, the rhetoric of written reception has reflected and promoted the values of the music under discussion. In a tone of high moral authority it has surrounded art music with the trappings of universality and timelessness. It has painted an elitist vision of music and infused it with an idealism that many find inspiring. This helped legitimate music at a time when it lost its aristocratic underpinning and moved into the unknown terrain of the public. In the early days, at least, the high-mindedness also served to legitimate the written reception itself.

The professional writer on music was a relatively new phenomenon and it was important that he establish his own validity.

Arguably professional music criticism became a genre in its own right, created by writers who could be considered an interpretive community. Although the term is not entirely clear, it seems to connote a group with some basis of commonality in response. Beyond that it is rather general. For example, would gender alone suffice as the criterion for an interpretive community? We will return to that later when discussing the relationships between women and reception. In practical terms we could call professional music critics an interpretive community on the basis of shared methods and structures, but one with the potential for substantial diversity.

The professional music critic has wielded considerable power. Since the late eighteenth century, the music critic has generally been a writer for widely disseminated print media, notably newspapers and magazines. Whereas some modern-day musicologists could be considered critics, much like academic literary critics, they are still few in number compared to the positivist mainstream. Furthermore, they reach a relatively limited, although influential, audience. Thus I am mainly referring to the first type. Critics have had enormous influence through the sheer numbers of people they reach and their ability to shape taste and "make or break" a composer, work, or performer. They seem to stand inside and outside the public at the same time. But this insider–outsider positioning differs from that associated with women: outside for the critic means power and status rather than marginalization. Critics are professional listeners, as it were, whose main goal is to propagate their own points of view, their own aesthetic paradigms. The one-way communication goes to countless anonymous individuals, who function as respondents twice-removed: the critic, as a respondent to a performance or work, is creating a work for other respondents.[17] While the dual-response structure of criticism raises some interesting theoretical possibilities, suffice it to say here that the respondent might begin the reading as some passive captive of the controlling, knowledgeable critic – knowledgeable in the sense that he or she attended the event. But in the process of response the reader becomes creator as well. Furthermore, equality might result if the reader also has first-hand acquaintance with the object under discussion. Yet in the aggregate, because of the extent of the readership and the regularity of the contribution, the critic has great control over what is basically a one-way process of communication. On the other hand, the critic does not operate in a cultural vacuum and has to be responsive to the desires of audiences and readers. This does not preclude some judgments that readers might not like, nor does it mean that the critic has to pander to common taste. But it does suggest that the critic is aware of the general aesthetic framework of art music and understands the boundaries beyond which he should not step. Of course, the critic does not come to his post as an outsider from another culture. He himself is part of the given culture and responds to many of the impulses that drive the tastes of audiences and others involved in music.

The critical establishment has been overwhelmingly male. The absence of women has meant the absence of a female voice and a female point of view, even if it is difficult to specify precisely what they might mean. As such, male modes of discourse have formed the basis of professional music criticism. By male modes we do not mean some essentialist traits but rather patterns that grow out of ideology and acculturation in Western society. It is also important to remember that male critics internalized musical values from male predecessors and contemporaries, and that conditions of response formed a pre-evaluative context for the structuring of their discourse.

How do women fit into this closed system? In fact there have been some female music critics, particularly in recent years: Harriet Johnson of the *New York Post*, Karen Monson of the now defunct *Chicago Daily News*, and Manuela Hoelterhof of *The Wall Street Journal* come readily to mind. Nonetheless, women still represent an exceedingly small segment of an overwhelmingly male profession. It is difficult for anyone to break into music criticism, man or woman, but women face added obstacles because of a strong male network.[18] But given a presence of women critics, the question to ask is what difference that could make. Is there, for instance, a specifically female point of view in music criticism? If we mean some viewpoint essential to women, even socialized women, the answer has to be no. Opinion will vary from woman to woman because of temperament and background. Furthermore, because such women themselves grew up in dominant culture, their value systems reflect that acculturation: as Judith Fetterley would put it, they have been immasculated. But in spite of the inevitable contradiction and dividedness that result in such situations, the voices of women betoken a more pluralistic field of reception. In addition, the kinds of subject positioning that women occupy have the potential to inflect the expectations and criteria they bring to musical experience. These may be subtle and variable, but they might indeed make a difference.

While discriminatory practices have kept women away from professional criticism, there are also ideological reasons why women have not functioned in that role. The role of critic implies authority. It connotes mind, wisdom, and judgment: an epistemological foundation for dispensing knowledge to others. This foundation hearkens back to the notion of God as the ultimate authority figure. But God is male, and thus women cannot hope to acquire the necessary moral foundation for dispensing knowledge. Written criticism is also a means of controlling knowledge, and in the case of music this means aesthetic as well as intellectual knowledge. Ideologically women have been separated from the realm of knowledge (see Chapter 2) and consequently seen as deficient in that area. They cannot control knowledge. Thus the ideological has laid a foundation for the practical, and the result is that there have been very few female critics.

The authority vested in the male critic has implications for women composers, who may find themselves objectified by the patriarchal subjectivity of the critic. Of course, a subject–object relation between critic and composer or critic and work is possible even if the composer is male. But the demarcation is much more sharply articulated in the case of a woman because of her representation in ideology. She is often portrayed as a subservient, daughterly figure to a wise yet authoritarian father: the daughterly female composer seeking legitimation from the fatherly male critic.[19] This can lead to a patronizing posture and mean marginalization for the composer. When the composer is male, however, a patriarchal relationship is less likely to occur. The subject and the potential object stand on a more equal ideological footing. But if the male composer is structured as an object, the relationship might seem like an imitation of the male–female power relationship in society at large. The male composer might feel feminized or even emasculated. Another possible scenario is that the authority vested in the critic triggers an Oedipal-like anxiety of influence in the male composer. In this situation the metaphoric murder is directed at the critic and not at some male-precursor.[20] What this discussion shows is that subtle factors of gender are at play in the critic's relationship with the composer. The obvious implications of maleness or femaleness have to be tempered with the dynamics of social process.

A review has various cultural implications. When first written it pertains to an event within the direct experience or potentially direct experience of the readers. It has a sense of immediacy, and the social context within which it was written will be relatively clear. But the meanings change as time passes. As the review becomes remote from the original event it begins to assume a life of its own. In part it takes on the form of a historical document, and in part its form becomes ambiguous. The implications for later readers are different from what they were for earlier readers. The later audience establishes a different relationship with that literary piece, and the critic is also endowed with different signs. If he or the material under review has gained in stature then the critic could become more of a transcendent persona. If the opposite, then he may resemble a historical footnote and lose much of his original power.

Women participate in various aspects of reception, as we have seen. Their presence can modify our understanding of how the elements of reception interrelate, and provide a more complete view of its contingency. For example, it is probably simplistic merely to speak of women's reception as some monolithic concept. There are female composers, female audiences, (a few) female critics, female performers, and representations of women in music itself. These elements can combine in various ways. In particular we could ask, how do audiences react to music by women? We could also ask, how do women listeners react to music? And each of these questions would require further definition and specificity. Yet they suggest the complexities of grappling with reception once gender is factored into the process.

Let us focus first on the female composer in reception. How audiences react to music by women is largely a consequence of other factors in canon formation. These elements ultimately come to define fundamental questions about the legitimacy and suitability of musical creation. Who is capable of being a worthy creator, a legitimate creator? Who is supposed to inhabit the public sphere and the professional ranks? Do audiences set up different expectations for a work when they find out it is written by a woman? Several previous comments, especially by Edith Borroff and Nancy Van de Vate (see Chapter 3), suggest that discovery of female authorship often modifies how a work is received. It is one of the main reasons why women have concealed their gender through the adoption of pseudonyms. The audience, like the composer herself, is influenced by societal constructions of woman and brings those images to the concert hall. With woman represented in the media as naughty temptress, for example, whose sexuality is to be consumed or controlled by men, it is no wonder that the public might find it difficult to accept a woman as a composer of art music. "Composer" conjures up images of the mind, not the body; of intellectual purity as opposed to base sexuality. In addition, the power of the author-function has turned the composer into a paragon of virtue and a force for ethical good. The composer through his art embodies the highest ideals of humankind, and in the West these have been separated from the degradations brought on by the flesh. Incidentally, this ideological separation may partially account for the strong reactions to explorations of sexuality in canonic composers.[21] In any event, perhaps I am painting an extreme picture. After all, women are portrayed in a variety of roles today and theoretically enjoy the freedom to choose from a variety of professional and personal pursuits. But the old ideologies still carry substantial weight – witness movies, MTV, and advertising – and they need not be present in full force to inflect perceptions of the woman composer. She is still received as an outsider, as an exception, and this may take a long time to change.

Certain themes in formal reception have had an impact on the perception of women and their music. The concept of genius became important in the early nineteenth century. Given the dislocation of the composer from court and Church, the concept of genius provided a way of positing authority and legitimation for the composer. Previously he occupied a particular niche in the social order and neither expected nor received special privilege. But after the political and social revolutions his place was uncertain. Social and moral identity was no longer defined by a secular or ecclesiastic patron. Furthermore, society itself was losing some of its own moral authority through increased secularization, and was attempting to define itself and find an identity. For the composer, one solution was to take on the attributes of divinity, of God. Genius meant divine powers of creativity and unquestionable moral authority. The composer, as it were, received inspiration directly from God and assumed awesome powers. The divine association also provided a solid basis for authority at a time when the composer lacked a respected figure, namely the royal patron, for his legitimation. On a more practical note, the notion of genius furnished a means of demarcating the composer from the public, the consumers of his music. In the past the composer had his own niche. But now the composer was a member of the middle class and hence the same population that made up the audience. He had to assert his authority through a separation, and an association with genius marked him off from the larger group. The attribute also had commercial advantages. It provided a vehicle for rhetorical distinction, and this could enhance the composer's reputation and sell his music.

The connections between genius and women are interesting. On the one hand, the association with God effectively signified male lineage and the exclusion of women. On the other hand, it is possible that the effusive rhetoric of the concept of genius actually stemmed from cultural representations of the feminine in ideology and language. If so, as Christine Battersby asserts,[22] then the concept of genius may be a prime example of appropriation whose content is turned against the original subject. In music and the other arts, genius has meant power, status, authority, and quality, and it has managed to perpetuate itself because of the almost mystical associations it evokes. The creator as divine and other-worldly has reinforced ideologies of masculinity and acted to suppress the possibility of a female creator.

Originality has functioned as another paradigm in formal reception. The concept of originality arose as a means of affirming the growing emphasis on the individual in capitalistic society – in particular the white middle-class male. For the composer it was useful as another means towards self-definition: of marking himself off from his audiences and from other composers, who now competed for attention in an open arena. In general, originality acts to set a style, an action, or a person apart because of qualities that are perceived as unique. It emphasizes difference rather than similarity and thus results in discontinuities more than continuities. As compared to the stylistic uniformity of the late eighteenth century, for example, the relative multiplicity of styles that blossomed in the nineteenth century and continued well into the twentieth testify to the change in ideology.[23] As discussed in Chapter 2, stylistic originality for the male composer may have been a necessary response to the burden of stylistic precursors: what Harold Bloom has dubbed an "anxiety of influence."

Originality is still touted as a positive attribute. Yet within the sweeping cultural critiques of the past quarter century, Barthes, for example, has rejected the concept of uniqueness in favor of structures of relationship: originality is replaced by intertextuality. Barthes is not implying that this is what should replace originality. Rather he is saying that originality itself is bogus and holds little or no aesthetic validity because every work is a product of highly interconnected social structures and stylistic relationships.[24]

Barthes's deconstruction of originality allies itself with feminist views of the concept. Literary critic Lillian Robinson makes the connection between originality and the isolation of the individual in capitalism. She wonders "whether the best role for the arts or for criticism is to celebrate that which is basic or that which is marginal, what is common or what is exceptional."[25] For Western women, who have been raised to value relationship and connectedness, artistic paradigms that stress uniqueness and individualism may raise difficulties. They have conflicted with ideologies that construct woman as nurturing and supportive. In such an environment, women composers may find themselves in a contradictory position. The emphasis on originality in formal reception implies that composition is a masculine terrain and is not "natural" to the female composer. Practically, however, women composers have been nurtured in male-defined norms also. Thus the actual distinction between male and female composers *vis-à-vis* originality is not clear.

Genius and originality have acted indirectly on the reception of women composers. More directly, however, women and their music have been objectified through a kind of sexual aesthetics that has attempted to regulate the gendered content of music.[26] In such assessments, which were particularly rampant around the turn of the century, male reviewers criticized women on the one hand for being too feminine in their music and not meeting male qualitative standards, and on the other for trying to be too masculine and thereby abandoning their natural feminine sweetness and charm. The following excerpts from contemporary reviews of Chaminade's music exemplify the dilemma:

[The *Concertstück* is] a work that is strong and virile, too virile perhaps, and that is the reproach I would be tempted to address to it. For me, I almost regretted not having found further those qualities of grace and gentleness that reside in the nature of women, the secrets of which she possesses to such a degree.[27]

[Her music] has a certain feminine daintiness and grace, but it is amazingly superficial and wanting in variety.... But on the whole this concert confirmed the conviction held by many that while women may some day vote, they will never learn to compose anything worthwhile. All of them seem superficial when they write music.[28]

By creating a no-win situation, the male establishment effectively kept women out and at the same time reaffirmed the supremacy of masculine values and male creative subjectivity.[29] A variation on that strategy is the "compliment" paid to a woman composer that she writes like a man. While expressed as flattery, it inculcates gender confusion as a woman is lulled into identifying with men against the lesser group, women, of which she is of course a member: another instance of immasculation. Perhaps this is occurring much less frequently, however. Composer Marilyn Ziffrin, for example, noted in 1981 how she used to be placed in this position quite often, but it eventually stopped. This is a positive sign.[30]

The contents of the canon indicate that women composers have not occupied a centered location as subjects in music history. Written reception is accordingly thin. Of course, the scarcity of written reception in fact helped to create that historical positioning. The relationship between women's contributions and their recognition in written form could be called a poetics of the under-reviewed or the non-reviewed. Written reception has belonged to the public sphere and served its component structures. It has favored the large forms, notably opera and symphony, and helped to maintain their respected status. Many women, however, have channeled their creative energies into other areas, including music for pegagogy, children, and social gatherings in more intimate settings. Formal criticism has generally passed over such activities, however. This means that such activities were not documented, at least with great regularity, and are difficult to find out about. But even more important for historiography, the absence of written reception itself reinforces the lowly position that these activities occupy on the hierarchy of musical value. It suggests that music for a specific purpose is suspect and that musical activity outside of major centers and concert halls is of lesser value. Such exclusions affirm the elitism of art music and sim-ultaneously enhance the prestige of the rhetoric and the author of the rhetoric. On the whole, written reception elevates art music to a centered and privileged position in Western culture, and affirms the exclusion of women from the center of the art form.

Yet we still have to question the assumption that reception is most valid in written form. Certainly for canon formation and for the study of history as presently practiced the absence of written evidence is a drawback. What can we use for evidence of a given practice in the past? How can we assemble material to study the assumptions and expectations of audiences in the past? There are several possibilities. We can look to other kinds of documents for source material, e.g. memoirs, diaries, and letters. These tell of experiences that escape the filters of professional music criticism. Activity in the home, the school, and other informal areas of musical life may find a place here. Other kinds of documents may also prove useful, such as household accounts. One practical problem, however, is that they may not be preserved, especially in middle- or lower-class contexts. But one advantage of informal documents is that they may illuminate the contributions of women as listeners in music. I do not mean as an individual respondent who happens to be a woman, but as a member of an interpretive community of women.

The notion of an interpretive community brings us to the second consideration laid out above: how women react to music. We have to define this carefully. Women have been part of mixed audiences and women-only audiences. As members of the former, women have participated in the public structures of art music and probably reacted much like any member of their class and environment. What I mean is that common aesthetic socialization suggests that women as a group do not exert any significant impact in processes of reception based upon the fact of essential traits specific to the group women. A given woman, of course, may respond in some way that pertains to her gender, but women in the mixed audience do not usually constitute an interpretive community that is necessarily marked off from the audience as a whole.

But in structures where women comprise the entire audience the situation may be different. Here we may be able to speak of an interpretive community that affects reception. This is because such communities have been cohesive and have established their own traditions and practices. Whether it be for teaching or entertainment, or the parlor or the music club, female interpretive communities have typically operated outside the mainstream and beyond the reach of the professional critic. Their activities may not be chronicled in the prestigious organs for art music, but there are other sources that can provide information. In addition to the kinds of personal documents listed above, there have been magazines devoted to women's activities. The long-lived *Etude*, for example (1896–1957), provides insight into the pedagogical and sociological aspects of the piano. *Etude* was aimed at female practitioners of all kinds, including teachers and performers, and embraces the mostly all-female audiences that were involved in these structures.

But despite the insights to be gained from such channels, there may still be recesses of female reception that are beyond the reach of written material. For instance, ultimately we may not know a great deal about the reception of Chaminade's character pieces among female audiences in France. We might be able to discover how many copies of a given piece were sold and draw inferences accordingly. But for clues to the affective and evaluative implications of this music for women we may be left with only bits and pieces of information. This is where oral evidence could be extremely important. But we face an obvious problem: how can we recapture oral history? In certain musical traditions this can occur through the oral chain that passes information from one generation to the next. But in the Western art tradition we cannot depend on this process because it does not characterize the main way that music has been preserved. We know of cases where a pedagogical technique or personal reminiscence has been passed on orally, as in the performance tradition handed down by the students of Franz Liszt; or instances where an oral tradition is later written down. When this happens we have a kind of hybrid record. In the end this may not be too dissimilar from the materiality of a taped version of oral testimony.

But my aim is not to focus on format. What is significant for canonicity is that reliance on formal reception for how music has been received represents a partial view of actual practice. For women as interpretive communities we may need to find other ways to discover their contributions to music. We must not conclude from an absence of formal reception that some practice did not exist or was not important. It may not have been important in terms of the paradigms of the professional world of public music but it may have been significant for other kinds of structures. And many of these involved women, as practitioners and as respondents. The canon represents the world of art music as culled from the typical path of creativity to evaluation. We should recognize its partiality and the ongoing efforts to preserve it through certain patterns of reception.

CHAPTER 6

The canon in practice

Chapters two through five have explored aspects and assumptions of canon formation in the Western art tradition that have had significant impact on women composers and their music. While the ordering of the chapters might suggest a linear progression, we have noted that several elements resist such a unitary model and instead imply multi-positionality. For example, the supposedly diachronic succession between creativity and reception actually turns out to be a multi-dimensioned relationship; beginning and end points do not exist. Yet the ordering of the chapters in some sense reflects what could be proffered as a sketch of stages on the way to canonicity.

Simply put, a work first has to be composed, then circulated, then reviewed. Of course, each of these steps implies a host of other factors that play important roles in various ways. For example, recognition and nurturing of talent to at least some extent are necessary. In addition, sound musical education serves as a desirable and probably necessary foundation behind a work that might reach the publication stage. We should recall that women have had to work "against the grain," to use Barthes's term, to gain credibility as potential creators. Many were denied access to education that supported and helped perpetuate the kinds of music that were most valued by the musical establishment. The next stage, circulation, involves publication and performance, especially repeat performance; these steps keep the work alive for potential canonic membership. Exceptions, of course, have occurred, as in the case mentioned earlier, Schubert's Symphony No. 9 in C. Attention in print comes next. Written recognition validates the worth of the work, prompts its repetition in performative and written forms, and eventually instills it as a norm or part of a larger norm – hence as a generator of similar exemplars.

This path seems fairly obvious. But as we have seen, many of the signposts contain hidden codes and assumptions. These underlay modes of relationality between women and the social fabric that can be different from those for men, i.e. categories such as causality, spatiality, temporality, and hierarchy. In my attempts to highlight the nature of these relationships certain theoretical frameworks have become thematic, almost paradigmatic. Somewhat surprisingly, they recur in discussions of diverse issues. Somewhat unsurprisingly, however, many replicate familiar themes in feminist theory and suggest that the seemingly disparate issues have more in common than would seem at first glance.

Issues of identity form a significant focus of the study. Many times I have asked "Who is ... ?", for example in attempting to describe the identity of a female listener (Chapter 5). Identity has assumed two forms: a woman's sense of her own identity, and a societal sense of woman's individual and collective identity. These might coincide or, more likely, differ to some extent. Identity figures prominently as a central issue in Western women's relationship with creativity and serves as a prime reason for a woman composer's desire and need for female creative traditions (Chapter 2). In the professional arena, at least partly in response to rather fixed societal notions of female identity, the adoption of pseudonyms bespeaks a woman's flexible yet contradictory sense of her identity (Chapter 3). Such objectification often situates her in a different subject position from that of a man. More generally, the concept of subject position offers an extremely valuable analytical tool for revealing how women have fared and functioned within male society. This is especially pertinent *vis-à-vis* dominant ideologies, male musical traditions, audiences, critics, gendered compositional codes, and their own pieces. Subject positions vary with the individual and within the individual. The relative weight of the determining factors can shift kaleidoscopically. Shunning fixity, subject positions tend to be dynamic, interactive, responsive, and flexible. For example, as discussed in Chapter 4, a composer can inhabit a range of positions on the insider–outsider spectrum, and can even be inside and outside at the same time.

While extremely powerful as a practical strategy, such dividedness can produce feelings of contradiction, another thematic element. The principal basis for contradiction is women's socialization in male conventions. Conflict arises when a woman has to identify against aspects of her woman-ness, which she does because of the strong pull of her socialization and its internalized values: what Judith Fetterley has termed "immasculation."[1] The notion of multiplicity also permeates many discussions. For example, the female listener might evince multiple subjectivity within the experience of perceiving a piece of music. A sense of movement characterizes other themes. For one, processes and conceptions tend to be dynamic rather than fixed, as in those concerned with reception/response (Chapter 5). For another, Nancy Chodorow's ideas on women's socialized proclivities emphasize structures of connectedness and continuity. A sense of movement lies behind the dynamics of many of the strategies that musical women have devised to negotiate their contradictory and multiple positions within male society. Resistance is one of the strategies I discussed in terms of the first movement of Chaminade's *Piano Sonata*.

Another thematic cluster centers on categorization. Binary oppositions are often harmful, and other modelings have been suggested. These include a continuum, a circle, and more complex structures such as three-dimensional designs and non-linear and non-vectored movement. Hierarchy typifies many binary oppositions, as in public–private, larger–smaller, and art–popular. It also characterizes the semiotics of some musical conventions, as in the tonal and gendered hierarchies of sonata form. Another categorical theme concerns large concepts that reveal significant problems when interrogated with new questions from new social positioning. Two major examples are professionalism and the *salon* (Chapter 3). I also critiqued the validity of some broad-based assumptions, for example the notion of the "centered author" (a term I never actually used) in my discussion of the author-function (Chapter 3).

In sum, what the arguments in the preceding chapters demonstrate is that Western women individually and collectively intersect with canonicity from different cultural perspectives from men. While this is a broad generalization that invites exceptions, it nonetheless sets us on a path toward making some final remarks about feasible modelings for women and canonicity. This is the main thrust of the chapter. Returning to some of the topics aired in Chapter 1, the first section briefly explores institutions of power in canon formation. The next section, occupying the lion's share of the chapter, focuses on canonic modelings and music by women in terms of the university music-history curriculum. Emphasizing historiographic possibilities and the realities of university pedagogy, the discussion brings together and often re-interprets many of the issues introduced earlier. The arguments center on three issues. The first concerns greatness and includes a discussion of valuation. The second is a critique of periodization and related aspects of chronological organization. The third proposes curricular models for music by women.

The third major section of the chapter explores the importance of women in structures associated with canonicity in music. And finally, akin to a coda, I comment on the usefulness and validity of canons. Canons are flawed, imperialistic, and power hungry: is it time to get rid of them? Perhaps by the end of the book there will be a more informed basis on which to make a decision.

INSTITUTIONS OF POWER IN CANON FORMATION

Canon formation is a complex process that exerts great power in shaping and perpetuating attitudes toward valuation and hence what gets enshrined as masterpieces. It includes performing organizations and personnel, critics, the publishing and recording industries, the academy, the musicological community, the public, and foundations and government agencies. Hardly synchronic, canon formation represents a dynamic process that builds on social and aesthetic belief systems of the past: not merely from when a piece originated but rather from the time before its composition to its preservation afterward, through the present. In this regard the Gadamer–Jauss notions of historical dialectics offer a helpful model.[2] In more tangible form, certain activities provide the visibility that represents and contributes to canonic status. Most obvious is what is performed and re-performed. This has a close relationship with other structures – for example the awarding of prizes, which in turn can lead to commissions. The career of contemporary composer Ellen Zwilich (b. 1939), for example, took flight after she won the Pulitzer Prize in 1983, for her Symphony No. 1. Today she counts as one of the most successful American composers, man or woman, and is able to make a living through commissions as a free-lance composer. Being anthologized and written about also function as signs of approval.

How one gets to that stage of recognition, however, is complicated. As I have argued, the formative processes are far from neutral and reflect cultural biases that have informed Western society. Gender figures prominently in the social relationships that underlie these processes. As Jane Tompkins demonstrates, received wisdom on the status of a given author can have more to do with fortuitous coincidence than intrinsic value.[3] Tompkins is not saying that authors considered canonic do not merit inclusion in the canon. What she is claiming is that previously respected names have often slipped into disfavor because of extraneous factors, and that value is an elusive notion that requires historical context for a fuller understanding of its meaning. Tompkins also discloses how the social relationships involved in the promotion of an author play a significant role in preservation.

The critic wields considerable power. This power derives not only from the message itself but from the asymmetrical position the critic occupies in relation to the work of art – one of subject to object – and from the ambiguous constituency the critic represents. For whom is the critic speaking?[4] The critic, who overwhelmingly has been male, may have a narcissistic need to mirror himself in the discourse of his critiques. This strong intrusion of ego suggests a masculinist attitude. It also means that such desires cannot be fulfilled as easily when the object of critique is female or created by a female: reflective identification is frustrated.[5] In this regard it is interesting to recall that many a male composer has functioned in the dual role of composer–critic. One need only recall Schumann, Berlioz, Wagner, Stravinsky, Schoenberg, Copland, or Virgil Thompson. Women have rarely enjoyed that outlet (Ethel Smyth is a notable exception). For the composer, the journalistic pen may not only have reinforced narcissistic desires, but practically speaking confirmed one's own aesthetics and thereby increased the possibility for acceptance and perpetuation of the values encoded in his music. Even when the male composer has not written for the public he might still enjoy the advantages of media coverage because of gender congruity with the critic.

Performance structures are major players in canon formation and linked with critics and publication. For example, how many times would orchestras play a work denounced by critics and rejected by publishers? The performer becomes a focus of interest. Does the performer exert power in canon formation, or do we have to move to the more organizational level of performance, such as conductor, impresario, or board member?[6] It would seem that the soloist, particularly the piano or vocal recitalist, has much greater autonomy and hence greater power. Yet I would suspect that the institutional and financial constraints on the average soloist are considerable and probably preclude the kinds of canonic power one might expect in an individual. Soloists of the stature of a James Galway or Itzhak Perlman, however, probably wield enormous power. I also wonder about the relative weight of a performer's ability to create and reflect attitudes about canonicity.[7]

Canonicity has a lot to do with tangible documents. As mentioned in Chapter 1, recordings as well as texted media belong to that category. Recordings preserve aural renditions that are repeatable and can themselves become canonic. Although a recorded rendition plays out in time, just like a live performance, it can be physically held or accessed, just like most texted media. This physical property has made recordings a marketable commodity distributed to various publics. As such, recordings have become an important means for audiences to get acquainted with compositions and their authors. Thus their enormous canonic power. The cultural power of recordings is especially strong for composers and works newly rescued from historical oblivion. For example, although the revival of interest in Clara Schumann and Fanny Hensel began with a few recordings and written treatments, the spate of recent music editions has gone a long way toward making these figures the "doyennes" of Western women composers. On a practical level, of course, it is difficult to produce recordings without the availability of printed music, especially modern editions. One or two recordings might emanate under more difficult circumstances, but the widespread issuing of works of a given figure would probably not happen. For Hensel the Mendelssohn-Archiv in Berlin has only recently begun to grant permission for microfilm duplication of unpublished works, and thus modern editions are now possible. These unpublished works are also being recorded, and they help strengthen the "author function" property of Hensel.

The academy and the field of musicology are interrelated structures with considerable power in canon formation. Immersed in received value systems, scholars, who are typically academics, make choices on whom and what to study, and which pieces to analyze and to prepare for publication. These decisions are shaped largely by disciplinary traditions, which also fashion the decorum on *how* topics are studied.[8] Scholarly behavior is also influenced by a sense of what is likely to be published and where. Through experience musicologists discern the goals and preferences of the possible outlets. If a given scholarly work is published and successfully distributed, it might well spur similar kinds of studies or generate further work on the topic. This can influence other scholars, graduate students, and the kinds of courses and the way they are taught at their own institution. As a teacher at the university level, the musicologist wields considerable power in imparting a sense of music as an art form with a past and a future. This is a huge challenge and responsibility. Preparation for the task not only calls for knowledge of bare facts but a feeling for the social, cultural, and aesthetic implications of music. Hopefully, musical characteristics such as sensitivity, a good ear, and performing ability are also present. Fortunately, graduate programs in musicology are broadening their curricula by incorporating pertinent methodologies from interdisciplinary theory.[9] These provide important tools for placing music within the larger cultural fabric.

The profession and the academy also have a lot at stake in the canon.[10] The canon, for example, helps to define the field of musicology. The kinds of works valued by the discipline reveal its goals and the way musicologists wish to define themselves professionally. The emphasis on the European art tradition and on works by male composers of the past reveals a desire to be associated with practices cultivated by the rich and powerful of the past. The professional definition is not only meaningful for practitioners but also serves to represent the field to other segments of the musical community and other disciplines.

The canon organizes subject matter within the discipline and simultaneously represents the organization of that material. It implies boundaries and provides relational links among the categories and paradigms developed over time. It helps to regulate the research of musicologists: what is studied, how it is studied, and how it is structured for presentation to others. These parameters are dependent on value systems that have grown up with the canon and go on to structure subsequent research. Canonic works and composers have been privileged in publications and conferences. One of the advantages of a body of preferences is that it gives the discipline a sense of shared knowledge: a commonality on which to build community, communication, and identity. It means that when one reads a journal or attends an annual meeting, one has a sense of what to expect and feels relatively confident of grasping the main points of someone's research, even if it lies outside one's expertise. If one went to an anthropology conference, in contrast, one would feel quite differently. Of course, some of the familiarity within musicology comes from knowing the disciplinary customs. But I would suggest that the content – the canon – and its cultural implications shape the customs to such a degree that it can be difficult to conceive of them as separate entities.

Yet the benefits afforded by the canon from shared structures do not necessarily mean that the profession is unified in its outlook. While a central metaphor, a canon in any field can hide ruptures or departures from disciplinary custom. In the case of musicology, a clear transitional phase is underway, such that it is difficult to speak of unity.[11] The positivist paradigms in place since the late nineteenth century are being challenged by a more pluralistic approach to research. The canon is of course centrally implicated in this crisis of identity. Like many effects of postmodernism, there is a kind of splintering into methodological multiplicity that challenges the authority of the received wisdoms associated with the European art-music tradition. This means that the tacit assumption of the canon as a vehicle of central control may be in jeopardy. As might be expected, a chink in the armor of the central metaphor can be threatening. It can seriously affect the identity of practitioners and their sense of what being a researcher means: what one studies, how one conducts research, and how one thinks about music in general. It can have political consequences as well. Canonic challenge can affect power structures in the field, for example who gets published by what press, who sits on editorial boards of which journal, and who gets elected to the Board of the professional society. On a personal level it can have profound consequences on a career. Should there be a sea change away from doing editions, for example, someone who still does that work could be evaluated negatively for tenure and promotion. Indeed, this may already be underway in academia. One has the impression that some universities, at least, are beginning to judge musicologists like humanists in other fields. They expect "cutting-edge" critical work and look with disfavor on positivist work.

Given the high stakes, it is not surprising that in many fields the canon is coming to represent a struggle among competing communities. Musicology is only now experiencing that process to any significant degree, having taken its belated cue from the field of literature. The extensive work beginning in the 1980s on women composers and their music, joined with the more recent interest in feminist methodology, has suggested an expanded field of study from that implied by the traditional canon. This is starting to trigger some serious reaction, as gauged, for example, by the recent article by Pieter van den Toorn in *The Journal of Musicology* and its response by Ruth Solie.[12] It is quite unusual for a musicological journal to print a full-fledged article in direct response to an article in a preceding issue. More likely there will be a response as a letter to the editor or a communication in the back of the journal. But what makes the pair even more extraordinary is that discourse is located well beyond "proper" musicological subjects of study: it embraces the personal and its relationship with the discipline. This is not an argument about objective phenomena like *musica ficta* in the fifteenth century or *notes inégales* in the seventeenth. It is a controversy about the implications of an expanded definition of the discipline, and this comes about at least partly from a reconceptualization of the meaning of the canon. We can expect a lot more controversy over the canon in the coming years.

For musicologists there is also a lot at stake in the canon as it functions in the academy. As John Guillory observes, "In teaching the canon, we are not only investing a set of texts with authority; we are equally instituting the authority of the teaching profession."[13] Once the canon has been formed – an ongoing process rather than some *fait accompli* – its prestige spills over into all who deal with it. This of course further perpetuates its authority. The validation of the professoriate reminds me of the validation of the professional music critic through the eminence accorded the formal criticism of art music (see Chapter 5). Both professions utilize the canon, and both become more prestigious through association with the canon. This has nothing to do with ulterior motives in specific cases. It is, rather, a comment on the cultural dynamics of the canon and its effect on the musical communities that participate in the Western art tradition.

The canon provides a basis for commonalities in the university curriculum. Canonic debates in literature have sent ripples through the academic community at large because of the central position that literature occupies in intellectual discourse. Literature has come to mean much more than fiction and includes areas of prime concern to Western civilization, including philosophy, religion, political science, and history. Canonic struggles in literature, therefore, often engage the university community as a whole and become power struggles of the first magnitude. With music we are not talking about matters of prime concern to the institution as a whole, although the conception of a canon in music means a great deal more than a mere list of compositions in some subsidiary discipline. But we are talking about the kind of shared tradition and knowledge discussed above in terms of the profession. The canon can standardize pedagogic practices within a department or school and produce a common body of knowledge among all the students who pass through the curriculum. Standardization also spills across institutional boundaries. This means that a student from "Y" university will have much the same historical foundation as a student from "Z" university. Granted that this is a questionable advantage and granted that there will be considerable variation in responses of teachers and students to the same material, still the canon represents a shared source of knowledge and experience. This can provide a basis for aesthetic exchange on the societal level. Widespread adoption of a given textbook and score anthology can further promote standardization.

As demonstrated in this study, gender functions as a major component of the social structures that affect the performance and historiography of music. But in practical terms, how does gender translate into the repertorial canon of the university curriculum? How do women and their works figure in what is taught and how it is taught? What kinds of canonic modelings would negotiate more successfully the mostly all-male canon currently in place and the implications of gender and the music of women? These fundamental questions form the basis of the next section, which begins with a critique of some of the current paradigms of music-history pedagogy.

CANONIC MODELINGS AND TEACHING

As of the early 1990s, the teaching of undergraduate music history in the university, at least in the United States, typically emphasizes the study of style in Western art music, in chronological order. Donald J. Grout's *A History of Western Music*, which first appeared in 1960 (4th ed. 1988), has played a major role in structuring that emphasis and assisting in its standardization. Proceeding chronologically from the

Greeks to roughly the present, Grout's *History* charts music history mainly through style: the significant stylistic aspects of significant musical works of significant composers. The narration proceeds in tandem with scores and recordings, and these provide a more direct acquaintance with the composition. A wealth of formats is possible within this basic approach, such as multi-media technology and live performance. Typical of its genre, Grout's *History* is organized in discrete chapters. These mirror accepted categories in musicological culture at large.

Are canonic choices in teaching finite? When teaching a survey course, for example, does the addition of "non-canonic" works mean the elimination of something previously present? Is it a matter of numbers or of paradigms? Does the model resemble something like the economic fear of native workers over displacement by immigrants, or the theory that new workers actually benefit everyone by expanding labor markets through creation of new jobs? When preparing a syllabus, one certainly makes choices regarding specific pieces or styles. And it would seem that if a new work is introduced then something old would have to be replaced. But that reasoning presupposes allotting the new work the same amount of time as the replaced work, and also keeping the time of the other works constant. But as I will argue later in the chapter, the incorporation of previously non-canonic works will probably modify many of the relationships among all the repertorial examples being used and this does not equate with elimination. Thus pedagogical canonicity can be elastic; new members enrich rather than replace.

The paradigms of "great composers," "great pieces"

The emphasis on style typically takes place within a framework of "great composers" and "great pieces," especially for later music. The significance of the composer as a category and a sign is often reflected in textbook organization. In Grout, for example, an entire chapter is devoted to one composer, "Beethoven"; another to Haydn and Mozart; and another to Rameau, Vivaldi, Bach, and Handel.[14] Other kinds of categories are prominent, especially organizing periods such as "Baroque era" or "Romantic era" and compositional classifications such as genres. Expectedly, certain style characteristics have become canonic, and these will vary from era to era, according to consensus on the era's distinguishing characteristics.

The "great composer" model – in reality the "great man" model – is a legacy from the nineteenth century and its idealization of the composer as a divinely inspired genius.[15] As discussed earlier, this was the period in which historicism began to flourish and influential biographies of past figures were written. The emphasis on the individual creator reflected societal respect for individual achievement, including economic fulfillment in a climate of free enterprise. In music, secularization and the rise of a public that functioned as a kind of collective patron probably provided a strong reason for the composer to make himself known as a separate persona and gain the attention of the public. As historicism gained a stronger hold and names from the past emerged, the composer began to see himself in terms of those individuals, in some sort of lineage.[16] History books written in the nineteenth century stressed individuals and their creative prowess. We have inherited that tradition, although the rhetoric has been objectified through the filters of modernism. Furthermore, the "great man" model presupposes a sharp division among the components that make up musical experience. Semiotically the great composer stands above and apart from the performer, the audience, and the critic. As J. Michèle Edwards and others have urged, we must dismantle those divisions and construct more interactive models.[17] To phrase it another way, the concept of the composer as a transcendent figure, removed from the dynamic, multiple processes of musical experience, must be modified. This is in line with my reasoning behind the need for a partial de-centering of the author and the author-function as understood in the West (Chapter 3). But what of the idea of the "great woman"? Might this not be an effective antidote to the invisibility of musical women from the Western canon? This will be discussed later.

The "great pieces" paradigm, underlying the notion of anthologized works, exerts tremendous power. A tacit assumption is that anthologized works embody high quality and exemplify the important stylistic and historical points that students should know. In varying proportions, each composition is deemed significant in its own right and representative of other works of like-minded values. Furthermore, inclusion implies that its composer as an individual and as part of the diachronic succession delineated via the other exemplars merits historical recognition. It suggests that the work and composer exemplify a style that influenced others; for works after 1800 add innovative and original.[18] But what of the pieces and composers who are not anthologized, not discussed in textbooks? Does this mean that they are of lesser quality, less "history worthy"? Does the fact that pieces have not survived, as is the case with numerous compositions by women, indicate lesser worth?[19] We might assume that if we have not heard of certain works or composers it means they have not endured because of deficient quality. They have failed the "test of time."

The phrase "test of time" connotes endurance: that a work withstands the vicissitudes of changing tastes over time because of its quality and universality. The paradigm operates under the assumption that the mechanisms that confer value are rational, high-minded, and focused exclusively on the inherent properties of the work. Like the classical theory of the *laissez-faire* economy, the model ignores constraints of a political, economic, or social nature. But the kinds of valuation involved in canon formation include social constraints, and many of those concerned with gender have been aired in previous chapters. They include negative stereotypes for women and creativity (Chapter 2), problematic notions of professionalism and of what public and private mean (Chapter 3), and the widely held assumption that music and the experiencing of music are gender-neutral (Chapters 4 and 5). Canonicity replicates and enshrines many of the values of a dominant cultural group. In the case of Western art music, where canonicity grew out of repertories formed in the nineteenth century amid emerging historicism, canonic values pertain most directly to values of middle- to upper-class white males. These groups were key participants in the new public structures that replaced the patronage of the aristocracy and Church.

The ideology of personal transcendence and its counterpart in political expansionism were mirrored in certain evaluative criteria in music: an exaltation of the persona of the composer; an emphasis on originality and innovation; a preference for the large over the small – in length, performing forces, and performing location; and recognition of the signs of participation in the public arena – professionalism, publication, reviews. These paradigms are socially contingent, not natural and universal. Furthermore, like canonic processes in general, they were absorbed and passed on. Soon they confirmed themselves retrospectively and actively created and affirmed value as new works and new eras ensued. Seen in this light the "test of time" represents the passing down of partial, biased, and socially contingent value systems that tend to replicate themselves, with modifications. It is not a question of a work's ability to withstand the onslaught of differing interpretations. Rather it is a question of differing ontologies of a work: the qualities valued in one era create one kind of work, and those valued in another era fashion another work.[20] Each ontology does different cultural work, and each must be considered within its particular historical context. Thus universality and timelessness are not inherent in the work. This does not mean that works in the canon do not necessarily merit inclusion, nor does it mean that there is no aesthetic basis for judgment. What it does mean is that we cannot ignore the importance of social context in the creation of value.

This brings us to works that are not canonic: what does the preceding imply about them? First there are works that were never published and thus well outside canonic borders. Given the partiality and biases surrounding publication, we have to resist the idea that if a work has not survived it cannot be any good. Another consideration is that certain kinds of works, such as improvisations or orally transmitted works, will not fit the model of permanence. Yet this bias is fundamental to Western canon formation. Second, there are those works with differing aims, such as utilitarian pieces written for children or for entertainment in mostly-female salons. Although published, many traveled different routes of circulation and eluded the pre-canonic track. There are also other conventions that one could cite. But whatever the particular circumstances, the contingent property of valuation means that a work has to be considered in terms of its social context.

After this analysis of the criterion of excellence one might infer that valuation has been reduced to meaningless relativism. Relativism might have a role to play but not in the ways one might expect. Recognition of the importance of social context in the formation of value does not mean that one work is as good (or bad) as another and that there are no qualitative differences that one can make between them. An individual, for example, makes choices based on preferences among aesthetic criteria. The bases for those choices can be varied. They can be based on cultural training or musical training; they can be based on inculcated notions of beauty or what is deemed worthy within the particular culture. These are not universal criteria. A lower-caste person in India, for example, might see little worthwhile in a Beethoven symphony or a Verdi opera. Of course, the ordering of preferences can vary from individual to individual within a culture. This could pose a theoretical problem for someone who holds firmly to a theory of valuational consensus – that the ordering of preferences must be uniform across a culture in order to be valid. But even within consensus there will be variation; it is a question of degree. The important point, however, is that qualitative distinctions are being made. Furthermore, consensus need not be a foundation for valuation, although traditionalists believe that consensus represents a fundamental characteristic of a canon.[21]

Another possible basis for valuation is consideration of a work in relation to how successfully it fulfills its purposes in comparison to like-minded works. Determining what the purposes are, of course, is difficult and involves many acts of judgment. Purpose seems to imply function, but it could also include aesthetic matters. For example, a seemingly functionless piece like a Chopin nocturne could be compared to other character pieces as to how well it sustains tension in its melodic contour. Historical remoteness could complicate the process, for distance means greater difficulty in discovering the original context of the work.[22] But awareness of that difficulty itself acts as an advantage; one will have increased sensitivity to the necessary intrusion of one's prejudices and biases.[23] The Gadamer–Jauss theories of the "hermeneutic circle" and the "horizons of expectation" can assist in bridging the gap.

Ultimately, however, one will probably have to negotiate some slippery slopes in the quest for meaningful valuation. Some feminists have put forward a rather extreme theory in which ranking itself is deemed patriarchal and therefore invalid. They argue that the creative work should be accepted for what it is: a product of a subject's creativity, to be valued for itself, without comparisons.[24] While the democratic implication is potentially attractive, the theory is not practicable as soon as one faces real situations, which inevitably involve choices. One has to sort out alternatives and make preferences. The bases for the choices, however, are variable, and this is where valuation becomes tricky.[25] But even if difficult to conceptualize and articulate, theories of valuation must come to grips with real situations.

While I have emphasized the role of social contingency in canon formation, it is critical to explore its relationship to valuation in greater detail. In the battles over the canon, valuation has been a hotly contested issue. Traditionalists, especially, consider it the heart of the disputes about canonicity. For them one of the main functions of a canon is to uphold standards and maintain quality. They claim that those who attack the canon or desire its elimination are not able to devise satisfactory alternatives that preserve this basic function of a canon. The other side, however, questions the claims put on quality in terms of how one defines quality and whether quality ultimately is critical as a defining property of a canonic work.

There are several key issues in the debates, some of which we have already mentioned. One is the relative importance of value in terms of the community and the individual: a desire for consensus versus a desire for individual authority in the determination and relevance of value. Another is the tension between a desire for absolute standards of value and a recognition that value grows out of socio-historical context – what Guillory terms intrinsic and extrinsic value.[26] While all but the most extreme partisans in the debates acknowledge that context shapes criteria for value, the question becomes to what extent that claim can apply to aesthetic valuation. Charles Altieri makes the perceptive point that there is a sliding scale of contingency.[27] Some expectations and assumptions derived from social context will be relatively short-lived while others may remain in force longer because they are more embedded in culture. He suggests that these be distinguished from each other. I sense that he believes the long-lived conventions resemble what others call "absolute" standards. Because the rate of change is virtually invisible and the relationship to context apparently so tenuous, such aesthetic criteria appear to be timeless, universal, and absolute. The third issue concerns value itself and the meanings ascribed to it. There is a great deal of confusion because value sometimes connotes quality, and sometimes content or other referential properties implied by the work. For the traditionalists value denotes quality and aesthetic valuation; for the liberals it is more pertinent to social content/context or other semiotic reference. The question becomes whether quality must be the prime characteristic of a canonic work, or whether other kinds of value are as important or even more important.

But while the debates seem to center around quality – whether a work meets certain standards, and how works are ranked relative to each other – the issue of valuation involves more. It suggests that issues of identity are at stake: who and what one wants to identify with in the past. The so-called "great" works imply certain values and an individual might want to bask in those ideals as well. An association with quality also suggests a certain moral authority that infuses the modern practitioner. Quality touches on desires of the present in relation to the past, and these assume some interesting forms. On the one hand, many see the present canon as a needed corrective to the past. On the other, some consider the past a needed corrective to the present and to the modern canon. Each can serve the needs of both sides of the canon debate. Adherents see the modern canon as a mechanism for capturing the best from the past and presenting it in its best light. They also look fondly to the glories of the past and see its preservation as a corrective to the ills of modern society. For detractors (or "canon-busters," according to Gerald Graff), the modern canon can rectify the past by recouping its forgotten works, particularly those of marginalized groups like women and minorities. Similarly, the new insights into diverse practices of the past help to correct modern notions of history and demonstrate that plurality should be emphasized in the present.

Although I have discussed many of the complexities of valuation, I have only summarized some of the major points. The rhetoric on the canon has become a genre in its own right and no one has "solved" the difficulties and contradictions surrounding valuation and context. My arguments suggest that I consider socio-historical contingency a major source of value, both aesthetic and otherwise. Yet contingency may not be able to account for certain kinds of aesthetic judgments, and it is here that we enter a grey area that cannot be easily solved. At this point we might do well to consider the practical approach of Gerald Graff.[28] He recognizes the gap between the two sides in the canon debate but comes to an interesting conclusion. Instead of choosing one side or the other, let's "teach the conflict." This aesthetic of contradiction has the distinct advantage of showing students that history is a construction, with considerable complexity. Understanding the factors behind each position is the key, as students become participants rather than onlookers in the debate. It can foster the kinds of creative thinking that will stand students in good stead throughout their lives. This attractive idea need not be confined to teaching, of course. An aesthetic of contradiction can infuse other forms of musicological activity, for example research. It ties in with many of the feminist positions described in this study and emphasizes process and possibility over fixity. It also underscores difference as a valid and significant cultural position.

Considerations of value are central to the paradigms of "great composers, great pieces.'' But there are other paradigms that underlie the pedagogical practices involved in the reification of the masterwork. Often unarticulated, the concept of influence structures a great deal of who and what are emphasized. Influence generally takes the form of stylistic influence: similarities traced from a forerunner or contemporary. It usually involves someone considered groundbreaking, whose innovative traits generate ripples throughout the musical community. We tend to concentrate on such an ''influential'' figure and his style, especially if canonic value has been placed in this kind of music. Beethoven and his instrumental music are a prime example. But the concept invites further thought. For example, assuming one accepts the notion of individual influence, how does influence get passed on? Personal acquaintance or widespread dissemination of one's work probably counts the most. But perhaps the model is more specific to the male composer, less pertinent to the female composer. For a line of personal acquaintance presupposes networks of colleagues. But for the female composer prior to the twentieth century, creative isolation was a real possibility. Influence suggests the assumption of lineage: that one is part of a discernible tradition. Yet the female composer might feel like an outsider and not think of herself as a link in a structure of influence. She might also resist the temptation to be innovative and stand out; patterns of socialization predicated on community and conformity might guide such a response.[29] As implied, I see influence bound up with the notions of innovation and originality, desiderata that rose to prominence in the nineteenth century and have become canonic. They pepper critical language, both in popular and scholarly venues, and play a significant role in what is emphasized in the teaching of music history. A related concept is the notion of genius, another Romantic construction that characterizes the semiotics of music.[30]

An interesting variation on the transcendent ''author-function'' in canon formation is the disparagement of the popular.[31] In this paradigm, composers extremely popular with the public at large are denigrated by musical connoisseurs – in this case, with musical academics. I can recall a few glaring instances of this inversion, which demonstrates the impact of modernism on canonic sensibilities. In the 1960s, for example, Tchaikovsky and Rachmaninoff were considered too accessible to the masses – too ''easy,'' too comfortable, too emotionally explicit – to be taken seriously by real devotees of music history. They were neither innovative nor influential but more like "culinary composers," in the Brechtian sense: too easily digested. Although postmodernism has rehabilitated Tchaikovsky (although perhaps not Rachmaninoff) the phenomenon is revealing. It highlights the elitist desire of the academy to separate itself from the tastes of the masses – Tchaikovsky and Rachmaninoff seen as icons of popular culture. It also displays the tendency of modernism to suppress accessibility in favor of alienation. But now that modernism itself has become passé, ease and accessibility have become acceptable, even valued.[32] The denigration of the popular recalls the historiographic reversals of Cécile Chaminade. Accorded regular press coverage in early career, while a composer of large-scale works, attention waned markedly after she became popular, especially with female audiences and performers. While the contexts do not exactly match, the consequences are nonetheless similar. This kind of inversion has also occurred in the field of literature. Jane Tompkins points out the critical bias against popular literary works, especially those by women. Although a *bona fide* genre in literary criticism, such popular fiction is often considered frivolous and thus cannot qualify for the canon.[33]

Some historical paradigms traditionally on the margins offer attractive possibilities for better reflecting the experiences of women in music. Particularly important is social history, which asks new questions.[34] Social history highlights configurations within and among groups of people. It reconceptualizes notions of what is "history worthy." In fact, the phrase seems irrelevant, as "history worthy" connotes traditional historical entities such as rulers, wars, military power, and geographical boundaries. Social history, however, starts from experiences of a particular group. It pays attention to all classes, not merely the upper echelons, and heeds the experiences of daily life, not only momentous events. For women, a meaningful focus might be their reproductive lives, their social mobility within family structures, their participation in economic structures, their creative activities, or their relationships with religious practice. As a result, the kinds of issues considered important would be quite different from those within more traditional notions of history. Process, interaction, and the personal might be more or at least as important as facts and dates. Historical women in music could benefit from this approach. It begins with women's actual experiences in music rather than some set of preconceived categories that reflect male experience. Social history would tend to lessen the hierarchies between women's activities and the privileged locus of the public arena. In fact, what is now called a division (and a hierarchy) between public and private might diminish in some other conceptualization that focuses on function rather than ranking. This would help to modify notions of professionalism so that they better reflect women's experiences. Social history also has the advantage of highlighting issues of access. Once again, however, the concept might not be called "access" any longer, for that implies some excluded entity that is attempting to enter the more accepted entity. In short, social history promotes breadth and flexibility in its categories and assumptions and thus accommodates a more diverse pool of social experience.

The advantages of social history are reinforced by the flexibility of an interdisciplinary approach, which offers attractive concepts from other fields. From anthropology, for example, the concept of the cultural group can be extremely useful for understanding some of the larger dynamics within society. Economics offers the framework of the market, which can be utilized to show the emergence of music as a public commodity. From sociology one can apply the concept of class and show how it has structured many of the fundamental assumptions we have about musical practice in the past.

Greater cognizance of the performative aspects of music could also be important for women.[35] Performance practice currently ranks as a canonic area of music study. But it has mostly emphasized *what* is performed in terms of the reconstruction of the musical text – the notes, the scoring, the ornaments, the tempo, the number and types of performers. What Jane Bowers and others are advocating is much broader: an ethnomusicological approach that pays greater attention to the sociological nuances that have characterized Western performance. These might include spatial relationships among performers, facial and bodily movement, clothing, and class and gender of the performers; one can extend the analysis to the audience. Such conventions can disclose a great deal about the varied social meanings of performance over time and round out our knowledge of the sorts of activities women were involved in. Performance conventions are particularly important because they reflect and re-construct societal value systems and power relations.[36] As a counter to the traditional emphasis on the composer, the approach reveals that women were quite active in music – much more than traditional histories would suggest. It also underscores the sociological proximity between

composing and performing. Indeed, their separation in the nineteenth century may have had a negative impact on women's status in
music.[37]

Periodization

History is a construction that we build from our values of the present
and our visions of the future.[38] It reflects our desires of what we would
like the past to represent, especially in relation to our identity in the
present. I like to think of the historical past as a vast panorama whose
details are filled in and rearranged according to new insights into
what went on in the past and what is going on in the present. It is a
framework that provides for great flexibility and the potential for
new meanings and relationships among its parts. For some, the parts
themselves or the aesthetic representation of the parts are the
members of the canon. While there is a diversity of opinion on who
the members of the canon should be and what a canon should
represent, many theorists offer an interesting description of the
import of a canon in terms of history. In this conceptualization the
canon becomes a total narrative or "meta narrative" of value,
interpretation, and ideology. Sometimes it is expressed as a large
work of art or one large book. Either way it suggests a kind of
coherence that for many characterizes history. It also implies a
convention whose prestige and power can be as great as history.

A narrative tells a story, and we have been telling many stories of
what the canon is and how it is formed. While the canon is capable
of many stories, one story implied by canon is the idea of history as a
unified whole. There are breaks inserted, in the form of periods, but
these disruptions seem to confirm the coherence of the whole.
Successive periods may introduce difference or contrast but if
anything they strengthen the integrity of the overarching framework.
Let me hasten to add that I do not necessarily subscribe to the notion
of historical unity, at least in the sense of congruity. I mention it here
because it is a fundamental assumption of many significant notions of
history. As Barthes notes, a paradigm of unity can mask ruptures that
represent the dynamics of how society actually operates.

Periodization is an important component of historical organization. The very fact that we classify in particular ways – according
to composers' names, genres, historical periods, functions, countries
– affects in fundamental ways how we structure material and what
kinds of knowledge we want our students to absorb. As Paul Lauter

notes, periods and other cultural classifications "shape significantly the ways in which we think about culture, emphasizing works that fit given frameworks, obscuring those which do not."[39] This means that evaluative and interpretive judgments have already been made; these function as the foundation behind the systems of classification.[40] Even the fact of certain kinds of pedagogical materials – narrative history texts, musical scores, recorded examples – represents the outcome of pre-evaluation on what is important.

Periodization is taken for granted in music history and in other fields as a way of dealing with vast expanses of historical time. Literary theorist Jean Rousset reminds us that modern conceptions of historical periods are just that: modern-day grids and "instruments of research" invented by us that provide "means of investigating" the past. Periods are not the past but only re-constructions of the past.[41] Periodization not only renders history accessible but as Frank Kermode observes, "makes it modern."[42] The criteria that demarcate periods from one another represent modern ideas of the past and what is important in the past. Without an organizing structure based in current values the past could well remain what it really is: temporally distant and foreign. It could keep us away from historical study. For Kermode, therefore, periodization is a necessary convention. But what does periodization mean? Is it equivalent with the notion of organizational categories for history?

In answering these questions we should recall that periodization entails chronology: boundaries placed around blocks of historical time. This seems obvious. But we need to explore how chronology is structured *vis-à-vis* periods. It is also important to consider the placement of boundaries and the names assigned the periods. Such choices are political,[43] and they reflect prevailing ideologies of what is considered important. Certain style traits are admired and become the basis for the archetypal properties of a given epoch. Works that differ tend to be ignored, excluded, and devalued. Thus periodization creates and perpetuates value. It is this canon-like power of periodization that has opened it to criticism. Lauter, for example, points out that periodization emphasizes differences, not continuities, and thus it can obscure certain kinds of historical experience that do not fit the model of contrast.[44] In music, for example, Friedrich Blume has shown how the labels "Classic" and "Romantic" for successive blocks of historical time conceal and distort the continued importance of sonata form in the nineteenth century. For Blume the solution is a larger "Classic-Romantic" era that combines the two.[45] This removes barriers that thwart recognition of an important stylistic commonality – one easily buried in the rhetoric about the innovation and excess of the nineteenth century.

Feminist historians have contributed their voices to the debate. Gerda Lerner and Joan Kelly have each asserted that traditional periodization reflects the history of men, as constructed by men. A history of women calls for new categories, new organization. As Lerner put it, what would history seen from the eyes of women be like?[46] It would probably emphasize social history, with women as primary subject; gender would be a major analytical category. Kelly did important work in showing how traditional historical periods not only make women invisible but frequently distort what was really happening to them. In a famous essay, Kelly demonstrates that women actually fared worse in so-called progressive eras, especially the Renaissance.[47] Similarly, Bonnie Anderson and Judith Zinsser claim that the beginning of the nineteenth century, a time of expanding opportunity for men, was "the nadir" for European women.[48] Thus traditional history and empirical evidence do not always coincide.

Periodization as an appropriate model for women is a complicated issue. One question is how chronology functions in historical organization. Another concerns the labels assigned historical groupings. Can traditional labels be retained for women's history? What are the criteria used to determine where the divisions are made? To answer these important questions I would like to discuss actual histories of women, from various fields.

I consulted five historical treatments of women in music and one each in literature and history. The seven display a range of formats, including prose anthology, score anthology, source anthology, and monograph. Two of the surveys – those edited by Jane Bowers–Judith Tick and James Briscoe – dispense with overarching categorization.[49] Although this can be attributed to the contents of each – the first is comprised of essays on selected topics while the second is a score anthology with brief introductions to each work – I believe that it also bespeaks an awareness that Western women's musical history does not lie comfortably within traditional historical divisions. Even if the editors did not discern direct contradiction, they probably decided that those categories would not strengthen the presentation. It is also interesting that they did not impose new organizing categories. Perhaps each hoped to leave some of the synthesizing to the reader: to challenge the reader, to allow for greater play of the imagination in making connections.

The other five histories utilize large organizing categories. The recent *Women in Music, A History* (Bloomington, 1991), by diverse authors under the editorship of Karin Pendle, has chronological divisions but assigns neutral labels: thus headings such as "Music of women of the 17th and 18th centuries," or "Music of women since 1918." Recognizing that women have participated in diverse musical activities, *Women in Music* includes sections on non-Western music, patronage, and feminist aesthetics. It seems to assume that a chronological approach is still best for a textbook aimed at undergraduates. Although most boundaries coincide with those of traditional periods, the labels medieval, Baroque, etc. are wisely avoided. These terms are deeply ingrained and call to mind traditional music history. This in turn suggests the categories, hierarchies, dualisms, and ideologies that lie behind traditional music history, including the male-dominated canon, and many have excluded women or relegated them to the periphery. Thus retention of these periods can further marginalize women and their music. For example, the Renaissance did not necessarily signal a rebirth of female activity, and placing women in this traditional category only masks the kinds of activities they did do. These include music-making in the courts, which continued through the seventeenth century; and music-making in the Church, which began well before 1400 and continued into the early eighteenth century. The notion of a Classic period for women can also be problematic. Women were active as Lieder composers, for example. But there is slight justification for considering these activities "classic" and imposing an artificial end point of *c.* 1820 when similar activities continued for at least thirty years more. Of course, this chronological problem with Lieder also applies to male composers. But this type of composition assumed a more prominent role in the totality of women's musical activities, and thus inappropriate periodization becomes that much more problematic for them.

The Norton Anthology of Literature by Women (New York, 1985) makes some departures from traditional periodization. As explained by the editors, Sandra Gilbert and Susan Gubar, "though conventional literary periodization does not suit women's literary history, women's history does have significant phases of its own. Thus, we have omitted references to the usual literary 'ages' (i.e., Augustan, Romantic, Victorian) and instead organized our authors by birthdate into six eras."[50] The categories are either bare chronological boundaries or descriptive labels based in aesthetic outlook or historical era: thus "Literature of the 19th century," and "Modernist literature" and "Literature of the Middle Ages and Renaissance." Like the Pendle history, this collection subscribes to chronological organization, perhaps largely for pedagogical purposes, but recognizes the need to avoid traditional labels and boundaries.

In contrast, two other histories reinforce traditional periodization to a much greater degree. *Women in Music: An Anthology of Source Readings from the Middle Ages to the Present*, edited by Carol Neuls-Bates, utilizes the labels medieval through Classic and for the other categories a range of years without labels (e.g. "1820–1920"). While this could be considered a conservative approach, the collection is early (1982) and groundbreaking, and adherence to mainstream periodization was common then. *Source Readings* is also important for its coverage of women as participants in varied areas of music and its emphasis on the sociology behind music-making. Diane Jezic's *Women Composers: The Lost Tradition Found*, a more recent contribution (1988), organizes biographies of twenty-five female composers mostly within traditional era categories.[51] Compared to the other narrative histories, the Jezic is more limited in scope with its straightforward life-and-works treatment of composers. Although the traditional periodization could be criticized, it is nevertheless consistent with the more traditional aims of the volume.

Although labels and points of demarcation may differ or be absent, each of the above books presupposes the primacy of chronological ordering and continuity. The seventh book, *A History of Their Own: Women in Europe* (2 volumes, 1988), by Bonnie Anderson and Judith Zinsser, makes significant departures from that organization and in so doing fashions a magnificent model for the presentation of women's history. With major headings such as "Women of the churches" and "Women of the salons and parlors: Ladies, housewives, and professionals," the study emphasizes function and place as criteria for historical organization. Periodization and chronological boundaries are absent. According to the authors, this kind of organization highlights the commonalities among European women across the centuries, which they found the most striking feature of their research. The situation differs from that of men, "who have been seen as divided by class, nation, or historical era": thus the appropriateness for men of what have come to be the standard conventions of writing history.[52] And because the most striking aspect of how women have been conceptualized in history is the very fact of their being women, gender functions as the major analytical category of the book. But in spite of the absence of chronological divisions *per se*, *A History of Their Own* pays attention to chronology, even if it is incidental. The ordering of the large sections is *roughly* chronological in relative time. Thus sections entitled "Noblewomen of the castles and manors" and "Women in the walled towns," concerned with earlier societies, occur well before "Women in the salons and parlors" and "Women of the cities," which pertain to more recent developments. Nonetheless, within each there can be a wide chronological spread. Furthermore, a wide-ranging chapter such as "Peasant women through the twentieth century," occurring very close to the beginning of volume 1, indicates strong resistance to the temptations of conventional categorization. Expectedly, organization within a section is often unusual. "Women of the cities," for example, begins in literary style, with an anecdotal comparison of the personal experiences of two ordinary women, one in the mid-nineteenth and the other in the mid-twentieth century: atypical "history worthy" figures. The style changes to historical narrative, with broad discussions on sociological trends from 1700 to the present. In sum, the historiographical assumptions underlying this study challenge traditional categories and methods. More importantly, they show how history can be written to reflect more faithfully the lived experiences of women.

The Anderson–Zinsser history raises questions about traditional conventions. I wonder, in particular, about the emphasis on linearity in the study of history. We are so accustomed to think about history in terms of direct succession that it almost seems a contradiction in terms to consider history in which temporal relationship can be more diverse. One does need to "package" the vast amount of material of the past in order to deal with it and make sense of it.[53] But the issue becomes *how* one packages that material, and that proceeds mostly from the values emphasized by the packaging. Traditional chronological organization, in terms of periods, is based on linear continuity that is simultaneously divided into large chronological blocks with specified beginning and end points. The linear continuity implies causal succession: that what comes next grows out of what came before. This succession is intercut with period divisions. Each is supposed to reflect attitudes and conditions that are distinctive enough to be demarcated as a particular period, and as such are different from those of a different period. Thus what we have is one pull toward continuity and wholeness, and another toward rupture and distinctness: an interesting tension. The Anderson–Zinsser approach crosscuts the horizontal tendency with vertical slices. In this way sociological themes rise to the top, like cream, and create their own versions of wholeness and succession. As a result, groups and issues previously obscured by the linearity–periodization model can become more visible, and this in turn suggests new questions and issues.

Linear succession need not occupy such a central position in the study of history. It emphasizes direct outgrowth, causality, and evolution, which suggest a common heritage and a continuous line of descent. It attempts to create a unity by reinforcing a central theme that can be traced in the unfolding of time. The central theme of general history has been political governance; yet women have had little involvement in such structures. In music the preferred central theme of late is the unfolding of style among composers visible in important power structures: the Church, the court, and the public arena. But this leaves out the experiences of most women in music. Furthermore, the direct continuity basic to linear organization can obscure connections that might be temporally remote from each other. For example, linearity could hide the functional similarity between the musical leadership of Hildegard in the convent and Hensel in the *salon*.

In short, history is the study of the past and not necessarily of a linear past. Events take place one after the other but their meaning in relationship with each other can assume many forms. Anderson and Zinsser seem to recognize that for women chronology can serve a function. Chronological placement and reference are present, to be sure, but large-scale understanding comes from relationships that resist linearity and rigid temporal boundaries.

How can the Anderson–Zinsser model be applied to the music of women? At the least, it suggests the avoidance of traditional period names and the creation of new labels. Pendle, for example, utilizes designations of century, a relatively neutral phrase. One could also modify the boundaries of divisions to suit women's experiences in music, as Pendle and others have done. One successful modification in the Pendle is a separate category for the period between *c.* 1880 and the end of World War I. For women composers in Europe, at least, this makes a great deal of sense. It was a period marked by a strong feminist movement, the drive for suffrage, and major advances in birth control. We see the modern woman emerging in figures like Ethel Smyth, Alma Mahler, and Lili Boulanger. To have to place them either in the Romantic period or in the twentieth century represents a distortion. Their confident sense of purpose clearly separates them from forerunners, yet their cultural roots lay in the nineteenth century and one would be hard-pressed to dub them modern figures.

Perhaps the strongest message from Anderson and Zinsser comes from their emphasis on function, place, and class. For music I can imagine fruitful categories such as the following, listed in random order: women in the *salons*, women in the Church, women in the courts, women as patrons, women and the voice, women and the theater, women as music teachers, women and folk traditions, women and jazz, women and reception, etc. Though challenging and time-consuming to plan, such modeling can work quite well in courses on women in music. Indeed, I sense that many courses on women have already utilized such categories but they have not yet had a major impact on disciplinary discourse. But how can such modeling affect historiography for musical traditions of both genders? Does it mean that mainstream music-history texts should get rid of linearity and traditional periodization? In fact, several music appreciation texts pay less attention to linearity and traditional periods than do texts geared to music majors. I will return shortly to a fuller discussion of the negotiation of female and male traditions. But let me say briefly that at the very least, awareness of alternatives and their advantages creates a sensitivity to the fact that the traditional paradigms are partial and constructed, and that other modelings can illuminate other kinds of knowledge. And even if traditional periods are in place, we can still utilize them differently. We might question their names, their boundaries, and their general applicability, and prompt our students to do the same. We might structure syllabi, lectures, discussions, and assignments differently in light of such questions: in effect "teach the conflict." As Gerald Graff notes, students might be better served by learning about the conflicts that go into periodization than merely memorizing the names, boundaries, and style traits of periods.[54]

In concluding this critique I would like to say a few words about general problems in traditional periodization, problems that are independent of modifications impelled by gender. They suggest other compelling reasons to re-think periodization. One difficulty concerns the names themselves and another the boundaries. Many of the labels derive from other fields and have little to do with what they have come to represent in music, for example "Baroque" from art history or "Classic" from German literature. While a label might pertain to some of the characteristics in its time frame, its nominative implications can distort the period as a whole and serve its constituents poorly. Are we comfortable with the attribution of "bizarre" to describe the music of Monteverdi, Corelli, Handel, and Bach? Are Haydn's symphonies more "classic" than Schubert's songs or Brahms's intermezzi? The other difficulty involves the placement of boundaries. When does an era end and another begin? What are the distinguishing characteristics that change to the extent that another era label should take over? These are difficult questions. I think of the problems with the Romantic era, for example. Not only is there the question of where it begins, an issue linked with the problem of how to categorize Beethoven, but difficulties arise in applying the label "Romantic" to the entire century. If one does, there is still the question of where the era ends. Is it at 1900? What about Mahler's later symphonies, Strauss's large operas? What about the so-called anti-Romantic currents, as represented by Debussy well before 1900? Of course, there are always some features that do not fit a particular era division, although the problems here seem to go well beyond expected inconsistencies. And after "Romantic," what are the categories and the boundaries? Is the twentieth century still one big expanse, or has it garnered enough years so that we can discern other divisions, such as "Modernism" and "Postmodernism"? And does a label such as "Twentieth-century music" indicate that we cannot push its characteristics into a Procrustean-like category comparable to the more suggestive names of earlier periods, e.g. Renaissance or Romantic?

Overall, history texts have devised various solutions to many of these problems. Perhaps categorization that pays greater attention to function or some other vertical parameter could alleviate the difficulties. Periodization in general can be an effective tool for approaching the past. But it should remain flexible enough to respond to changing views of the meanings of the past.

A place for women and their music

Music by women has had little if any presence in the canons of Western music. This is not unique to music, and feminists in general have been concerned with proposing ways of negotiating women and their works with existent canons. They have typically focused on the two positions of mainstreaming and separatism: the incorporation of new works into existent canons and the establishment of separate repertories.[55] These are often placed in an either/or and sometimes oppositional relationship. To summarize briefly the main points of each, mainstreaming affords a realistic way of providing visibility and eventually acceptance of previously obscured or lost figures. It integrates women into well-known historical structures and shows how they relate stylistically to male composers and their music. Mainstreaming is premised on the notion that society embraces two genders that partake of common cultural institutions. It tends to unite rather than separate. It avoids a sense of opposition, confrontation, or hierarchy that could result from separate repertories. Advocates of separatism, however, see great advantages in their system, which Lillian Robinson has dubbed a "counter canon."[56] Like the arguments advanced on behalf of women's colleges or black colleges, separatists believe that only through distinct structures can minority interests be preserved against the imperialistic tendencies of the mainstream. They fear that individualism and identity cannot avoid being compromised once their culture is incorporated into established conventions. Separatist repertories promote group identity and distinct traditions. They create a kind of intertextuality among pieces by women; as Virginia Woolf sees it, women's works "continue each other."[57] They allow for a historiography that grows out of the particular characteristics of the group rather than one that is forced to adopt dominant ideologies. But a separate repertory runs the danger of being viewed as marginal or unimportant, and hence ignored, because it lies outside the mainstream. As a practical political strategy, therefore, separatism may be self-defeating. But separatists might respond that since they do not aspire to success in the social mainstream, such supposed political practicality is meaningless and therefore poses few problems.

Separatism and mainstreaming do not spell opposition nor are they necessarily either/or or hierarchical. Yet minority traditions are often constructed as "Other" to more dominant traditions. Philip

Bohlman, for example, has explored the dominance of musicology over ethnomusicology and has shown how the disciplinary canons of ethnomusicology have become "Other" to those of musicology, which tends to annex territory like an imperialistic ruler.[58] Consequently, ethnomusicology must rediscover its own ways and emerge as a strong subject.[59] In an example from another field, the collection *Displacements* discusses empowering strategies that strengthen the subjectivity of what is inherently "Other," namely French literature by women as taught in the United States. Here Otherness is twice-told. First, the repertoire by women stands within a male-saturated canon; second, French literature outside France connotes a kind of exile status. And finally, in a somewhat different inflection on canonic Otherness, Allan Bloom asserts that the passion in Western intellectual life is dependent on the existence of an Other, "closet" tradition for the tensions it will produce with the mainstream. Such tensions are needed for intellectual stimulation and to keep alive the great themes in Western culture. Bloom blames the recent de-stigmatization of taboo traditions for many of the problems in American education.[60]

In the following discussions I would like to offer models that mediate the seeming distance between mainstreaming and separatism. More importantly, however, these ideas amount to practical ways of negotiating music by women and the traditional canon of Western art music. The suggestions pertain most directly to music-history pedagogy at the university level, although the general principles are relevant to other situations as well.[61]

Thus far I have framed mainstreaming and separatism as alternative options. But that exclusive model is much less attractive than the inclusive model that embraces both concepts. It is not a matter of hierarchy; indeed, both offer real advantages. Together they provide the female teacher–student–respondent a perspective of fluidity from/in which to move through the nuances of insider and outsider in relation to the two models.[62] She works two fields, so to speak, and occupies a mobile subject position whose particular location can be dependent on her desires, on what she wants to accomplish. While aware of the importance of studying a discrete female tradition, she is equally aware that, like herself, the historical players and institutions have been socialized to varying degrees in masculine culture. This means not only that a female tradition is inflected with contradictions that may have their basis in patriarchy, but that it cannot be studied entirely divorced from the masculine tradition. I am not implying that a separate female tradition should be collapsed. Rather I am saying that it operates as one of the sights in the "double vision" that the female (and male) student brings to the historical field. The model also applies to other so-called muted cultures, as Henry Louis Gates, Jr. eloquently states in relation to black literature:

It is a question of perspective, a question of emphasis. Just as we can and must cite a black text within the larger American tradition, we can and must cite it within its own tradition, a tradition not defined by a pseudoscience of racial biology, or a mystically shared essence called blackness, but by the repetition and revision of shared themes, topoi and tropes, the call and response of voices, their music and cacophony.[63]

This kind of musicality exists not only within a tradition. It also meanders between the two traditions and resembles interweaving or contrapuntal texture. "A female creator needs to be slotted into the context of male traditions. But to understand what that artist is doing ... she will also have to be located in a separate female pattern that, so to speak, runs through the first in a kind of contrapuntal way."[64] Here Christine Battersby is grounding the counterpoint in *ad hoc* historical traditions. But I would like to suggest counterpoint or interweaving as a metaphor that describes the active processes of relating the two traditions to each other. Flexibility, fluidity, and irregularity characterize the processes, as now one or now another strand can rise in prominence and then fade to the background. The terms also allow for a multiplicity of historical strands. These can obscure a sense of binary opposition between the two traditions and simultaneously suggest a broad spectrum of subtleties between and around them. In addition, the properties of interweaving replicate those associated with subject position. It, too, is flexible, fluid, and irregular in its possibilities for movement to a different location.

But negotiation of two traditions constitutes only one element of a larger two-pronged approach to canonicity. The second is grounded in the practical situation of teaching a music-history survey course that is not devoted specifically to the activities of women. This approach is not necessarily an alternative or addition to the first, but perspective and intent are more fixed and defined. It pertains to the very real situation of teaching music history rooted in the traditional canon. What kinds of practical strategies can be devised to bring in the music of women? Is it merely a matter of having works by women replace works by men and of ending up with a more balanced numerical representation?

While substitution has been an important step toward increasing the visibility of women and their music, it does not go far enough. What happens is that the new work becomes integrated into the canonic pantheon and as such is discussed in the same terms, according to the same paradigms and categories, as works by men. This has the effect of keeping women and their music in an "Other" or peripheral position in relation to the mainstream, which is defined by and based on masculine conventions. It tends to thwart an understanding of women *as women* and of the importance of gender and socialization on how and why music is produced. It assumes universal meanings, responses, and valuation of music. In short, it tends to obliterate difference and social specificity and their importance in understanding music as cultural activity. But the answer to the above difficulties is not necessarily to withdraw to a separatist position and defend the territory. As we saw above, fluid perspective and positioning can negotiate effective interweaving between the two traditions. But within a framework of teaching the inherited tradition, works by women can indeed play an important role. Not only do they introduce new questions for themselves, but they have the very real power of modifying the discourse for the entire canon so that a fuller range of human expression is being represented. Let me give some examples.

In the case of Fanny Hensel, discussed earlier in the study,[65] lack of public visibility and of publications during her lifetime would seem to mean lack of skill. Discussion of mechanisms of professionalism and familial prohibitions would be a good start toward explication and prove interesting to the students. But further analysis of Hensel's situation could lead to important questions about the desirability of publication and permanence, the attractiveness of private modes of creativity for nineteenth-century women, and the general privileging of composition over other kinds of musical activity. These questions could similarly infuse discussions of traditionally canonic composers and works and thereby provide additional frameworks for an understanding of musical practices in the nineteenth century. The second example involves Cécile Chaminade's *Piano Sonata*, discussed in Chapter 4. Following up on the analysis of the first movement in terms of a possible response to the gendered codes of masculine and feminine themes in sonata form, we could apply similar methodology to other examples of sonata form in the nineteenth century, particularly in compositions written by a man. We might speculate on his strategies toward those conventions, which might differ from a woman's and also differ from composer to composer and possibly piece to piece within a given composer. Similarly we might discuss analogous codes of gender, even if unarticulated, in other musical conventions. These explorations would underscore the point that musical structures, while not essentially male or female, can be vehicles for compositional strategies that relate to one's identity and position within society. They also demonstrate the central role that gender plays in music itself.

The third and last example concerns Alma Mahler-Werfel and one of her extraordinary songs, "Ansturm." Composed in 1911 and published as number 3 of the *Vier Lieder* (1915), "Ansturm" could well be one of the earliest works by a woman set to a text on sexual desire and release.[66] Its brilliant musical contrasts would provide fodder enough for lively discussion of style. But arguably its frank expression of forbidden subject matter is much more important and opens the door to larger questions. What did it mean for a woman around 1900 to openly express sexual desire and release? How were women of her background and class conceptualized sexually? What about constructions of sexuality in contemporary works, for example Strauss's *Der Rosenkavalier*, Mahler's late symphonies, Schoenberg's Expressionist works, or the songs of Dutch composer Anna Cramer (1873–1968)?[67] What these queries suggest is that music as lived practice represents much more than style, formalism, and a succession of great names and works.

But at the same time that women and their works are helping to broaden the canonic fields of discourse, another kind of activity must be taking place: exploration of the social values underlying current works in the canon. Susan McClary has been a driving force behind this strategy and I have come to agree with her on its necessity. For canonic works come to be canonic not through some abstract notion of quality, but largely through the accretion of value systems the work encodes and endorses. As Jane Tompkins would express it, works of art perform "cultural work" that makes them effective and successful in the context in which they originated.[68] What helps make them canonic, however, is that certain of those values continue to be esteemed over time and conferred with the seal of quality. Thus, for example, McClary shows how phallic violence underlies Beethoven's

Ninth Symphony, and by implication, this is one of the underlying codes that has helped keep the work canonic. Or, in another essay, she explores chromaticism in two late nineteenth-century works and its cultural meaning in patriarchal constructions of female sexuality.[69] These studies help shatter the myth of music as an autonomous art, divorced from social conventions, and as a result clear a space for new works to participate.[70] Jonathan Culler carries the idea further when he observes that the old works in the canon function as the "most powerful demystifiers of the ideologies they have been said to promote."[71] In other words, the contingency of the works themselves *vis-à-vis* socio-historical context will refute the notion of transcendence implied in canonicity.

As part of the process of bringing works by women into the canon it is important to expose students to the very idea of a canon: that what they take for granted as a familiar body of works actually represents a cultural construction that is complex and dependent on social values. This makes possible the notion of multiple canons. As Eve Sedgwick asserts, the very act of giving a name to these canons, and especially to the "Master canon," is a crucial step toward instilling a sense of the role of social contingency in canon formation.[72] The process introduces students to important concepts such as permanence and repeatability – ideas we tend to intuit rather than rationalize. In my music-history surveys I have found students extremely interested in such concepts and, without exaggerating their reactions, I would guess that many will give the notion of canonicity additional thought beyond the classroom.

Just as making students aware of canonicity involves the introduction of new historiographic ideas, so the strategy of incorporation and paradigm modification will result in some new ways of studying music history. Social history will play a greater role. This will include increased attention to issues of gender and class. Music as a discourse that involves representation will become more significant. Processes of music, including communication, response, and performance, will receive greater emphasis. Less time might be devoted to formalist analysis divorced from social context. The study and performance of music by women will assist in its valuation and promote a sense of valuation as part of a process rather than an objective set of aesthetic criteria. I have fewer realistic expectations regarding linearity and periodization, however. Our current period divisions and labels are fraught with difficulty and new ones would probably be an improvement. But that is very difficult to bring about, and I do not anticipate major changes in the near future. In the meanwhile, the difficulties can be put to good pedagogical use in discussions of the bases of the difficulties. For the instructor, however, it will be a challenge not to fall back into the comfort of traditional structures.

One of the major advantages of this discussion about a place for women in canonicity is the "putting into discourse of 'woman'," to quote Alice Jardine.[73] It places her front and center stage. It also suggests the question of a woman's subject position in relation to the canon. What I mean here is a historical woman and not the present-day woman approaching the canon (see also Chapter 5). Through inclusion in the canon does she now occupy a centered position within it? Does she stand at other positions? I believe that she, like a present-day female subject approaching the canon, occupies a position of fluidity. At times it might be centered, at other times not, and the many gradations in between allow for a flexibility that resists rigid categorization in relation to male structures and conventions. For women, perhaps the only kind of canon in which they are usually centered is that of an all-female canon. But in saying that historical women might now occupy the center occasionally I am not suggesting that they are still "Other" and should be viewed as "Other." Rather I am assuming a more complex positional field in which duality is absent and flow and multiplicity are possible.

Claiming that women cannot be viewed as "Other" any longer, Battersby advocates that the historical female artist be viewed dually: as an individual and as part of a collective tradition.[74] In making this proposal Battersby is resisting rigid positioning. While I agree with this position, I do not concur with her thesis that we view the subjectivity of the female artist within the framework of "genius." She sees this as a practical strategy of appropriation. Perhaps this is Battersby's way of turning the tables, so to speak, on the male appropriation of genius at the end of the eighteenth century. At that juncture many of the qualities that characterized genius were modeled on supposedly feminine attributes (p. 103). Battersby goes to great lengths to separate her notion from the common understandings of the term, among them that of the transcendent, divinely gifted (male) creator. But ultimately I fear that the label of genius could only hurt historical women: genius would inevitably be associated with transcendence. Thus I cannot agree with Battersby on the exaltation of the female artist's subjectivity. Instead, the partial de-centering put forward in Chapter 3 provides a means of creating space for the modelings that can in the end afford women greater visibility.

What might be the response of students to these kinds of expanded canons? I already cited the positive reactions of undergraduate students to assumptions associated with canonicity. My sense is that students of both genders had a similar response. When I have presented music by women and framed discussions in terms of a female point of view, I have also sensed interest from both genders but a special kind of curiosity from women. It seems as if some desires toward identification with the material under study are being affirmed. A female student realizes, perhaps for the first time, that women have played an important role in the history of music and serve as foremothers to their own desires to become musicians. They yearn to be part of a tradition with which they can identify. An all-male canon can produce feelings of alienation and contradiction beneath the surface as a woman wonders how she is to relate to such a tradition. In addition, her negative depiction, as a woman, in many masterworks can lead to further confusion.[75] Thus new ways of reading old works can position the female student more centrally in relation to the past. As for the male student, I suspect that he would be interested in having a more diverse picture of Western music history, although if this is his first acquaintance with the study of music history then he (and she) is likely to assume that "this is the way it is." That is, the student will not view this as some kind of alternative historiography but accept it as "regular" music history.[76] But I am not naive enough to anticipate no resistance. This might come from students with prior study of music history or those with extensive informal acquaintance with the Western musical heritage. I am including both genders in these statements. Furthermore, if the professor is female, there is always the possibility that resistance might be channeled into the assumption that she is somehow making a plea in favor of special interests of her liking but that this amounts to her own bias and should be considered less valid.

While I do not believe that this situation would occur often, especially if the professor is generally sensitive to students and encourages their input, it nonetheless underscores the role of the professor in the new canonic modelings. As things stand at present it takes a major commitment of time and energy to execute such a course. A large part of the substantial investment comes from the fact that the current array of materials – textbooks, score anthologies, recordings, and possibly source anthologies as well – generally support and reaffirm the traditional canon and its categories. It is not merely a matter of a meager number of available compositions by women. It also concerns the emphases and assumptions behind the organizing and structuring of the material. Given the realities of students' expectations toward course materials, a teacher might still prefer traditional materials as a base and supplement as needed. But that is cumbersome and potentially illegal if extensive duplication is entailed. Furthermore, the use of dispersed materials as the basis for assignments might discourage some students from doing the work. Thus materials are a very real problem. It requires a strong desire on the part of the teacher to surmount the difficulties.

In addition to the practical problems, the instructor might also face a formidable psychological hurdle: the Oedipal-like fear of confronting the father-like symbol of Musicology-and-Its-Canon in such a direct way. It is almost an act of daring to rethink the historiographic values in which we were trained and nurtured, and to expose that restructuring so blatantly.[77] Here again the desire must be considerable. But even if the desire is present, an instructor might be at pains to find the kinds of material that provide him or her with the needed information. For example, are there easily accessible sources on women as patrons in the nineteenth century in Europe, or on constructions of gender in Mozart operas? For the first one would have to know about Eva Rieger's fine book, *Frau, Musik und Männerherrschaft*, still unavailable in English and difficult to obtain in the United States. I am happy to report that the recent history edited by Pendle does provide some information on female patronage. And for the Mozart, no one source that I know of addresses the issue. One could do a fair amount of analysis and thinking on one's own and piece together tidbits from various sources. There is Clément's feminist critique of opera in general, but it falls short on the musical end. McClary has written a brief essay on the topic, but unfortunately it appears in a source with limited visibility to musicologists.[78] So basically the task would fall to the teacher. And given the pressures of two or three preparations a week for a given course, not to mention the other classes, committee work, and miscellaneous duties that befall a professor, the scales might tip in favor of yet another semester in the traditional mold. On the other hand, such a change might provide just the sort of rejuvenation a professor needs in the throes of mid-career burnout. After "x"-number of years of teaching music-history surveys, a new approach might inject vigor into the presentation of the material, as the teacher more than ever becomes a pupil along with the students.

THE PRESENCE OF WOMEN

Just as inclusion of women in music history is crucial toward understanding more fully musical activity of the past, so too a presence of women in the study and dissemination of music is critical. Their visibility as well as the climate surrounding women working in music influence general receptiveness to modification of the canon.[79] In this brief section I will concentrate on the field of musicology.

In the United States, which serves as the basis of my remarks, there has been a marked increase in the number of women engaged in musicology. I have been attending annual conventions of the American Musicological Society for over twenty years. In the early period hardly any female faces were to be found among the established figures. One would usually know who they were and where they taught. Similarly, there were relatively few junior scholars and graduate students who were women. Having been a junior scholar (female) for several years, I can remember those feelings of being an outsider. The annual meetings, of course, are formidable for any newcomer. But they were particularly difficult for a young woman for she tended to feel isolated. But at some point, perhaps in the early 1980s, I began to notice many women at the meetings, and the perception has only strengthened ever since. Women presently make up approximately 38 per cent of the membership, with a higher proportion in the junior ranks.[80] The increased presence of women has helped fuel a growing interest in historical women and their music as a research area. While several men are doing fine research on women or gender, most of the work has been conducted by women. For them (us), such research can bring a pleasure derived from a special woman–woman relationship forged with the object of study. Our visibility in musicology also suggests that women today have an important place within Western music, and this in turn can make the musical community more receptive to music by women.

But how is the musicologist who specializes in women reflected in musicological structures? One indicator is her definition in job classification.[81] Despite recent excitement in musicology over inter-disciplinary work, job classification still adheres mainly to traditional period names, such as medieval, Baroque, and Romantic, and there is no slot for feminist musicology. A specialist in the area is more likely to find a home in a joint appointment with another department or in an interdisciplinary women's studies program. The absence of categorical recognition has significant consequences. First, it means that graduate students interested in feminism as a research area should be aware of the special challenges they face in the job market. Although a temporally limited topic could be packaged in a traditional period and thus belong to a standard job category, a broad thematic study could mean exclusion. Women's studies programs, however, might be attracted to this kind of approach. It might fall under a category like "critical studies," which is beginning to appear in job notices in musicology. These pertain mainly to the top schools, however, and as of yet very few seem particularly interested in feminist work. Second, feminist research might prove problematic in tenure and promotion decisions. Colleagues in musicology might not be qualified to assess such work nor be favorably disposed toward it. There is still considerable resistance to feminist musicology,[82] although I sense less bias against studies of women that utilize more traditional methodology. Overall, however, the situation is gradually improving. Although most universities still pattern their hiring on traditional periods, which reflect curricular structure, feminist musicology is slowly gaining a place in the academy. Its presence can make a difference in the hospitality accorded historical women.

As several studies indicate, musicological work on women has increased dramatically.[83] The 1988 annual meeting of the AMS served both as litmus test and catalyst.[84] Interest exploded again in the summer of 1991 with three major conferences devoted to women in music, all organized and directed by women.[85] In the meantime, monographs, collections, and editions of music are appearing with greater frequency. But while this list seems impressive and com-prehensive, there is one obvious omission: journal articles. This is not to say that articles on women have not appeared in journals — many have.[86] But even given the growing acceptance rate of feminist work I believe it is easier for a book to get published than an article, at least in many of the top musicological journals. One notable exception is *The Journal of Musicology*, under Marian Green. The asymmetry between journals and books results partly from the fact that musicology has relatively few journals and thus there is great competition for available space. The difficulty with journals also involves the review process and the presence of women as editors and members of the editorial board. Of course, the mere presence of women does not ensure greater acceptance of articles on women although it might suggest a greater sensitivity to the relatively new area. Perhaps more important is whether there is a feminist musicologist on the editorial board or in a pool of reviewers. Books are more attractive as an outlet largely because of the dynamics of the market. While journals aim for prestige, book publishers pay attention to the potential profitability of a book. It is true that there is not a lot of money to be made in musicological books in general. Yet publishers sense a pent-up demand in this research area that might yield good returns, and are especially interested in projects that entail critical theory. Feminist musicology and the field as a whole will reap the benefits.

A presence of women is also important in other facets of musicology: in leadership and governance in the AMS, in review panels for grants, and particularly in universities. Women professors provide strong and needed role models for female students. They demonstrate to all students that women participate in the discourse of history and by extension in history itself. Female teachers might also be more receptive to promoting a less hierarchical environment inside (and outside) the classroom: what has been called a feminist environment. Some suggest this as a necessary correlate or even pre-condition for the kinds of historiographic changes detailed earlier in the chapter.[87] In any case, the female professor, like the other categories of women discussed in the book, stands in a potentially different subject position from men in relation to the material under study. This can play a role in how she views history and sees herself in relation to that history. Consequently, the incorporation of music by women and the attendant paradigm changes might have a different resonance, a special inflection. I do not mean necessarily better; I mean different. Perhaps the main persons to feel that difference are students. This contributes yet another element to the broad range of experiences and knowledge that the university is specially equipped to provide: a situation in which women and men are seen as participants in the cultural life of the present and past and by implication the future as well.

CODA: USEFULNESS AND VALIDITY OF CANONS

As this study has shown, canonicity is a cultural concept with enormous power. It represents certain interests and excludes others, suggests a veneer of excellence, and even carries a certain moral force. Furthermore it perpetuates itself. Changes may occur over time but the canon tends to resist major change in the short term. It earns additional respect by virtue of its roots in ecclesiastical law. On a practical level, canonicity has validated certain kinds of music through inclusion and discredited others through exclusion. Music by women has largely fallen outside the paradigms and assumptions central to canon formation, and as a result a substantial portion has been ignored, forgotten, or concealed. These paradigms and assumptions are biased and partial, however, for they reflect only certain segments of society. In the Western art tradition they emphasize the centrality of the middle- to upper-class white male and the subordination of women, resulting in an asymmetric power relationship. With this disappointing record, is it any wonder that some would like to eliminate the notion of canon altogether – that artifact that Lillian Robinson has dubbed a "gentleman's agreement"?[88]

While elimination might seem attractive in the abstract, I do not believe it is feasible or desirable. One reason is that humans display strong tendencies to make preferences, and this will involve ranking; we could call those choices that stand at the top a part of a canon. In this sense, then, a canon is a resultant concept. Of course canonicity is much more, for the resultant property becomes predictive and normative. But if we were to throw out the notion of canon there would still be the resultant function, although it would be called something else. All this might seem like a circular maze with no way out. But I believe the answer lies in modifying some of the aspects of canonicity, not eliminating the concept altogether. One element that goes a long way toward loosening the cultural stranglehold of canonicity is the recognition that a canon is a socially contingent notion, and that it does not (and cannot) claim to be universal or neutral. It is contingent upon a mediation between the past as it has sifted down to us and the present.

It might be useful to look to canons for their idealism, but this has the danger of whitewashing the cultural complexity of the past, present, and future. It is not necessarily a contradiction to aspire to ideals and to attempt to represent musical experience in its diversity.

Indeed, it can be argued that one major ideal of a canon should be a recognition of the strength to be found in diverse practices. Nonetheless, I am making this argument mainly in response to one of the major points put forward by adherents of a traditional canon.[89] The idealizing function of a canon may be a reality of the traditional canon, but for the kind of canon I desire this plays a decidedly lesser role. But even if some should feel the need to construct them as opposing concepts, idealism and diversity can be negotiated in the classroom and in musicological discourse within an aesthetic of contradiction that takes advantage of the tension between the two.

I can imagine that some might agree with my modifications about canonicity but argue that they cannot occur under the words canon and canonicity because of their traditional meanings. I appreciate this viewpoint and might even agree with it. Perhaps a semantic replacement is needed. But what I am really concerned with is the cultural power of canonicity as it presently exists, not the labels. One measure of this distinction is the fact that until approximately a decade ago canon and canonicity were strangers to musicological discourse, but the processes they represent have been operative for two hundred years.

Canonicity is an *ad hoc* concept, an analytical construction. Like similar constructions it can help us organize the past. It is a way of imposing our desires on the past.[90] Hence it is our collective and individual desires that need modification: what we wish the past to be, how we want it to relate to the present, and how we shape the future. In discussing canonicity we are talking about the direction and future of the field of musicology: about methodologies, paradigms, education, and above all, openness to change. We are also talking about ideologies encoded in music and the performance of music. May the conversation continue.

Notes

INTRODUCTION

1 *Critical Inquiry* 10/1 (1983), 107–25.
2 These studies form the basis of *Disciplining Music: Musicology and Its Canons*, ed. Katherine Bergeron and Philip V. Bohlman (Chicago, 1992).
3 There has been an outpouring of studies devoted to the politics of the canon and its meaning to us as a culture. I found the following especially helpful: Jan Gorak, *The Making of the Modern Canon: Genesis and Crisis of a Literary Idea* (London, 1991); John Guillory, "Canonical and non-canonical: A critique of the current debate," *English Literary History* 54/3 (1987), 483–527; *Canons*, ed. Robert von Hallberg, (Chicago, 1984); Paul Lauter, *Canons and Contexts* (New York, 1991); Herbert Lindenberger, *The History in Literature: On Value, Genre, Institutions* (New York, 1990); and Christopher Ricks, "What is at stake in the 'Battle of the books'?" *New Criterion* 8 (1989), 50–54. See also Robert Scholes, "Aiming a canon at the curriculum," *Salmagundi* No. 72 (1986), 101–17, and the articles in the same issue in response: E. D. Hirsch, Jr., "'Cultural literacy' does not mean 'canon'"; Marjorie Perloff, "An intellectual impasse"; Elizabeth Fox-Genovese, "The claims of a common culture: Gender, race, class and the canon"; John P. Sisk, "What is necessary"; and J. Mitchell Morse, "Some variations on – and from – Scholes' theme."
4 Guillory, "Canonical and non-canonical," p. 494.
5 For a history of the canon debates see especially Gorak, *The Making of the Modern Canon*, pp. 221–34.
6 See especially Ann Clark Fehn, "Relativism, feminism, and the 'German connection' in Allan Bloom's *The Closing of the American Mind*," *German Quarterly* 62 (1989), 384–94.
7 For an analysis of the canon debate in terms of territory see Susan Hardy Aiken, "Women and the question of canonicity," *College English* 48 (1986), 288–301.
8 For a review see Ruth Solie and Gary Tomlinson, "Women's studies in a new key," *National Women's Studies Action* 2/1 (1989), 6.
9 See *The Journal of Musicology* 9/4 (1991) for reviews of three conferences: Alice H. Cash on "Feminist theory and music: Toward a common

language," University of Minnesota, Minneapolis (521–32); and my report on "Beyond biography: Seventh international congress on women in music," Utrecht, The Netherlands; and "Music and gender conference," King's College, University of London (533–43).

10 "Gender, professionalism, and the musical canon," *The Journal of Musicology* 8/1 (1990), 102–17.

11 See, for example, Elaine Showalter, "Introduction: The rise of gender," *Speaking of Gender*, ed. Showalter (New York, 1989), 1–16; Joan Scott, "Introduction," *Gender and the Politics of History* (New York, 1988), pp. 2–3; Judith Butler, *Gender Trouble: Feminism and the Subversion of Identity* (New York, 1990); and Tania Modleski, "Postmortem on post-feminism," *Feminism Without Women* (New York, 1991), 3–22.

12 Showalter, "The feminist critical revolution," *The New Feminist Criticism: Essays on Women, Literature, and Theory*, ed. Showalter (New York, 1985), p. 4.

13 Many feminist scholars have addressed the complexities of women/ woman and the general category of woman. See, for example, Janet Todd, *Feminist Literary History* (New York, 1988), p. 4; Denise Riley, *"Am I That Name?" Feminism and the Category of "Women" in History* (Minneapolis, 1988); and Janet Wolff, *Feminine Sentences: Essays on Women and Culture* (Berkeley, 1990), pp. 81–2. My thanks also to Ruth Solie for her helpful comments on the two terms.

14 See Sandra M. Gilbert and Susan Gubar, *The Madwoman in the Attic: The Woman Writer and the Nineteenth-Century Literary Imagination* (New Haven, 1979).

1 CANONIC ISSUES

1 An ardent case for a canon's ability to embody these qualities is made by Charles Altieri, "An idea and ideal of a literary canon," *Critical Inquiry* 10/1 (1983), 37–59.

2 "A few canonic variations," *Critical Inquiry* 10/1 (1983), pp. 107 and 112.

3 For another critique of Kerman's distinctions see William Weber, "The eighteenth-century origins of the musical canon," *Journal of the Royal Musical Association* 114/1 (1989), p. 6.

4 Its validity is discussed in the last section of Chapter 6.

5 Smith, "Contingencies of value," *Critical Inquiry* 10/1 (1983), p. 23. See also the discussion on genre in Chapter 4.

6 "Race and gender in the shaping of the American literary canon: A case study from the twenties," *Feminist Studies* 9/3 (1983), pp. 452–6. Genre functions as another major kind of classification within canonicity; see especially the discussion "Theories of genre," in Chapter 4.

7 See, for example, Sandra Harding, *The Science Question in Feminism* (Ithaca, 1986); Evelyn Fox Keller, *Reflections on Gender and Science* (New Haven, 1985); *Feminism and Science*, ed. Nancy Tuana (Bloomington, 1989); and Joan Kelly, *Woman, History, and Theory: The Essays of Joan Kelly* (Chicago, 1984).

8 See more in Chapters 5 and 6. Although flawed, their ideas are useful for mediating a temporally distant past with the present.

9 See Jane Tompkins, *Sensational Designs: The Cultural Work of American Fiction* (New York, 1985); and Lauter, "Race and gender." See also the following articles, published in the "Canons" issue of *Critical Inquiry* 10/1 (1983): Smith, "Contingencies of value"; Richard Ohmann, "The shaping of a canon: U.S. fiction, 1960–1975," 199–223; and Arnold Krupat, "Native American literature and the canon," 145–71.

10 Lauter, "Race and gender," p. 435.

11 Succeeding chapters illuminate many of the cultural processes and institutions that contribute to the formation of canonic value systems.

12 See Ohmann, "Shaping of a canon," p. 209. Roland Barthes has underscored the significance of the academy in the dissemination of literary value in his observation that "the 'teaching of literature' is for me almost tautological. Literature is what is taught, that's all." Quoted in Krupat, "Native American literature," p. 146.

13 See below in this chapter and also Chapter 6 for discussions of powerful groups in musical canon formation.

14 Tompkins, *Sensational Designs*, p. 196. See also Smith, "Contingencies of value," pp. 29–30. See Chapter 6 for a fuller discussion of valuation and canonicity, including more on the "test of time."

15 See especially Susan Hardy Aiken, "Women and the question of canonicity," *College English* 48 (1986), 288–301; Henry Louis Gates, Jr., "'What's love got to do with it?': Critical theory, integrity, and the Black idiom," *New Literary History* 18 (1986–7), 345–62; Krupat, "Native American literature"; Lawrence Lipking, "Aristotle's sister: A poetics of abandonment," *Critical Inquiry* 10/1 (1983), 61–81; Lillian Robinson, "Treason our text: Feminist challenges to the literary canon," *Tulsa Studies in Women's Literature* 2 (1983), 83–98; and Showalter, "Women and the literary curriculum," *College English* 32 (1970–71), 855–62.

16 For Afro-American literature, for example, see the work of Gates, including "'What's love got to do with it?'"; and "Whose canon is it, anyhow?" *New York Times Book Review* (26 February 1989).

17 For a study of musicology's disciplinary canons see Randel's "The canons in the musicological toolbox," article drawn from remarks at the annual meetings of the American Musicological Society in 1987 (New Orleans) and 1988 (Baltimore), published in *Disciplining Music: Musicology and Its Canons*, 10–22.

18 Feminism, of course, is part of the challenge. See, for instance, Joseph Kerman, "American musicology in the 1990s," *The Journal of Musicology* 9/2 (1991), 131–44. A special issue of *Current Musicology*, entitled "Musicology in the year 2000," is intended as an assessment of the field in light of the many paradigm shifts that are taking place.

19 See the discussion below on the role of the public, and also Peter Burkholder, "Brahms and twentieth-century classical music," *Nineteenth Century Music* 8/1 (1984), 75–83.

20 "Canonic variations," p. 119. He quotes composer Roger Reynolds, who declares that in such situations the recording "becomes the work."

21 See Kerman, "Canonic variations," pp. 118–19. "Text" has become a loaded term. Traditionally it has meant a written record or document, but it has acquired an expanded meaning in recent discourse. Now "text" can be applied to various phenomena, not necessarily written, and the attributes of a traditional text – for example readability, narrativity, coherence, grammar, and vocabulary – are applicable to their analysis. To avoid confusion I have tried whenever possible to substitute a term that more precisely reflects my meaning. In those places where "text" remains, however, it represents the best choice in the given context. Hopefully the reader can ascertain my particular intent. See also the discussion below on transmission.

22 The canon of theory pedagogy often overlaps, but I am reluctant to lump them together as the pedagogic aims are not equivalent and thus the repertorial membership will tend to differ.

23 For an interesting discussion of the changing values behind the adoption and abandonment of certain works in literary anthologies, see Lauter, "Race and gender."

24 Hugo Riemann's three-volume *Musikgeschichte in Beispielen* (Leipzig, 1911–12, with several later editions) might have been the first significant anthology.

25 Edith Borroff's *A History of Music in Europe and the United States* (1971) is one of the first survey texts to incorporate folk and popular elements, particularly in its treatment of American traditions.

26 The Outreach Committee of the American Musicological Society, as of this writing, is attempting to encourage these kinds of professional interactions with the community.

27 The following writings are especially pertinent to this discussion: Elliott Carter, "The orchestral composer's point of view," *The Writings of Elliott Carter: An American Composer Looks at Modern Music*, ed. Else Stone and Kurt Stone (Bloomington, 1977), 282–300; Aaron Copland, *Music and Imagination* (New York, 1952); Edward J. Dent, "The historical approach to music," *The Musical Quarterly* 23 (1937), 1–17; Allen Edwards, ed., *Flawed Words and Stubborn Sounds: A Conversation with Elliott Carter* (New York, 1971); Paul Hindemith, *A Composer's World* (Cambridge, Mass., 1952); Bernard Holland, "Composers rediscover the public," *The New York Times* (21 May 1991); Paul Henry Lang, ed., *Problems of Modern Music: The Princeton Seminar in Advanced Musical Studies* (New York, 1962), especially Elliott Carter, "Shop talk by an American composer" (51–63) and Roger Sessions, "Problems and issues facing the composer today" (21–33); Henry Pleasants, *The Agony of Modern Music* (New York, 1955); George Rochberg, *The Aesthetics of Survival: A Composer's View of Twentieth-Century Music* (Ann Arbor, 1984); Arnold Schoenberg, *Style and Idea*, ed. Leonard Stein, trans. Leo Black (Berkeley, 1984), especially "My public," 1930 (96–8) and "Criteria for the

evaluation of music," 1946 (124–36); Roger Sessions, *Questions About Music* (New York, 1971); and miscellaneous excerpts from *Music in the Western World: A History in Documents*, ed. Piero Weiss and Richard Taruskin (New York, 1984).

28 "Reflections on Schoenberg" (1972), *The Aesthetics of Survival*, pp. 52–3.

29 See also the discussion on anxiety of influence, in Chapter 2.

30 "My public," in *Style and Idea*, p. 96.

31 See excerpts of the 1912 performance in London and of the "Statement of Aims" for the Verein für Musikalische Privataufführungen, in Weiss and Taruskin, *Music in the Western World*, pp. 428–32.

32 Edwards, ed., *A Conversation with Elliott Carter*, p. 36.

33 "The composer as specialist" (1958), in Weiss and Taruskin, *Music in the Western World*, p. 533.

34 "Music: Science vs. humanism," excerpt in Weiss and Taruskin, *Music in the Western World*, pp. 534–8.

35 See also Paul Henry Lang, "Introduction," *Problems of Modern Music*, 7–16.

36 See also Chapter 6.

37 Suzanne Cusick, in a private communication, cleverly dubbed these writings a kind of embryonic canon.

38 See especially "The eighteenth-century origins of the musical canon"; "Mentalité, tradition et origines du canon musical en France et en Angleterre au XVIIIe siècle," *Annales. Economies. Sociétés. Civilisations* 44/4 (1989), 849–73; "Mass culture and the reshaping of European musical taste, 1770–1870," *International Review of the Aesthetics and Sociology of Music* 8 (1977), 5–21; and "The rise of the classical repertoire in nineteenth-century orchestral concerts," *The Orchestra: Origins and Transformations*, ed. Joan Peyser (New York, 1986), 361–86.

39 According to Tompkins, most literary anthologizers believe that quality is their main criterion for inclusion (*Sensational Designs*, p. 192). For a perceptive exploration of the relationship between historicism and the notion of repeating classics in music see Burkholder, "Museum pieces: The historicist mainstream in music of the last hundred years," *The Journal of Musicology* 2/2 (1983), 115–34. Kerman's "Canonic variations" also discusses historicism in the nineteenth century. See also Chapter 6 for a critique of the criterion of quality.

40 See Burkholder, "Museum pieces." Literary critic Charles Altieri believes that one of the two main functions of canons is curatorial, a function he clearly endorses. See his "Literary canon," pp. 47–8.

41 *Music and Imagination*, p. 27.

42 For a witty account of the sociological role of the piano in the music business see Arthur Loesser, *Men, Women, and Pianos: A Social History* (New York, 1954). For a thorough study of the socio-economic environment surrounding musicians in early nineteenth-century Vienna see Alice M. Hanson, *Musical Life in Biedermeier Vienna* (Cambridge, 1985).

43 Weber, "Rise of the classical repertoire," p. 367.
44 In the twentieth century *The Musical Quarterly*, through the mid-1980s, was published by G. Schirmer. A similar situation exists today with scholarly journals published by scholarly presses. One might wonder whether books issued by that press receive greater attention, particularly in the form of reviews. For literature see Ohmann, "Shaping of a canon."
45 Kerman, "Canonic variations," pp. 111–12.
46 Leon Plantinga, *Romantic Music*, p. 13.
47 See Edward Dent, "The historical approach to music," pp. 4–6. The theme is echoed in the crisis of modernism in the mid-twentieth century; see, for example, Hindemith, *A Composer's World*, p. 63.
48 See also Chapter 5.
49 For additional discussions of genius see Chapters 5 and 6, and also Christine Battersby, *Gender and Genius: Towards a Feminist Aesthetics* (London, 1989).
50 See Chapter 4.
51 For perceptive essays on the new challenges the composer faced in a time of growing historicism see Burkholder, "Museum pieces" and "Brahms and twentieth-century classical music."
52 "Rise of the classical repertoire," p. 371; and "Wagner, Wagnerism, and musical idealism," *Wagnerism in European Culture and Politics*, ed. David C. Large and William Weber (Ithaca, 1984), pp. 33–6.
53 "The historical approach to music."
54 Romy Kozak, "The composition of women in the Paris Conservatory," Paper presented at the Feminist Theory and Music Conference, University of Minnesota, Minneapolis, June 1991.
55 Dent considers this event important as the first trace in England of a reverence for older works; see "The historical approach to music," p. 5. I am making the connection with nationalism. Later work by William Weber places the English reverence for older works much earlier in the century.
56 Kerman, "Canonic variations," pp. 112–13.
57 For a summary of the varied functions of scores see Leo Treitler, "Transmission and the study of music history," *International Musicological Society. Twelfth Congress, Berkeley 1977: Report* (Kassel, 1981), 202–11.
58 Arguably the reader or respondent is constructing the work; see Chapter 5, "Reception."
59 Philosopher Karey Harrison presents a feminist critique of the epistemological basis of the visual, in "Reason embodied," Paper delivered at Rice University in April 1989. Smith has observed that it is difficult for Westerners to comprehend the notion that non-written structures – objects, events, and processes – can encompass the kind of canonic meaning and reverence we accord figures like Homer and Shakespeare ("Contingencies of value," p. 31). Ethnomusicologist Judith Becker emphasizes the eclecticism of cognitive experiences that underlie

musical perception, in her paper "Some thoughts on 'non-verbal' communication," presented at the annual meeting of the American Musicological Society/Society for Music Theory/Society for Ethnomusicology, Oakland, November 1990. See also John Shepherd, "Music and male hegemony," *Music and Society: The Politics of Composition, Performance, and Reception*, ed. Richard Leppert and Susan McClary (Cambridge, 1987), p. 155, and my discussion of oral traditions below.

60 It is interesting that Philip Bohlman links canonicity in ethnomusicology only with disciplinary paradigms and not with any concept of repertories. See his "Ethnomusicology's challenge to the canon, the canon's challenge to ethnomusicology," paper presented at the annual meeting of the American Musicological Society, New Orleans, October 1987; published in *Disciplining Music: Musicology and Its Canons*, 116–36.

61 For a perceptive discussion of models of transmission and their importance for Western historiography, see Treitler, "Transmission and the study of history," 202–11.

62 Mantle Hood has commented on the negative effect of creating written records of oral traditions, in *Perspectives in Musicology*, ed. Barry Brook, Edward Downes, and Sherman Van Solkema (New York, 1972), pp. 203–4; quoted in Kerman, "Canonic variations," pp. 107–8. See also Charles Seeger, "Oral tradition in music," *Funk and Wagnall's Standard Dictionary of Folklore, Mythology, and Legend*, ed. Maria Leach (New York, 1950), 825–9.

63 Some theories of response place the principal creative role in the respondent; see Chapter 5 for a discussion of response as creativity.

64 See my arguments in Chapters 3 and 6 regarding a de-centered author.

65 Of course, there are often problems in ascertaining the actual version of a piece of music. An example is Schumann's Symphony No. 4. See, for example, Linda Roesner's paper, "Aesthetic ideals and structural goals: Schumann's d-minor Symphony at mid-century," delivered at the annual meeting of the American Musicological Society, Austin, October 1989.

66 See, for example, Treitler, "Transmission and the study of music history."

67 See Treitler, "Homer and Gregory: The transmission of epic poetry and plainchant," *The Musical Quarterly* 60 (1974), 333–72. For a more general application of the theory see Margaret Murata, "Scylla and Charybdis, or steering between form and social context in the seventeenth century," *Explorations in Music, The Arts, and Ideas*, ed. Eugene Narmour and Ruth Solie (New York, 1988), pp. 75–8.

68 In a private communication, where she pointed out that a common male fantasy in the late Renaissance was the achievement of reproduction without women.

69 See Chapter 6 for extended discussion of the issues raised in this paragraph.

70 See also Diane Jezic and David Binder, "A survey of college music textbooks: Benign neglect of women composers," *The Musical Woman: An International Perspective*. Vol. II: *1984–85*, ed. Judith Lang Zaimont, Catherine Overhauser, and Jane Gottlieb (Westport, Ct., 1987), 445–69. The statistical approach in this study was criticized by Richard Taruskin in his review of the volume, in *Opus* 4/2 (1988), p. 64.

71 As described in the abstract for her paper, "Teaching the history of women in music," presented at the Gender and Music Conference, King's College, University of London, July 1991.

2 CREATIVITY

1 *A Room of One's Own* (New York, 1929), pp. 48–58.

2 See especially Sandra M. Gilbert and Susan Gubar, *The Madwoman in the Attic: The Woman Writer and the Nineteenth-Century Literary Imagination* (New Haven, 1979).

3 See, for instance, Lawrence Lipking, "Aristotle's sister: A poetics of abandonment," *Critical Inquiry* 10/1 (1983), pp. 67–8.

4 This is linked to the notion of genius, which is discussed in Chapters 5 and 6.

5 "Creativity and the childbirth metaphor: Gender difference in literary discourse," *Speaking of Gender*, ed. Elaine Showalter (New York, 1989), pp. 75–6.

6 On literary creativity and childbirth see Nina Auerbach, "Artists and mothers: A false alliance," *Women and Literature* 6/1 (1978), 3–15. Elaine Showalter discusses these issues in terms of valuation of the Victorian woman writer, in "Women writers and the double standard," *Woman in Sexist Society: Studies in Power and Powerlessness*, ed. Vivian Gornick and Barbara K. Moran (New York, 1971), 333–6.

7 As Susan Gubar notes, "the female body has been feared for its power to articulate itself" ("'The blank page' and the issues of female creativity," *Critical Inquiry* 8 [1981], p. 76). Elizabeth Wood hypothesizes male fear of the female body as one reason for the awe accorded the female singer throughout history, in her paper "The odyssey of sirens and songbirds: Opera and its prima donnas," presented at the open meeting of the Committee on the Status of Women, annual meeting of the American Musicological Society, Austin, October 1989.

8 As quoted in Gilbert and Gubar, *Madwoman in the Attic*, p. 3. See also "The great 'I am'," Chapter 5 in Christine Battersby, *Gender and Genius: Towards a Feminist Aesthetics* (London, 1989), pp. 43–51.

9 *The Magic Flute, Masonic Opera* (English translation, New York, 1971). Yet the Queen of the Night, the main representative of the female side (along with the evil Monostatos, for example), is not fashioned by Mozart and Schikaneder–Gieseke as a benevolent "earth-mother" type. On the contrary, her range and style are constructed to make her into a shrew, despite justifiable horror over her daughter's abduction.

See also Catherine Clément, *Opera, or the Undoing of Women*, trans. Betsy Wing (Minneapolis, 1988), pp. 73–7. Ingmar Bergman's film version attempts to provide some justification for the abduction by making Sarastro the father of Pamina. Arguably, however, the filmmaker's conception heightens the misogyny of the work. See, for example, Rose Laub Coser, "The principle of patriarchy: The case of *The Magic Flute*," *Signs* 4/2 (1978), 337–48. As for *The Ring*, although Erda has a placid, soothing *Leitmotif*, she is not portrayed consistently as a soothing female presence. She is often capricious and willful. See also Clément, *Opera, or the Undoing of Women*, p. 145.

10 Constance Jordan, *Renaissance Feminism: Literary Texts and Political Models* (Ithaca, 1990), pp. 86–91. My thanks to Suzanne Cusick for bringing this to my attention.

11 Christine Froula, "When Eve reads Milton: Undoing the canonical economy," *Canons*, ed. Robert von Hallberg (Chicago, 1984), 149–75. See also Mieke Bal, "Sexuality, sin, and sorrow: The emergence of female character (A reading of Genesis 1–3)," *The Female Body in Western Culture: Contemporary Perspectives*, ed. Susan Rubin Suleiman (Cambridge, Mass., 1986), 317–38; Gilbert and Gubar, "How are we fal'n?: Milton's daughters," *Madwoman in the Attic*, 187–310; and Madelon Sprengnether, "(M)other Eve: Some revisions of the fall in fiction by contemporary women writers," *Feminism and Psychoanalysis*, ed. Richard Feldstein and Judith Roof (Ithaca, 1989), 298–322.

12 Susan McClary, "This is not a story my people tell: Musical time and space according to Laurie Anderson," *Feminine Endings: Music, Gender, and Sexuality* (Minneapolis, 1991), pp. 132–4.

13 For a fascinating critique see Adrienne Rich, "Hands of flesh, hands of iron" and "Alienated labor," *Of Woman Born: Motherhood as Experience and Institution*, Tenth Anniversary Edition (New York, 1986), 128–55 and 156–85.

14 Although we should not discount the possibility of advances in biotechnology that might make it a reality.

15 Genevieve Lloyd, *Man of Reason: "Male" and "Female" in Western Philosophy* (Minneapolis, 1984), p. 10.

16 From Nietzsche's "The Greek Woman" (1871), as quoted in Lloyd, *Man of Reason*, pp. 1–2. Rousseau's glorification of nature might imply elevation of women's theoretical status, but it too leaves women in a compromised position. See Lloyd, *ibid.*, pp. 58–64; and also Maurice Bloch and Jean H. Bloch, "Women and the dialectics of nature in eighteenth-century French thought," *Nature, Culture and Gender*, ed. Carol MacCormack and Marilyn Strathern (Cambridge, 1980), 25–41.

17 Sherry Ortner, "Is female to male as nature is to culture?" *Feminist Studies* 1/2 (1974), p. 14.

18 This discussion of nature and culture is based largely on Ortner's important essay, "Is female to male as nature is to culture?" For a later overview of the issue see Ynestra King, "Healing the wounds: Feminism,

ecology, and nature/culture dualism," *Gender/Body/Knowledge: Feminist Reconstructions of Being and Knowing*, ed. Alison M. Jaggar and Susan R. Bordo (New Brunswick, 1989), 115–41.

19 *Gender and Genius*, p. 160.

20 This has been a major theme in the work of Susan McClary. See, for instance, "Introduction: A material girl in Bluebeard's castle," *Feminine Endings*, pp. 17–18. Philip Brett has explored the relationship in terms of music and homophobia; see "Musicality, essentialism, and the closet," paper presented at Gender and Music Conference, King's College, University of London, July 1991.

21 Gilbert and Gubar, *Madwoman in the Attic*, p. 187; and Catherine Parsons Smith, "On feminism and American art music," Paper delivered at the annual meeting of the American Musicological Society, Austin, October 1989, published in *Cecilia: Exploring Gender and Music*, ed. Susan Cook and Judy Tsou (Urbana, 1993). Similarly, Judith Tick has cited Frank Rossiter on how Charles Ives divided music into male and female traits and rejected the classical tradition because it was too feminized; untitled presentation on "Interdisciplinary roundtable: Toward a theoretical framework for the study of gender and music," annual meeting of the American Musicological Society/Society for Ethnomusicology/Society for Music Theory, Oakland, November 1990.

22 The male fear of being considered women can be seen in general attitudes towards a man dressing up as a woman. He is seen as socially deviant and becomes an object of ridicule. The reaction is quite different when a woman dresses up as a man. While she may elicit laughter, the inversion is much more acceptable. The former situation is threatening, the latter is cute.

23 Quoted in Rozsika Parker and Griselda Pollock, *Old Mistresses: Women, Art and Ideology* (London, 1981), p. 83.

24 See, for instance, Susan Gubar, "'The blank page'," p. 77.

25 *Ibid.*, p. 86.

26 See Susan Bordo, "The Cartesian masculinization of thought," *Signs* 11/3 (1986), 439–56; the expansion in *The Flight to Objectivity: Essays on Cartesianism and Culture* (Albany, 1987); and Lloyd, *Man of Reason*.

27 Lloyd, *Man of Reason*, p. 2.

28 "Cartesian masculinization," p. 450.

29 Lloyd, *Man of Reason*, p. 49. Mark Johnson shows how Western reasoning is steeped in spatial conceptualizations of the body. Thus reasoning is embodied. See his major study, *The Body in the Mind: The Bodily Basis of Meaning, Imagination, and Reason* (Chicago, 1987), which formed a basis for Robert Walser's paper, "The body in the music: Epistemological challenges for ethnomusical semiotics," delivered at the AMS/SEM/SMT annual meeting, Oakland, November 1990.

30 See, for example, George Upton's influential *Woman in Music* (Boston, 1880).

31 Ruth Ginzberg, "Gender, rationality, and mathematics," Paper presented at Rice University in March 1989.

32 Friedman, "Creativity," p. 76.

33 See, for example, Ann Rosalind Jones, "Writing the body: Toward an understanding of *l'écriture féminine*," *The New Feminist Criticism*, ed. Elaine Showalter (New York, 1985), 361–78; and Domna C. Stanton, "Language and revolution: The Franco-American dis-connection," *The Future of Difference*, ed. Hester Eisenstein and Alice Jardine (New Brunswick, 1985), 73–87.

34 See Elaine Showalter, "Feminist criticism in the wilderness," *The New Feminist Criticism: Essays on Women, Literature, and Theory* (New York, 1985), p. 249; and Alice A. Jardine and Anne M. Menke, "Exploding the issue: 'French' 'women' 'writers' and 'the canon'?" *Displacements: Women, Traditions, Literatures in French*, ed. Joan DeJean and Nancy K. Miller (Baltimore, 1991), 275–307.

35 The term comes from Gilbert and Gubar, *Madwoman in the Attic*. See especially Chapter 2, "Infection in the sentence: The woman writer and the anxiety of authorship," pp. 45–92.

36 Both quotations come from Elaine Barkin, ed., "In response" *Perspectives of New Music* 20–21 (1981–2), 288–329.

37 Letter of 1 July 1829, in *Letters of Fanny Hensel to Felix Mendelssohn*, ed. Marcia J. Citron (New York, 1987), p. 60.

38 See especially the introductory essays in my *Letters* volume, and also my article, "Felix Mendelssohn's influence on Fanny Mendelssohn Hensel as a professional composer," *Current Musicology* No. 37–8 (1984), 9–17.

39 For an elegant analysis of the gaze in the discourse of music, see Lawrence Kramer's discussion of the second movement, "Gretchen," of Liszt's *A Faust Symphony*, in *Music As Cultural Practice, 1800–1900* (Berkeley, 1990), 102–34.

40 In Nancy Reich, *Clara Schumann: The Artist and the Woman* (Ithaca, 1985), p. 228; Reich is quoting from Berthold Litzmann's two-volume biography (1902–8).

41 Reich, *Clara Schumann*, pp. 228–9.

42 See my essays, "Corona Schröter: Singer, composer, actress," *Music and Letters* 61 (1980), 15–27; and "Women and the Lied, 1775–1850," *Women Making Music: The Western Art Tradition*, ed. Jane Bowers and Judith Tick (Urbana, 1986), p. 230.

43 Of course, not all female composers have felt ambivalent about the act of creating, especially more recent composers. We will take this up later, in "Professionalism."

44 See Carol Neuls-Bates, ed., *Women in Music: An Anthology of Source Readings from the Middle Ages to the Present* (New York, 1982), pp. 220–22.

45 Romy Kozak, "The composition of women in the Paris Conservatory," Paper presented at the Feminist Theory and Music Conference, University of Minnesota, Minneapolis, June 1991.

46 "Women composers: Reminiscence and history," *College Music Symposium* 15 (1975), p. 27.

47 From *Female Pipings in Eden* (London, 1933), as quoted in Neuls-Bates, *Women in Music*, p. 286.

48 Barbara Herrnstein Smith, "Contingencies of value," *Critical Inquiry* 10/1 (1983), p. 23. I added the variable of gender to Smith's list.

49 From *Female Pipings in Eden*, as excerpted in Neuls-Bates, *Women in Music*, pp. 287–8. Many women writers, however, hid their femaleness under a male pseudonym, such as the three Brontë sisters, who wrote under the names Acton Bell, Currer Bell, and Ellis Bell. See Chapter 3.

50 Rozsika Parker and Griselda Pollock, *Old Mistresses*, pp. 32–4; and Linda Nochlin, "Why have there been no great women artists?" *Art and Sexual Politics*, ed. Thomas B. Hess and Elizabeth C. Baker (New York, 1973), pp. 24–7.

51 Valuation of these characteristics is also discussed in the section "Theories of genre," in Chapter 4.

52 Diane Jezic, *Women Composers: The Lost Tradition Found* (New York, 1988), p. 166.

53 For example in my study, "Women and the Lied."

54 Alma Mahler Werfel, *And The Bridge is Love* (New York, 1958), p. 9.

55 See Chapter 6 for a brief discussion of her song "Ansturm."

56 For an excellent study of Boulanger, the first based on family documents, see Léonie Rosenstiel's *The Life and Works of Lili Boulanger* (Rutherford, N.J., 1978).

57 Nancy Chodorow, *The Reproduction of Mothering: Psychoanalysis and the Sociology of Gender* (Berkeley, 1978), p. 169.

58 See, for example, the critique of Chodorow in Nancy Fraser and Linda J. Nicholson, "Social criticism without philosophy: An encounter between feminism and postmodernism," *Feminism/Postmodernism*, ed. Nicholson (New York, 1990), pp. 29–34.

59 See, for instance, the pioneering article of Gerda Lerner, "Placing women in history: A 1975 perspective," *Liberating Women's History*, ed. Berenice A. Carroll (Urbana, 1976), 357–67; and in the same collection, Hilda Smith, "Feminism and the methodology of women's history," 368–84. Ruth Solie has written eloquently on what it is to write a woman's life, in her review of Nancy Reich's biography, *Clara Schumann*; see *Nineteenth-Century Music* 10/1 (1986), 74–80.

60 For a full discussion of Bargiel see Reich's *Clara Schumann*, especially pages 32–6.

61 *Clara Schumann*, p. 36.

62 For a perceptive discussion of Hensel's many female familial influences see Carol Quin, "Fanny Mendelssohn Hensel: Her contributions to nineteenth-century musical life," unpublished Ph.D. dissertation, University of Kentucky (1981), pp. 25–6, 32–6.

63 That Lea actually studied with Kirnberger seems a bit unlikely, as Kirnberger died in 1783, which would have made Lea five years old at the most when she studied with him. Nonetheless, this information appears in a reliable source, Eric Werner's *Mendelssohn: A New Image of the Composer and His Age*, trans. Dika Newlin (Westport, Ct., 1978; reprint of 1963 edition), p. 10.

64 Unpublished letter of 7 June 1837, no. 44 of vol. vi in the Green Books collection of Mendelssohn correspondence in the Bodleian Library, Oxford.

65 Dorothea, who married Schlegel in 1804, was treated as the black sheep of the family. But interestingly, she was the only family member to attend Felix's wedding, which took place in Frankfurt, where she was living, in March 1837. Some bad feelings among members of the family led to this absence; see, for instance, Hensel's letter to Mendelssohn of 2 June 1837 in my edition of *Letters*, pp. 233-8.

66 See my essays "The relationship between Fanny and Felix," in *Letters*, pp. xxxi-xliv; and "Felix Mendelssohn's influence on Fanny Mendelssohn Hensel." Abraham Mendelssohn's views reflected those of his father, the philosopher–theologian Moses Mendelssohn, which in turn derived from Enlightenment thought about proper female roles, as uttered by Rousseau, Kant, and others.

67 See Borroff, "An American parlor at the turn of the century," *American Music* (1986), 302-8.

68 "Ink is inaudible, and no music exists without sound; a printed score is like a portrait, able to conjure up an image of the beloved but not to be courted or made love to" (*ibid.*, p. 307).

69 Adrienne Fried Block discusses the relationship between Amy Beach (1867-1944) and her mother, Clara Cheney, in an essay in *Cecilia Reclaimed: Feminist Perspectives on Gender and Music* (Urbana, 1993). For a few women the maternal influence has been detrimental, as in the case of Mary Carr Moore (1873-1957); see Catherine Parsons Smith and Cynthia S. Richardson, *Mary Carr Moore, American Composer* (Ann Arbor, 1987), especially pages 62-8.

70 Jane Marcus, "Virginia Woolf and her violin," *Mothering the Mind: Twelve Studies of Writers and Their Silent Partners*, ed. Ruth Perry and Martine Watson Brownley (New York, 1984), 180-203.

71 *Madwoman in the Attic*, p. 49. See also "Lack of models" in Joanna Russ, *How to Suppress Women's Writing* (Austin, 1983), pp. 87-96.

72 Nicola LeFanu has commented on her frustration at not finding any sources that discuss the existence of a female tradition in Britain in the twentieth century, in "Master musician: An impregnable taboo?" *Contact: Journal of Contemporary Music* No. 31 (1987), p. 6.

73 Lockwood's extremely interesting comments form one of the nineteen responses to a questionnaire on aspects of being a woman composer, sent to selected female composers by Elaine Barkin, composer and then co-editor of *Perspectives of New Music*. The responses, in prose form and unedited, appear in *Perspectives* 20-21 (1981-2), 288-329.

74 *Perspectives* survey. Campus under-representation of female composers surfaces in many responses. See Chapter 6 for a discussion of the importance of the visibility of female musicologists in the academy.

75 See Rae Linda Brown, "Selected orchestral music of Florence B. Price (1888-1953) in the context of her life and work," unpublished Ph.D.

dissertation, Yale University (1987); Mildred Denby Green, *Black Women Composers: A Genesis* (Boston, 1983); Barbara Garvey Jackson, "Florence Price, composer," *The Black Perspective in Music* 5/1 (1977), 30–43; and Eileen Southern, *The Music of Black Americans*, 2nd ed. (New York, 1983).

76 I refer the reader to Chapter 6 for a fuller airing of the complexities involved in the notion of history as a constructed entity.

77 *A Room of One's Own*, p. 77.

78 See also John Berger's theory regarding women's double consciousness, as discussed in Elaine Showalter, *The Female Malady: Women, Madness, and English Culture, 1830–1980* (New York, 1985), p. 212.

79 *Musical Courier* 46/11 (18 March 1903), p. 12, in Neuls-Bates, *Women in Music*, p. 226.

80 See also the discussion on a female aesthetic in Chapter 4.

81 See Gilbert and Gubar, *Madwoman in the Attic*, pp. 46–53.

82 See the discussion of originality in Chapter 5.

83 *Madwoman in the Attic*, p. 50.

84 Heidi Waleson, "Women composers find things easier – sort of," *The New York Times* (28 January 1990), sec. 2, p. 30. See also Chapter 6.

85 See also the discussion on Schoenberg in Chapter 1.

86 See *Old Mistresses*, pp. 115–33. See also Pollock, *Vision and Difference: Femininity, Feminism and Histories of Art* (London, 1988), pp. 85–90.

87 "Archimedes and the paradox of feminist criticism," *The Signs Reader*, ed. Elizabeth Abel and Emily K. Abel (Chicago, 1983), p. 77.

88 Friedman, "Creativity," p. 91.

89 See, for instance, Upton, *Woman in Music*. For a recent analysis see Roberta Lamb, "Questioning the canon: Women and music education," presentation at Bergamo Conference at Queen's University, Kingston, Ontario, October 1989. My thanks to Professor Lamb for sharing a typescript of the paper.

90 See especially Clément, *Opera, or the Undoing of Women*; and Susan McClary, "Sexual politics in classical music," *Feminine Endings*, 53–79. McClary's analysis of *Carmen* in "Sexual politics" is expanded to a full-length feminist exploration in a forthcoming monograph for Cambridge's Opera Handbook Series. See also Mary Ann Smart, "Azucena's excess: Memory and voice in *Il Trovatore*," Paper presented at Feminist Theory and Music Conference, University of Minnesota, Minneapolis, June 1991; and Eva Rieger, "The role of music in Alfred Hitchcock's cinema films seen from a feminist perspective," presented at the same conference.

91 See, for instance, Edward J. Dent, *Mozart's Operas: A Critical Study*, 2nd ed. (London, 1947), p. 190; Alfred Einstein, *Mozart: His Character, His Work*, trans. Arthur Mendel and Nathan Broder (London, 1945), pp. 443–4; and Wolfgang Hildesheimer, *Mozart*, trans. Marion Faber (New York, 1982), p. 286. Beethoven and Wagner were some of the main critics of the opera.

92 Even though in a word like this the "i" ending would typically be

understood as gender inclusive, there is still the possibility that it could be taken to mean men only. In this case my suggestion could not apply. However, Professor Anna Caflisch of Rice University, a native Italian and member of the Italian Department, assures me that the first meaning is the common interpretation. My thanks to her for her expertise.

93 Andrew Steptoe discusses the literary origins of two important plot elements – the wager and the test of fidelity – in "*Così fan tutte* and contemporary morality," *The Mozart-Da Ponte Operas: The Cultural and Musical Background to Le nozze di Figaro, Don Giovanni, and Così fan tutte* (Oxford, 1988), 121–39. He notes in passing that the woman who is unfaithful was a convention in opera buffa at the time (p. 138).

94 Even Wye Allanbrook's balanced treatment finds her a bit ridiculous: "She is a woman of great passion and not a little madness; she is completely vulnerable because she looks to Heaven for her principles, yet cannot control her willful and susceptible heart. It is a measure of the bleak perspective of *Don Giovanni* that such high excesses are rendered as near-comic idiosyncrasies by the stiff-gaited rhythms of an antique style." This quotation appears in a discussion of the aria No. 8, which is notable for Baroque mannerisms. Such stylistic features can create parody; this happens also in Bartolo's archaic aria (No. 4) in *Figaro*. See *Rhythmic Gesture in Mozart: Le Nozze di Figaro and Don Giovanni* (Chicago, 1983), p. 238. Regarding hysteria see, for instance, Ian Maclean, *The Renaissance Notion of Woman: A Study in the Fortunes of Scholasticism and Medical Science in European Intellectual Life* (Cambridge, 1980), p. 41.

95 See Hoffmann's essay, "Don Juan," originally in the *Allgemeine musikalische Zeitung* 15/13 (31 March 1813); and Kierkegaard's "The immediate stages of the erotic," *Either/Or* (1843). It is Mozart's Don in particular that Kierkegaard considers the embodiment of these features. His thesis reflects evolutionary tendencies of the time as it demonstrates how other Mozart operas, namely *The Magic Flute* and *The Marriage of Figaro*, respectively represent earlier stages leading up to the full flowering of desire in *Don Giovanni*. The only problem with this sequence, of course, is that *The Magic Flute* was later than *Don Giovanni*. But this temporal anachronism is irrelevant given the symbolic nature of the theory.

96 See also Clément, *Opera, or the Undoing of Women*, pp. 33–7.

97 See Judith Fetterley, *The Resisting Reader: Feminist Approaches to American Fiction* (Bloomington, 1978); and Elaine Showalter, "Women and the literary curriculum," *College English* 32 (1970–71), 855–62.

98 The concept of suture comes from film theory. For the interplay among identification, desire, and narrative, see especially Teresa de Lauretis, "Desire in narrative," *Alice Doesn't: Feminism, Semiotics, Cinema* (Bloomington, 1984), 103–57; Tania Modleski, *The Women Who Knew Too Much: Hitchcock and Feminist Theory* (New York, 1988); and Kaja Silverman, *The Subject of Semiotics* (Oxford, 1983).

99 Lipking, "Aristotle's sister: A poetics of abandonment," p. 79.

100 As Suzanne Cusick reminds me, the *virtuose* of the late sixteenth and early seventeenth centuries apparently knew each other well. These women, including Francesca Caccini (1587–*c.* 1640), were singer-composers who were also familiar with female musicians from the preceding generation. Perhaps with the fragmentation that came with public music and the growing division between creating and performing, female composers found themselves more isolated from each other than before.

101 See also Elaine Showalter, *A Literature of Their Own* (Princeton, 1977); and Janet Todd, *Women's Friendship in Literature* (New York, 1980).

102 Neuls-Bates, *Women in Music*, p. 218.

103 From *Female Pipings in Eden*, as excerpted in Neuls-Bates, *Women in Music*, p. 295.

104 *Perspectives* responses.

105 Many cultural critics and feminists have proposed this strategy. See, for example, Judith Fetterley, *The Resisting Reader*; and Jeffrey Kallberg, "The harmony of the tea table: Gender and ideology in the piano nocturne," *Representations* 39 (1992), 102–33.

106 Elisabeth Lutyens describes how, as a teen, she was composing in secret, in *A Goldfish Bowl* (London, 1972), as excerpted in Neuls-Bates, *Women in Music*, p. 315.

107 For additional discussions on marginalization and separatism see Chapter 6.

3 PROFESSIONALISM

1 For example Elisabeth Jacquet de la Guerre (*c.* 1666–1729) or Antonia Bembo (*b.* 1670).

2 See excerpts from her *Female Pipings in Eden* (London, 1933), in Carol Neuls-Bates, *Women in Music: An Anthology of Source Readings from the Middle Ages to the Present* (New York, 1982), pp. 278–96.

3 At least on any regular basis. Chaminade, for one, conducted a few concerts in Switzerland in the 1890s and was considered a real novelty. See my *Cécile Chaminade: A Bio-Bibliography* (Westport, Ct., 1988), p. 12.

4 As observed in 1981 by Nancy Van de Vate, in Neuls-Bates, *Women in Music*, pp. 325–6. The observations have been documented in a few studies, including Adrienne Fried Block's "Women in composition," *The Status of Women in College Music: Preliminary Studies*, ed. Neuls-Bates, College Music Society Report No. 1 (1976); and Block's expanded report, "The status of women in college music, 1986–87," *Women's Studies/Women's Status*, College Music Society Report No. 5 (1988). Ellen Zwilich (*b.* 1939) is one of the few successful contemporary composers who is managing to earn a living as a free-lance composer, without academic affiliation.

5 In our own time, Van de Vate candidly airs her views on the practical ramifications of the category "amateur" for twentieth-century women; see her interview in Neuls-Bates, *Women in Music*, pp. 323–5.

6 Diane Thome, in the responses by women composers in *Perspectives of*

New Music, as gathered by Elaine Barkin: volume 20–21 (1981–2), 288–329.

7 *Perspectives of New Music* survey.

8 *The Resisting Reader: A Feminist Approach to American Fiction* (Bloomington, 1978).

9 *Perspectives of New Music* survey.

10 "Master musician: An impregnable taboo?" *Contact: A Journal of Contemporary Music* No. 31 (1987), 4–8.

11 *Perspectives of New Music* survey.

12 *Ibid.*

13 See Nancy Reich's *Clara Schumann: The Artist and the Woman* (Ithaca, 1985).

14 See Phyllis Benjamin's fascinating discussion of Hensel and young motherhood, based on a newly found source, in "A diary-album for Fanny Mendelssohn-Bartholdy," *Mendelssohn-Studien* 7 (1990), 178–217.

15 Quoted in Jane Weiner Le Page, ed., *Women Composers, Conductors, and Musicians of the 20th Century*, vol. 1 (New York, 1980), p. 214.

16 See the interview with Chaminade in *The Washington Post* (1 November 1908), "Magazine" section, p. 4; see also Citron, *Cécile Chaminade*, pp. 13–14.

17 See Diane Jezic, *Women Composers: The Lost Tradition Found* (New York, 1988), p. 159. Clarke's radio interview with Robert Sherman in 1976, excerpts of which appear on volume 1 of the Leonarda Sampler Cassette, is a valuable piece of oral history that presents her views on gender discrimination experienced in her earlier years.

18 Laura Mitgang, "Germaine Tailleferre: Before, during, and after *Les Six*," *The Musical Woman: An International Perspective*, vol. II, ed. Judith Lang Zaimont, Catherine Overhauser, and Jane Gottlieb (Westport, Ct., 1987), 177–221.

19 See Walter B. Bailey, "The triumph of modernism: Parallels and divergences in the musics and careers of Radie Britain and Ruth Crawford," unpublished manuscript.

20 Ray Wilding-White, "Remembering Ruth Crawford Seeger: An interview with Charles and Peggy Seeger," *American Music* (1988), p. 445.

21 Matilda Gaume, "Ruth Crawford Seeger," *Women Making Music: The Western Art Tradition, 1150–1950*, ed. Jane Bowers and Judith Tick (Urbana, 1986), p. 382; and *Ruth Crawford Seeger: Memoirs, Memories, Music* (Metuchen, 1986), p. 56.

22 "'Spirit of me... Dear rollicking far-gazing straddler of two worlds': The 'Autobiography' of Ruth Crawford Seeger," Paper presented at Gender and Music Conference, King's College, University of London, July 1991.

23 "Transformation of the American orchestra: Gender issues," Paper presented at the Gender and Music Conference, King's College, University of London, July 1991.

24 Letter of 29 May 1948, in Ruth Crawford-Seeger collection, music

division, Library of Congress. Quoted with the permission of Michael Seeger. Published in Neuls-Bates, *Women in Music*, p. 309.

25 Gaume, "Ruth Crawford Seeger," pp. 380–82. Judith Tick's forthcoming biography (Oxford University Press) will no doubt shed considerable light on the contradictions inherent in this fascinating figure.

26 Introduction by Charles Slater to the Da Capo reprint edition, *Agathe Backer-Grøndahl: Piano Music* (New York, 1982), n. p.

27 In *Perspectives of New Music* survey. Although gender dynamics change considerably in Lesbian relationships, still the issue of children, possibly adopted, has an impact on the making of professional choices. Furthermore, the issue of the role of a supportive partner in a Lesbian relationship could also be considered in this discussion. As an example of this kind of work as applied to historical women, a recent "coming-out" phenomenon in musicology, see Elizabeth Wood's fascinating work on Ethel Smyth, including "Lesbian fugue: Ethel Smyth's contrapuntal arts," presented at the Seventh International Congress on Women in Music, Utrecht, May 1991.

28 Heilbrun, *Writing a Woman's Life* (New York, 1988), pp. 109 and 118. In a 1987 interview, composer Barbara Kolb remarked on the disparity between successful female and male composers in terms of practical recognition – i.e., monetary remuneration. See the excerpt from the article in the *Hartford Courant* (7 April 1987), in Jezic, *Women Composers*, p. 197.

29 "Master musician," p. 6.

30 Interview of 7 October 1981, in Neuls-Bates, *Women in Music*, p. 324.

31 *Writing a Woman's Life*, p. 121.

32 For a perceptive analysis of this phenomenon see Rose Laub Coser, "The principle of patriarchy: The case of *The Magic Flute*," *Signs* 4/2 (1978), 337–48.

33 In some groups in Latin America there is also a matrilineal succession in name.

34 "Women writers and the double standard," *Women in Sexist Society: Studies in Power and Powerlessness*, ed. Vivian Gornick and Barbara K. Moran (New York, 1971), p. 325. See also Naomi Schor, "Female fetishism: The case of George Sand," *The Female Body in Western Culture: Contemporary Perspectives*, ed. Susan Rubin Suleiman (Cambridge, Mass., 1986), 363–72.

35 Sandra M. Gilbert and Susan Gubar, *The Madwoman in the Attic: The Woman Writer and the Nineteenth-Century Literary Imagination* (New Haven, 1979), p. 65.

36 Charlotte Brontë remarked on this as a reason why the three sisters donned male identities, as quoted in Showalter, "Women writers and the double standard," p. 325.

37 Rollo Myers, "Augusta Holmès: A meteoric career," *The Musical Quarterly* 53 (1967), p. 371. I have not been able to corroborate the

accuracy of this statement. Aaron Cohen's *International Encyclopedia of Women Composers* includes a two-page list of pseudonyms; see 2nd edition, vol. II (New York, 1987), pp. 854–5. A word of caution, however: while admirable in its comprehensiveness, the study as a whole is unfortunately riddled with errors.

38 Mentioned in Clarke's radio interview with Robert Sherman. See also Jezic, *Women Composers*, p. 159. In a similar vein, Judith Tick describes how some American male composers published parlor music under female pseudonyms. Stephen Foster apparently issued a song under the anonymous atttribution "a Lady," probably because the custom of concealed authorial identity rested mainly with women at that time, and perhaps because its style affirmed feminine stereotypes in music. Tick also provides an interesting summary of the varied practices women engaged in with regard to authorial identity. See *American Women Composers Before 1870* (Ann Arbor, 1983), pp. 74–5.

39 Edith Borroff, "Women composers: Reminiscence and history," *College Music Symposium* 15 (1975), p. 27. Similarly, Emily Brontë received more favorable reviews when she published under a male pseudonym; see Carol Ohmann, "Emily Brontë in the hands of male critics," *College English* 32 (1971), 906–13.

40 Interview in Neuls-Bates, *Women in Music*, p. 330.

41 See *Letters of Fanny Hensel to Felix Mendelssohn*, ed. Marcia J. Citron (New York, 1987), pp. 100–101.

42 See Chapter 6 of Heilbrun's *Writing a Woman's Life*, especially pp. 116 and 114.

43 Linda Nicholson, *Gender and History: The Limits of Social Theory in the Age of the Family* (New York, 1986). The following discussion is based largely on Nicholson's arguments. For another feminist interpretation, see historian Joan Kelly's hypothesis that "a new division between personal and public life" occurred during the Renaissance, in "Did women have a Renaissance?" (1977), in *Women, History, and Theory: The Essays of Joan Kelly* (Chicago, 1984), p. 47.

44 Locke's dualism bears obvious affinities with the mind–body dualism promulgated earlier in the century by René Descartes (see Chapter 2). Nicholson notes a psychoanalytic analogue to public–private in the theories of Nancy Chodorow: "young girls learn concretely how to be adult women in the context of their initial familial setting. Young boys have to 'achieve' gender identity by breaking out of this setting. They are thus led to create extrafamilial 'public' associations whose construction or entrance into represents an accomplishment. Such associations are defined in part oppositionally to the family and to women" (Nicholson, *Gender and History*, p. 75).

45 Nicholson attributes the exposure of this contradiction to Marxism; see *Gender and History*, p. 2.

46 *Ibid.*, p. 3.

47 *The Social Production of Art* (New York, 1984).

48 See Nicholson, *Gender and History*, especially Chapter 2, pp. 43–68. This related to the so-called "cult of domesticity," especially in nineteenth-century America, and to the "eternal feminine" principle, ideologically pervasive in European Romanticism.

49 See Rosaldo's "The use and abuse of anthropology: Reflections on feminism and cross-cultural understanding," *Signs* 5/3 (1980), 389–417. A groundbreaking study that posits that the notion of separate spheres in the United States was in many respects an enabling convention that fostered intimate, supportive friendships between married women is Carroll Smith Rosenberg, "The female world of love and ritual: Relations between women in 19th-century America," *Signs* 1 (1975), 1–29. For an overview of separate spheres as a historical construction see Linda K. Kerber, "Separate spheres, female worlds, woman's place: The rhetoric of women's history," *Journal of American History* 75/1 (1988), 9–39.

50 Nancy Fraser makes a convincing case for new modelings in "What's critical about critical theory? The case of Habermas and gender," *Feminism as Critique*, ed. Seyla Benhabib and Drucilla Cornell (Minneapolis, 1988), 31–56.

51 See especially Janet Wolff, "Women's knowledge and women's art," *Feminine Sentences: Essays on Women and Culture* (Berkeley, 1990), p. 71.

52 Imogen Fellinger, "Die Begriffe *Salon* und *Salonmusik* in der Musikanschauung des 19. Jahrhunderts," *Studien zur Trivialmusik des 19. Jahrhunderts*, ed. Carl Dahlhaus (Regensburg, 1967), pp. 131–2.

53 In a letter from Paris to his family of 9 May 1825, Felix Mendelssohn makes a clear distinction between *salons*, which are "social gatherings," and *soirées*, which are "concerts for money." See Sebastian Hensel, *Die Familie Mendelssohns (1729–1847)*, 3rd ed., 2 vols (Berlin, 1882), I, p. 148. Mendelssohn was chiding Fanny Hensel for presuming to know more about Paris than he did; see Citron, *Letters of Fanny Hensel*, p. 14.

54 See Jeffrey Kallberg's perceptive essay, "The harmony of the tea table: Gender and ideology in the piano nocturne," *Representations* 39 (1992), 102–33. Kallberg shows how the nocturne, a major genre of Chopin, was considered a feminine *topos*.

55 Eric Werner believes that Mendelssohn was passed over for the position of head of the Berlin Singakademie, in 1833, because of anti-Semitism; see his *Mendelssohn: A New Image of the Composer and His Age*, trans. Dika Newlin (New York, 1963), pp. 229–33.

56 For more insight, see, for example, Hilde Spiel's *Fanny von Arnstein, oder die Emanzipation* (Frankfurt, 1962); Arnstein, incidentally, was a maternal great-aunt to Fanny Hensel, and provided the source for Hensel's first name. A general study is Deborah Hertz's *Jewish High Society in Old Regime Berlin* (New Haven, 1988). For French *salonières* see Dena Goodman, "Enlightenment salons: The convergence of female and philosophic ambitions," *Eighteenth-Century Studies* 22/3 (1989), 329–50.

57 See Citron, *Letters of Fanny Hensel*. The diaries, only excerpts of which

were published by her son Sebastian in his *Die Familie Mendelssohns*, have been largely unavailable for consultation, and are in private hands or in the Mendelssohn Archive of the Staatsbibliothek, Berlin.

58 Johanna Kinkel (1810–1858), herself a composer, commented favorably on Hensel's conducting. See Eva Rieger, *Frau, Musik und Männer-herrschaft*, 2nd ed. (Kassel, 1988), p. 231; this excerpt is taken from Else Thalheimer, *Johanna Kinkel als Musikerin* (Bonn, 1924).

59 See Maynard Solomon, "Franz Schubert and the peacocks of Benvenuto Cellini," *Nineteenth Century Music* 12/3 (1989), 193–206. See also Susan McClary, "Making a difference in the music: The relevance of sexuality to compositions by Laurie Anderson and Schubert," paper delivered at the annual meeting of the American Musicological Society, Oakland, November 1990. For a thorough exploration of the socio-economic background of this period see Alice M. Hanson, *Musical Life in Biedermeier Vienna* (Cambridge, 1985).

60 Fellinger's study, "Die Begriffe *Salon* und *Salonmusik*," shows the various meanings and valuations accorded the *salon* in the nineteenth century. For example, she cites Robert Schumann's classification of three types of *salon* music in 1836 and his statement the next decade that *salon* music has declined (pp. 132–5). For the activities of female composers and performers in the American parlor see Tick, *American Women Composers Before 1870*.

61 "An American parlor at the turn of the century," *American Music* (1986), 302–8.

62 Many European *salons* around 1900 were criticized for their inclusion of "Unterhaltungsmusik," or light music; see Fellinger, "Die Begriffe *Salon* und *Salonmusik*," pp. 139–41. Perhaps the greatest exception in late nineteenth-century art music would be Italian opera, especially Verdi. The Italian tradition is much more rooted in populism and inclusive of all classes. Opera seems to grow naturally out of folk idioms. Folk styles also played a substantial role in other European cultures of the period, but they were often more a self-conscious gesture than an integrated idiom. Composers like Brahms and Mahler also utilized folk idioms. With Brahms, the works consciously modeled on folk music often seem like the work of another composer – they are quite different from his more "learned" works. Yet many of these incorporate folk styles in an unselfconscious way. In the Second Symphony or the Violin Concerto, for example, the distinction between art and folk style is often blurred to the point where the distinction collapses.

63 See Chapter 6 for a discussion of modernism's view of popularity as a negative factor in valuation and hence canonicity.

64 Critiques pointed to "Hausmusik" – music-making in the home or some other domestic environment, as well as styles that suggest such a setting – as indicative of lesser value. But some kinds of *salons* earned greater respect, including those sponsored by upper-class patrons who used such occasions to further the careers of aspiring soloists. Critics looked for the

presence of "Bildung" – a combination of education, refinement, and taste – as a measure of artistic quality. See Fellinger, "Die Begriffe *Salon* und *Salonmusik.*" Carl Dahlhaus observes that the bourgeois *salon* and its *Hausmusik* were an imitation of the social functions and the kinds of music performed at the aristocratic counterparts; see "Zur Problematik der musikalischen Gattungen im 19. Jahrhundert," *Gattungen der Musik in Einzeldarstellungen: Gedenkschrift Leo Schrade*, ed. Wulf Arlt, Ernst Lichtenhahn, and Hans Oesch (Berne, 1973), p. 866.

65 Gustave Ferrari in *Grove's Dictionary of Music and Musicians*, 2nd edn, ed. J. A. Fuller Maitland, 5 vols. (New York, 1911), vol. 1, p. 496; the entry in the 6th edition has an updated bibliography by Jean Mongrédien (London, 1980), IV, p. 125.

66 As in his definition of "pseudo-music," in *Music Since 1900*, 4th ed. (New York, 1971), p. 1484.

67 "Ophelia's songs in *Hamlet*: Music, madness, and the feminine," Paper presented at Feminist Theory and Music Conference, University of Minnesota, Minneapolis, June 1991.

68 See also the discussion of hierarchy of genre in Chapter 4.

69 Letter to Lea Mendelssohn, 24 June 1837, in the New York Public Library; incorrectly dated 2 June and published in Felix Mendelssohn-Bartholdy, *Briefe aus den Jahren 1830–1847*, ed. Paul Mendelssohn Bartholdy and Carl Mendelssohn, 3rd ed. (Leipzig, 1875), vol. II, pp. 88–9 (translation mine).

70 For a more detailed study see my essay, "Felix Mendelssohn's influence on Fanny Mendelssohn Hensel as a professional composer," *Current Musicology* No. 37/8 (1984), 9–18.

71 A verbal comment made to me by the great-granddaughter of Fanny Hensel, the Berlin historian Cécile Loewenthal-Hensel, in early 1983.

72 My thanks to Suzanne Cusick for this idea.

73 An idea offered in a critique of an early draft of the manuscript. For more on artistic ownership and permanence see Roland Barthes, "From work to text," *Textual Strategies: Perspectives in Post-Structuralist Criticism*, ed. Josué Harari (Ithaca, 1979), 73–81; Simon Frith, "Towards an aesthetic of popular music," *Music and Society: The Politics of Composition, Performance and Reception*, ed. Richard Leppert and Susan McClary (Cambridge, 1987), 133–50; Edward Lippman, "Permanence," *A Humanistic Philosophy of Music* (New York, 1977), 196–241; and Edward Said, "The text, the world, the critic," *Textual Strategies*, 161–88.

74 See "What is an author?" (1969), in *Textual Strategies*, 141–60.

75 See, for example, Hans Lenneberg, "The myth of the unappreciated (musical) genius," *The Musical Quarterly* 66 (1980), 219–31. Even more pertinent is Christine Battersby, *Gender and Genius: Towards a Feminist Aesthetics* (London, 1989).

76 Althusser's ideas are discussed in Wolff, *The Social Production of Art* (New York, 1984), pp. 129–32.

77 "The orchestral composer's point of view," *The Writings of Elliott Carter*, ed. Else Stone and Kurt Stone (Bloomington, 1977), p. 285.

78 *Questions About Music* (New York, 1971), p. 129.
79 "The historical approach to music," *The Musical Quarterly* 23 (1937), p. 7.
80 Foucault, "What is an author?".
81 See Chapter 6 for a discussion of the pedagogical paradigm of the "great composer."
82 Barthes, "The death of the author" (1968), in his *Image, Music, Text*, trans. Stephen Heath (New York, 1977), 142–8.
83 Nancy Miller later explained that when Barthes wrote his essay he was specifically reacting to certain French laws regarding authorial rights; see "Changing the subject: Authorship, writing, and the reader," *Feminist Studies/Critical Studies*, ed. Teresa de Lauretis (Bloomington, 1986), p. 118, n. 2. Miller is shrewd in grounding Barthes's pronouncements, for in some later essays he seems to rejoice in the mystical properties of the creator. I am specifically thinking of his essays on music, from the mid-1970s, especially "Loving Schumann." Here Barthes virtually idolizes Schumann as he gushes and effuses much like a Romantic writer. This includes the attribution of almost mythical creative powers to the composer. See, for example, this essay in *The Responsibility of Forms: Critical Essays on Music, Art and Representation*, trans. Richard Howard (New York, 1985).
84 "Aristotle's sister: A poetics of abandonment," *Critical Inquiry* 10/1 (1983), p. 73. The views of Barthes and Foucault are also grounded in a critique of the notion of the unified subject, which they claim has been implicit in the Western concept of the author. In varying ways, both wish to show that subjectivity is multiple, partial, and contradictory, and that much more is involved in the meaning and in the coming into existence of an art work than the persona of the individual author. See, for example, Wolff, *The Social Production of Art*, especially Chapter 6; and Cheryl Walker, "Feminist literary criticism and the author," *Critical Inquiry* 16/3 (1990), 551–71.
85 As discussed in Herbert Lindenberger, *The History in Literature: On Value, Genre, Institutions* (New York, 1990), p. 157.
86 Other artistic fields have also begun to pose feminist inquiries regarding the cultural emphasis on the author. For art history see Rozsika Parker and Griselda Pollock, *Old Mistresses: Women, Art and Ideology* (New York, 1981), pp. 68–9. For film studies see Teresa de Lauretis, "Aesthetic and feminist theory: Rethinking women's cinema," *Feminist Art Criticism: An Anthology*, ed. Arlene Raven, Cassandra L. Langer, and Joanna Frueh (Ann Arbor, 1988), p. 139; and for an interesting critique of Barthes's theories in relation to the presence of a gendered film-maker, Kaja Silverman, "The female authorial voice," *The Acoustic Mirror: The Female Voice in Psychoanalysis and Cinema* (Bloomington, 1988), 187–234.
87 Nancy Miller, "Changing the subject"; and Elizabeth Fox-Genovese, "The claims of a common culture: Gender, race, class, and the canon," *Salmagundi* No. 72 (1986), p. 134. See also Battersby, *Gender and Genius*, pp. 146–53.

88 See Foucault, "What is an author?"; and Wolff, *The Social Production of Art*, especially Chapter 6, "The death of the author."

4 MUSIC AS GENDERED DISCOURSE

1 In "The death of the author" (1968), in his *Image, Music, Text*, trans. Stephen Heath (New York, 1977), 142–8.

2 Barbara Herrnstein Smith, "Contingencies of value," *Critical Inquiry* 10/1 (1983), p. 23. The topic has since been expanded into a full-length study, with the same title. See also Janet Todd, *Feminist Literary History* (New York, 1988), p. 99.

3 See Edward Lippman, *A Humanistic Philosophy of Music* (New York, 1977), p. 334.

4 See Carl Dahlhaus, "Gattung," *Brockhaus Riemann Musiklexikon*, ed. Dahlhaus and Hans Heinrich Eggebrecht, 2 vols. (Wiesbaden, 1978), I, p. 452. On the relationship between title and genre see, for example, his *Esthetics of Music*, trans. William Austin (Cambridge, 1982), p. 15; and Jim Samson, "Chopin and genre," *Music and Analysis* 8/3 (1989), p. 217. A significant degree of change brings up the issue of what constitutes genre in the first place. Dahlhaus distinguishes genre from form-types and musical processes, such as fugue, in "Was ist eine musikalische Gattung?" *Neue Zeitschrift für Musik* 135 (1974), 620–25.

5 In addition to "Was ist eine musikalische Gattung?" he has discussed genre in broader studies and in other essays devoted specifically to the topic. Among them are *Esthetics of Music*; *Foundations of Music History*, trans. J. B. Robinson (Cambridge, 1983); "Gattung" in *Brockhaus Riemann Musiklexikon*; "Zur Problematik der musikalischen Gattungen im 19. Jahrhundert," *Gattungen der Musik in Einzeldarstellungen: Gedenkschrift Leo Schrade*, ed. Wulf Arlt, Ernst Lichtenhahn, and Hans Oesch (Berne, 1973), 840–95; and "New music and the problem of musical genre," *Schoenberg and the New Music*, trans. Derrick Puffett and Alfred Clayton (Cambridge, 1987), 32–44.

6 For Dahlhaus see especially "Was ist eine musikalische Gattung?" especially pp. 621–2. For Kallberg see his essays, "The rhetoric of genre: Chopin's Nocturne in G Minor," *Nineteenth Century Music* 11/3 (1988), 238–61; and "The harmony of the tea table: Gender and ideology in the piano nocturne," *Representations* 39 (1992), 102–33. Jim Samson also discusses mixed genres in "Chopin and genre."

7 See also Lippman, *A Humanistic Philosophy*, p. 170.

8 Julia P. Stanley and Susan J. Wolfe (Robbins) consider this a male approach to aesthetics: "Toward a feminist aesthetic," *Chrysalis* 6 (1978), pp. 62–3. This point was also made by Lilian Robinson, "Who speaks for women – and is it poetry?" Paper presented at the annual meeting of the Modern Language Association, New York, in December 1976. For substantial excerpts see the article by Stanley and Wolfe. See also Jane Tompkins, *Sensational Designs: The Cultural Work of American*

Fiction 1790–1860 (New York, 1985), p. xvi. I take up the issue again in the last section of Chapter 5.

9 Kallberg discusses this idea of Dahlhaus, in "The rhetoric of genre," p. 240.

10 On a link between female writers and a traditionally male genre see Susan Stanford Friedman, "Gender and genre anxiety: Elizabeth Barrett Browning and H. D. as epic poets," *Tulsa Studies in Women's Literature* 5 (1986), 203–29. For a more general literary study that includes a chapter on hierarchy of genre and its relationship with canonicity see Alastair Fowler, *Kinds of Literature: An Introduction to the Theory of Genres and Modes* (Cambridge, Mass., 1982). Jacques Derrida has made playful semantic associations between genre and female gender, based on the female gender of the word "law" (*la loi*), in his essay "The law of genre," in *On Narrative*, ed. W. J. T. Mitchell (Chicago, 1981), 51–77.

11 In a pun on the arts and crafts distinction, Rozsika Parker and Griselda Pollock entitle the chapter that treats the different valuation accorded particular genres, "Crafty women and the hierarchy of the arts," in their *Old Mistresses: Women, Art, and Ideology* (New York, 1981), 50–81.

12 *William Morris, Selected Writings and Designs*, ed. Asa Briggs (Baltimore, 1962), p. 84, as quoted in Parker and Pollock, *Old Mistresses*, pp. 50–51.

13 The depiction of daily life and its citizens was a specialty of the Dutch, who were looked down upon by the Italians. See Svetlana Alpers, "Art history and its exclusions," in *Feminism and Art History: Questioning the Litany*, ed. Norma Broude and Mary D. Garrard (New York, 1982), 183–200. For "genre painting" see the entry "Genre and secular subjects" in *Encyclopedia of World Art* (London, 1962), VI, p. 82.

14 See Chapter 2 for more on women artists' training from the nude. For a fascinating analysis of female objectification as nudes in art works by men and of resistance to the convention in recent works by women, see the chapter "Painted ladies," pp. 114–33, in Parker and Pollock, *Old Mistresses*. For a feminist perspective on the conventions and semiotic codes of sculpture see Eva Rieger, *Frau, Musik und Männerherrschaft*, 2nd ed. (Kassel, 1988), p. 148; and Parker and Pollock, *ibid.*, pp. 103–4.

15 Parker and Pollock, *ibid.*, p. 37.

16 For more on Lady Butler see Ann Sutherland Harris and Linda Nochlin, *Women Artists: 1550–1950* (Los Angeles, 1976), pp. 53–4.

17 The following discussion is drawn largely from Parker and Pollock, *Old Mistresses*, pp. 51–70.

18 *Ibid.*, p. 58.

19 *Ibid.*, p. 59. For a full study of women and embroidery see Rozsika Parker, *The Subversive Stitch* (London, 1984).

20 Architecture of course is grounded in functionality: structures in which people live, work, pray, and spend leisure time. Yet many of architecture's famous edifices, at least before the twentieth century, are honored largely because of exterior and interior beauty and less so by

way of functional strength. Thus, in the artistic canon, buildings tend to be viewed more as visual phenomena – textualized, if you will – than as phenomenological embodiments of function.

21 *Old Mistresses*, p. 51.

22 For a discussion of women's relationship with a hierarchy of film images see Teresa De Lauretis, "Aesthetic and feminist theory: Rethinking women's cinema," *Feminist Art Criticism: An Anthology*, ed. Arlene Raven, Cassandra L. Langer, and Joanna Frueh (Ann Arbor, 1988), 133–52.

23 For an attempt at categorization of contemporary popular idioms see John Shepherd, "Music and male hegemony," *Music and Society: The Politics of Composition, Performance, and Reception*, ed. Richard Leppert and Susan McClary (Cambridge, 1987), pp. 165–8. In the same collection, Simon Frith suggests that popular genres might be classified "according to their ideological effects"; see his "Towards an aesthetic of popular music," p. 147. Of course, one could hypothesize various other binary divisions among these types of music. Furthermore, most can be subdivided, and the proliferation offers further possibilities for relationship. A recent study in psychology has attempted to discern gender preferences of college students toward various genres of popular music. See Peter G. Christenson and Jon Brian Peterson, "Genre and gender in the structure of music preferences," *Communication Research* 15/3 (1988), 282–301.

24 In the past twenty-five years or so, considerable discussion has taken place on the viability of these genres within the styles and aesthetics of contemporary musical idioms. Both symphony and opera stand as aesthetic and sociological holdovers from the nineteenth century. Nonetheless, as mentioned earlier and also observed by others, art music as currently practiced *still* has many of its basic structures from the nineteenth century, for example the quasi-religious experience of the symphony concert or the elitist ritual of opera in the purportedly egalitarian opera house. Both symphony and opera have given their names to the two major kinds of performance structures within art music; certainly this, if nothing else, demonstrates the resilience of the genres. It is also important to note that the hegemony of these genres has not been constant and universal since *c.* 1800 but has varied according to many factors, notably country and era. In nineteenth-century France, for example, opera reigned supreme while the symphony enjoyed lesser status, at least until the later part of the century.

Leonard Meyer notes the contradiction between Romantics' professed desire to eliminate generic distinctions and their reinforcement of such distinctions in actual practice (*Style and Music: Theory, History, and Ideology* [Philadelphia, 1989], p. 179). Furthermore, the division into large and small genres described here pertains to accumulated historiographical understanding since the nineteenth century rather than to music written today. Perhaps other hierarchic divisions are taking its place.

25 *Style and Music*, p. 204.

26 For more on the relationship between musical genres and contemporary societal processes see Rieger, *Frau, Musik und Männerherrschaft*, especially pp. 124–50. Susan McClary has also isolated musico-social correspondences in "Sexual politics in classical music," *Feminine Endings: Music, Gender, and Sexuality* (Minneapolis, 1991), 53–79; and "The blasphemy of talking politics during Bach year," *Music and Society: The Politics of Composition*, 13–62.

27 Dahlhaus notes that it was Schubert who transformed the genre of Lied from a folk-like style of low rank to an art song that became worthy of the label "masterpiece" and thus high rank. See "Zur Problematik der musikalischen Gattungen im 19. Jahrhundert," p. 860.

28 Dahlhaus has pointed out how concert halls, which proliferated in the nineteenth century, functioned as temples of art music. Their architecture aimed for the monumental and was often neo-Classical, like many a religious temple. This secular religion functioned as replacement for the lessened emphasis on formal religion. See *The Idea of Absolute Music*, trans. Roger Lustig (Chicago, 1989), especially Chapter 5 (pp. 78–87); and *Nineteenth Century Music*, trans. J. Bradford Robinson (Berkeley, 1989), p. 44. Eva Rieger also discusses this new function of music in *Frau, Musik und Männerherrschaft*, p. 136.

29 "Contingencies of value," p. 23. For a discussion of complexity see Dahlhaus, *Esthetics of Music*, pp. 91–3.

30 In contrast, music composed only some twenty years earlier was subject to negative criticism for being complex. *The Marriage of Figaro*, for example, was criticized for being texturally too complex: it had "too many notes."

31 As in the summary assessment of Cécile Chaminade's music in *The New Grove Dictionary of Music and Musicians* (vol. IV, p. 125). This entry basically repeated the contents from earlier editions of *Grove's* (authored by Gustave Ferrari). Hopefully the assessment will be more even-handed in the forthcoming *New Grove Dictionary of Women Composers*, ed. Julie Sadie and Rhian Samuel.

32 Leo Treitler discusses an interesting expression of the masculine–feminine power relationship, in the nineteenth century, as the dualism Europe–Orient: "The politics of reception: Tailoring the present as fulfilment of a desired past," *Journal of the Royal Musical Association* 116 (1991), p. 291.

33 See Peter Bloom, "Communication," *Journal of the American Musicological Society* 27 (1974), p. 162. For a discussion of Reicha in relation to Marx and Czerny and a facsimile of Reicha's diagram of sonata form, see William S. Newman, *The Sonata Since Beethoven* (Chapel Hill, 1969), pp. 32–3. See also Hans H. Eggebrecht, ed., "Exposition" in *Handwörterbuch der musikalischen Terminologie*, vol. II, n.d., pp. 5–6.

34 An interesting idealization of "maternal" in relation to music occurs in Roland Barthes's essay, "Loving Schumann" (1979), *The Responsibility of Forms: Critical Essays on Music, Art and Representation*, trans. Richard Howard (New York, 1985), p. 298.

35 "In diesem Paar von Sätzen ist … der Hauptsatz das zuerst, also in erster Frische und Energie Bestimmte, mithin das energischer, markiger, absoluter Gebildete, das Herrschende und Bestimmende. Der Seitensatz dagegen ist das nach der ersten energischen Feststellung Nachge-schaffne, zum Gegensatz dienende, von jenem Vorangehenden Bedingte und Bestimmte, mithin seinem Wesen nach nothwendig das Mildere, mehr schmiegsam als markig Gebildete, das Weibliche gleichsam zu jenem vorangehenden Männlichen. Eben in solchem Sinn ist jeder der beiden Sätze ein Andres und erst beide miteinander ein Höheres, Vollkommneres." *Die Lehre von der musikalischen Komposition*, part 3 (Leipzig, 1845), p. 273.

36 "In der Regel ist die Sonatenform so angelegt daß einem kraftvollen, charakteristischen, ersten Thema sozusagen dem Vertreter des männlichen Prinzips, ein gesangvolleres, weicheres gegenübertritt, als Repräsentant des weiblichen Prinzips, regelmäßig in anderer, aber verwandter Tonart." *Katechismus der Musik* (*Allgemeine Musiklehre*) (Leipzig, 1888), p. 128.

37 "Aber das zweite Thema in seiner Gegensätzlichkeit zum ersten gemildert durch Annahme von dessen Tonart oder durch möglichste Annäherung an dieselbe" (*ibid.*, p. 128).

38 "A mesure que les deux idées exposées et développées dans les pièces de forms Sonate se perfectionnent, on constate en effet qu'elles se comportent vraiment comme des êtres vivants, soumis aux lois fatales de l'humanité: sympathie ou antipathie, attirance ou répulsion, amour ou haine. Et, dans ce perpétuel conflit, image de ceux de la vie, chacune des deux idées offre des qualités comparables à celles qui furent de tout temps attribuées respectivement à l'homme et à la femme.

Force et énergie, concision et netteté: tels sont à peu près invariablement les caractères d'essence *masculine* appartenant à la *première idée*: elle s'impose en *rythmes* vigoureux et brusques, affirmant bien haut sa propriété tonale, une et définitive.

La *seconde idée*, au contraire, toute de douceur et de grâce *mélodique*, affecte presque toujours par sa prolixité et son indétermination modulante des allures éminemment *féminines*: souple et élégante, elle étale progressivement la courbe de sa mélodie ornée; circonscrite plus ou moins nettement dans un ton voisin au cours de l'exposition, elle le quittera toujours dans la réexposition terminale, pour adopter la tonalité initiale occupée dès le début par l'élément dominateur masculin, seul. Comme si, après la lutte active du développement, l'être de douceur et de faiblesse devait subir, soit par la violence, soit par la persuasion, la conquête de l'être de force et de puissance.

Telle paraît être du moins, dans les Sonates comme dans la vie, la loi commune, en dépit de quelques rares exceptions où le rôle respectif des deux idées semble moins tranché, parfois même interverti." *Cours de composition musicale*, Book 2, part 1 (Paris, 1909), p. 262.

39 Entry "Form," by Joseph Müller-Blattau, vol. iv, col. 549 (Kassel,

1955): "Zwei Grundprinzipe des Menschen sollen in den beiden Hauptthemen Gestalt werden: das tätig nach außen drängende männliche (1. Thema) und das still in sich beruhende weibliche (2. Thema) .... [Das 2. Thema] soll vor allem ein 'Folgethema' sein, ein solches von geringerer Selbständigkeit, das erste abwandelnd und doch Ausdrucksgegensatz zu ihm."

40 *The Classical Style* (New York, 1971), p. 81.

41 "D'après les notes prises aux Classes de Composition de la Schola Cantorum en 1899–1900," on title page of book 2, part 1.

42 Some modern descriptions of Romantic sonata form list a third theme in the exposition, which could be thought of as an expansion of the closing theme in late eighteenth-century practice. See, for example, *MGG*, vol. IV, col. 548. James Webster discusses this trait in "Schubert's sonata form and Brahms's first maturity," *Nineteenth Century Music* 2 (1978–9), 18–35; and 3 (1979–80), 52–71. As an extension of the implications of the second theme, the third theme would also be an "Other" to the first theme and at least partially dependent on it.

43 As discussed in the introductory chapter and several essays in *Feminine Endings*.

44 Ernst H. Meyer, *Musik im Zeitgeschehen* (Berlin, 1952), as quoted in Rieger, *Frau, Musik und Männerherrschaft*, p. 141.

45 Charles Rosen, *Sonata Forms* (New York, 1980), p. 222.

46 Donald Francis Tovey, "Sonata style," *Encyclopedia Britannica*, 13th edn (Chicago, 1957), vol. xx, p. 978; Webster, "Sonata form," *The New Grove Dictionary of Music and Musicians* (London, 1980), vol. xvii, p. 498. Leonard Meyer characterizes a principal difference between eighteenth- and nineteenth-century sonata form as the later era's conception of the two themes in conflict, not just contrast, with each other. Meyer, incidentally, admits the existence of gendered labels for the two themes, although like other twentieth-century scholars (e.g. William S. Newman in *The Sonata Since Beethoven*) he questions its validity and creates authorial distance by placing quotation marks around masculine and feminine. See *Style and Music*, p. 203.

47 Charles Rosen, for example, has remarked, "I do not want to turn Haydn, Mozart, and Beethoven into Hegelians, but the simplest way to summarize classical form is as the symmetrical resolution of opposing forces": *The Classical Style*, p. 83. See also Leonard Meyer's discussion of Hegelian views toward the form in the nineteenth century, in *Style and Music*, pp. 308–9.

48 The association of first with male and with better apparently was a long-held assumption through the Renaissance, as noted by Constance Jordan in *Renaissance Feminism: Literary Texts and Political Models* (Ithaca, 1990). With regard to the musical Renaissance, the absorption of material from a second key into a first key that is linked with male conquest of the female was a device in some late dramatic works, including the intermedi of 1589 and the *Euridice* scores of both Peri and

Caccini. My thanks to Suzanne Cusick for providing these valuable connections.

49 See Carl Dahlhaus, *The Idea of Absolute Music.*

50 See Rieger, *Frau, Musik und Männerherrschaft*, p. 147. See also my discussions in Chapter 2.

51 Philip Brett notes how abstraction in music, i.e. absolute music, served as a crafty means of driving out the irrationalism of music itself; see his paper "Musicality, essentialism, and the closet," presented at Gender and Music Conference, King's College, University of London, July 1991.

52 Dahlhaus, *The Idea of Absolute Music*, p. 81.

53 Another contradictory aspect of absolute music concerns the more intrusive presence of the composer as compared with the late eighteenth century. Such personal intrusion contradicts the attribute of autonomy supposedly present in absolute music. This intrusion is a characteristic I have discussed in my classes for years, and I was happy to see it aired by Rose Subotnik, with regard to Beethoven, in "The cultural message of musical semiology: Some thoughts on music, language, and criticism since the Enlightenment," *Critical Inquiry* 4/4 (1978), p. 756.

54 For music-as-religion in the early nineteenth century see Meyer, *Style and Music*, especially Chapter 6, "Romanticism – the ideology of elite egalitarians," pp. 163–217; Dahlhaus, *The Idea of Absolute Music*; Rieger, *Frau, Musik und Männerherrschaft*, especially section 2, "Musik als Trägerin geschlechtsspezifischer Ideologien," pp. 105–69. Related to women's exclusion from creative identification with God are statements such as that by Jean-Jacques Rousseau from the mid-eighteenth century, in which he asserts that women cannot create because they do not possess that "celestial fire" that sparks creativity. See his *Lettre à M. d'Alembert sur les spectacles* (Amsterdam, 1758), p. 193n.

55 Carol Gilligan, *In A Different Voice* (Cambridge, Mass., 1982). See also the discussion of Nancy Chodorow in Chapter 2 of the present study.

56 In a refreshing change from the typical operatic protagonist, performance artist Meredith Monk has fashioned an unusual opera, *Atlas*, whose hero on a quest for personal meaning is in fact a heroine. A powerful and imaginative work, which premièred at Houston Grand Opera in February 1991, *Atlas* challenges the typical association of quest and males in Western society.

57 Published by Da Capo, New York, 1979. I know of four recorded renditions: Doris Pines on "Jewels from la belle époque," Genesis 1024; Danielle Laval on "Pièces pour piano – Cécile Chaminade," EMI C069 16410; Judith Alstadter on "Romantic Women Composers," Educo 3146; and Nancy Fierro, Pelican 2017.

58 For McClary see especially "Sexual politics in classical music," where she discusses the first movement of Tchaikovsky's Symphony No. 4; in *Feminine Endings*, pp. 69–79. For Kallberg see "The harmony of the tea table."

59 See Citron, *Cécile Chaminade: A Bio-Bibliography* (Westport, Ct., 1988), p. 38.

60 See items B76 and B254 (pp. 124 and 156) in my *Cécile Chaminade*.

61 All five musical examples are from the Da Capo Press reprint (1979); used with permission.

62 Desire fulfilled or denied on the part of the spectator has formed a major theme in feminist film theory. See, for example, Teresa de Lauretis, "Desire in narrative," in her collection *Alice Doesn't: Feminism, Semiotics, Cinema* (Bloomington, 1984), 103–57. Susan McClary is working on a major study of desire in seventeenth-century music. At an open forum sponsored by the Committee on the Status of Women at the 1990 annual meeting of the American Musicological Society, McClary suggested how de Lauretis's ideas could be utilized in the study of music.

63 By the mid-nineteenth century, according to Rieger, the fugue carried a semiotic association of glorification of male power through exaltation of God, who was male; see *Frau, Musik und Männerherrschaft*, p. 137. More generally, the musical competitiveness in fugues reflected the rise of male individualism in Western society after 1700. Elizabeth Wood points out another association with the fugue, although a less historically specific link: its function as a metaphor of the hunt, and by extension of sexual mounting. See "Lesbian fugue: Ethel Smyth's contrapuntal arts," Paper presented at the Seventh International Congress on Women and Music, Utrecht, 31 May 1991.

64 This quality occurs occasionally in nineteenth-century music, particularly in the music of Chopin. See Rose Rosengard Subotnik, "On grounding Chopin," *Music and Society: The Politics of Composition, Performance and Reception*, 105–31.

65 Fetterley, *The Resisting Reader: A Feminist Approach to American Fiction* (Bloomington, 1978).

66 For an interesting discussion of subjective flexibility see Rachel Blau DuPlessis, in shared authorship with members of Workshop 9, "For the Etruscans: Sexual difference and artistic production – the debate over a female aesthetics," *The Future of Difference*, ed. Hester Eisenstein and Alice Jardine (New Brunswick, 1980), p. 149.

67 William S. Newman notes the difficulty in discovering the precise and relative functions of the sonata in the Romantic era, but points out "its increasing functions as diversional and as pedagogic material, and now more than ever as solid fare in public and private recitals" (*The Sonata Since Beethoven* [Chapel Hill, 1969], pp. 50–51). This implies a growing split or hierarchy between the two main types. Presumably the concert sonatas are technically and expressively more complex, the pedagogic sonatas easier and simpler. The latter type was probably aimed largely at women in their roles as teachers, students, and purveyors of music as an accomplishment in private gatherings. But Chaminade's sonata aims technically for at least the advanced pianist (the last movement is particularly demanding) and expressively for a mature player; it would

suit a professional setting such as the concert hall. It is interesting that Newman's study reinforces the split by covering only the concert types, and thereby reflects and reaffirms the canonic view of the sonata and the sonata aesthetic as high art music. Because of women's major participation in piano pedagogy and the fact that many women, including Chaminade, composed pieces expressly for children, it is likely that the relationship between woman's subject position, as composer and performer, to the semiotics of the pedagogic sonata would make a fascinating study. In any case, in the present discussion I am assuming the more canonic view of the sonata as a complex work compositionally, and one intended largely for the professional in the concert hall. Another aspect of the sonata as more of a public, professional genre in the nineteenth century as compared to the eighteenth century is that the marginalizing codes of gender in sonata form could have arisen when they did as a means of controlling women's presence in public music.

68 Rieger, "'Ich recycle Töne': Schreiben Frauen anders? Neue Gedanken zu einem alten Thema," *Neue Zeitschrift für Musik* (February 1992), p. 15. Nancy Reich's passing reference to this work states that it was incomplete (*Clara Schumann: The Artist and the Woman* [Ithaca, 1985], p. 246).

69 Gerd Nauhaus, Introduction to the score of the Piano Sonata in g minor (Wiesbaden, 1991).

70 Christine Battersby, *Gender and Genius: Towards a Feminist Aesthetics* (London, 1989), p. 154.

71 "To the familiar saying of the East German musicologist Brockhaus that there exists neither a capitalist or socialist interval of a third, we should add that there can be neither a female or male interval of a third" (Rieger, *Frau, Musik und Männerherrschaft*, p. 130). An indication of the interest in the issue is the notice inserted in the June 1989 issue of the CMS *Bulletin* by the editors of *The Musical Woman*, vol. 3, soliciting opinions from readers on the matter. In a similar vein, editors of *In Theory Only* asked the readership for input on whether there exists feminist music theory (9/8 [May 1987], 3–4).

72 "'Ich recycle Töne'." Rieger's oral presentation on the topic offers some additional points. While noting the difficulty of positing a female aesthetic yet believing that there are similarities or tendencies within much of women's music, Rieger emphasizes seven attributes of what she calls a "restricted aesthetics." These include emphases on functionalism, communication, substance rather than innovation, "Ganzheitlichkeit" (holism), and a close relationship with their bodies and the human voice; "Is there a female aesthetic in music?" presented at Seventh International Congress on Women in Music, Utrecht, May 1991.

73 *The Reproduction of Mothering: Psychoanalysis and the Sociology of Gender* (Berkeley, 1978).

74 "'Ich recycle Töne'," p. 17.

75 Letter to Felix Mendelssohn of 17 February 1835. "I've reflected how I, actually not an eccentric or overly sentimental person, came to write pieces in a tender style. I believe it derives from the fact that we were young during Beethoven's last years and absorbed his style to a considerable degree. But that style is exceedingly moving and emotional. You've gone through it from start to finish and progressed beyond it in your composing, and I've remained stuck in it, not possessing the strength, however, that is necessary to sustain that tenderness." Hensel then links this trait with a flaw in her approach to life, and claims that as a result she is weak at sustaining musical ideas. In Citron, *Letters of Fanny Hensel to Felix Mendelssohn* (New York, 1987), p. 174.

76 Material attributed to Marga Richter comes from Jane Weiner Le Page, *Women Composers, Conductors, and Musicians of the Twentieth Century: Selected Biographies*, vol. 1 (Metuchen, 1980), pp. 222–3, as quoted in Diane Jezic, *Women Composers: The Lost Tradition Found* (New York, 1988), p. 204.

77 See the discussion of female traditions in Chapter 2.

78 The phrase comes from DuPlessis, "Etruscans," p. 151.

79 Cox, "A gynecentric aesthetic"; my thanks to Professor Cox for sharing the typescript. For the published version see *Hypatia: The Journal of Feminist Philosophy* 5/2 (1990), 43–62. For more on feminist perspectives regarding counterpoint, see Rieger, *Frau, Musik und Männerherrschaft*, pp. 137–8; and McClary, "The blasphemy of talking politics during Bach year." Among the thoughtful studies that note the difficulties in identifying a female aesthetic are essays in the collection *Feminist Aesthetics*, ed. Gisela Ecker (Boston, 1985): Ecker's "Introduction," pp. 15–22; Silvia Bovenschen's "Is there a feminine aesthetic?" pp. 23–50; Heide Göttner-Abendroth, "Nine principles of a matriarchal aesthetic," pp. 81–94; and Eva Rieger, "'*Dolce semplice*'? On the changing role of women in music," pp. 135–49. See also Stanley and Wolfe (Robbins), "Toward a feminist aesthetic"; Rachel Blau DuPlessis and members of Workshop 9, "For the Etruscans"; and Teresa de Lauretis, "Aesthetic and feminist theory."

80 Janet Wolff, *Feminine Sentences: Essays on Women and Culture* (Berkeley, 1990), p. 69. For more detailed discussion see Elaine Showalter, "Feminist criticism in the wilderness," *The New Feminist Criticism: Essays on Women, Literature, and Theory* (New York, 1985), pp. 261–7.

81 See her "Foreword" to Catherine Clément, *Opera, or the Undoing of Women*, trans. Betsy Wing (Minneapolis, 1988), p. xv. See also Gisela Ecker's "Introduction" to *Feminist Aesthetics*, pp. 19–20.

82 Wolff, *Feminine Sentences*, p. 131.

5 RECEPTION

1 Robert C. Holub, *Reception Theory: A Critical Introduction* (New York, 1984).

2 Among the most useful are *The Reader in the Text: Essays on Audience and Interpretation*, ed. Susan Rubin Suleiman and Inge Crosman (Princeton, 1980); *Reader-Response Criticism: From Formalism to Post-Structuralism*, ed. Jane Tompkins (Baltimore, 1980); Terry Eagleton, *Literary Theory: An Introduction* (Minneapolis, 1983); Nancy Hogan, "Towards a better definition of 'audience': Hans Robert Jauss's *Rezeptionsästhetiks* theory," M.A. thesis, philosophy, Rice University (1989); Hans-Robert Jauss, *Toward an Aesthetic of Reception*, trans. Timothy Bahti (Minneapolis, 1982); Janet Wolff, *The Social Production of Art* (New York, 1984); Roland Barthes, "From work to text" (1971), *Textual Strategies: Perspectives in Post-Structuralist Criticism*, ed. Josué Harari (Ithaca, 1979), 73–82; *Gender and Reading: Essays on Readers, Texts, and Contexts*, ed. Elizabeth A. Flynn and Patrocinio Schweickart (Baltimore, 1986); Holub, *Reception Theory*; and various essays in *Music and Society: The Politics of Composition, Performance and Reception*, ed. Richard Leppert and Susan McClary (Cambridge, 1987).

3 McClary's essay is in *Feminine Endings: Music, Gender, and Sexuality* (Minneapolis, 1991), 112–31; Taruskin's and Abbate's essays are in *Nineteenth Century Music* 12/3 (1989), 241–56 and 221–30.

4 McClary is doing important work on the role of pleasure in the meanings of music. See various essays and especially "Introduction: A material girl in Bluebeard's castle," *Feminine Endings*, 3–34.

5 Most of the literary sources are cited elsewhere in the notes to this chapter; see also Kamuf, "Writing like a woman," *Women and Language in Literature and Society*, ed. Sally McConnell-Ginet, Ruth Borker, and Nelly Furman (New York, 1980), 284–99. In other fields see Dolan, *The Feminist Spectator as Critic* (Ann Arbor, 1988); Parker and Pollock, *Old Mistresses: Women, Art, and Ideology* (New York, 1981); De Lauretis, *Alice Doesn't: Feminism, Semiotics, Cinema* (Bloomington, 1984); and Modleski, *The Women Who Knew Too Much: Hitchcock and Feminist Theory* (New York, 1988).

6 Art is often categorized as a non-temporal medium. Yet, as in literature, temporality is engaged in the process of perceiving an art work: viewing a painting, a building, a piece of sculpture. Perhaps a principal difference lies in the fact that one knows that the art work exists intact, in front of one, quickly verifiable by sight, whereas in music, unless one is referring to the score, a visual representation once-removed from the composition, one cannot grasp it quickly. It must play out in time, and often very lengthy time. See also discussions of transmission in Chapter 1.

7 See also John Mowitt, "The sound of music in the era of its electronic reproducibility," *Music and Society*, 173–97.

8 In "Musica practica" (1970), an essay that praises Beethoven's late style for its "tangible intelligibility, with the intelligible as tangible" (p. 153), Barthes declares that this music, exemplified by the Diabelli Variations, can best be grasped by "reading" and not by performance or hearing. "This is not to say that one has to sit with a Beethoven score and get from

it an inner recital ...; it means that with respect to this music one must put oneself in the position or, better, in the activity of an operator, who knows how to displace, assemble, combine, fit together; in a word ... who knows how to structure .... Reading this Beethoven is *to operate* his music ...." Barthes goes on to assert that "to compose ... is *to give to do*, not to give to hear but to give to write." Thus for Barthes, at least in this rather limited body of music, response is active, constructing, and creative in the sense of an assemblage of given elements. It would be interesting to know what Barthes would have in mind for other music. See *Image, Music, Text*, trans. Stephen Heath (New York, 1977), 149–54.

9 Some music of the late twentieth century fosters shared creativity with the performer, who can alter substantially the "text" of the composition in each performance. Stockhausen's *Klavierstück XI* is such an example. Joke Dame underscores the authorial role of Cathy Berberian in her astounding rendition of Berio's *Sequenza III*, in "Voices within the voice: Geno-text and pheno-text in *Sequenza III*," presentation at Feminist Theory and Music Conference, University of Minnesota, Minneapolis, June 1991.

10 Barthes, in contrast, does not really consider the performer a listener ("Musica practica," p. 149).

11 "Reading ourselves: Toward a feminist theory of reading," *Gender and Reading*, ed. Flynn and Schweickart, p. 56.

12 *On Deconstruction: Theory and Criticism after Structuralism* (Ithaca, 1982), 43–64.

13 "Reading as a woman," p. 58.

14 Culler's essay sparked a number of responses. One of the first is Elaine Showalter's "Critical cross-dressing: Male feminists and the woman of the year," *Men in Feminism*, ed. Alice Jardine and Paul Smith (New York, 1987), 116–32. Showalter focuses on male appropriation of feminism in both popular and scholarly treatments and mostly approves of Culler's contribution, although men speaking as feminists causes her unease. Tania Modleski criticizes both Culler and Showalter in "Feminism and the power of interpretation: Some critical readings," *Feminist Studies/Critical Studies*, ed. Teresa de Lauretis (Bloomington, 1986), 121–38. Robert Scholes provides a male critique of Culler, in "Reading like a man," *Men in Feminism*, 204–18. Diana Fuss uses Scholes as her point of departure in "Reading like a feminist," *Differences* 1/2 (1989), 77–92. Nancy Miller also shares Showalter's concern over male appropriation, in "Rereading as a woman: The body in practice," *The Female Body in Western Culture: Contemporary Perspectives*, ed. Susan Rubin Suleiman (Cambridge, Mass., 1986), 354–62. The notion of the hypothesized woman comes from Showalter, in a different context. See her "Towards a feminist poetics," *Women Writing and Writing About Women*, ed. Mary Jacobus (New York, 1979), 22–41. In music, Don Randel geared a few of Culler's points toward a template for gendered response in music. See "The canons in the musicological toolbox,"

article drawn from remarks at the 1987 and 1988 annual meetings of the American Musicological Society, and published in *Disciplining Music: Musicology and Its Canons*, 10–22.

15 Modleski, "Feminism and the power of interpretation," p. 132.

16 This idea of Barthes is discussed in Eagleton, *Literary Theory*, p. 138. See also Barthes, "From work to text," p. 77.

17 As Terry Eagleton notes, "there is no clear division... between 'criticism' and 'creation'..." in a post-structuralist view of literature; *Literary Theory*, p. 139.

18 See Barbara Jepson, "Women music critics in the United States," *The Musical Woman: An International Perspective*, vol. 1, ed. Judith Lang Zaimont, Catherine Overhauser, and Jane Gottlieb (Westport, Ct., 1984), 244–64; and Karen Monson, "Byline Monson: Music critic," in vol. 2 of the same series (1987), 59–70.

19 As Jepson remarks concerning critics in general, they "have traditionally been viewed as authority figures" ("Women music critics," p. 244).

20 These two fascinating possibilities were suggested by Suzanne Cusick. See also Chapter 2.

21 See, for example, Edward Rothstein's review of the hostile reception accorded presentations on Schubert's homosexuality, at a conference on Schubert at the 92nd Street "Y" in New York in February 1992: "Was Schubert gay? If he was, so what?" *The New York Times* (4 February 1992), B3.

22 See *Gender and Genius: Towards a Feminist Aesthetics* (London, 1989).

23 J. Peter Burkholder has pointed out the pervasiveness of stylistic commonalities in the nineteenth century in spite of the paradigm of originality; see his "Museum pieces: The historicist mainstream in music of the last hundred years," *The Journal of Musicology* 2/2 (1983), 115–34.

24 See Eagleton, *Literary Theory*, p. 138. Carl Dahlhaus provides a brief discussion of originality in "The value judgment: Object or premise of history?" in *Foundations of Music History*, trans. J. B. Robinson (Cambridge, 1983), p. 95.

25 Lillian Robinson, "Who speaks for women – and is it poetry?" Paper presented at Modern Language Association, New York, December 1976, as quoted in Julia Penelope Stanley and Susan J. Wolfe (Robbins), "Toward a feminist aesthetic," *Chrysalis* 6 (1978), pp. 62–3. See also Paul Lauter, "Race and gender in the shaping of the American literary canon: A case study from the twenties," *Feminist Studies* 9/3 (1983), pp. 452–6; and Jane Tompkins, *Sensational Designs: The Cultural Work of American Fiction 1790–1860* (New York, 1985), p. xvi.

26 The term has been used extensively in studies of female musicians and may have been coined by Judith Tick or Carol Neuls-Bates in the early 1980s. See, for example, Neuls-Bates's collection, *Women in Music: An Anthology of Source Readings from the Middle Ages to the Present* (New York, 1982).

27 "Quatorzième concert populaire," *Angers Revue* [late February 1989].
28 "Music and drama: Mme. Chaminade's concert," *New York Evening Post* (26 October 1908), p. 7.
29 For the effects of exclusion in literary modernism see Sandra Gilbert and Susan Gubar, *No Man's Land: The Place of the Woman Writer in the Twentieth Century*, Vol. 1: *The War of the Words* (New Haven, 1987). For its application to musical modernism see Catherine Smith, "On feminism and American art music," Paper delivered at annual meeting of the American Musicological Society, Austin, October 1989, published in *Cecilia Reclaimed: Feminist Perspectives on Gender and Music*, ed. Susan Cook and Judy Tsou (Urbana, 1993).
30 "In response," ed. Elaine Barkin, in *Perspectives of New Music*, vols. 20–21 (1981–2), 288–329.

6 THE CANON IN PRACTICE

1 *The Resisting Reader: A Feminist Approach to American Fiction* (Bloomington, 1978).
2 See Chapter 5.
3 See her discussions on the divergent changes over time that befell the reputations of two contemporary nineteenth-century American authors, Nathaniel Hawthorne and Susan Warner, in *Sensational Designs: The Cultural Work of American Fiction 1790–1860* (Oxford, 1985).
4 See Chapter 5.
5 See Nancy K. Miller, "Men's reading, women's writing: Gender and the rise of the novel," *Displacements: Women, Tradition, Literatures in French*, ed. Joan DeJean and Miller (Baltimore, 1991), p. 49. Eva Rieger sees narcissism as a possible reason for the male composer's penchant for stylistic novelty, in conjunction with his desire for career advancement: "Is there a female aesthetic in music?" Paper presented at the Seventh International Congress on Women in Music, Utrecht, May 1991.
6 J. Michèle Edwards discusses aspects of the cultural and sexual power of the orchestral conductor in the modern American orchestra, in her paper "Transformation of the American orchestra: Gender issues," presented at Gender and Music Conference, King's College, University of London, July 1991. She cites Joan Tower's important observation that visibility breeds activity: that a mere presence of women will create other opportunities, small and large, for women in the field of music. On a related topic, Odaline de la Martinez explores how the organization of the modern orchestra is based on a pyramid structure typical of big business, in "Women and the orchestra as a hierarchical structure," Paper presented at the same conference.
7 Some performers, however, seem to specialize in the music of women. These include, among others, pianists Virginia Eskin, Sylvia Glickman, Rosario Marciano, and Selma Stein. They make vital contributions to the visibility and dissemination of women's music, especially through

recordings. Yet I do not think I am doing them a disservice by saying that they are known to relatively small segments of the public and are not in the superstar rank. Although they may not reach the numbers of listeners of the superstars, they are nonetheless making a difference that over time can influence the repertoire of "the big boys."

8 See Don Randel, "The canons in the musicological toolbox," Paper delivered at the annual meeting of the American Musicological Society, New Orleans, October 1987. Published in *Disciplining Music: Musicology and its Canons*, 10–22.

9 See my essay, "Gender, professionalism, and the musical canon," *The Journal of Musicology* 8/1 (1990), pp. 115–16.

10 The following literary sources lay down some of the general principles used in this discussion on the stakes of canonicity in the profession and the academy: George Allan, "The process and reality of an educational canon," *Contemporary Philosophy* 12/9 (1989), 3–8; Lawrence Buell, "The extra: Literary history without sexism? Feminist studies and canonical reconception," *American Literature* 59 (1987), 102–14; John Clifford, "A response pedagogy for noncanonical literature," *Reader*, issue "Teaching noncanonical literature," No. 15 (1986), 48–61; Henry Louis Gates, Jr., "Whose canon is it, anyhow?" *New York Times Book Review* (26 February 1989); Jan Gorak, *The Making of the Modern Canon: Genesis and Crisis of a Literary Idea* (London, 1991); John Guillory, "Canonical and non canonical: A critique of the current debate," *English Literary History* 54/3 (1987), 483–527, and "The ideology of canon-formation: T. S. Eliot and Cleanth Brooks," *Canons*, ed. Robert von Hallberg (Chicago, 1984), 337–62; Frank Kermode, *Forms of Attention* (Chicago, 1985), and *History and Value* (Oxford, 1988); Paul Lauter, *Canons and Contexts* (New York, 1991); John Schilb, "Canonical theories and noncanonical literature: Steps toward a pedagogy," *Reader*, issue "Teaching noncanonical literature," No. 15 (1986), 3–23; Robert Scholes, "Aiming a canon at the curriculum," *Salmagundi* No. 72 (1986), 101–17; and Cornel West, "Minority discourse and the pitfalls of canon formation," *The Yale Journal of Criticism* 1/1 (1987), 193–201.

11 See Joseph Kerman, "American musicology in the 1990s," *The Journal of Musicology* 9/2 (1991), 131–44.

12 "Politics, feminism, and contemporary music theory," *The Journal of Musicology* 9/3 (1991), 275–99; and "What do feminists want? A reply to Pieter van den Toorn," *The Journal of Musicology* 9/4 (1991), 399–411.

13 "The ideology of canon-formation: T. S. Eliot and Cleanth Brooks," p. 351.

14 The Beethoven emphasis is affirmed, for example, by *The Age of Beethoven* volume in the series, *The New Oxford History of Music* (1954 –). Many of the volumes in its predecessor series, *The Oxford History of Music* (1901–5), bear titles of composers' names.

15 Philip Brett utilizes the colorful phrase "fetishization of the great composer," a metaphor I find apt, in his paper "Musicality, essential-

ism, and the closet," presented at Gender and Music Conference, King's College, University of London, July 1991.

16 See the discussions in Chapter 2 on the importance of a tradition with which a composer can identify.

17 These ideas were expressed in "Sonic exploration, women, and feminist issues," presented at the Seventh International Congress on Women in Music, Utrecht, May 1991.

18 See the discussion on originality in Chapter 5 and also below.

19 As Barbara Herrnstein Smith asserts, "the repeated inclusion of a particular work in literary anthologies not only promotes the value of that work but goes some distance toward creating its value, as does also its repeated appearance on reading lists or its frequent citation or quotation by professors, scholars, and academic critics ... . The converse side to this process is well known. Those who are in positions to edit anthologies and prepare reading lists are obviously those who occupy positions of some cultural power; and their acts of evaluation – represented in what they exclude as well as in what they include – constitute not merely recommendations of value, but, for the reasons just mentioned, also determinants of value." See *Contingencies of Value: Alternative Perspectives for Critical Theory* (Cambridge, Mass., 1988), p. 46.

20 See Tompkins, *Sensational Designs*, pp. 35–7.

21 For a perceptive discussion of the meaning of consensus in terms of value see Guillory, "Canonical and non canonical."

22 See Kermode, *History and Value*, p. 85. While admitting that this is impossible, Kermode's discussion leads him to say that a work that was canonic in the past and continues to remain so has passed the test of time. His views contrast with my own and also those of Jane Tompkins (see discussion above). Barbara Herrnstein Smith casts her discussion of the test of time mainly in terms of the perpetuating properties of those values, representing dominant cultural groups, that made the work canonic in the first place; see *Contingencies of Value*, pp. 51–3.

23 See Tompkins, *Sensational Designs*, p. 193.

24 As proposed, for example, by Regina Himmelbauer in her presentation, "Without a picture the mirror breaks: The use of her story," delivered at the Seventh International Congress on Women in Music, Utrecht, June 1991.

25 For more on valuation, see Tompkins, *Sensational Designs*, pp. 186–7; and Kermode, *History and Value*.

26 "Canonical and non-canonical," pp. 491–4.

27 *Canons and Consequences: Reflections on the Ethical Force of Imaginative Ideals* (Evanston, 1990), pp. 84–8.

28 See especially "Other voices, other rooms: Organizing and teaching the humanities conflict," *New Literary History* 21/4 (1990), 817–39; *Professing Literature: An Institutional History* (Chicago, 1987); and "The university and the prevention of culture," *Criticism in the University*, ed. Graff and Reginald Gibbons (Evanston, 1985), 62–84.

29 See Chapter 4. See also Tompkins, *Sensational Designs*, p. xv; and Lawrence Lipking, "Aristotle's sister: A poetics of abandonment," *Critical Inquiry* 10/1 (1983), 61–81.

30 See the discussions on genius in Chapter 5 and below. For a fascinating feminist exploration see Christine Battersby, *Gender and Genius: Towards a Feminist Aesthetics* (London, 1989).

31 This discussion is influenced by Peter Gay's interesting article, "Aimez-vous Brahms? On polarities in modernism," *Freud, Jews and Other Germans* (Oxford, 1978), 231–56.

32 In our postmodern age, we have the phenomenon of Mozart as a "pop" phenomenon of mass culture, as in the movie *Amadeus* and also in the cult-like celebrations of the bicentennial of his death. Yet Mozart still commands enormous respect from musicians and academics. For an interesting analysis of the cultural need for the Mozart craze see Geraldine Finn, "Music, Mozart, and men," Paper presented at Feminist Theory and Music Conference, University of Minnesota, Minneapolis, June 1991, and at Gender and Music Conference, King's College, University of London, July 1991.

33 *Sensational Designs*, p. xiv.

34 See also Jane Bowers, "Feminist scholarship and the field of musicology: I," *College Music Symposium* 29 (1989), 81–92.

35 Jane Bowers has long been an advocate of this approach; see, for instance, "Feminist scholarship and the field of musicology: I," p. 83.

36 See Carol E. Robertson, "Power and gender in the musical experiences of women," *Women and Music in Cross-Cultural Perspective*, ed. Ellen Koskoff (Westport, Ct., 1987), 225–44.

37 Besides Robertson's article, other essays in the Koskoff collection address the cultural meanings of woman's musical performance; see Koskoff's fine introduction to the volume (pp. 1–23). See also Jennifer Post, "Erasing the boundaries between public and private in women's performance traditions," *Cecilia Reclaimed: Feminist Perspectives on Gender and Music*, ed. Susan Cook and Judy Tsou (Urbana, 1993). In addition, exciting work is being done on the semiotics of woman's singing voice in the Western tradition. See, for example, Elizabeth Wood, "The odyssey of sirens and songbirds: Opera and its prima donnas," Paper presented at the Open Meeting of the Committee on the Status of Women, at the Annual Meeting of the American Musicological Society, Austin, October 1989. Dutch musicologist Joke Dame is exploring several facets of the cultural meanings of the female voice: "Unveiled voices: Sexual difference and the castrato," Paper presented at the Seventh International Congress on Women in Music, Utrecht, May 1991; "Voices within the voice: Geno-text and pheno-text in *Sequenza III*," Paper presented at Feminist Theory and Music Conference, University of Minnesota, Minneapolis, June 1991, and at Gender and Music Conference, King's College, University of London, July 1991.

38 For these general characteristics of history and canon see Gorak, *The*

Making of the Modern Canon, pp. 178–82 and 254–60; Kermode, *History and Value*, pp. 108–27; and Lauter, *Canons and Contexts*, p. 257.

39 "Race and gender in the shaping of the American literary canon: A case study from the twenties," *Feminist Studies* 9/3 (1983), p. 452.

40 Barbara Herrnstein Smith, *Contingencies of Value*, p. 43.

41 "La définition du terme 'Baroque,'" article in *Actes du IIIe Congrès de l'Association Internationale de Littérature Comparée* (1962), as quoted in Kermode, *History and Value*, p. 122.

42 *History and Value*, pp. 121 and 123.

43 *Ibid.*, p. 123.

44 "Race and gender," p. 456.

45 *Classic and Romantic Music* (New York, 1970), which combines Blume's articles on the two eras that originally appeared in *Die Musik in Geschichte und Gegenwart*.

46 *The Majority Finds Its Past* (New York, 1979), p. 168.

47 "Did women have a Renaissance?" *Women, History, and Theory: The Essays of Joan Kelly* (Chicago, 1984), 19–50.

48 *A History of Their Own: Women in Europe from Prehistory to the Present*, 2 vols. (New York, 1988), vol. 2, p. xviii.

49 *Women Making Music: The Western Art Tradition, 1150–1950* (Urbana, 1986); *Historical Anthology of Music by Women* (Bloomington, 1987).

50 "Preface," *The Norton Anthology of Literature By Women: The Tradition in English* (New York, 1985), p. xxviii.

51 Medieval, Baroque, and Classical are utilized. The Romantic era is coupled with genre or medium in two separate chapters, and the second incorporates the early twentieth century as well. The title "Six living U.S. composers" represents twentieth-century music.

52 Page xii.

53 Kermode, *History and Value*, p. 108.

54 *Professing Literature*, pp. 258–62.

55 Among the many sources that discuss these models are, in alphabetical order, Battersby, *Gender and Genius*; James Briscoe, "Integrating music by women into the music history sequence," *College Music Symposium* 25 (1985), 21–7; Susan C. Cook, "Women, women's studies, music and musicology: Issues of pedagogy and scholarship," *College Music Symposium* 29 (1989), 93–100; Gates, "Whose canon is it, anyhow?"; Kermode, *History and Value*; Miller, "Men's reading, women's writing: Gender and the rise of the novel," *Displacements*, 37–54; Carol Neuls-Bates, "Creating a college curriculum for the study of women in music," *The Musical Woman*, vol. 1, ed. Judith Lang Zaimont, Catherine Overhauser, and Jane Gottlieb (Westport, Ct., 1983), 265–82; Lillian Robinson, "Treason our text: Feminist challenges to the literary canon," *Tulsa Studies in Women's Literature* 2 (1983), 83–98; Eve Kosofsky Sedgwick, "Introduction: Axiomatic," *The Epistemology of the Closet* (Berkeley, 1990), 1–63; and Elaine Showalter, "Women and the literary curriculum," *College English* 32 (1970–71), 855–62.

56 "Treason our text." Elizabeth Wood uses the standpoint of a women's studies program, in which she teaches, for her views on canonic models that place women's historical activities in music in a holistic female context. For a summary see Cook, "Women, women's studies, music and musicology," pp. 95–6.

57 See Chapter 2 for more on the importance of a female tradition.

58 The metaphor of imperialism is borrowed from Randel's essay, "The canons in the musicological toolbox."

59 "Ethnomusicology's challenge to the canon, the canon's challenge to ethnomusicology," Paper presented at the Annual Meeting of the American Musicological Society, New Orleans, October 1987; *Disciplining Music: Musicology and Its Canons*, 116–36. My thanks to the author for graciously sharing a copy of the manuscript.

60 See Bloom's *The Closing of the American Mind* (New York, 1987). Eve Sedgwick sees this as a "closet" metaphor because it has to do with forbidden sexual acts that were kept secret. See her critique of Bloom in *The Epistemology of the Closet*, p. 50. For another critique of Bloom see Ann Clark Fehn, "Relativism, feminism, and the 'German connection' in Allan Bloom's *The Closing of the American Mind*," *German Quarterly* 62 (1989), 384–94.

61 My remarks obviously pertain to the history of Western art music. Yet I am well aware that remodeling of the canon can also involve a broadening that goes beyond the limitations of "Western" and "art music." This means consideration of non Euro-American cultures, such as Eastern, Middle Eastern, African, and native American traditions. Many of these, of course, divide further, for example into Japanese, Chinese, and Indonesian musics in the East. It also means musics with a social base other than that of the upper- to middle-class white. This brings in popular music, with its many subdivisions, as well as folk music and jazz. While there are numerous advantages to such an expansion, many of which reinforce the points I make in this chapter, I am afraid that the enormity of this project precludes its treatment here.

62 Joan Kelly used the term "doubled vision" to describe the dual perspective of women. See, for instance, the "Introduction" by colleagues to a posthumous collection of her essays, *Women, History, and Theory: The Essays of Joan Kelly*, p. xxiv.

63 "Whose canon is it, anyhow?" p. 45.

64 *Gender and Genius*, p. 152.

65 See Chapters 2 and 3.

66 Reprinted in *Sämtliche Lieder*, Universal Editions, 1984; recorded on Leonarda LPI 118. See also my discussion in "European composers and musicians, 1880–1918," in *Women and Music, A History*, ed. Pendle, pp. 133–7; and Edward Kravitt, "The Lieder of Alma Maria Schindler-Mahler," *The Music Review* 49 (1988), 190–204.

67 Relatively little is known of Cramer, who studied in Amsterdam. Several of her wonderful songs, which were mostly composed between 1905 and

1910, were performed at the Seventh International Congress on Women in Music, May 1991, in Utrecht.

68 *Sensational Designs.*

69 See, respectively, "Getting down off the beanstalk: The presence of a woman's voice in Janika Vandervelde's *Genesis II*," pp. 128–30; and "Sexual politics in Classical music," 53–79; both essays in *Feminine Endings: Music, Gender, and Sexuality* (Minneapolis, 1991). Other imaginative examples are Robert Fink's analysis of desire in Brahms's First Symphony, in a paper presented at Feminist Theory and Music Conference, University of Minnesota, Minneapolis, June 1991; and Lawrence Kramer's explorations of several works, in *Music as Cultural Practice, 1800–1900* (Berkeley, 1990).

70 As expressed so eloquently in a private communication of McClary. Feminists in other fields have called for similar modeling, for example French literary critic Nancy K. Miller, "Men's reading, women's writing," p. 51; and Eve Sedgwick, *The Epistemology of the Closet*, p. 50.

71 From Culler's *Framing the Sign: Criticism and Its Institutions* (Norman, Okla., 1988), as quoted by Kermode, *An Appetite for Poetry* (Cambridge, Mass., 1989), p. 14.

72 *The Epistemology of the Closet*, p. 50. Gates affirms this point of view, in "Whose canon is it, anyhow?" p. 45.

73 Susan Rubin Suleiman quotes Jardine, in "A double margin: Reflections on women writers and the avant-garde in France," *Displacements*, p. 183.

74 *Gender and Genius*, p. 157.

75 See Chapter 2, including the analyses of negative depictions of women in Mozart's operas. For an early exploration of female students' position in relation to the literary canon, see Showalter, "Women and the literary curriculum."

76 This view emerged as the consensus opinion of seven graduate students, all but one performance majors, enrolled in the "Women composers" seminar I taught in the Fall 1990 semester. There was no disagreement by gender (six women, one man). My thanks to the participants for their input: Christi Campbell, Ramona Galey, Katie Powell, Chris Rose, Kathy Ross, Connie Slaughter, Mary Thornton.

77 This idea of Oedipal-like fear in confronting Musicology-the-Father was suggested by Suzanne Cusick, in a private letter, with regard to a similar situation. See also my application of Oedipal killing to women and their prior depiction in opera, in Chapter 2.

78 "Mozart's women," *Hurricane Alice* 3 (1986), 1–4.

79 In the last few years, much of the emphasis of the Committee on the Status of Women in the American Musicological Society seems premised on the converse: that promoting research on women has a positive impact on the status of women in general in musicology, whatever their area of specialty.

80 The demographics of women earning doctorates in musicology is not the

only factor to account for higher percentages of women in the lower ranks. It also has to do with the fact that women have greater difficulty making it to the top ranks. The reasons for this are many and complex, but they have included discouragement, discrimination, and personal factors. A tight job market since *c.* 1970 is also a factor. See Report No. 5 of the College Music Society, *Women's Studies/Women's Status* (Boulder, 1988). In addition, I would guess that many women have felt uncomfortable in the masculinist environment of the field.

81 See also my "Gender, professionalism, and the musical canon."
82 For example, Van den Toorn, "Politics, feminism, and contemporary music theory."
83 See, for instance, Bowers, "Feminist scholarship and the field of musicology"; and Nancy Reich, ed., "An annotated bibliography of recent writings on women in music," *CMS Report Number 5*, pp. 1–78.
84 See, for example, the review by Ruth Solie and Gary Tomlinson, "Women's studies in a new key," *National Women's Studies Action* 2/1 (1989), 6.
85 They were the Seventh International Congress on Women in Music, Utrecht, The Netherlands; Feminist Theory and Music Conference, University of Minnesota, Minneapolis; and Gender and Music Conference, King's College, University of London.
86 See a partial list in Bowers, "Feminist scholarship and the field of musicology." See also the bibliography compiled by Nancy Reich (see n. 84).
87 See Susan Cook's descriptions of her own approach to teaching in "Women, women's studies, music and musicology," pp. 97–8. See also Madeleine R. Grumet, *Bitter Milk: Women and Teaching* (Amherst, 1988); Roberta Lamb, "Questioning the canon: Women and music education," Paper presented at Bergamo Conference, Queen's University, Kingston, Ontario, October 1989 (my thanks to Professor Lamb for sharing a typescript of her paper); Elizabeth Minnich, *Transforming Knowledge* (Philadelphia, 1990); and especially Constance Penley, "Teaching in your sleep: Feminism and psychoanalysis," *The Future of An Illusion: Film, Feminism, and Psychoanalysis* (Minneapolis, 1989), 165–84.
88 "Treason our text," p. 84.
89 See especially Altieri, *Canons and Consequences*; Roger Kimball, "The academy debates the canon," *New Criterion* 6 (1987), 31–43; and Christopher Ricks, "What is at stake in the 'Battle of the books'?" *New Criterion* 8 (1989), 40 44.
90 Kermode, *History and Value*, p. 18.

Bibliography

Anthologies and edited volumes are listed under their title

Abert, Hermann. *Mozart's Don Giovanni*, trans. Peter Gellhorn, London, 1976

Adams, Hazard. "Canons: Literary criteria/power criteria," *Critical Inquiry* 14 (1988), 749–64

Aiken, Susan Hardy. "Women and the question of canonicity," *College English* 48 (1986), 288–301

Allan, George. "The process and reality of an educational canon," *Contemporary Philosophy* 12/9 (1989), 3–8

Allanbrook, Wye. *Rhythmic Gesture in Mozart: Le Nozze di Figaro and Don Giovanni*, Chicago, 1983

Allen, Warren Dwight. *Philosophies of Music History: A Study of General Histories of Music, 1600–1960*, New York, 1962

Altieri, Charles. *Canons and Consequences: Reflections on the Ethical Force of Imaginative Ideals*, Evanston, 1990

"An idea and ideal of a literary canon," *Critical Inquiry* 10/1 (1983), 37–59

Anderson, Bonnie S. and Judith P. Zinsser. *A History of Their Own: Women in Europe from Prehistory to the Present*, 2 vols., New York, 1988

Auerbach, Nina. "Artists and mothers: A false alliance," *Women and Literature* 6/1 (1978), 3–15

Bailey, Walter B. "The triumph of modernism: Parallels and divergences in the musics and careers of Radie Britain and Ruth Crawford," Unpublished manuscript

Bal, Mieke. "Sexuality, sin, and sorrow: The emergence of female character (A reading of Genesis 1–3)," *The Female Body in Western Culture: Contemporary Perspectives*, ed. Susan Rubin Suleiman, Cambridge, Mass., 1986, 317–38

Barthes, Roland. "The death of the author," *Image, Music, Text*, trans. Stephen Heath, New York, 1977, 142–8

"From work to text," *Textual Strategies: Perspectives in Post-Structuralist Criticism*, 73–81

"Loving Schumann," *The Responsibility of Forms: Critical Essays on Music, Art and Representation*, trans. Richard Howard, New York, 1985, 292–8

"Musica practica," *Image, Music, Text*, trans. Stephen Heath, New York, 1977, 149–54

Battersby, Christine. *Gender and Genius: Towards a Feminist Aesthetics*, London, 1989

Becker, Judith. "Some thoughts on 'non-verbal' communication," Presentation at annual meeting of AMS/SMT/SEM, Oakland, 1990

Benjamin, Phyllis. "A diary-album for Fanny Mendelssohn-Bartholdy," *Mendelssohn-Studien* 7 (1990), 178–217

Bloch, Maurice and Jean H. Bloch. "Women and the dialectics of nature in eighteenth-century French thought," *Nature, Culture and Gender*, ed. Carol MacCormack and Marilyn Strathern, Cambridge, 1980, 25–41

Bloom, Allan. *The Closing of the American Mind*, New York, 1987

Bloom, Peter. "Communication," *Journal of the American Musicological Society* 27 (1974), 161–3

Blume, Friedrich. *Classic and Romantic Music*, New York, 1970

Bohlman, Philip V. "Ethnomusicology's challenge to the canon; the canon's challenge to ethnomusicology," Presentation at annual meeting of the American Musicological Society, New Orleans, October 1987; and published in *Disciplining Music: Musicology and Its Canons*, 116–36

Bordo, Susan. "The Cartesian masculinization of thought," *Signs* 11/3 (1986), 439–56

Borroff, Edith. "An American parlor at the turn of the century," *American Music* (1986), 302–08
  "Women composers: Reminiscence and history," *College Music Symposium* 15 (1975), 26–33

Bovenschen, Silvia. "Is there a feminine aesthetic?" *Feminist Aesthetics*, ed. Gisela Ecker, Boston, 1985, 23–50

Bowers, Jane. "Feminist scholarship and the field of musicology," *College Music Symposium* 29 (1989), 81–92 (part 1)

Brett, Philip. "Musicality, essentialism, and the closet," Presentation at Gender and Music Conference, King's College, University of London, July 1991

Briscoe, James. "Integrating music by women into the music history sequence," *College Music Symposium* 25 (1985), 21–7

Brown, Rae Linda. "Selected orchestral music of Florence B. Price (1888–1953) in the context of her life and work," Ph.D. dissertation, Yale University (1987)

Broyles, Michael. "The musical canon in Europe and America: Differences and implications," Presentation at the annual meeting of the American Musicological Society, Chicago, November 1991

Buell, Lawrence. "The extra: Literary history without sexism? Feminist studies and canonical reconception," *American Literature* 59 (1987), 102–14

Burkholder, J. Peter. "Brahms and twentieth-century classical music," *Nineteenth Century Music* 8/1 (1984), 75–83
  "Museum pieces: The historicist mainstream in music of the last hundred years," *The Journal of Musicology* 2/2 (1983), 115–34

Butler, Judith. *Gender Trouble: Feminism and the Subversion of Identity*, New York, 1990

Canons, ed. Robert von Hallberg, Chicago, 1984

"Canons" issue of *Critical Inquiry* 10/1 (1983)

Carter, Elliott. "The orchestral composer's point of view," *The Writings of Elliott Carter: An American Composer Looks at Modern Music*, ed. Else Stone and Kurt Stone, Bloomington, 1977

Cash, Alice H. Conference Report on "Feminist theory and music: Toward a common language," University of Minnesota, Minneapolis, *The Journal of Musicology* 9/4 (1991), 521–32

Cecilia Reclaimed: Feminist Perspectives on Gender and Music, ed. Susan Cook and Judy Tsou, Urbana, 1993

Chailley, Jacques. *The Magic Flute, Masonic Opera*, New York, 1971

Chodorow, Nancy. *The Reproduction of Mothering: Psychoanalysis and the Sociology of Gender*, Berkeley, 1978

Citron, Marcia J. *Cécile Chaminade: A Bio-Bibliography*, Westport, Ct., 1988

Conference Report on "Beyond biography: Seventh international congress on women in music," Utrecht, The Netherlands, 29 May to 2 June 1991; and "Music and gender conference," King's College, University of London, July 1991, *The Journal of Musicology* 9/4 (1991), 533–43

"Corona Schröter: Singer, composer, actress," *Music and Letters* 61 (1980), 15–27

"European composers and musicians, 1880–1918," *Women and Music, A History*, ed. Pendle, 123–41

"Felix Mendelssohn's influence on Fanny Mendelssohn Hensel as a professional composer," *Current Musicology* No. 37/8 (1984), 9–17

"Gender, professionalism, and the musical canon," *The Journal of Musicology* 8/1 (1990), 102–17

"Women and the Lied, 1775–1850," *Women Making Music: The Western Art Tradition*, ed. Bowers and Tick, 224–48

Clément, Catherine. *Opera, or the Undoing of Women*, trans. Betsy Wing, Minneapolis, 1988

Clifford, John. "A response pedagogy for noncanonical literature," *Reader*, issue "Teaching noncanonical literature," No. 15 (1986), 48–61

Cook, Nicholas. *Music, Imagination, and Culture*, Oxford, 1990

Cook, Susan C. "Women, women's studies, music and musicology: Issues of pedagogy and scholarship," *College Music Symposium* 29 (1989), 93–100

Copland, Aaron. *Music and Imagination*, New York, 1952

Coser, Rose Laub. "The principle of patriarchy: The case of *The Magic Flute*," *Signs* 4/2 (1978), 337–48

Cox, Renée. "A gynecentric aesthetic," *Hypatia: The Journal of Feminist Philosophy* 5/2 (1990), 43–62

"Recovering *Jouissance*: Feminist aesthetics and music," Presentation at Feminist Theory and Music Conference, University of Minnesota, Minneapolis, June 1991

Criticism in the University, ed. Gerald Graff and Gerald Gibbons, Evanston, 1985

Culler, Jonathan. "Reading as a woman," *On Deconstruction: Theory and Criticism after Structuralism*, Ithaca, 1982, 43–64

D'Indy, Vincent. *Cours de composition musicale*, Book 2, part 1, Paris, 1909

Dahlhaus, Carl. *Esthetics of Music*, trans. William Austin, Cambridge, 1982

   Foundations of Music History, trans. J. B. Robinson, Cambridge, 1983

   "Gattung," *Brockhaus Riemann Musiklexikon*, ed. Dahlhaus and Hans Heinrich Eggebrecht, 2 vols., Wiesbaden, 1978, vol. 1, p. 452

   The Idea of Absolute Music, trans. Roger Lustig, Chicago, 1989

   Schoenberg and the New Music, trans. Derrick Puffett and Alfred Clayton, Cambridge, 1987

   "Was ist eine musikalische Gattung?" *Neue Zeitschrift für Musik* 135 (1974), 620–25

   "Zur Problematik der musikalischen Gattungen im 19. Jahrhundert," *Gattungen der Musik in Einzeldarstellungen: Gedenkschrift Leo Schrade*, ed. Wulf Arlt, Ernst Lichtenhahn, and Hans Oesch, Berne, 1973, 840–95

Dame, Joke. "Unveiled voices: Sexual difference and the castrato," Presentation at Seventh International Congress on Women in Music, Utrecht, May 1991

   "Voices within the voice: Geno-text and pheno-text in Berio's *Sequenza III*," Presentation at Feminist Theory and Music Conference, University of Minnesota, Minneapolis, June 1991

Dent, Edward J. "The historical approach to music," *The Musical Quarterly* 23 (1937), 1–17

   Mozart's Operas: A Critical Study, 2nd edn, London, 1947

Derrida, Jacques. "The law of genre," *On Narrative*, ed. W. J. T. Mitchell, Chicago, 1981, 51–77

Dinnerstein, Dorothy. *The Mermaid and the Minotaur*, New York, 1976

Disciplining Music: Musicology and Its Canons, ed. Katherine Bergeron and Philip V. Bohlman, Chicago, 1992

Displacements: Women, Tradition, Literatures in French, ed. Joan DeJean and Nancy Miller, Baltimore, 1991

Dolan, Jill. *The Feminist Spectator as Critic*, Ann Arbor, 1988

Donovan, Josephine. *Feminist Theory: The Intellectual Traditions of American Feminism*, New York, 1985

Dubrow, Heather. *Genre*, London, 1982

Dunn, Leslie. "Ophelia's songs in *Hamlet*: Music, madness, and the feminine," Presentation at Feminist Theory and Music Conference, University of Minnesota, Minneapolis, June 1991

DuPlessis, Rachel Blau. "For the Etruscans: Sexual difference and artistic production – the debate over a female aesthetics," *The Future of Difference*, ed. Hester Eisenstein and Alice Jardine, New Brunswick, 1980, 128–56

Eagleton, Terry. *Literary Theory: An Introduction*, Minneapolis, 1983

"Editorial," *In Theory Only* 9/8 (1987), 3–4

Edwards, J. Michèle. "Sonic exploration, women, and feminist issues,"

Presentation at Seventh International Congress on Women in Music, Utrecht, May 1991

"Transformation of the American orchestra: Gender issues," Presentation at Gender and Music Conference, King's College, University of London, July 1991

Eggebrecht, Hans H. *Handwörterbuch der musikalischen Terminologie*, n. d.

Einstein, Alfred. *Mozart: His Character, His Work*, trans. Arthur Mendel and Nathan Broder, London, 1945

Ezell, Margaret. "The myth of Judith Shakespeare: Creating the canon of women's literature," *New Literary History* 21/3 (1990), 579–92

Fehn, Ann Clark. "Relativism, feminism, and the 'German connection' in Allan Bloom's *The Closing of the American Mind*," *German Quarterly* 62 (1989), 384–94

Fellinger, Imogen. "Die Begriffe *Salon* und *Salonmusik* in der Musikanschauung des 19. Jahrhunderts," *Studien zur Trivialmusik des 19. Jahrhunderts*, ed. Carl Dahlhaus, Regensburg, 1967

Feminism and Science, ed. Nancy Tuana, Bloomington, 1989

Feminism/Postmodernism, ed. Linda J. Nicholson, New York, 1990

Feminist Aesthetics, ed. Gisela Ecker, trans. Harriet Anderson, Boston, 1985

Fetterley, Judith. *The Resisting Reader: A Feminist Approach to American Fiction*, Bloomington, 1978

Finn, Geraldine. "Music, Mozart, and men," Presentation at Feminist Theory and Music Conference, University of Minnesota, Minneapolis, June 1991, and at Gender and Music Conference, King's College, University of London, July 1991

Flawed Words and Stubborn Sounds: A Conversation with Elliott Carter, ed. Allen Edwards, New York, 1971

Foucault, Michel. "What is an author?" *Textual Strategies: Perspectives in Post-Structuralist Criticism*, ed. Harari, 141–60

Fowler, Alastair. *Kinds of Literature: An Introduction to the Theory of Genres and Modes*, Cambridge, Mass., 1982

Fox-Genovese, Elizabeth. "The claims of a common culture: Gender, race, class and the canon," *Salmagundi* No. 72 (1986), 131–43

Fraser, Nancy and Linda J. Nicholson. "Social criticism without philosophy: An encounter between feminism and postmodernism," *Feminism/Postmodernism*, 19–38

Fraser, Nancy. "What's critical about critical theory? The case of Habermas and gender," *Feminism as Critique*, ed. Seyla Benhabib and Drucilla Cornell, Minnesota, 1988, 31–56

Friedman, Susan Stanford. "Creativity and the childbirth metaphor: Gender difference in literary discourse," *Speaking of Gender*, ed. E. Showalter, New York, 1989, 73–100

"Gender and genre anxiety: Elizabeth Barrett Browning and H. D. as epic poets," *Tulsa Studies in Women's Literature* 5 (1986), 203–29

Frith, Simon. "Towards an aesthetic of popular music," *Music and Society: The Politics of Composition, Performance and Reception*, 133–50

"What is good music?" *Canadian University Music Review* 10/2 (1990), 92–102

Froula, Christine. "When Eve reads Milton: Undoing the canonical economy," *Canons*, ed. Robert von Hallberg, Chicago, 1984, 149–75

Fuss, Diana. "Reading like a feminist," *Differences* 1/2 (1989), 77–92

Gates, Henry Louis, Jr. "Introduction: 'Tell me, sir...what *is* "Black" literature'?" *Proceedings of the Modern Language Association* (1990), 11–22

"'What's love got to do with it?': Critical theory, integrity, and the Black idiom," *New Literary History* 18 (1986–7), 345–62

"Whose canon is it, anyhow?" *New York Times Book Review* (26 February 1989)

Gaume, Matilda. *Ruth Crawford Seeger: Memoirs, Memories, Music*, Metuchen, 1986

"Ruth Crawford Seeger," *Women Making Music: The Western Art Tradition 1150–1950*, ed. Bowers and Tick, 370–88

Gay, Peter. "Aimez-vous Brahms? On polarities in modernism," *Freud, Jews and Other Germans*, Oxford, 1978, 231–56

Gender and Reading: Essays on Readers, Texts, and Contexts, ed. Elizabeth A. Flynn and Patrocinio Schweickart, Baltimore, 1986

Gender/Body/Knowledge: Feminist Reconstructions of Being and Knowing, ed. Allison Jaggar and Susan Bordo, New Brunswick, 1989

Gilbert, Sandra M. and Susan Gubar. *The Madwoman in the Attic: The Woman Writer and the Nineteenth-Century Literary Imagination*, New Haven, 1979

No Man's Land: The Place of the Woman Writer in the Twentieth Century. Volume I: The War of the Words, New Haven, 1987

"Tradition and the female talent," *The Poetics of Gender*, ed. Nancy Miller, New York, 183–207

Gilligan, Carol. *In a Different Voice*, Cambridge, Mass., 1982

Ginzberg, Ruth. "Gender, rationality, and mathematics," Presentation at Rice University, March 1989

Goehr, Lydia. "Being true to the work," *Journal of Aesthetics and Art Criticism* 47/1 (1989), 55–67

Golding, Alan C. "A history of American poetry anthologies," *Canons*, ed. Robert von Hallberg, Chicago, 1984, 279–308

Gomez, Edward M. "Quarreling over quality: A feminist critique blasts old assumptions about how we judge an artist's works," *Time*, Issue on Women (1990), 61–2

Goodman, Dena. "Enlightenment salons: The convergence of female and philosophic ambitions," *Eighteenth-Century Studies* 22/3 (1989), 329–50

Gorak, Jan. *The Making of the Modern Canon: Genesis and Crisis of a Literary Idea*, London, 1991

Göttner-Abendroth, Heide. "Nine principles of a matriarchal aesthetic," *Feminist Aesthetics*, ed. Ecker, 81–94

Graff, Gerald. "Debate the canon in class," *Harper's Magazine* 282 (1991), 31–35

Literature Against Itself: Literary Ideas in Modern Society, Chicago, 1979

"Other voices, other rooms: Organizing and teaching the humanities conflict," *New Literary History* 21/4 (1990), 817–39

Professing Literature: An Institutional History, Chicago, 1987

Green, Mildred Denby. *Black Women Composers: A Genesis*, Boston, 1983

Grumet, Madeleine R. *Bitter Milk: Women and Teaching*, Amherst, 1988

Gubar, Susan. "'The blank page' and the issues of female creativity," *Critical Inquiry* 8 (1981), 73–93.

Guillory, John. "Canonical and non-canonical: A critique of the current debate," *English Literary History* 54/3 (1987), 483–527

"The ideology of canon-formation: T. S. Eliot and Cleanth Brooks," *Canons*, ed. Robert von Hallberg, Chicago, 1984, 337–62

Hanson, Alice M. *Musical Life in Biedermeier Vienna*, Cambridge, 1985

Harding, Sandra. *The Science Question in Feminism*, Ithaca, 1986

Harris, Ann Sutherland and Linda Nochlin. *Women Artists: 1550–1950*, Los Angeles, 1976

Harrison, Karey. "Reason embodied," Presentation at Rice University, April 1989

Heilbrun, Carolyn. *Writing a Woman's Life*, New York, 1988

Hensel, Sebastian. *Die Familie Mendelssohns (1729–1847)*, 3rd edn, 2 vols., Berlin, 1882

Hertz, Deborah. *Jewish High Society in Old Regime Berlin*, New Haven, 1988

Hildesheimer, Wolfgang. *Mozart*, trans. Marion Faber, New York, 1982

Himmelbauer, Regina. "Without a picture the mirror breaks: The use of her story," Presentation at the Seventh International Congress on Women in Music, Utrecht, June 1991

Hindemith, Paul. *A Composer's World: Horizons and Limitations*, Cambridge, Mass., 1952

Hirsch, E. D. "'Cultural literacy' does not mean 'canon'," *Salmagundi* No. 72 (1986), 118–24

Historical Anthology of Music by Women, ed. James Briscoe, Bloomington, 1987

Hoffmann, E. T. A. "Don Juan," *Allgemeine musikalische Zeitung*, 15/13 (31 March 1813)

Hogan, Nancy. "Towards a better definition of 'audience': Hans Robert Jauss's *Rezeptionsästhetiks* theory," M.A. thesis, philosophy, Rice University (1989)

Holland, Bernard. "Composers rediscover the public," *The New York Times* (21 May 1991)

Holub, Robert. *Reception Theory: A Critical Introduction*, New York, 1984

Hood, Mantle. "The reliability of oral tradition," *Journal of the American Musicological Society* 12 (1959), 201–9

Howe, Florence. "Those we still don't read," *College English* 43 (1981), 12–16

"In response," ed. Elaine Barkin, *Perspectives of New Music* 20–21 (1981–2), 288–329

Jackson, Barbara Garvey. "Florence Price, Composer," *The Black Perspective in Music* 5/1 (1977), 30–43

Jardine, Alice A. and Anne M. Menke. "Exploding the issue: 'French'

'women' 'writers' and 'the canon'?" *Displacements*, ed. DeJean and
    Miller, 275–307
Jauss, Hans-Robert. *Toward an Aesthetic of Reception*, trans. Timothy Bahti,
    Minneapolis, 1982
Jehlen, Myra. "Archimedes and the paradox of feminist criticism," *The
    Signs Reader*, ed. Elizabeth Abel and Emily K. Abel, Chicago, 1983,
    69–96
Jepson, Barbara. "A woman's place is on the podium," *The Wall Street
    Journal* (18 December 1991), A4
    "Women music critics in the United States," *The Musical Woman: An
    International Perspective*, vol. I, ed. J. L. Zaimont, C. Overhauser, and
    J. Gottlieb, Westport, Ct., 1984, 244–64
Jezic, Diane and David Binder. "A survey of college music textbooks:
    Benign neglect of women composers," *The Musical Woman: An
    International Perspective*, vol. II, ed. J. L. Zaimont, C. Overhauser, and
    J. Gottlieb, Westport, Ct., 1987, 445–69
Jezic, Diane. *Women Composers: The Lost Tradition Found*, New York, 1988
Johnson, Mark. *The Body in the Mind: The Bodily Basis of Meaning, Imagination,
    and Reason*, Chicago, 1987
Jones, Ann Rosalind. "Writing the body: Toward an understanding of
    l'écriture féminine," *The New Feminist Criticism*, ed. Showalter, 361–78
Jordan, Constance. *Renaissance Feminism: Literary Texts and Political Models*,
    Ithaca, 1990
Kallberg, Jeffrey. "The harmony of the tea table: Gender and ideology in
    the piano nocturne," *Representations* 39 (1992), 102–33
    "The rhetoric of genre: Chopin's Nocturne in G Minor," *Nineteenth
    Century Music* 11/3 (1988), 238–61
    "Understanding genre: A reinterpretation of the early piano nocturne,"
    *Proceedings of the XIV Congress of the International Musicological Society,
    Bologna 1987*, Forthcoming
Kamuf, Peggy. "Writing like a woman," *Women and Language in Literature
    and Society*, ed. Sally McConnell-Ginet, Ruth Borker, and Nelly
    Furman, New York, 1980, 284–99
Kaplan, Cora. *Sea Changes: Essays on Culture and Feminism*, London, 1986
Keller, Evelyn Fox. *Reflections on Gender and Science*, New Haven, 1985
Kelly, Joan. *Women, History, and Theory: The Essays of Joan Kelly*, Chicago,
    1984
Kerber, Linda. "Separate spheres, female worlds, woman's place: The
    rhetoric of women's history," *Journal of American History* 75 (1988),
    9–39
Kerman, Joseph. "American musicology in the 1990s," *The Journal of
    Musicology* 9/2 (1991), 131–44
    Contemplating Music, Cambridge, Mass., 1985
    "A few canonic variations," *Critical Inquiry* 10/1 (1983), 107–25
    "How we got into analysis, and how to get out," *Critical Inquiry* 7 (1980),
    311–31

Kermode, Frank. *An Appetite for Poetry*, Cambridge, Mass., 1989
  Forms of Attention, Chicago, 1985
  History and Value, Oxford, 1988
Kimball, Roger. "The academy debates the canon," *The New Criterion* 6 (1987), 31–43
King, Ynestra. "Healing the wounds: Feminism, ecology, and nature/culture dualism," *Gender/Body/Knowledge*, 92–114
Kolb, Harold H., Jr. "Defining the canon," *Redefining American Literary History*, ed. A. La Vonne Brown Ruoff and Jerry W. Ward, New York, 1990, 35–51
Kolodny, Annette. "Dancing through the minefield: Some observations on the theory, practice, and politics of a feminist literary criticism," *The New Literary Criticism*, ed. Showalter, 144–67
  "Respectability is eroding the revolutionary potential of feminist criticism," *The Chronicle of Higher Education* (4 May 1988), A52
Kozak, Romy. "The composition of women in the Paris Conservatory," Presentation at Feminist Theory and Music Conference, University of Minnesota, Minneapolis, June 1991
Kramer, Lawrence. *Music as Cultural Practice, 1800–1900*, Berkeley, 1990
Kravitt, Edward. "The Lieder of Alma Maria Schindler-Mahler," *The Music Review* 49 (1988), 190–204
Krupat, Arnold. "Native American literature and the canon," *Critical Inquiry* 10/1 (1983), 145–71
Lamb, Roberta. "Questioning the canon: Women and music education," Presentation at Bergamo Conference at Queen's University, Kingston, Ontario, October 1989
Lauretis, Teresa de. "Aesthetic and feminist theory: Rethinking women's cinema," *Feminist Art Criticism: An Anthology*, ed. Arlene Raven, Cassandra L. Langer, and Joanna Frueh, Ann Arbor, 1988, 133–52
  "Desire in narrative," *Alice Doesn't: Feminism, Semiotics, Cinema*, Bloomington, 1984
  Technologies of Gender: Essays on Theory, Film, and Fiction, Bloomington, 1987
Lauter, Estella and Carol Schreier Rupprecht. *Feminist Archetypal Theory: Interdisciplinary Re-Visions of Jungian Thought*, Knoxville, 1985
Lauter, Paul. *Canons and Contexts*, New York, 1991
  "The literatures of America: A comparative discipline," *Canons and Contexts*, 48–96
  "Race and gender in the shaping of the American literary canon: A case study from the twenties," *Feminist Studies* 9/3 (1983), 432–63
LeFanu, Nicola. "Master musician: An impregnable taboo?" *Contact: A Journal of Contemporary Music* No. 31 (1987), 4–8
Lenneberg, Hans. "The myth of the unappreciated (musical) genius," *The Musical Quarterly* 66 (1980), 219–31
Le Page, Jane Weiner. *Women Composers, Conductors, and Musicians of the Twentieth Century: Selected Biographies*, vol. 1, New York, 1980

Lerner, Gerda. *The Majority Finds Its Past*, New York, 1979
    "Placing women in history: A 1975 perspective," *Liberating Women's History*, ed. Berenice A. Carroll, Urbana, 1976, 357–67
Letters of Fanny Hensel to Felix Mendelssohn, ed. and trans. Marcia J. Citron, New York, 1987
Levy, Janet. "Covert and casual values in recent writings about music," *The Journal of Musicology* 5/1 (1987), 3–27
Levy, Kenneth. "On Gregorian orality," *Journal of the American Musicological Society* 43/2 (1990), 185–227
Lindenberger, Herbert. *The History in Literature: On Value, Genre, Institutions*, New York, 1990
Lipking, Lawrence. "Aristotle's sister: A poetics of abandonment," *Critical Inquiry* 10/1 (1983), 61–81
Lippman, Edward. *A Humanistic Philosophy of Music*, New York, 1977
Lloyd, Genevieve. *Man of Reason: "Male" and "Female" in Western Philosophy*, Minneapolis, 1984
Loesser, Arthur. *Men, Women, and Pianos: A Social History*, New York, 1954
Macarthur, Sally. "Celebrating difference in music at the 1991 Gender and Music Conference," *Sounds Australian* (1992), 5–9, 12
Maclean, Ian. *The Renaissance Notion of Woman: A Study in the Fortunes of Scholasticism and Medical Science in European Intellectual Life*, Cambridge, 1980
Mahler Werfel, Alma. *And the Bridge is Love*, New York, 1958
Marcus, Jane. "Virginia Woolf and her violin," *Mothering the Mind: Twelve Studies of Writers and Their Silent Partners*, ed. Ruth Perry and Martine Watson Brownley, New York, 1984, 180–203
Martinez, Odaline de la. "Women and the orchestra as a hierarchical structure," Presentation at Gender and Music Conference, King's College, University of London, July 1991
Marx, A. B. *Die Lehre von der musikalischen Komposition*, Part 3, Leipzig, 1845
McClary, Susan. "The blasphemy of talking politics during Bach year," *Music and Society: The Politics of Composition, Performance and Reception*, 13–62
    Feminine Endings: Music, Gender, and Sexuality, Minneapolis, 1991
    "Making a difference in the music: The relevance of sexuality to compositions by Laurie Anderson and Schubert," Presentation at annual meeting of the American Musicological Society, Oakland, November 1990
    "Mozart's women," *Hurricane Alice* 3 (1986), 1–4
Mendelssohn-Bartholdy, Felix. *Briefe aus den Jahren 1830–1847*, 3rd edn, pt. 2, ed. Paul Mendelssohn-Bartholdy and Carl Mendelssohn-Bartholdy, Leipzig, 1875
Meyer, Leonard. "Innovation, choice, and the history of music," *Critical Inquiry* 9 (1983), 517–44
    Music, The Arts, and Ideas, Chicago, 1967
    Style and Music: Theory, History, and Ideology, Philadelphia, 1989
Miller, Nancy. "Changing the subject: Authorship, writing, and the

reader," *Feminist Studies/Critical Studies*, ed. Teresa de Lauretis, Bloomington, 1986, 102–20

"Men's reading, women's writing: Gender and the rise of the novel," *Displacements*, ed. DeJean and Miller, 37–54

"Rereading as a woman: The body in practice," *The Female Body in Western Culture: Contemporary Perspectives*, ed. Susan Rubin Suleiman, Cambridge, Mass., 1986, 354–62

Minnich, Elizabeth Kamarck. *Transforming Knowledge*, Philadelphia, 1990

Mitgang, Laura. "Germaine Tailleferre: Before, during, and after *Les Six*," *The Musical Woman: An International Perspective*, vol. 2, 1987, 177–221

Modleski, Tania. "Feminism and the power of interpretation: Some critical readings," *Feminist Studies/Critical Studies*, ed. Teresa de Lauretis, Bloomington, 1986, 121–38

"Postmortem on postfeminism," *Feminism Without Women*, New York, 1991

The Women Who Knew Too Much: Hitchcock and Feminist Theory, New York, 1988

Monson, Karen. "Byline Monson: Music critic," *The Musical Woman: An International Perspective*, vol. 2, ed. Judith Lang Zaimont, Catherine Overhauser, and Jane Gottlieb, Westport, Ct., 1987, 59–70

Morse, J. Mitchell. "Some variations on – and from – Scholes' theme," *Salmagundi* No. 72 (1986), 148–63

Müller-Blattau, Joseph. "Form," *Die Musik in Geschichte und Gegenwart*, vol. 4, col. 549, Kassel, 1955

Murata, Margaret. "Scylla and Charybdis, or steering between form and social context in the seventeenth century," *Explorations in Music, The Arts and Ideas*, ed. Eugene Narmour and Ruth Solie, New York, 1988, 67–85

Music and Society: The Politics of Composition, Performance, and Reception, ed. Richard Leppert and Susan McClary, Cambridge, 1987

Music in the Western World: A History in Documents, ed. Piero Weiss and Richard Taruskin, New York, 1984

"Musicology in the year 2000," Special issue of *Current Musicology*, Forthcoming

Myers, Rollo. "Augusta Holmès: A meteoric career," *The Musical Quarterly* 53 (1967), 365–76

Nettl, Bruno. "Some notes on the state of knowledge about oral transmission in music," *International Musicological Society, 12th Congress, Berkeley, 1977: Report*, Kassel, 1981, 139–44

Neuls-Bates, Carol. "Creating a college curriculum for the study of women in music," *The Musical Woman*, vol. 1, ed. J. L. Zaimont, C. Overhauser, and Jane Gottlieb, Westport, Ct., 1983, 265–82

The New Feminist Criticism: Essays on Women, Literature, and Theory, ed. Elaine Showalter, New York, 1985

Newman, William S. *The Sonata Since Beethoven*, Chapel Hill, 1969

Nicholson, Linda J. *Gender and History: The Limits of Social Theory in the Age of the Family*, New York, 1986

Nochlin, Linda. "Why have there been no great women artists?" *Art and Sexual Politics*, ed. Thomas B. Hess and Elizabeth C. Baker, New York, 1973, 1–39

The Norton Anthology of Literature by Women: The Tradition in English, ed. Sandra M. Gilbert and Susan Gubar, New York, 1985

Ohmann, Carol. "Emily Brontë in the hands of male critics," *College English* 32 (1971), 906–13

Ohmann, Richard. "The shaping of a canon: U. S. fiction, 1960–1975," *Critical Inquiry* 10/1 (1983), 199–223

Ong, Walter. *Orality and Literacy: The Technologizing of the Word*, London, 1982

Ortner, Sherry. "Is female to male as nature is to culture?" *Feminist Studies* 1/2 (1974), 5–31

Parker, Rozsika and Griselda Pollock. *Old Mistresses: Women, Art and Ideology*, London, 1981

Parker, Rozsika. *The Subversive Stitch*, London, 1984

Pascall, Robert. "Genre and the finale of Brahms's Fourth Symphony," *Music Analysis* 8/3 (1989), 233–45

Pendle, Karin. "Teaching the history of women in music," Presentation at Gender and Music Conference, King's College, University of London, July 1991

Penley, Constance. "Teaching in your sleep: Feminism and psychoanalysis," *The Future of an Illusion: Film, Feminism, and Psychoanalysis*, Minneapolis, 1989, 165–84

Perlmutter, Donna. "The composer in a gender ghetto?" *The Los Angeles Times* (6 April 1986), "Calendar" section, 55–6

Perloff, Marjorie. "An intellectual impasse," *Salmagundi* No. 72 (1986), 125–30

Platoff, John. "Writing about influences: *Idomeneo*, a case study," *Explorations in Music, The Arts, and Ideas*, ed. Eugene Narmour and Ruth Solie, New York, 1988, 43–65

Pleasants, Henry. *The Agony of Modern Music*, New York, 1955

Pollock, Griselda. *Vision and Difference: Femininity, Feminism and Histories of Art*, London, 1988

Problems of Modern Music: The Princeton Seminar in Advanced Musical Studies, ed. Paul Henry Lang, New York, 1962

Quin, Carol. "Fanny Mendelssohn Hensel: Her contributions to nineteenth-century musical life," Unpublished Ph.D. dissertation, University of Kentucky (1981)

Randel, Don. "The canons in the musicological toolbox," Presentation at annual meeting of the American Musicological Society, New Orleans, 1987; and published in *Disciplining Music: Musicology and Its Canons*, 10–22

"Defining music," *Notes* 43/4 (1987), 751–66

The Reader in the Text: Essays on Audience and Interpretation, ed. Susan Rubin Suleiman and Inge Crosman, Princeton, 1980

Reader-Response Criticism: From Formalism to Post-Structuralism, ed. Jane Tompkins, Baltimore, 1980

Reich, Nancy. *Clara Schumann: The Artist and the Woman*, Ithaca, 1985
    "The professional woman musician in nineteenth-century Europe: Problems of class and gender," Forthcoming in *Musicology and Difference*, ed. Ruth Solie

Rich, Adrienne. *Of Woman Born: Motherhood as Experience and Institution*, Tenth Anniversary Edition, New York, 1986

Ricks, Christopher. "What is at stake in the 'Battle of the books'?" *New Criterion* 8 (1989), 40–44

Rieger, Eva. "'Dolce semplice?': On the changing role of women in music," *Feminist Aesthetics*, ed. Ecker, 135–49
    Frau, Musik und Männerherrschaft, 2nd edn, Kassel, 1988
    "'Ich recycle Töne': Schreiben Frauen anders? Neue Gedanken zu einem alten Thema," *Neue Zeitschrift für Musik* (February, 1992), 14–18
    "Is there a female aesthetic in music?" Presentation at Seventh International Congress on Women in Music, Utrecht, May 1991
    "The role of music in Alfred Hitchcock's cinema films seen from a feminist perspective," Presentation at Feminist Theory and Music Conference, University of Minnesota, Minneapolis, June 1991

Riemann, Hugo. *Katechismus der Musik (Allgemeine Musiklehre)*, Leipzig, 1888

Riley, Denise. "*Am I That Name?*" *Feminism and the Category of "Women" in History*, Minneapolis, 1988

Robertson, Carol E. "Power and gender in the musical experiences of women," *Women and Music in Cross-Cultural Perspective*, ed. Koskoff, 225–44

Robinson, Lillian. "Is there class in this text?" *Tulsa Studies in Women's Literature* 5/2 (1986), 289–302
    "Treason our text: Feminist challenges to the literary canon," *Tulsa Studies in Women's Literature* 2 (1983), 83–98
    "Who speaks for women – and is it poetry?" Presentation at the annual meeting of the Modern Language Association, New York, December 1976

Rochberg, George. *The Aesthetics of Survival: A Composer's View of Twentieth-Century Music*, Ann Arbor, 1984

Rosaldo, Michelle. "The use and abuse of anthropology: Reflections on feminism and cross-cultural understanding," *Signs* 5/3 (1980), 389–417

Rosen, Charles. *The Classical Style*, New York, 1971
    Sonata Forms, New York, 1980

Rosen, Judith and Grace Rubin-Rabson. "Why haven't women become great composers?" *High Fidelity* 23/2 (1973), 46–53

Rosenfelt, Deborah S. "The politics of bibliography: Women's studies and the literary canon," *Opportunities for Women's Studies Research in Language and Literature*, New York, 1982, 11–35

Rosenstiel, Léonie. *The Life and Works of Lili Boulanger*, Rutherford, 1978

Rothstein, Edward. "Was Schubert gay? If he was, so what?" *The New York Times* (4 February 1992), B3

Rousseau, Jean-Jacques. *Lettre à M. d'Alembert sur les spectacles*, Amsterdam, 1758

Russ, Joanna. *How To Suppress Women's Writing*, Austin, 1983

Ruthven, K. K. *Feminist Literary Studies: An Introduction*, Cambridge, 1984

Said, Edward. "Music [discussion of feminine musical style and gender in music]," *Nation* 244 (7 February 1989), 158–60

    Musical Elaborations, New York, 1991

    "The text, the world, the critic," *Textual Strategies: Perspectives in Post-Structuralist Criticism*, ed. Harari, 161–88

Samson, Jim. "Chopin and genre," *Music and Analysis* 8/3 (1989), 213–31

Schlueter, June. *Modern American Drama: The Female Canon*. Rutherford, 1990

Schoenberg, Arnold. *Style and Idea*, ed. Leonard Stein, trans. Leo Black, Berkeley, 1984

Scholes, Robert. "Aiming a canon at the curriculum," *Salmagundi* No. 72 (1986), 101–17

    "Reading like a man," *Men in Feminism*, ed. Alice Jardine and Paul Smith, New York, 1987, 204–18

Schor, Naomi. "Female fetishism: The case of George Sand," *The Female Body in Western Culture: Contemporary Perspectives*, ed. Susan Rubin Suleiman, Cambridge, Mass., 1986, 363–72

Schulte-Sasse, Jochen. "Imagination and modernity: Or the taming of the human mind," *Cultural Critique* 5 (1986–7), 23–48

Scott, Derek B. "Music and sociology for the 1990s: A changing critical perspective," *The Musical Quarterly* 74 (1990), 385–410

Scott, Joan. *Gender and the Politics of History*, New York, 1988

Sedgwick, Eve Kosofsky. *The Epistemology of the Closet*, Berkeley, 1990

Seeger, Charles. "Oral tradition in music," *Funk and Wagnall's Standard Dictionary of Folklore, Mythology, and Legend*, ed. Maria Leach, New York, 1950, 825–9

Sessions, Roger. *Questions About Music*, New York, 1971

Shepherd, John. "Music and male hegemony," *Music and Society: The Politics of Composition, Performance and Reception*, 151–72

Showalter, Elaine. "Critical cross-dressing: Male feminists and the woman of the year," *Men in Feminism*, ed. Alice Jardine and Paul Smith, New York, 1987, 116–32

    The Female Malady: Women, Madness, and English Culture, 1830–1980, New York, 1985

    "The feminist critical revolution," *The New Feminist Criticism: Essays on Women, Literature, and Theory*, 3–18

    "Feminist criticism in the wilderness," *The New Feminist Criticism: Essays on Women, Literature, and Theory*, 243–70

    A Literature of Their Own, Princeton, 1977

    "Towards a feminist poetics," *Women Writing and Writing About Women*, ed. Mary Jacobus, New York, 1979, 22–41

"Women and the literary curriculum," *College English* 32 (1970–71), 855–62

"Women writers and the double standard," *Woman in Sexist Society: Studies in Power and Powerlessness*, ed. Vivian Gornick and Barbara K. Moran, New York, 1971, 323–43

Silverman, Kaja. *The Acoustic Mirror: The Female Voice in Psychoanalysis and Cinema*, Bloomington, 1988

The Subject of Semiotics, Oxford, 1983

Sisk, John P. "What is necessary," *Salmagundi* No. 72 (1986), 144–7

Slater, Charles. "Introduction" to Reprint Edition of *Agathe Backer-Grøndahl: Piano Music*, New York, 1982

Slonimsky, Nicholas. *Music Since 1900*, 4th edn, New York, 1971

Smart, Mary Ann. "Azucena's excess: Memory and voice in *Il Trovatore*," Presentation at Feminist Theory and Music Conference, University of Minnesota, Minneapolis, June 1991

Smith, Barbara Herrnstein. "Contingencies of value," *Critical Inquiry* 10/1 (1983), 1–35

Contingencies of Value: Alternative Perspectives for Critical Theory, Cambridge, Mass., 1988

Smith, Catherine Parsons and Cynthia S. Richardson. *Mary Carr Moore, American Composer*, Ann Arbor, 1987

Smith, Catherine Parsons. "On feminism and American art music," Presentation at the annual meeting of the American Musicological Society, Austin, October 1989

Smith, Hilda. "Feminism and the methodology of women's history," *Liberating Women's History*, ed. Berenice A. Carroll, Urbana, 1976, 368–84

Smith-Rosenberg, Carroll. "The female world of love and ritual: Relations between women in 19th-century America," *The Signs Reader*, ed. Elizabeth Abel and Emily K. Abel, Chicago, 1983, 27–56

Solie, Ruth and Gary Tomlinson. "Women's studies in a new key," *National Women's Studies Action* 2/1 (1989), 6

Solie, Ruth. Review of Nancy Reich's *Clara Schumann: The Artist and the Woman*, *Nineteenth Century Music* 10/1 (1986), 74–80

"What do feminists want? A reply to Peter van den Toorn," *The Journal of Musicology* 9/4 (1991), 399–411

Solomon, Maynard. "Franz Schubert and the peacocks of Benvenuto Cellini," *Nineteenth Century Music* 12/3 (1989), 193–206

Southern, Eileen. *The Music of Black Americans*, 2nd edn, New York, 1983

Speaking of Gender, ed. Elaine Showalter, New York, 1989

Spiel, Hilde. *Fanny von Arnstein, oder die Emanzipation*, Frankfurt, 1962

Sprengnether, Madelon. "(M)other Eve: Some revisions of the fall in fiction by contemporary women writers," *Feminism and Psychoanalysis*, ed. Richard Feldstein and Judith Roof, Ithaca, 1989, 298–322

Stanley, Julia P. and Susan J. Wolfe (Robbins). "Toward a feminist aesthetic," *Chrysalis* 6 (1978), 57–76

Stanton, Domna C. "Language and revolution: The Franco-American dis-connection," *The Future of Difference*, ed. Hester Eisenstein and Alice Jardine, New Brunswick, 1985, 73–87

The Status of Women in College Music: Preliminary Studies, ed. Carol Neuls-Bates, College Music Society Report No. 1 (1976)

Steptoe, Andrew. *The Mozart-Da Ponte Operas: The Cultural and Musical Background to Le nozze di Figaro, Don Giovanni, and Così fan tutte*, Oxford, 1988

Stout, Janis P. *Strategies of Reticence: Silence and Meaning in the Works of Jane Austen, Willa Cather, Katherine Anne Porter, and Joan Didion*, Charlottesville, 1990

Straus, Joseph N. "The 'anxiety of influence' in twentieth-century music," *The Journal of Musicology* 9/4 (1991), 430–47

Subotnik, Rose Rosengard. "The cultural message of musical semiology: Some thoughts on music, language, and criticism since the Enlightenment," *Critical Inquiry* 4/4 (1978), 741–68

Developing Variations, Minneapolis, 1991

"On grounding Chopin," *Music and Society: The Politics of Composition, Performance and Reception*, 105–31

"The role of ideology in the study of Western music," *The Journal of Musicology* 2 (1983), 1–12

Tambling, Jeremy. *Opera, Ideology, and Film*, New York, 1987

Taruskin, Richard. Review of *The Musical Woman*, vol. 2, *Opus* 4/2 (1988), 64

Teaching Noncanonical Literature, ed. Elizabeth Flynn, Issue of *Reader Magazine*, No. 15 (1986)

Textual Strategies: Perspectives in Post-Structuralist Criticism, ed. Josué Harari, Ithaca, 1979

Tick, Judith. *American Women Composers Before 1870*, Ann Arbor, 1983

"'Spirit of me ... Dear rollicking far-gazing straddler of two worlds': The 'Autobiography' of Ruth Crawford Seeger," Presentation at Gender and Music Conference, King's College, University of London, July 1991

Todd, Janet. *Feminist Literary History*, New York, 1988

Women's Friendship in Literature, New York, 1980

Tompkins, Jane. *Sensational Designs: The Cultural Work of American Fiction 1790–1860*, New York, 1985

Toorn, Pieter Van Den. "Politics, feminism, and contemporary music theory," *The Journal of Musicology* 9/3 (1991), 275–99

Tovey, Donald Francis. "Sonata style," *Encyclopedia Britannica*, 13th edn, vol. 20, Chicago, 1957, 977–85

Treitler, Leo. "Homer and Gregory: The transmission of epic poetry and plainchant," *The Musical Quarterly* 60 (1974), 333–72

Music and the Historical Imagination, Cambridge, Mass., 1989

"The politics of reception: Tailoring the present as fulfilment of a desired past," *Journal of the Royal Musical Association* 116 (1991), 280–98

"Transmission and the study of music history," *International Musicological Society, Twelfth Congress, Berkeley 1977: Report*, Kassel, 1981, 202–11

Upton, George. *Woman in Music*, Boston, 1880

Waleson, Heidi. "Music, maestra, please," *The New York Times* (16 April 1989), sec. 2, pp. 1 and 36

"Women composers find things easier – sort of," *The New York Times* (28 January 1990), sec. 2, p. 30

Walker, Cheryl. "Feminist literary criticism and the author," *Critical Inquiry* 16/3 (1990), 551–71

Walser, Robert. "The body in the music: Epistemological challenges for ethnomusical semiotics," Presentation at annual meeting of AMS/SEM/SMT, Oakland, 1990

Weber, William. "The eighteenth-century origins of the musical canon," *Journal of the Royal Musical Association* 114/1 (1989), 6–17

"Mass culture and the reshaping of European musical taste, 1770–1870," *International Review of the Aesthetics and Sociology of Music* 8 (1977), 5–21

"Mentalité, tradition et origines du canon musical en France et en Angleterre au XVIIIe siècle," *Annales. Economies, Sociétés, Civilisations* 44/4 (1989), 849–73

Music and the Middle Class, New York, 1975

"The rise of the classical repertoire in nineteenth-century orchestral concerts," *The Orchestra: Origins and Transformations*, ed. Joan Peyser, New York, 1986, 361–86

"Wagner, Wagnerism, and musical idealism," *Wagnerism in European Culture and Politics*, ed. David C. Large and William Weber, Ithaca, 1984, 28–71

Webster, James. "Schubert's sonata form and Brahms's first maturity," *Nineteenth Century Music* 2 (1978–9), 18–35

Werner, Eric. *Mendelssohn: A New Image of the Composer and His Age*, trans. Dika Newlin, New York, 1963

West, Cornel. "Minority discourse and the pitfalls of canon formation," *The Yale Journal of Criticism* 1/1 (1987), 193–201

Whelchel, Marianne. "Transforming the canon with nontraditional literature by women," *College English* 46 (1984), 587–97

Wilding-White, Ray. "Remembering Ruth Crawford Seeger: An interview with Charles and Peggy Seeger," *American Music* (1988), 442–54

Wolff, Janet. *Feminine Sentences: Essays on Women and Culture*, Berkeley, 1990

The Social Production of Art, New York, 1984

Women and Music, A History, ed. Karin Pendle, Bloomington, 1991

Women and Music in Cross-Cultural Perspective, ed. Ellen Koskoff, Westport, Ct., 1988

Women in Music: An Anthology of Source Readings from the Middle Ages to the Present, ed. Carol Neuls-Bates, New York, 1982

Women Making Music: The Western Art Tradition, 1150–1950, ed. Jane Bowers and Judith Tick, Urbana, 1986

Women's Studies/Women's Status, College Music Society Report No. 5, Boulder, 1988

Wood, Elizabeth. "Lesbian fugue: Ethel Smyth's contrapuntal arts,"

Presentation at the Seventh International Congress on Women in Music, Utrecht, May 1991

"The odyssey of sirens and songbirds: Opera and its prima donnas," Presentation at the open meeting of the Committee on the Status of Women, annual meeting of the American Musicological Society, Austin, October 1989

Woolf, Virginia. *A Room of One's Own*, New York, 1929

Worbs, Hans-Christoph. "Le tribut à la mode: Die Anfänge der Salonmusik," *Neue Zeitschrift für Musik* 132 (1971), 128–33

The Writings of Elliott Carter, ed. Else Stone and Kurt Stone, Bloomington, 1977

Index

power of, 168, 180–1, 194, 268 n. 19
relationship with listeners, 180
relationship with musical work, 194
subject–object positioning, 12, 182
women as, 181–2
see also music criticism; professionalism;
reception
music education, 59–60, 190
and education in other arts, 60–1
and stylistic paradigms, 61, 130–2
music history
location with respect to center, 187
see also canonicity; canons; canon
formation; historiography; music-
history pedagogy
music-history pedagogy, 4, 12–13, 24–5
canonic modelings, 199–228; as finite,
200
emphasis on style, 199–200, 216
materials, 227–8; and copyright, 25;
textbooks, 24–6, 42, 236 n. 25; *see also*
anthologies
and music by women, 219–28; counter
canon, 219; dangers of mere
incorporation, 42–3, 222;
mainstreaming/separatism, 13, 219–20;
other options, 217, 220–8; *see also* dual
perspective
new modelings, 12–13, 220–8
paradigm of great works: *see* greatness;
masterpiece
see also periodization; social history
music publishers, 25, 229–30, 238 n. 44
music theory, 236 n. 22
see also feminist music theory
musical analysis, 37, 116, 158, 224
contradiction in, 145–6, 158
and gender, 145–59, 222–3
importance for works by women, 6, 144
multiple interpretations, 145, 158
see also Chaminade, Cécile; music;
representation
musical canon, 16, 22–41
defines field, 196
not confined to Western art music, 274 n.
61
origins of, 9, 31–7
properties of, 13, 196–7
and social conditions, 3
types of, 5–6
and women, 4, 9, 41–3, 201, 219–28
works omitted from, 203
see also canon formation; canonicity;
canons; music; music by women;
music-history pedagogy

The Musical Quarterly, 238 n. 44
musical work, 120
beyond original milieu, 111, 174
and discourse, 10
functionality of, 35–6, 215–17, 259 n. 28;
see also periodization
as gendered, 122–3
and ideology, 121–3, 144
and meaning, 120, 158, 223–4
ownership of, 112, 116
and representation, 121; *see also*
representation
in response, 172
and social referentiality, 120–2
see also musical analysis
musicologist, 196, 198
musicology, 37, 102–3, 232
and identity, 196–7
job classifications of, 228–9
paradigms, 39, 235 n. 18
and positivism, 197
presence of women in, 13, 41, 228–30,
275–6 n. 80
self-definition of, 196
unity of, 197
see also feminist musicology; musical
canon

nationalism, 36–7, 130
nature, *see* dualisms: culture–nature
Neuls-Bates, Carol, *Women in Music: An
Anthology of Source Readings from the
Middle Ages to the Present*, 214
*The New Grove Dictionary of Music and
Musicians*, 108, 117, 132
New Oxford History of Music, 115
New York Post, 181
The New Yorker, 167
Newman, William S., *The Sonata Since
Beethoven*, 116, 261 n. 46
Nicholson, Linda, 100–2, 251 n. 44
Nietzsche, Friedrich, 49
Nin, Anaïs, 46
Nissen, Georg Nikolaus, 114
Norton Anthology of Literature by Women, The,
213
Norton Anthology of Western Music, 42
Norton Scores, The, 42

Oates, Joyce Carol, 97
Oberlin Conservatory, 59
Oedipal relationship, 50, 68, 69–70, 71, 160,
182
Oliveros, Pauline, 66
opera, 247 n. 93